Game Development and Production

Erik Bethke

VCTC Library
Hartness Library
Vermont Technical College
Randolph Center, VT 05061

Wordware Publishing, Inc.

Library of Congress Cataloging-in-Publication Data

Bethke, Erik.
    Game development and production / by Erik Bethke.
        p. cm.
    ISBN 1-55622-951-8
    1. Computer games--Design.   2. Computer games--Programming.
    3. Project management.   I. Title.
    QA76.76.C672 B47 2002
    794.8'1526--dc21   2002153470
                                                                        CIP

© 2003, Wordware Publishing, Inc.

All Rights Reserved

2320 Los Rios Boulevard
Plano, Texas 75074

No part of this book may be reproduced in any form or by any means
without permission in writing from Wordware Publishing, Inc.

Printed in the United States of America

ISBN 1-55622-951-8

10 9 8 7 6 5 4 3 2 1
0301

Product names mentioned are used for identification purposes only and may be trademarks of their respective companies.

All inquiries for volume purchases of this book should be addressed to Wordware Publishing, Inc., at the above address. Telephone inquiries may be made by calling:

(972) 423-0090

Contents

Foreword

It is a great honor to write a foreword for a book on game production, as this is a subject that is very close to our hearts. We have played a very small part in helping Erik with this book—he has accomplished a Herculean task in a relatively short period of time. We believe this book will serve as an excellent foundation for mastering the art of game production.

A multitude of books have been written on the specific disciplines of art, programming, and design for games, but few, if any, have ever tackled game production as a topic. Perhaps this is because there isn't a standardized way of referring to production in a manner similar to programming and art. Programming is done in C and C++ and usually follows standards that have been carefully crafted over many years. Art uses both traditional media and a narrow range of digital art tools, such as 3D Studio Max and Maya, and is often practiced by individuals with formal art training at their disposal. Perhaps game design is most similar to game production in that, until recently, there haven't been formal programs in game design, and it is somewhat of an "arcane art" that could be realized in any potential medium. At the current time there aren't any formal training programs for game production, though there are various courses available in project management. Project management doesn't fully encompass the skills needed to manage game development, but it does provide some. Appropriately, this book includes elements of project management, engineering discipline (a tribute to Erik's engineering background), and a lot of common sense (an essential ingredient in game production).

Erik explained that his goal with this book was to fully realize the discipline of game production in a formal, yet widely appealing treatment. We were quite impressed with his ambition, as we've learned over the years (via our work on games like Baldur's Gate, MDK2, Neverwinter Nights, and Star Wars: Knights of the Old Republic) that game production is a huge area. Erik further explained that he was going to provide additional information on topics such as outsourcing and detailed production frameworks. During our review of the manuscript, we learned a number of things that we're going to be able to apply to development at BioWare. We're also more excited than ever in seeing the final work with all of the graphs, diagrams, and illustrations accompanying the text.

In conclusion we believe you, the reader and presumed game producer or game developer, will learn a great deal by reading this book. Its contents cover a wide range of topics and contain pearls of knowledge that will be of value to not only new game producers but also to experienced game developers. Read and enjoy!

Dr. Greg Zeschuk and Dr. Ray Muzyka
Joint CEOs and co-executive producers, BioWare Corp.

Preface

Who Is This Book For?

This is a book about the making of digital interactive entertainment software—games! Specifically, this book is for people who want to lead the making of games: programmers, designers, art directors, producers (executive, associate, line, internal development, external development), project managers, or leaders on any type of entertainment software.

- Are you a talented individual working on a mod to your favorite commercial game who needs to understand how a game is put together?
- Are you working with a small team across the Internet on a total conversion like Day of Defeat that will grip gameplayers and game developers alike—but are wondering how to motivate your team members and articulate your vision for your total conversion?
- Are you running your first game, with six or more developers working on your game?
- Have you been at work for a few months, and everything felt great at the beginning, but now you are wondering if you are on time?
- Are you just starting your second game project and determined to plan it right this time?
- Are you a successful executive producer who is now responsible for overseeing several projects and want to know how you can get more clarity on your project's success?
- Are you an external developer and want to know how you can best manage risks and meet your milestones?
- Is your project late?
- Are you a member of a game development team and have a vested interest in the success of this game?
- Are you thinking of joining the industry as a producer and need a producer's handbook?

The point is there are many different types of people responsible and accountable for the production of a game project.

This book gives you specific tools for the management of your game, methods to create a project plan and track tasks, an overview of outsourcing parts of your project, and philosophical tools to help you solve abstract production problems.

The author's personal experience producing the hit series Starfleet Command and other projects, as well as extensive interviews with many other producers in the game industry, backs up this advice with real-world experience.

Games are incredible products of creativity requiring art, science, humor, and music—a true blend of the mind. Managing this effort presents the producer with many challenges, some specific and some vague. While this book will answer many specific questions and give guidance in some of the general ideas, the tough calls are still yours.

Acknowledgments

I have been very fortunate in the writing of this book and I was able to lean on quite a number of folks from the game development community to answer questions and supply material for this book. I would especially like to thank the following individuals: Chip Moshner, Jarrod Phillips, Jason Rubin, Kevin Cloud, Ken Levine, James Masters, Lorne Lanning, David Perry, Nate Skinner, Nigel Chanter, Steve Perkins, Chris Taylor, Trish Wright, Beth Drummond, and John Carmack.

I would like to thank Chris Borders for his lengthy interview on voice in games; Adam Levenson and Tommy Tallarico for their interviews on sound effects and music; and Scott Bennie for his generous response on writing.

I would like to thank Steve McConnell for writing all of his books on software project management.

I would like to thank all of the employees of Taldren who entrust in me every day the responsibility to lead the team.

At Wordware I gratefully thank Jim Hill for the opportunity to write this book and I also thank Wes Beckwith for being a wonderful development editor and so supportive of writing this book. I also would like to thank Beth Kohler and Dianne Stultz for the amazing editing job they performed.

A most outstanding thank you to Greg Zeschuk and Ray Muzyka who have given so generously of their time and minds to make this book a much better book.

My two dear partners, Sean Dumas and Zachary Drummond, are due my heartfelt thanks for all of their support and just plain kicking ass every day.

And finally, I dedicate this book to my wife, Kai-wen, and my son, Kyle, who is younger than this book.

Part I

Introduction to Game Development

> >

Chapter 1 > > > > > > > > > > > > > > > >

What Does This Book Cover?

How to Make a Game

Fairly audacious heading, huh? There are a lot of books out there that are introductions to C++ or Direct3D, or discuss the construction of a real-time strategy game. What these books do not cover is which development methodologies you should employ in creating your game and how to be smart about outsourcing portions of it.

This book is not a vague list of good ideas and suggestions; rather it gets down and dirty and discusses failed and successful project management techniques from my own experience as well as the experience of a multitude of other development studios.

First Have a Plan

Games that have a poor development methodology (or none at all) take much longer than they should, run over budget, and tend to be unreasonably buggy. The majority of commercial games fail to turn a profit.

Figuring out what your game needs to do is called "requirements capture." This book will show you how to use formalized methods such as the Unified Modeling Language's use case diagrams to quickly collect your requirements and communicate them

effectively to your team and other project stakeholders.

Even if you are working on a solo project, you must still take your game's project planning seriously. A mere demo of your capabilities to show a prospective employer would be created with higher quality and with more speed if you follow the techniques presented here.

These are just the earliest elements of an entire game project production methodology that is developed throughout this book.

< < < < < < < < < < < < < < < < < < < < < < < < <

Organize Your Team Effectively

Once you have a plan in hand, full game production commences. This is the most exciting time for a game project. Literally every day new features will come online, and on a healthy project, the team will feed itself with new energy to propel forward. This book discusses how to create task visibility so everyone knows what he or she needs to do and how far along the rest are in their tasks.

Controlling feature creep, reaching alpha, and freezing new features are critical to finishing your game. All of the mega-hits in our industry kept their feature sets narrow and the polish deep. I will point this out again: The mega-hits such as Doom, Warcraft, Myst, Gran Turismo, Mario64, and The Sims are not small games; rather their feature set is small but polished to a superior degree. This book will show you how to get a grip on your features.

If you think about it, teams with one developer must use their time even more effectively than a fat 30-person production. All the methods of creating achievable tasks, measuring progress, and controlling features are even more critical for very small teams.

Game Development Is Software Development

Games are certainly special; however, a point I will be making repeatedly throughout this book is that game development is software development. Games are software with art, audio, and gameplay. Financial planning software is software that is specialized for financial transactions and planning, expert systems are software with artificial intelligence, and cockpit instrumentation is software dedicated to flying an aircraft. Too often game developers hold themselves apart from formal software development and production methods with the false rationalization that games are an art, not a science. Game developers need to master their production methods so that they can produce their games in an organized, repeatable manner—a rigorous manner that creates great games on budget and on time.

Where to Turn for Outside Help

The game industry is maturing rapidly. With this growth, outside vendors that are experts in the fields of cinematics, character modeling, motion capture, sound effects, voice-over, language localization, quality assurance, marketing, and music composition have produced mature, cost-effective solutions for the largest to the smallest team.

Do you know how many moves you need to capture for your game or how much they will cost? Do you need to record in high fidelity 120 frames per second, or will buying a library of stock moves be the best solution? I will show you how to specify what you need and give you an idea of how the bid will break down in costs. Interviews by major vendors in these areas will highlight major gotchas where projects went afoul and explain how to avoid them.

> >

How to Ship a Game

So you have finished your game, eh? You've coded it all up and played through it a bunch, and your friends like it, but how do you know when it is ready to ship? I will show you how to track bugs, prioritize your bugs effectively, task your bugs, and review your final candidates for readiness.

All game projects can benefit from beta testing. I will show you how to effectively solicit help from beta testers. Respect them and you will be repaid in help beyond measure. Let your beta testers lie fallow or fail to act meaningfully on their suggestions and your game will suffer. Beta testers are project stakeholders too; you must communicate with them effectively, explain to them your decisions, and show strength of leadership.

Post-Release

After a game ships you will often have a responsibility and an opportunity to support your game. This is especially true for the PC game market where it is possible to patch bugs, fine-tune the balance, and add new features or content. The new content can take the form of free downloads or larger packages that can be sold as expansions to your game. These are the straightforward tasks; true mega-hits transcend the status of just a game to play through and become a hobby. Enabling players to modify the game through the creation of new levels, new modules, new missions, or even total conversions keeps your game alive far beyond the life expectancy of a game without user-extensible elements. Pioneered to great success, id Software's Doom and Quake series coined the term *level designer* as an occupation. Arguably, the greatest strength of Chris Taylor's Total Annihilation was its aggressive design for user modification. Chapter 9 discusses the technical design, and it is here, in the earliest stages of architecture for your game, that you must plan for user modification. Waiting until the end of your project is not a valid method for adding user-extensibility to your game.

Fan communication is critical to long-term success; set up an Internet message board for your fans to trade ideas, tips, gripes, rants, stories, challenges, and new content.

Success and the Long Race

The deeper message I am presenting in this book is that successful game making is a long race rather than a sprint to fast cash. Any attempt to take a shortcut for poor motives will manifest itself in a sickly, failed game project. Take your time to figure out the context of your game project. Discover why you are making this game. What is the vision? What are your true profit goals? Are they reasonable? What should you accomplish in this game? Where does this game you are making fit into a chain of game projects?

< < < < < < < < < < < < < < < < < < < < < < < < < < < <

How to Use This Book

I suggest you first lightly skim through the entire book cover to cover to get a cursory exposure to formalized game development.

Parts I and II discuss the challenges of game development thoroughly and introduce you to effective methods of game development to use on your project.

The early chapters of Part III should be read thoroughly at the beginning of your game project to create a detailed project plan that will give your project the best start possible.

Part IV is a resource guide to getting outside help on your project. This material should be reviewed carefully in the second half of your preproduction phase to flesh out your production plan.

Part III should remain handy during production to help with organizing your team, wrestling with Microsoft Project, Unified Modeling Language, Excel, and other tools for measuring progress, and for controlling the scope of your project.

Review the later chapters of Part III as production reaches alpha and it is time to figure out how to ship your game.

The methods presented in this book have been boiled down in a distilled format in the Game Project Survival Test included in Chapter 4.

> >

Chapter 2 > > > > > > > > > > > > > > > >

Why Make Games?

To Share a Dream

Creative people love to share their dreams, thoughts, and worlds. Artists want to show you the world, musicians want you to feel the world, programmers want you to experience the world, and game designers want you to be there.

Games are deeply rewarding because they appeal on so many different levels: They are stories to be caught up in, action sequences to live, stunning visuals to experience, and they challenge our minds by exploring our strategy and tactical skills. Games hold the unique position, of all the different entertainment mediums, of having the most interactivity with the audience. This is a very special quality; it makes the player the most important part of the story—the hero. Novels are interactive with the reader, as no two readers will visualize a narrative in the same way. Music is interactive for the rhythm, mood, and inspiration to dance that it charges humans with. Games are very special—only in a game can a player try different actions, experience different outcomes, and explore a model of a world.

Games Teach

Games and stories are deep elements of human culture. Peek-a-boo and its more sophisticated cousin hide-and-seek teach the elements of hunting prey and evading predators. The oldest complete game set discovered so far is the Royal Game of Ur, an ancient Sumerian game dating back to 2500 B.C. The rules for this game are unknown, but the conjecture is that it was a betting game about moving a piece around a track of squares, perhaps as a very early predecessor to backgammon. Wei-Ch'i, or Go, can be traced back by one legend to 2200

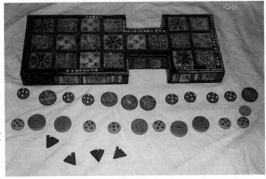

The Royal Game of Ur with permission from James Masters

B.C. China where Emperor Shun supposedly used the game to train his son for assuming leadership of the state. Chess has a rich history throughout the Middle Ages, the Renaissance, and through to modern times as the most celebrated game of strategic thinking.

Longer histories of games are available; the point I am making here is that games have held an intimate role in our intellectual growth from the earliest ages. We modern game makers are carrying on an honorable, historic role.

Game Genres Satisfy Different Appetites

Electronic games are usually described by their genre—strategy, adventure, role-playing, action, and simulation. These genres are a direct reflection of the source material for the game. Military and sports simulations; gambling, parlor, and puzzle games; storytelling; toys; and children's games comprise some of the major branches of influence for the creation of electronic games.

Modern computer games have a rich history; some of the earliest games (1970s) were text adventure games such as Adventure, crude arcade games like Pong, and a little later, multiplayer games such as NetTrek. These early games explored storytelling, strategy, tactics, and the player's hand-eye coordination. The sophistication of these games was, of course, limited by technology—a limit that is constantly being pushed back.

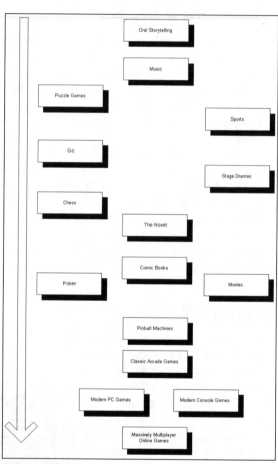

Background and influences on modern game genres

Gambling, Puzzle, and Parlor Games

Games evolved from elegant board games full of culture to a wide variety of wagering games involving dice or cards. Games like Parcheesi and Scrabble took solid form during the 1800s and early 1900s. Parcheesi is the father of board games and requires the players to navigate their tokens around the board like Monopoly and Candy Land. These games themselves have been directly ported as electronic games, but it is the fast-paced puzzle games like Tetris that have developed new ground in this genre.

As I type these words, over 110,000 people are playing straightforward conversions of the classic card and board games online at Microsoft MSN Gaming Zone (http://zone.msn.com/ql.asp). These games have entertained families and friends throughout the ages and teach deduction, probability, and social skills. The folks at Silver Creek

Entertainment (http://www.silvercrk.com) have taken the concept of spades and hearts and have crafted the finest versions of these games, complete with a rich set of features for social interaction including chat, ratings, and blasting your opponents with fireballs.

One of the coolest parlors (in my opinion) happening right now is the Internet Chess Club (http://www.chessclub.com) with over 1,000 players currently connected and 26 Grand Masters and International Masters playing online. The ICC boasts an impressive chat system, automated tournaments, over 30 flavors of chess, anytime control, and impressive library and game examination features. Automated chess courses are broadcast throughout the day, and many titled players turn their mastery into cash by teaching chess using the shekel—the unit of currency on the ICC. It is an exciting place where you have the choice of watching GMs and IMs or playing in tournaments around the clock. Instead of dusty annotated chess columns in the newspaper, try some three-minute blitz action with the best players in the world.

A partial listing of games and gamers on Microsoft's Gaming Zone

A dwarf and a fireball from Silver Creek Entertainment's Hardwood Spades

< < < < < < < < < < < < < < < < < < < < < < < < < < < <

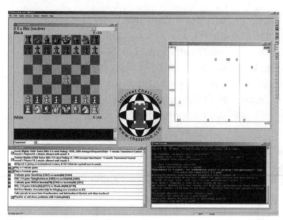

Various windows of the Blitz interface to the Internet Chess Club

Military and Sports Simulations

Games have long been providing simulations of real-life experiences that many of us do not get to experience in daily life. There are simulations for white-water kayaking, racing minivans at night on the streets of Tokyo, fantastic-looking detailed professional football simulations, skateboarding simulators, star fighter sims; in short, any sport, military action, or transportation method is a good candidate for an electronic simulation.

Flight simulators have been the staple of computer simulations since the early '80s. Microsoft enjoys the #1 spot with Microsoft Flight Simulator, which they release new versions of every even-numbered year—the latest being FS 2002 (http://www.microsoft.com/games/fs2002). Microsoft Flight Simulator has a huge following including hundreds of virtual airlines and air traffic controllers, and half a dozen or so books are available for Flight Simulator.

Austin Meyer of Laminar Research is the author of the most realistic and user-extensible flight simulator, X-Plane (http:// www.x-plane.com). Aside from

the obligatory features of impressive 3D plane graphics, great looking scenery, and a realistic flight model, the truly impressive features of X-Plane involve its expandability. Hundreds of planes and other features created by devoted fans are available for X-Plane, including real-time weather that is downloaded to your computer while flying! The author put his time into creating the first simulation of what it would be like to fly on Mars: real flight with the gravity, air density, and inertia models of flight on Mars.

A screen shot collage from X-Plane

Through the '70s and '80s Avalon Hill produced a vast array of detailed military board games that covered all aspects of war making from the Bronze Age to the Jet Age. Avalon Hill's crowning achievement is perhaps the most detailed board game ever created: Advanced Squad Leader (ASL). ASL is also the most detailed squad-level military board game simulation ever

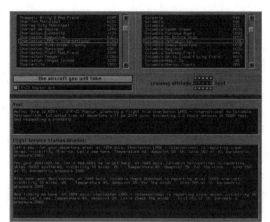

A screen shot from the real-time weather display for X-Plane

Virtual airlines from X-Plane

My company, Taldren, was founded on the success of our team's Starfleet Command game, which is a 3D real-time interpretation of the rule set of Star Fleet Battles from Amarillo Design Bureau. Star Fleet Battles is a detailed simulation of starship naval combat based on the *Star Trek* television show and was created by Steven Cole. The board game translated well into a real-time 3D strategy game in part because the pen and paper board game itself broke the turns of the game into 32 "impulses" of partial turns to achieve a serviceable form of real-time simulation. The game itself was usually played as a scenario re-enacting a "historical" battle between star empires of the Star Trek universe. The game was so detailed in its mechanics a simple cruiser-on-cruiser skirmish could take two to fours hours to resolve, and a fleet action such as a base assault was a project for the entire weekend and a bucket of caffeine. We developed the Starfleet Command series that draws upon this rich heritage and delivers a compelling career in one of eight star empires or pirate cartels. As the players get caught up in epic struggles between the star empires, they earn prestige points for successful completion of their missions, which can be used to repair their ships, buy supplies, and upgrade to heavier class starships. This electronic game blends a television show telling the story of exploring the galaxy with the detail of a war game.

developed. Countless modules expand the game and the rules to take into account the differences of individual operations in World War II. There are zillions of rules (and errata!) for everything from ammo types to night combat rules. Military buffs have been playing war games for hundreds of years, but the developments that led to ASL carried forward into electronic gaming. Currently there is a rage going on about WWII squad games such as Microsoft's Close Combat and Cornered Rat's World War II: Online. The most hardcore of them all is Combat Mission: Barbarossa to Berlin by Battlefront.com.

< < < < < < < < < < < < < < < < < < < < < < < < < < < < < <

Car racing has been a staple of games from the days of Monaco GP and Pole Position in the arcade to the state-of-the-art Gran Turismo 3 by Sony. Gran Turismo 3 features hundreds of hours of gameplay, the most realistic driving physics model, and graphics so compelling you can feel the sunlight filtered through the pine trees.

Electronic Arts, the largest software company in the games business, sells about $3 billion in games a year. Electronic Arts is both publisher and developer of countless games dating back to the early '80s. EA has done very well across all platforms and all genres; however, it is the simulation of sports—professional sports—that is EA's cash cow. Madden NFL Football (http://madden2002.ea.com) has been published for years and has been released on every major platform including the PC, PlayStation, PlayStation 2, N64, Game Boy Color, GameCube, and Xbox.

Role-Playing Games

No discussion of game making could be complete without discussing storytelling. Sitting around a fire and spinning a tale is one of the oldest forms of entertainment. Shamans acted out roles as gods, animals, and warriors to explain our world, teach us history, and to fuel our imaginations after the sun went down. With the advent of writing, authors could now tell stories across time—longer, deeper stories than a single dry throat could repeat. J.R.R. Tolkien's *Lord of the Rings* trilogy: Here we drank wine with nearly immortal elves, fought epic battles with orcs, and saved the world from ultimate evil through careful use of a ring. Science fiction and fantasy exploded in the

second half of the twentieth century to become the dominant market of fiction.

Reading a novel is wonderful, but would it not be better to slay the dragon yourself and take the loot home to your castle? In the early '70s, Gary Gygax created Dungeons and Dragons and showed us how to slay the dragon. Dungeons and Dragons was very special because you did not compete against the other players; rather you *acted* or *role-played* a *character* in a fantasy world. You wrote a backstory for your elven ranger, what motivated him, why he must slay the orcs of the Fell Lands. You then joined up with the characters of your friends and role-played through an adventure run by your Dungeon Master, or referee.

Dungeons and Dragons has been played by virtually everyone in the game industry, and it is a keystone of the role-playing game genre. Text adventures such as Zork and graphic adventures such as the King's Quest series gave us choices for how the story would turn out. As capabilities expanded, breakthrough games such as Bard's Tale, written by the infant Interplay and published by Electronic Arts, were later followed up by important games like the Ultima and Wizardry series. Role-playing games took a brief slumber in the early '80s when first-person shooters dominated the PC market, and the format of the computer RPG remained fairly stale in the early '90s. Starting around 1997 role-playing games made a big comeback in the form of three hugely important games: Baldur's Gate developed by BioWare, Diablo developed by Blizzard, and Ultima Online developed by Origin. Baldur's Gate brought us a gorgeous game with intuitive controls and mechanics and lavish production values that brought the Dungeons and Dragons world of the Forgotten Realms to life. Diablo stunned the game industry with the simple and addictive gameplay of the tight user interface and online multiplayer dungeon hacking. Ultima Online was the first commercially viable massively multiplayer role-playing game. I spent probably 80 hours of my life there, mining virtual iron ore to get ahead in a virtual economy where I paid a real $10 a month for the privilege of exploring my mining fantasies.

Looking back to pen and paper role-playing games and fantasy fiction, I am excited to see the future of role-playing games with the release of Neverwinter Nights developed by BioWare, where the tools of game mastering are part of the game. Scores of players will participate together in user-created adventures online. These online role-playing games are fantastic in scope compared to the multi-user Dungeons available on Unix systems on the Internet, but the story experience is just as compelling. I look forward to seeing the massively multiplayer virtual reality games as depicted in Tad Williams' Otherland fiction series, where we become true avatars. Gas Powered Games' release of Dungeon Siege, building on the groundbreaking immediacy of Diablo, will be the slickest action/RPG today with breathtaking 3D graphics and strong online multiplayer matchmaking that will satisfy the dungeoneer in all of us.

Youth Making Games

You have to have the bug to make games. The talent usually begins at a young age. Like countless other game developers who made goofy games on early computers, I had a Commodore Vic20 and C64 on which I created text adventure games and crude bitmap graphic maze adventures. In fourth grade I produced a fairly elaborate board game series that involved adventuring through a hostile, medieval fantasy world with various characters very similar to the Talisman board game. In eighth grade my friend Elliott Einbinder and I created a wireframe, first-person maze game; you used the keyboard to navigate through the maze. A most embarrassing flaw was in our maze game: We could not figure out how to prevent the player from cheating and walking through the walls! We kept asking our computer science teacher how we could query the video display to find out if we drew a wall. We had no concept of a world model and a display model!

On Money

In this whole discussion I have not talked about the money to be made in making games. Game making is both an art and a science. If you are honest with yourself, your team, the customer, and to the game, you will make a great game. In all art forms, excellence is always truth.

Honesty, truth, and clarity are all interrelated, and they are important not because of moral standards; they are important because only with the ruthless pursuit of a clean, tight game can you hope to make a great game.

The rest of this book will focus on how to get maximum value for your development dollars with outsourcing, how to decide which features to cut, and how to track your tasks; all these activities are heavily involved with money. That being said, look deeper and understand that I am helping you realize the true goals for your game project and to reach these goals as efficiently as possible.

Great games sell just fine, and the money will come naturally enough; focus on making a great game.

Why Make Games?

You should make games because you love to. Making a game should be a great source of creative release for you. You love to see people enthralled by your game, playing it over and over, totally immersed in the world and the challenges you have crafted for their enjoyment. You should make games if there is something fun you can visualize in your mind, something fun you would like to experience, and you want to share that experience with others.

Chapter 3 > > > > > > > > > > > > > > > >

What Makes Game Development Hard?

The Importance of Planning

What does it take to make great games? Brilliantly optimized graphics code? Stunning sound effects, clever artificial intelligence routines, lush artwork, or simply irresistible gameplay? Well, you need all of that of course, with gameplay one of the most important factors. However, behind the scenes you are going to need a trail guide and a map to get there.

You might be working alone on a great mod to a commercial game, or you might be working with an artist on a cool online card game, or you might be the director of development at

Blizzard. The size of your project or your role does not matter; you still need a plan to create your game.

Why must you have a plan? With the smallest of projects the plan will likely be to get a prototype of the game going as soon as possible and then just iterating and playing with the game until it is done. This method works well if the game you are making is a hobby project, or your company is funded by a seemingly unlimited supply of someone else's money and you are not holding yourself financially accountable.

Very Few Titles Are Profitable

Many people do not realize how few games are profitable. In 2001 over 3,000 games were released for the PC platform; it is likely only 100 or so of those titles turned a profit, and of those only the top 50 made significant money for the developers and publishers.

In 2000 an established developer in North America would likely receive between $1 million and $3 million in advances paid out over 12 to 36 months for the development of a game. The typical publisher will spend between $250,000 and $1.5 million in marketing

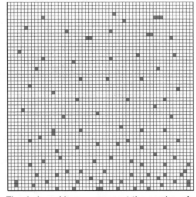

The darkened boxes represent the number of successful games published each year.

and sales development ("sales development" is the euphemistic term for the money the publisher must spend to get the game actually on the shelf at the retailer and well positioned). The box, CDs, maps, manual, and other materials in the box cost between $1.50 and $4.00 collectively. The royalties an established developer could expect vary widely, from 10 to 30 percent, depending on many factors including how much of the financial risk the developer is assuming and the types of deductions to the wholesale price. Let's take a look at what these numbers mean for a game that has an average retail price of $35 over the life of sales in the first 12 to 24 months after release. Table 1 summarizes the financial assumptions behind this hypothetical project.

Table 1—PC Game Project Financial Basics

Average Retail Price	$35.00
Wholesale Price	$21.00
Developer Advance	$1,500,000
Developer Royalty	15%

Table 2—Game Project Payoffs at Various Sales Targets

Units	Royalty	Less Advance
10,000	$ 31,500	$ (1,468,500)
30,000	$ 94,500	$ (1,405,500)
100,000	$ 315,000	$ (1,185,000)
200,000	$ 630,000	$ (870,000)
300,000	$ 945,000	$ (555,000)
500,000	$ 1,575,000	$ 75,000
1,000,000	$ 3,150,000	$ 1,650,000
2,000,000	$ 6,300,000	$ 4,800,000

500,000 Units to Break Even?

Take a long hard look at Table 2. Notice that not until 500,000 units have been sold does the developer see a royalty check. This is a $75,000 check that is likely to be issued to you between 9 and 18 months after release of the title. The conclusion from this is that royalties alone will not feed you and your team post-release. "No problem," you think, "my title will sell millions!" Unfortunately, even good games don't always sell many units. As an example, the excellent developer Raven sold a little over 30,000 units of the strong game Hexen II. Messiah, the long-anticipated edgy first-person shooter, saw fewer than 10,000 units sold in its first three months (most games make the large bulk of their sales in the first 90 days of release). Fallout 1 enjoyed a loyal fan following and strong critical reviews and sold a little more than 120,000 units in its first year. The author's Starfleet Command 1 sold over 350,000 units its first year without counting the Gold Edition and the Neutral Zone expansion. However, the sequel, Starfleet Command 2, has sold 120,000 units in its first six months of release. Sure, Diablo II from Blizzard enjoyed over 2 million units of orders on day one of release, and The Sims has been in the top 3 of *PC Data* for almost *a year and a half*. These titles have clearly made a ton of money. In fact, those orders that Blizzard had for Diablo II on day 1 had a value that exceeds the market capitalization of

Interplay Entertainment[1]—a publisher with a rich publishing history spanning over 15 years.

Employee Compensation and Royalties

Table 2 has other implications. Many development houses share royalties they receive with their employees by some fraction. Many developers go even further and offset the often too-low salaries paid in the highly competitive game business with overly optimistic promises of future royalty payments. These promises are meaningless in many cases: After the employees crunch through development and release and even during post-release, supporting the fans, these expectations of monetary rewards for their labor turn out to be false. Then these employees turn from energetic, highly productive creative developers to disenfranchised employees looking for a new job.

What Are the Financial Expectations for Your Game?

A recurring theme throughout this book is managing expectations of all project stakeholders through high-quality communication that is clear and honest. That is why I am presenting this sobering information so early in this book. You must be clear about why you are creating your game. Do you expect to make a profit? Are you depending on the royalties (or direct sales in the case of software sold as shareware or by other direct sales methods) to support yourself and your development staff? Is this project only a hobby and any money it produces a happy bonus? Is a publisher funding the project or do you have an investor backing your project?

Knowing your financial expectations—not your hopes and dreams—for your game project is critical to achieving success. Establishing these expectations will determine the scope of the project. With the scope of the project in mind, an estimation of the number of developers required to create the game and how long it will take is established. This estimate should then be compared to the financial goals one more time to establish a baseline for cost, time, and scope.

The Scope of the Game Must Match Financial Parameters

Most game projects fail to meet their financial expectations because the developers fail to articulate clearly and honestly what the implications of their expectations are. This is such an obvious statement, but virtually every game project I know of suffers from a disparity between what the expectations are for the project and the resources and time allocated to the project. Some of the very well-endowed developers such as Blizzard, BioWare, and id are famous for the "When it's done" mantra. There is little doubt that a project from Blizzard, BioWare, or id will be of the highest quality and most

---

1   This statement sounded a lot more impressive when I wrote it in the summer of 2001; as of October 2002 Interplay has been delisted from NASDAQ.

< < < < < < < < < < < < < < < < < < < < < < < < < < < < <

undoubtedly be very profitable. However, Blizzard, BioWare, and id also have a large amount of working capital on hand and have dedicated that working capital to making killer games.

If you do not have an unlimited supply of working capital on hand, then I strongly suggest you take on a different mantra than "When it's done." Most likely you have a budget of both time and money to work with, so what you need to do is figure out what is the "best" game you can make within budget. Remember, id founders once created games for $6 an hour for a long-forgotten publisher, SoftDisk, and Blizzard once worked as a developer for Interplay. There are steppingstones on the way to greatness; too many developers try to take the gaming world by storm in one ambitious step.

Why Your Game Should Profit

Part II, How to Make a Game, will show how we take these baselines and develop a project plan and then execute the development of a game project. Beyond just running a single game project, I will discuss how your game project should fit into a greater plan of growth for yourself, your company, and/or your team. The dot-com era has distorted many people's expectations of what it takes to make a business. Too many dot-coms were based on business plans about gaining "mind share" or "market presence," or were just plain hype. Many overnight millionaires were made, so this style of business creation certainly worked for some, but for the vast majority of dot-coms, bankruptcy and bust was the end. These dot-coms failed to create a product or service that people would actually pay money for and be able to deliver it in such a manner that they could *make a profit*. Making a profit is not an evil thing to do for a bunch of creative game developers. Making a profit enables you to store up capital to handle the period of time between projects. A capital reserve allows you to respond more gracefully to project slippage due to unexpected turnover or other unforeseen events. Profit allows you more tactical and strategic maneuvering room for your game company. This store of capital enables you to make more ambitious games in the future, retain employees, hire new talent, and make capital improvements to your workplace for greater efficiency. Too many game developers pour their heart and soul into game projects that have no real likelihood of making a profit.

Maybe you do not care about profit. Maybe it is of secondary or even tertiary importance to you. I still urge you to run your game project with the rigor and the earnestness of a small business that needs to deliver on expectations, on budget, and on time.

Following are two unprofitable attitudes when approaching game development.

Feature Storm

Attitude #1: "Hey! What about quality? You are leaving me cold here, Erik. My game is going to rock; it is going to be massively multiplayer, with magic, martial arts, and small arms combat. I am going to have vehicles, and you can go to any planet you want and even fly a starship to get there! Erik, you dork, of course my game is going to make a ton of money; people are going to lay down $10 a month to play it, and I will port it over to the PS2 and Xbox and pick up the juicy console money too. Sheesh! Making a profit, that is going to be a side effect of my vision, Erik. I do not need to worry about that!"

What is wrong with attitude #1 is that the designer has not looked into the costs for developing every feature under the sun. There is a reason why Warcraft is a tight game about managing humans and orcs gathering stone, gold, and wood. There is a reason why Quake is a tight game about first-person combat. Creating a game that people want to play means fully *delivering on every expectation* you create in your game design. If your game design has martial arts combat, then your fans will want a very playable martial arts simulation. If you also have starfighters to pilot in your game, your game better be competitive with FreeSpace 2 in its

execution of starfighter combat. Otherwise you will end up creating a bunch of open expectations that you will not be able to fulfill. The market will crush you for creating unmet hype.

If the Game Is Worth Making, Make It Excellent

Attitude #2: "I am just making a little spades game to get my feet wet. I am never going to show it to anyone, and no one is going to play it, so who cares if I make a profit?"

The problem with attitude #2 is that it ignores the strong wisdom that says if something is worth doing, it is worth doing well. A weak demonstration of your programming skills will demonstrate that you are a weak programmer. An incomplete game design document will demonstrate that you make incomplete designs. Art that does not appear competitive shows that you do not have the artistic talent to compete.

Excellence in Spades

Take a look at Hardwood Spades from Silver Creek Entertainment (http:www.silvercrk.com). This is by far the most polished execution of spades the world has ever seen. A core team of just three developers has put out an incredible series of classic card games, where the quality of the executed games is way over the top. They have added a ton of small, tight features and improvements to the playing of spades such as casting a fireball or a shower of flowers at another player. This spades game is multiplayer and is played 24x7 on servers hosted by these folks. They do not take advance money from a publisher

but sell their games direct to the consumer online. They have slowly built up a following over the years and are now quietly selling hundreds of units a month for each of their titles. I have the utmost respect for these folks. They had a vision for creating the highest quality classic card games on the planet and have executed that dream step-by-step, building up their capital, fan base, and quality level as they went. Notice that they did not pitch the idea of the world's most gorgeous card games for $2 million up front to a publisher and then go find an artist, programmer, game designer, and fan base. Instead,

< < < < < < < < < < < < < < < < < < < < < < < < < < <

they released their first game, Hardwood Solitaire, in 1997, which had moderate success and enabled them to build upon this experience. I have no idea what their future plans are, but notice that they have built up a strong collection of popular titles and a successful brand, and are now in the powerful position of continuing to build up their brand and products, licensing their products for a distribution deal, or perhaps selling themselves in whole to a larger company to lock in a strong return on their years of investment.

Game Making Is a Long Race of Many Game Projects

Investing over time is what it takes to make it big in the game industry. It is a very long race in a very small world; do not burn any bridges, and try to make as many friends as possible along the way.

Some of you may be familiar with the games I have produced—the Starfleet Command series. Some of you might say, "Hey, Erik, didn't SFC1 and SFC2 have a bit too many bugs? How do you account for that? Oh, and didn't SFC2 not ship with a functional Dynaverse 2, the hyped, massively multiplayer-lite metagame? If you are so wise, Erik, explain what happened."

No problem, hang on a moment and listen to what I have to say.

This is a book wrought from my experience and the experience of other developers—experience of both success and failure.

What I have to share with you in this book is not wisdom I received in college, nor did my boss train me when I first led a game project. This is hands-on, face-the-challenges-as-you-go advice. Much of what I have learned has come from taking the time to analyze what happened and discussions with my teammates and other game developers to figure out what went wrong and how we could have done better. In many ways this book represents a field manual of essential game production that I would have appreciated reading when I started leading game projects. Throughout this book I will discuss the Starfleet Command series and the decisions I have made along the way as a producer. You will be able to run shotgun and role-play an armchair executive producer!

There are books out there that will attempt to teach you to design and program a real-time strategy game or write the rasterizer for a software first-person shooter. You can also find books telling you how to design and architect your game, and some books have made strong efforts as a resource guide for finding sources of art, music, and code. However, these books do not address *how to make a game*.

> >

A Brief History of Software Development

How to make a game, I believe, is the most elusive question in the game industry. In fact, the software industry at large is relatively open and up-front about how immature the software engineering processes are as a whole. Take a look at *After the Gold Rush* by Steve McConnell for an excellent discussion of the much-needed maturation in the software industry. Much development in the software engineering community is going into improving the process of how we go about making software. During the '60s and '70s great strides were made in increasing the strength of the programming languages from Fortran and COBOL to C. During the '80s the microcomputer created tremendous improvements in the programming workplace. Each developer could have his own workstation where he edited, ran, and debugged code. During the late '80s and early '90s the leading edge of the software development community got charged with the efficacy of object-oriented programming and the large-project strength of C++. Improvements continued with integrated editors, debuggers, and profilers. Optimizing compilers have almost made assembly programming obsolete, and visual interface layout tools have made programming rather pleasant for business applications. With all of these fantastic improvements to the software development process, software project budgets have only gotten larger and have only slipped by longer amounts of time and by greater numbers.

Overly Long Game Projects Are Disastrous

Take a look at Table 3 listing game projects, how long they took to release, and the outcome.

This table is a Who's Who of games that have run horribly over budget, and only two games on that list have made significant money: The Sims and Baldur's Gate. The best-selling game on the list, The Sims, has made and is continuing to make a huge fortune for Electronic Arts. Why is it that The Sims has made the most money on that list? Because Electronic Arts was very fortunate that no one else (that statement is worth repeating) no one in the entire PC game industry of some 3,000 titles a year for five years in a row has released a title even remotely competitive to The Sims, filling a vastly

Table 3—Long Game Projects

Stonekeep 1	5 years of development	Weak sales
Daikatana	4 years of development, fantastic cost overruns	Weak sales
Messiah	5 years of development	Weak sales
Max Payne	5 years of development	Just released
The Sims	5 years of development	Amazing sales
Baldur's Gate	3+ years of development	Very strong sales
Duke Nukem Forever	5+ years of development	Yet to be released
Stonekeep 2	5 years of development	Project cancelled
Ultima Online 2	4 years of development	Project cancelled

< < < < < < < < < < < < < < < < < < < < < < < < <

underserved market of women who are consumers waiting for games to be designed for them. And with the right title EA can make tons of money due to its marketing and sales strength; this cannot be underestimated.

Also note that Maxis released something like ten games in the sims genre and only two of these, SimCity and The Sims, have generated great returns over ten years. The rest of the sim-type games were relatively poor sellers. This is something that seems to be forgotten by a lot of people—that Will Wright has been experimenting with this type of game for ten + years before hitting a home run with The Sims.

Max Payne has just been released, and we need a little time to see how the market will respond to this adventure shooter with amazing graphics (I expect this game to do well). The other successful title on the list, Baldur's Gate, had a number of delays and development extensions but ultimately was still successful: The Baldur's Gate series (BG with its expansion pack and sequel/expansion pack) has sold nearly 4 million units worldwide. It came at the right time for role-playing games and was a quality title with a strong license (Advanced Dungeons and Dragons) behind it.

As for the rest of the titles, they were simply too-little too-late titles that had to compete against stronger games that were produced faster and for less money. Or in the case of Stonekeep 2 and Ultima Online 2, there were millions of dollars of game development and even the hype of game magazine covers that the publishers had to walk away from when the games were cancelled!

What Late Games Do to Publishers

When projects run over, even by less than three years, they hurt the industry at large. Consumers are tired of being frustrated by overly hyped games that are late. The publishers are constantly attempting to make realistic financial projections to manage their cash flow and maintain investor confidence. With poor cash flow or low investor confidence, a publisher is often forced into publishing more titles. More titles mean each receives less attention at every stage of development. This in turn weakens the publisher more, as titles begin to ship before they are ready in order to fill gaps in the quarter. This creates a vicious feedback cycle that pressures the publisher to publish even more titles.

Our Project Plan Behind Starfleet Command

Interplay was impressed with our quick execution of Caesars Palace W95 while working for another developer, and after doing various contracting and working on our own demo of a game, we joined Interplay in the summer of 1998. Interplay presented me with

running Starfleet Command and the opportunity to work with Sean, Zach, and other folks I had worked with before. We jumped at the opportunity to work on a big title at a big publisher. When we got into it, we realized that Interplay was a big company with many

> >

Starfleet Command

different games in production. Our sister project, Klingon Academy, was making impressive success in the damage effects of its 3D engine and its cinematic cut scenes. Starfleet Command, on the other hand, was considered a niche game appealing only to the most hardcore of game players—fans of Star Fleet Battles. This turned out to be a great advantage on several different levels at the same time. The first benefit is that Brian Fargo, the founder and CEO of the company, left the project's vision entirely in my hands while Klingon Academy received more of Interplay's attention. The other benefit was of course the built-in base of Star Fleet Battles fans who had waited 20 years for a computerized version of their favorite, ultra-detailed naval starship simulation set in the original series' *Star Trek* universe.

The Vision for Starfleet Command

Starfleet Command was my first big title to manage; I was very excited and determined to do a good job. I wanted

to earn Interplay's respect so that they would trust us enough to fund a future game concept of ours. SFC itself was an exciting title for us to work on, but for every game project you must know why you are doing it. For Starfleet Command our goal was to create the most faithful, highest fidelity modeling of naval starship combat set in the *Star Trek* universe. We were not trying to make a Star Trek game, we were not trying to make a 3D game, and we were not trying to make a real-time strategy game like StarCraft. As we worked on our vision statement, we developed the term *real-time tactical* to describe our gameplay. Our game was all about tactical starship combat. We did not send teams down to planets, we did not have the player act as a courier and carry goods across the galaxy, and we did not allow the scavenging of enemy vessels to build a Frankenstein ship. No, instead you were a naval officer in one

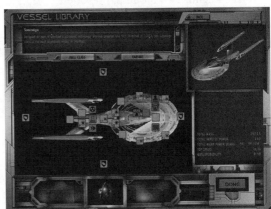

The vessel library screen from Starfleet Command

of six star empires carrying out combat missions on behalf of your empire.

Over 1,000 starships were modeled in our game, with over 100 missions to test your tactics and strategy. The player role-played a captain enjoying a career of over 30 years in the service of his empire. That was what Starfleet Command was about, that was our goal, and we delivered on that.

Constraints Give Much Needed Focus

Starfleet Command went on to be a stunning success. The press at the time was stunned to see a Star Trek game that was actually fun. The secret to our success was following our vision. We had no budget for fancy movies to tell a story, so we did not try to create a game with a linear story line that depended on movies. Instead we developed a random mission/campaign generator with linear story missions embedded like raisins in pudding. You must look at every constraint on your project as an opportunity to focus your game on its key features.

On Bugs Shipped in Starfleet Command

High-quality games with ultra-low bug counts like Quake and Diablo sell very well. However, Quake and Diablo sell strongly for quite a few good reasons working together. We had a fixed timeline; in fact, the Starfleet Command project was already late before I took it over. After reviewing where the project was for two months, I decided on a delivery date of summer 1999 given a lot of extra programming and art resources. Interplay granted the resources but in turn needed the date to be unmoving. We had a project with a flexible feature set but a fixed timeline. We essentially put too many features in the game and coded too late into the production process. We were still coding heavily two weeks from final master and worked on the first patch all the way through manufacturing. We fixed so many bugs in the last three months of development that we honestly thought we had a game with a fairly low bug count and a ton of features. After a week of it being on the street, I developed a new realization of how high a quality standard software must have in order to work on anyone's computer, in any manner the user could come up with. We did have to ship with known bugs though, and the consumers had to deal with those too. We were fast with the patches, and altogether the public enjoyed a game that was original and fun to play. Starfleet Command went on to sell over 350,000 units in its first year, and at that time at Interplay, SFC was the second most successful title, behind Baldur's Gate developed by BioWare. Also it is a fact that there are more bugs inherent to games with more complex systems; for example, SFC is much more complex and detailed than Quake and therefore needs additional QA attention. Role-playing games like BG are also more complicated and required additional QA time and completely different QA processes. Treating all games in an identical manner from a QA perspective is just plain wrong (but it happens all the time).

> >

Well-Met Goals Enable Future Successes

Based on the success of Starfleet Command, Interplay's management was very receptive to our pitch to do Starfleet Command 2 as a wholly independent developer. See Chapter 27 to see how we set up as Taldren and how we structured our company for the development of Starfleet Command 2.

Strong Game Developers Have Strong Foundations

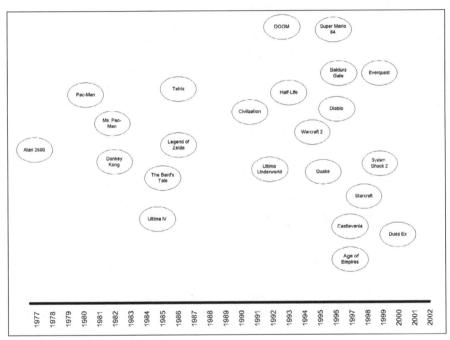

A small chronicle of great games

The above figure chronicles just a few of the most successful and influential games over the years.

The Tension between Preproduction and Production

Bridges for the most part stoically support their loads across their spans. Dams rarely burst, flooding entire cities. Why do civil engineering projects seem to be routinely successful when software engineering projects routinely go over budget, take too long, and generally underperform or are just buggy? The difference is in process and methodologies. Performing something complex that requires the efforts of many skilled humans over an extended period of time necessitates breaking up the large, complex task into a series of small, achievable, measurable tasks. Ideally, figuring out what you are doing should come before you do it; the game industry term for this phase of work is *preproduction*, or the vision or design phase. We have a name for it sure enough, but too many projects violate their preproduction phases and move straight to production. Twenty years ago preproduction would have been a sketch of the game screen on a napkin and a couple of experimental routines to get the idea straight. Ten years ago preproduction was largely about the art of the proposed game. Now preproduction is usually a playable demo.

True preproduction would be the distillation of all the game's requirements, an analysis stage to determine the implications of these requirements, a culling stage to meet the business parameters, and a detailed game, art, audio, and technical design to detail the requirements. Preproduction would still not be done, however, for these detailed game, art, audio, and technical designs would uncover new details about the project requiring another revision of the feature set to meet the business requirements.

Any risky areas of the project need to be explicitly called out, and alternative plans need to be formulated to get around these risks. Finally the plan needs to be presented to all stakeholders including the development team, the publisher, and the marketing, press relations, and sales forces.

Games are big productions, and successful games require the full effort of many individuals spanning many companies. In my opinion, preproduction is the most important stage of the project. I would like to see the day when a project spends a full 25 to 40 percent of its overall prerelease time in preproduction. During production there should be relatively few surprises. The developers should be able to work eight hours a day, take vacations, and pick up their children from school. Instead, the industry responds to the intense competition by compressing preproduction into the shortest period of time possible. There is no hype, celebration, visibility, or honor in the game industry as a whole for preproduction. In my opinion, everyone would make a lot more money if instead of 3,000 game projects being launched a year, 4,000 or 5,000 game projects could receive two to nine months of preproduction and *get cancelled*, and only the top 400 to 800 would get produced and released. Publishers' net revenues would be five to ten times higher if their hit projects were not bogged down by four to ten failed projects.

The Power of the Console

The console side of the business does manage itself a lot stronger than the PC world in this regard. The answer lies in the hardware vendors; they do not allow a title to be released unless they approve. A console title must be presented to the hardware vendor several times along the way and can be sent back for revision or altogether cancelled by the hardware vendor with no

> >

recourse for the publisher except to work harder. This added rigor in the console world allows far fewer titles to be produced, but the net revenues across all console titles are reported to be seven times more profitable.

Why Aren't All Publishers Using Preproduction?

If preproduction is so compelling, why isn't every publisher using it? Actually publishers have a twist on this process, called *green-light meetings*. Some projects have only one at the beginning of a project; other companies have a series of green-light meetings acting as gates that the project must pass through. However, these meetings are just meetings. There are a bunch of executives with too much work to do trying to figure out if they should cancel a project or not. To help them make a positive decision, the developers, producers, and executive producers at the publishing house spend a lot of development energy making bits of software and art that hopefully make a striking impression on the executive's mind. This is accurately enough called "eye candy."

> **JARGON**: A *green-light meeting* is a meeting at which a body of decision makers at the publisher decide whether or not to publish a game.

Instead of one of these green-light meetings, I think each game project should undergo a green-light miniphase where each portion of the project, such as art, game design, and technical, present their detailed plan on how to get their job done to one or more experts in that field. It should be the composite findings of these experts that is shown to the executives. It could be that diagrams, charts, concept sketches, and even demonstrations of eye candy are appropriate, but the eye candy should be presented in the context of an overall production plan. If this level of rigor were followed, we would all be making stronger games resulting in much stronger sales and much saner schedules. Unfortunately the experts you would need to employ would have to be so skilled that they would most likely be art directors or technical directors, or running their own development company. The usual process is that game projects are ignored by the executives in the early stages when there are other more pressing fires to be put out, or the executives tend to focus on what they see in the form of eye candy.

The Process Is Changing

The game development process is one of the hotter topics that publishers now look for in a developer. Microsoft, for instance, sends a solid team of experts down to a prospective developer and interviews the house for a day or two. Microsoft also appears to be the publisher that respects preproduction the most by giving each project at least two or three months of real, funded preproduction. The actual presentation to the executives of the preproduction is more of a team affair involving the developer, the producers, as well as early reports of something called usability.

Having far less development resources to tap than Microsoft, Eidos calls upon the heads of their various studios to pass judgment at the greenlight meeting. Each of these studio heads has a strong development background and his or her gut reactions are fairly good divining rods of a game's success when you only have 20 minutes to review a title.

Look for more publishers changing their project review process as they try to cull their failing projects before release, and ideally, early in production.

A Strong Plan Makes Game Development Easy

This is not a chapter of gloom and doom; rather this chapter points out the larger pitfalls in game development. The whole book is dedicated to taking a proactive, forward-looking approach to game development. Chapters 8 and 9 detail the role of the game design and technical design documents. Chapter 10 discusses how the game design and technical design documents are synthesized into a project plan. Chapter 17 delves deeper into the rigor that should be put into preproduction with an introduction to Unified Modeling Language in the form of use cases and how they are used to perform your requirements capture.

Chapter 16 discusses how critical the game design document is in shaping the team's vision for the game. If everyone knows what the game is supposed to be like, they will make it a lot faster and better. Chapter 16 presents specific steps you should take when constructing your game design document; other leaders in the game industry will discuss what material they think is critical in the game design document.

Technical design is presented in Chapter 18, a thick chapter with a lot of discussion of large project object-oriented technical design. Unified Modeling Language is revisited here to see how it is used to model the software from different views, such as static views of deployment, packages and class diagrams, and the dynamic views of activity and sequence diagrams.

Developing accurate time estimates is addressed in Chapter 19, including classic questions such as how much to pad or whether one should one pad at all.

Wrestling all of this data together into a digestible project plan is discussed in Chapter 20.

The Gravitational Pull of Feature Creep

Even if you have the best-constructed production plan this industry has ever seen, your project still needs to be organized. Do not think that production is the time to go get your plan professionally printed and sent to all of your friends while you work on getting your A licenses in Gran Turismo 3. Rather, production is the time to put your plan to work; Chapter 22 tells you how to get a grip on feature creep.

> >

Task Visibility for Team Motivation and for Progress Tracking

Task visibility is my passion. There is a deep satisfaction I get as a producer when I know my team members know their own tasks and the tasks that the others have to do. When each person is humming along, tearing through the project with the utmost confidence in his or her team members, it seems like anything and everything can be done. As the leader of a team or a subteam, your job is to monitor this well-being. Too many times a project's Gantt chart (discussed in Chapters 10 and 20) is posted on a wall and updated only once a month. Task visibility means a lot more than the manager keeping track of progress and reporting to the executive management. The development team is the most important customer to report the project's progress. Chapter 10 gives an introduction to task tracking, while Chapter 21 provides detailed task management techniques from various top studios.

Use Your Core Competencies and Outsource the Rest

A large portion of this book is an in-depth guide to outsourcing parts of your development from cinematics and motion capture to music and sound effects. Figuring out what you should outsource is discussed in Chapter 12. Chapter 12 introduces outsourcing, and Chapters 28 through 33 give specific advice on where to get your outsourcing done and how to do business with these vendors.

A Pitfall of Success—Fan-Requested Features and Changes

Ironically, making a hit game brings with it the challenges of meeting a fan base with an insatiable appetite for more, bigger, faster, and cooler features. Endless debates discussing your game balancing skills and astonishing acts of generosity from your most dedicated fans will test the depth of your commitment to your game, which is now their game. Mastering the post-release fan relationship is a lot more than issuing a patch and crawling back into your cave of creativity. Now that your game has enjoyed success, it is time to open your shop door, so to speak, and take your relationship with the fans to a deeper level that will carry forward to your next title. Chapter 24 discusses the issues involved in this relationship and some specific advice from successful game developers.

The Relentless Pace of Technology

Game making is a creative art form that competes with other media such as novels, television, movies, and music. While technology has had dramatic effects on how music is recorded, how film is taped, how television is delivered, and even how a novel is typed, none of these other art forms have to compete with technology to nearly the pace game making does.

Movies are probably the closest art form in scope, cost, and high-level production methods. That being said, camera technology stays stable for 20 years at a stretch, lights are lights, and microphones are microphones. Right now the movie industry is looking at using digital film, but again, this is technology that has been in regular use for 20 or more years.

In the past 25 years that electronic games have been a consumer entertainment medium, they have gone through nearly countless technological evolutions including text adventures, 2D graphic adventures, turn-based strategy games, 3D action games, smooth-scrolling 3D action games, ray-casting engines, binary space-partition engines, and I could go on and on listing the different game engines that have been created.

Each new game must develop its own tools first and then create its content. Future add-on and expansion packs will often use the same engine, and in some cases the sequel will use a modified version of the prior game. It has become increasingly common in the last five years to license whole game engines such as Quake and Unreal to act as the foundation engine to build a game. A game requires not only a solid design but also a completed engine and tool path prior to entering the implementation or production phase; otherwise the inevitable result seems to be redoing work over and over, which is demoralizing, expensive, and a waste of time.

This shifting engine technology is not seen in any other consumer software product. There is no consumer operating system, word processor, or spreadsheet that has required the computing power of the last five or ten years of Intel's advances to the x86 line of chips. It is games that drive our voracious appetites for more RAM to hold our textures, gigabytes of hard drive space to hold our gigabyte installs, and the fastest CPU on the planet to simulate our fantasy worlds.

The dark side of this technological advance on the PC side of the game business is that we do not know what hardware the consumers will have before they install and run our software. We do not know if they have 64 MB of RAM, 128 MB, or just 32 MB of main memory. We do not know if they have a 3D accelerator card with 8 MB of RAM, 32, 64, or no 3D card at all! We do not know if they will have enough space to install our game in its full glory, so we have multiple install options. We do not know if their graphics card chipset will support the subset of features we want for our game. We do not even know how fast the target CPU is. In fact we do not even know what *operating system* they will be running our game on. Sure it will be a Windows variant, but there must be big differences between Windows 95, Windows 98, Windows NT, Windows 2000,

> >

Windows ME, and Windows XP or Microsoft would not have put thousands of man-years into these operating systems. These operating systems have major differences on critical low-level functionality like how memory is accessed and protected, how timers are created, what their resolution is, and the efficiency of storing and retrieving data from the hard drive. There are people out there playing Starfleet Command 1 with the graphics options turned low on laptops with only a Pentium 90 MHz and no 3D card, and there are also folks out there with a Pentium IV 1.7 GHz with a GeForce 3 card that has 64 MB of memory just on the card. Depending on which metric you use, the Pentium IV 1.7 GHz is nearly *twenty times* more powerful than the Pentium 90. This is called Moore's Law, stating that the computing power of computers doubles every 18 months.

With all of these unknowns, we need to create a game that will run substantially well and deliver the same play experience on the greatest number of machines out there. This is where minimum requirements and clever use of scalability in performance-intensive features such as graphics and artificial intelligence comes to play. Hardcore games typically have the most aggressive schedule for culling older machines from the minimum requirements. This, however, cuts into sales for mass-market games, and a delicate balance exists between pushing the edge of the performance bar in order to gain exposure and adoption by the hardcore players, and planning for broad sales by supporting as many older systems as possible. Games that are strong examples of this are The Sims, StarCraft, and Baldur's Gate I and II, which

work on quite low-end systems. Much of their success in the mass market may relate to the fact that people with lower end systems can still play them.

The final challenge in the fast pace of technological change is that your requirements will often change mid-project or very late in your project. With less than six weeks to go on Starfleet Command 1, I was informed that Interplay signed a ten-product agreement to support AMD's 3DNow chip set. With little time left before code freeze, we were forced to optimize just a handful of low-level vector and matrix routines to take advantage of the 3DNow feature set.

The console market is considerably different. When you make a game for the PlayStation 2 you know exactly how fast it will be, how much video RAM you will have, and every other detail of the console at the time of producing the game. (Except when a developer is working on a game for a console that has not been released yet to the public. In the case of Taldren, we are working on an Xbox game, and I get packages from Microsoft every so often with a revision to the software running the box. At larger intervals the hardware itself changes.) This factor, combined with much more stringent QA from the console manufacturers themselves, makes console games practically bug-free in comparison to PC games.

Console developers have a strategic advantage in that their platform is known and immutable, but also a disadvantage in that their platform may be supplanted by new consoles such as the recently released GameCube/Xbox, which technologically are far superior to the PS2. The console developers must then go through an awkward

‹ ‹

stage of trying to prove to the publishers that they are capable of developing on the new console platform.

The only way to deal with these technological changes is to plan for them. You need to build profiling and diagnostic tools straight into your game so that you can understand how it is performing under various game conditions. You need to allow time in your schedule to support the odd piece of software or hardware that is strategically important to your publisher. You will also need to develop your minimum requirements as early in your schedule as possible. The sooner you set the goal of meeting a specific minimum requirement, the closer you will be to actually achieving that goal.

The Art of War and Games

Around 500 B.C. Sun Tzu Wu spelled out five essential points to follow for victory in battle:

1. He will win who knows when to fight and when not to fight.
2. He will win who knows how to handle both superior and inferior forces.
3. He will win whose army is animated by the same spirit throughout all the ranks.
4. He will win who, prepared himself, waits to take the enemy unprepared.
5. He will win who has military capacity and is not interfered with by his sovereign.

"Victory lies in the knowledge of these five points." Sun Tzu

Only after writing the first draft of this chapter did I pick up my copy of *The Art of War* and flip through it. Notice how well this advice that is over 2,500 years old neatly describes the fundamental challenges of game development. Preproduction was so valued by Sun Tzu that he felt point #1 was insufficient and added point #4 with the admonishment of not hyping your game too early. Point #2 succinctly reminds you to create a game in response to the financial parameters of your game project. Point #3 clearly supports strong task visibility and a production plan signed off by the whole team. And I see point #5 as the combination of building your game development experience and not being forced to follow inefficient production methods due to inexperience on the part of the publisher.

二十

故知勝有五：知可以戰與不可以戰者勝；識
眾寡之用者勝；上下同欲者勝；以虞待不虞者
勝[1]；將能而君不御者勝[2]。此五者，知勝之
道也。

Sun Tzu's five essential points in Chinese

Chapter 4 > > > > > > > > > > > > > > > >

Game Project Survival Test

This test is an adaptation of the software project survival test that can be found in Steve McConnell's *Software Project Survival Guide*. The idea behind this test is to quickly get a rough guide to the overall preparedness of yourself and your team for the game project at hand. I suggest taking the test at the beginning, middle, and end of each of your projects as a reminder of good practices.

The Game Project Survival Test

As you read through the questions below, score 3 points if you are comfortable answering yes, score 2 points if you feel your team is partially addressing the question but more work could be done, and score 1 point if you really want to say yes, but it would be a lie. If the question is referring to something that occurs mid-project, answer the question according to your current plans.

Game Requirements

___ 1.   Is there a clear, unambiguous vision statement for the game?

___ 2.   Do all team members believe that this vision is realistic?

___ 3.   Does the project have a reasonable expectation of being profitable for both the publisher and the developer?

___ 4.   Has the core gameplay and user interface of the game been fleshed out so that everyone clearly understands what the game is and why it is fun?

___ 5.   Do the team members think the game will be fun?

Planning

___ 6.   Does the game have a detailed, written game design document?

___ 7.   Does the game have a detailed, written technical design document?

___ 8.   Does the game have a detailed, written art production plan?

___ 9.   Do you have a detailed, integrated project schedule that lists all of the tasks that need to be performed, and have the dependencies between various team members been indicated?

< < < < < < < < < < < < < < < < < < < < < < < < <

___ 10. Does your project schedule include tasks like press tours? E3? The Game Developers Conference? Installer? Auto-patcher? Submission to hardware manufacturer approval?

___ 11. Were the schedule and the budget for the game officially updated and discussed between the publisher and the developer at the end of the latest milestone—even if to say, "Yes, everything is on track"?

___ 12. Are the features of the game tagged with core, secondary, and tertiary levels of priority to facilitate feature trimming if necessary to maintain the schedule?

___ 13. Does the game have a written quality assurance plan? Does it handle beta testers? In-house testing? Automated test suites?

___ 14. Does the game have a detailed milestone plan? Does it clearly describe what will be delivered and reviewable at each milestone?

___ 15. Does the schedule allow enough time for balance, tuning, and tweaking of features to ensure that it is fun?

___ 16. Does the schedule account for sick days, holidays, and vacation time? Are the developers tasked at less than 100 percent? Are the leads tasked at less than 75 or 50 percent depending on their responsibility sets?

___ 17. Has the game design, technical design, art production plan, QA plan, and all of the rest of the composite game development team signed off on the plan?

Project Control

___ 18. Does the game have a single executive—the project leader or lead designer or producer? Whatever you call the job at your shop, has this person been given full authority, responsibility, and accountability for the success of this game? And is the person enthusiastically embracing this authority, responsibility, and accountability?

___ 19. Does this project leader have the right workload? Does she have the adequate amount of time to perform at her highest level of project management?

___ 20. Have the milestones been laid out with clear, measurable deliverables that can easily be quantified as done or not done?

___ 21. Are the milestones being delivered to the publisher in such a manner as to make it easy for them to review the milestones and measure the progress of the project for themselves?

___ 22. Do the developers have access to an anonymous communication channel where they can report problems without fear?

___ 23. Does the game project plan have a written plan for controlling feature creep in the game?

___ 24. Does the game project have a clearly defined method of how changes will be reviewed by development team leads such as the art and technical directors?

> >

____ 25. Are all of the game design, technical design, schedule, art production, QA, and all other planning materials easily accessible to all development team members? Are they encouraged to read the material?

____ 26. Is all source code under version control software?

____ 27. Are all of the binary assets such as textures, models, music files, and sound effects also stored under version control software?

____ 28. Do all of the team members have the tools to do the job such as workstations, PS2 and Xbox development kits, 3D Studio Max or Maya seats, bug tracking software, and scheduling software?

Risk Management

____ 29. Does the game project have a written risks document with possible solutions?

____ 30. Is this risks document updated at the completion of every milestone?

____ 31. Does the game project have a risks officer who is encouraged to scout ahead for risks on the project?

____ 32. If the project is using subcontractors, is there a written plan for how to manage the subcontractors? For each subcontractor is there a single member of the development team who is responsible for that subcontractor?

Personnel

____ 33. Does the game development team have all of the expertise needed to complete the game?

____ 34. Does the game development team have a management team that is experienced with managing game development? In other words, are the developers able to concentrate on developing rather than worrying about the state of their game development shop?

____ 35. Does the game have a lead programmer who is capable of leading the programmers of the team to making a kick-ass game?

____ 36. Are there enough developers to do all of the work?

____ 37. Do all of the development team members get along with each other?

____ 38. Is each team member committed to staying with the game until it successfully ships?

Calculating Your Project's Score

____ **Subtotal:** Add the points above (ranges from 38 to 114).

____ **Development team size factor:** If your game project has fewer than nine full-time developers, including all artists, programmers, designers, QA, and audio people, use 1.5. If your team has fewer than 19 full-time developers, use 1.2.

____ **Grand total:** Multiply your subtotal by the team size factor.

What Does My Score Mean?

Scores: 102+   AAA—Your game has every possible resource, tool, and plan it will take to make a hit game on time and on budget.

Scores: 91-101   AA—Your game is being managed on a level much higher than the industry norm and is most likely to be a successful project with only a minor amount of difficulty in schedule or budget. Anticipate cost and schedule overruns of at most 5 to 10 percent above baseline.

Scores: 68-90   A—Your game is being managed better than the average game project. Significant challenges will pop up from time to time; however, you stand a strong chance of mastering these challenges. Anticipate cost and schedule overruns limited to 25 percent above the baseline amount.

Scores: 45-67   B—This is about the typical level of management a game project is provided with. This game will certainly face significant challenges at some point. The project will be run with unnecessary risk, frustration, and stress. Some degree of team burnout will occur. Anticipate some turnover at the end of the project. It is without question that the project will be over budget and will take considerably longer than planned at the start of the project. Anticipate cost overruns between 50 and 100 percent of the baseline planned.

Scores below 45   C—Games with these scores are at high risk of being cancelled by the publisher due to poor progress visibility, feature creep, and cost overruns. Only a team without financial concerns will be able to plow through these challenges without being cancelled. These types of projects always result in developer burnout, and some turnover will occur at the end of the project and to some degree in the middle of the project. These projects are advised to get serious planning and management happening immediately or be cancelled and save the industry from one more crappy game.

Part II > > > > > > > > > > > > > > > > > > >

How to Make a Game

> >

Chapter 5 > > > > > > > > > > > > > > >

What Is a Game Made Of?

The Extended Development Team

Before you tear off into preproduction of your game, I want to show you all the parts that go into a game. Whether your background is art, programming, design, marketing, or sales, you will tend to view a game project as a medium of art, software with game design, a game design in motion, or a product to be marketed or sold. The big picture of game development involves a team effort of many individuals spanning dozens of professions all across our industry and spilling into other industries. When you see what it takes to make a modern commercial game, I hope you get a more balanced view of the various roles to be played to carry out a hit game.

That Lever 2000 soap commercial is bouncing around my head right now with its silly jingle of all your 2,000 parts. So, following that jingle, let's take a look at all of the parts of a game.

Game Production Parts

Surely a game project is all about producing a great game. If not for the developers, there would be no product to sell! I am biased as I am a developer, and so yes, I do think game development is the most critical component of a successful electronic entertainment product. However, the developers hold a sacred trust given to them by the rest of the project stakeholders that they will be able to develop a compelling and competitive game, on budget and on time. This is a sacred trust that has been violated more times than it has been honored. We developers must perform to the best of our ability to deliver the strongest game on time and on budget.

Design Parts

1. Lead Designers/Visionary
2. Game Mechanics
3. Level/Mission Designers
4. Story and Dialogue Writers

< < < < < < < < < < < < < < < < < < < < < < < < < < <

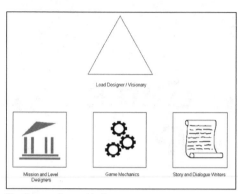

The flavors of game designers

Where Do Lead Designers Come From?

We have to design a game first and foremost. Some games have a key visionary who has been kicking around an idea for a long time; others are more of a collaborative process with a leader. There is probably no single more difficult task in the industry than being able to create an original game of your own design and see it through to commercial release (only a nitpicker would point out that seeing your game become a mega-hit would be harder). Each game has its own story of how it got to be funded and made. However, it is usually the publisher or the studio head of a successful game development company that has finally arranged for all the business points to be in place in order to kick off their game.

If the publisher suggests the game concept, then the developer will supply the lead designer. Often the founder of a game development company will act as a lead designer on the project.

The lead designer's job is to coordinate the design staff in the effort to create timely, thorough, compelling game design specifications that the rest

of the team can readily use and is readily understood by the game's publisher and other key stakeholders. The lead designer is not responsible for designing the whole game; rather it is the lead designer's role to be a director and sculpt not only what goes into a game, but also what does not belong and should be cut. (In practice, the lead designer also picks up any design tasks that the rest of the team is not able to do.)

How Do You Nail Down the Game Mechanics?

Each game usually has a lead game mechanics designer. This person often has a game programming background, as programmers are the ones most likely to implement the game mechanics in the code. This person receives direction from the lead designer, solicits engineering feasibility from the programming staff, and confers with the mission or level designers to find out their requirements. Depending on the type of game, the game mechanics designer often plays with Excel, trying to achieve a rough balance to the game and simulating portions of the game to get an idea of how some of their mechanics will play both for single player and multiplayer.

Who Are the Level and Mission Designers?

Some games have levels, others have missions, and quite a few have neither. Whatever game you have, it can almost always be broken down into a series of smaller challenges, puzzles, levels, or missions for the player to complete. Level and mission designers are sometimes programmers writing scripting code for a mission. Sometimes these

> >

designers are artists laying out tiles of a map and designing triggers, and sometimes they work in pure text, describing to others how the game should be laid out.

Story and Dialogue Writers Are Writers for Interactivity

Writing a compelling narrative that is formatted for the high degree of interactivity found in games is a wholly different skill than writing the narrative of a short story or novel or a motion picture screenplay. A writer for games needs to spend a lot of time with the lead designer for direction on where to take the story arc, and he or she needs to spend even more time with the mission and story writers to determine what is possible and not possible to do in the scripting language, map editor, or level building tool.

Writing natural sounding language for characters is not the same as just listening to people talk and writing it down; it is a talent for having an ear that sets the right rhythm of tone and balance for their characters to speak in a fantasy world in a believable manner.

I am discussing design roles that people will play, not saying that each project will literally divide its design tasks into discrete people; in other words, designers will cross over back and forth through these roles.

Coding Parts

I detailed game designers first, as the designers define the spirit of the game; however, I have often been caught saying the ultimate designers on a project are the programmers and the artists. The designers can write documents and create specifications until they turn blue, but the game will not be anything

other than what the programmers and artists create. I am not trying to cast programmers as an uncooperative bunch; I am a programmer myself. What I am trying to say is that the programmers and artists are very special people and often need to be convinced of the designer's vision. Most often the final implementation is a blend of the designers', programmers', and artists' collective vision.

The programmers' roles are to obviously create the code: the 3D engine, the networking library, art asset converter, and such, to realize the vision for the game. Games are often late, over budget, or buggy as I mentioned earlier. Games are hardly ever late two months while they wait for the tile artist to get her act together, and games are hardly ever late by a month because the audio guys have not mastered your sounds yet. It is a rare project that is delayed due to sheer asset production deficiencies, and even when that occurs the programmers are not idle. Why? Because electronic games boil down to just code—code with art, code with sound, code with gameplay, yes, but it is still just code. Even with code being the main deliverable, why does it always have to be late? This is an issue that is larger than the game industry. In Steve McConnell's *Rapid Development*, he writes that 50 to 90 percent of general software engineering projects are significantly late. Software engineering projects, in general, are chronically failing. The reason for this is that we game developers are part of a larger industry—software development—that is in turn an immature branch of the engineering discipline. The processes in specifying software, the processes for creating software, and the processes for testing software and even establishing skill levels in programmers have yet to be established! You have to be a licensed engineer to pilot a ship for commercial transport, to build a bridge or a skyscraper, or even analyze the soil on a hill for a single-family dwelling. In fact, in California and in most states you must have a license to cut someone's hair. No one needs a license to write code.

The idea of licensing game programmers may seem, at first, ridiculously out of place in the game industry. The lifeblood, the very soul of the industry is founded on clever people dropping out of whatever they were doing before and putting their heart and soul into creating a fun game. Why do I advocate the clearly un-fun part of getting a license to write code?

Imagine a future of game development where each game project has a licensed software engineer as the lead programmer or technical director (with the license administered much like a professional engineering license). With this type of person a very important safety structure has been put into place. Someone is responsible for the technical soundness of a project, and not only is her name and reputation on the line for this project, but her license to operate as a professional engineer could be revoked if she is shown to be manifestly negligent in her role as a technical director. I know I am way out on my own here with this opinion, but I really think this would protect not just the programming staff from unreasonable schedules, but the *publishers* themselves. They could lay down some outline of a feature set, quality level, budget, and timeline and say go make

the game, but it would be so much stronger if they had to have the signature of the lead programmer (a licensed software engineer) to sign off on the project before the project could continue past preproduction and into production.

Microsoft employs a version of this method where Microsoft employees have to sign off on a developer for technical, artistic, design, and project management competence before any funding of the team can commence.

Well, enough of my diatribe on the merits of licensing programmers, let's go see what they actually do on a project.

Lead Programmers and Technical Directors

The lead programmer has traditionally been the most experienced programmer on the team (from the 1970s through the 1980s, he or she could have been the only programmer). The lead programmer usually takes on the programming tasks that are the most challenging of the project. The quintessential examples of lead programmers are John Carmack of id and Tim Sweeney of Epic. These guys are usually the heroes of the projects, and many teams are structured around the lead programmer.

Some games tend to have a large programming staff, such as the massively multiplayer game Ultima Online or EverQuest, or the single-player/multiplayer game Neverwinter Nights with *over 25 programmers*. These large projects typically employ a technical director that oversees the programmers and reports directly to the project manager. The technical director title implies much less coding being

> >

performed by the individual and more management of programmers and code creation. Sometimes smaller projects employ a technical director when the lead programmer is handling a tricky part of the project she does not care for or has no time for, or is otherwise not suitable for project management. Another model is to have a series of "assistant leads" who are all responsible for different aspects of a programming task—i.e., functional leads—who each in turn manage a few programmers and who ultimately report to the lead programmer. This is the model at BioWare and at Taldren.

The lead programmer is like the queen in chess; she might be your most productive programmer on the project, but you must use her time wisely. Technical directors, on the other hand, act as scouts on behalf of the programming staff, looking ahead, lining up dependencies between programmers, and coordinating the development of the software.

The rest of the programming positions I describe below are not necessarily distinct humans on every project; rather they are common programming roles that most projects have. A lot of projects, for example, have the 3D graphics programmer and the lead programmer be one and the same, or the game mechanics and user interface programmer could be the same person.

Game Mechanics Programmer

The game mechanics programmer is the one who converts the "real meat and potatoes" of the game design into playable code. This person usually models the physics of the game world, how objects such as weapons and potions work, and how the protagonists and antagonists function.

The game mechanics programmer can usually be seen near one of the project's designers, debating the merits of the designer's weapon mechanics and such. The game mechanics position is usually a mid-level programming job that ambitious scripters and mission programmers often grow into.

The great thing about being the game mechanics programmer is you are the one who really puts the game into the game. You are the first one to see a lightning bolt strike the ogre, the first to see a tank shell a building, and the first to see the health pack heal the character. This is a fun job.

3D Graphics Programmer

The 3D graphics programmer is one of the most highly respected positions in the industry. 3D graphics programmers must have a strong comfort level in mathematics including calculus, vector and matrix math, trigonometry, and algebra. The 3D graphics programmers enjoy seeing their work come vividly into being in lush 3D graphics, immersing the player in environments they can only dream about.

Artificial Intelligence Programmer

The demands on the artificial intelligence programmer vary from game to game and from genre to genre. Steven Polge, now working with Epic, has written some truly impressive bits of AI code such as the Reaper bot. Also, the AI programmers are usually the folks who have the proper skills to write scripting languages and other tools used by the designers.

User Interface Programmer

The user interface programmer is the person who has the tricky job of developing the software that bridges the game mechanics of the fantasy world with a slick implementation of the user interface through the controls, in-game panels, and HUD elements, as well as the shell or navigational menus. The UI programmer is the expert on the UI library and usually maintains it by extending its functionality. The UI programmer position is one that is likely to have been gained through experience in the industry. UI programming is often hard to get precisely right and is often underappreciated.

Audio Programmer

The audio programmer is the person who codes up the 3D sound effects, the voice-over tag system, and the music playback system. Often this position is a light position due to strong, widely used audio libraries available such as the Miles Sound System from RAD Tools.

Tools Programmer

Michael Abrash once told me that id spends greater than 50 percent of its programming resources creating tools. This is a significant statement. Most game companies do not commit this level of programming resources to their games. BioWare has a large tools department as well, over ten people, who make tools for all of BioWare's games. They have found this saves a lot of time and rework by designers and artists. The fact that id is arguably the most successful developer ever, with many mega-hits of their own as well as a prosperous licensing program that

includes other mega-hits such as Half-Life, seems to say that every programmer on the project should be a tools programmer half of the time.

Most teams do not have full-time tools programmers, although if the team is part of a larger house, there might be a tools department. Still, every solid game company builds up its own toolset over time to get graphics on the screen, get audio out the speakers, and get the characters in the game to have interesting behavior.

A game development organization should have short-term and long-term tools production goals. I suggest a Gantt chart produced in MS Project be printed out and hung on a wall to indicate the internal tools development in your organization. This visibility will help everyone see how the tools are integral to the growth of your team and how things are planned to get better in the future.

Mission/Level Editor Programmer

The mission editor programmer is just one of the tools positions; however, for many games with a mission or level editor, the editor will be released to the public with the game's release. Developing a mission editor or level editor that is robust and easy to use is the work of creating another piece of commercial software. The UnrealEd level editor for the creation of Unreal Tournament levels by Epic is a fine example of a 3D solid constructive geometry modeling and scripting tool that is extremely powerful, robust, and easy to use by both industry professionals and by fans who want to make new content for their favorite games. Some development houses organize a world-building tool as part of the main

> >

game team, and others put this work in the tools group if they were rigorous in the technical design of the world editor to make it truly useful for other game projects.

Network, Server, or Client Programmer?

The network programmer writes the low-level and application-level code to get games running between a small number of players using modems, a local area network, or across the Internet. In the past the network programmer had to master a variety of protocols such as IPX, and serial and modem protocols. Modern games are now run almost exclusively on TCP/IP and UDP, the networking protocols of the Internet.

The multiplayer architecture of games can be broken down into two main structures: peer-to-peer and client-server.

Peer-to-peer structures have all of the player machines simulating their own copy of the game and use a variety of algorithms to keep the states on the different computers as close as possible. The peer-to-peer machines all talk directly to every other computer in the network. The bandwidth required to service this model of game grows exponentially with each added player. That is an unfortunate side effect as you try to handle more players.

The client-server structure divides up the computing of game simulation into a server, which handles the actual simulation, and the client, which is the viewer, or browser, of the world events. There are several benefits to this structure, including the fact that the bandwidth requirement grows only linearly with the number of players, and the

game can also be protected from quite a few forms of cheating by having it run on a trusted and secure server. (Remember, in a peer-to-peer game each machine is running its own copy of the world and has authority on some portion of the world. This authority can easily be abused by running a rogue version in the peer-to-peer network.)

Why are not all games client-server? Arguably they all should be; however, depending on the game, the client-server architecture is much more complex and requires divorcing the simulation and the presentation along much stricter object-oriented lines. Today's massively multiplayer games are a prime example of the complexity of client-server games. Literally dozens of machines, running a score or more instances of servers, carry out different operations such as player authentication, version checking, cheat detection, game simulation, chat hosting, database transactions, and more. Peer-to-peer games are much more similar to traditional single-player games with the exception of the games periodically making corrections to be more in line with each other's view of the world.

Art Parts

The artists of an electronic game may wear a host of different titles just like the programmers. Games used to have a single artist drawing the character sprites and the world backdrops for these electronic heroes to carry out their missions. In the earliest days the programmer, designer, and artist were one and the same person. Starting in the mid-'80s small teams of artists, usually no more than three, would work on a project. Starting in the early '90s game projects grew substantially in their art requirements and budgets. Famous examples of these are Wing Commander IV by Origin, where over $10 million was spent by Chris Roberts on chasing the dream of the fabled movie-in-a-game; Mario64, rumored to have a budget of over $20 million; and finally the Japanese epics in the Final Fantasy series and Shenmue, which have had gargantuan budgets.

Artists are now differentiated by their skill sets. It is interesting to know that many artists can build 3D models of the most arcane objects quite accurately and swiftly without being able to sketch them. The domain of the artist now covers a wide enough area that you will need to plan your art team carefully to be sure you have enough bandwidth of skill and talent across your art requirements.

Art Director

The art director is the manager for the art team, scouting ahead to be sure that project dependencies are taken care of ahead of time and that the artists produce their art assets on time for the rest of the game project. The other, arguably more important role is to look at every art asset as it is being constructed to be sure it is consistent in quality and theme with the rest of the game.

The art director job should be given to the artist with the most industry experience, tempered with people skills, and the person who best enjoys the entire team's respect.

Concept Artist

The concept artist is gathering visibility. In the past a few sketches would convey the look of the major characters

and locations, and the game was off into production. Now with project budgets 10 and 20 times larger than in 1995, the stakes are much larger and the penalty for getting the art wrong is often fatal to a project. This is where the concept artist saves the day. High-quality black-and-white drawings are often colorized (color comp) to accurately convey to the art director, the producer, and the major project stakeholders what the look of an art asset will be before it is created. For example, on our Starfleet Command series, we needed to create a black-and-white sketch for each and every proposed ship model we wanted to introduce into our Star Trek game. These black-and-white sketches first made the rounds of the team to be sure we liked them, then the sketch went on to Interplay's upper management, then on to Paramount's interactive licensing director, and on to even Rick Berman, the producer of the *Star Trek* television show and movies now at Paramount. Only when we received approval from all these folks did we start to colorize the sketch and start the approval process once again for the colorized sketch. Once this was approved, we were permitted to actually begin work on an art asset that would make it into the game. (The resulting 3D model would of course need to make this same approval-seeking trip.)

This approval process is even more stringent at LucasArts on *Star Wars* properties, and Japanese games are very much oriented around the concept artist, such as Yoshitaka, best known in the game industry for his work on the Final Fantasy series.

> >

2D Artist/Interface Designer

The 2D artist is an expert in classical sketching and painting. These artists are capable of painting backdrops, creating character portraits, and creating tiles and sprites for use in non-3D game engines. These artists used to use Deluxe Paint in the golden age of game development and have now moved on to Photoshop, Illustrator, and other packages.

Even in a 3D game, the 2D artist is an incredibly versatile and important member of the team, producing high-res artwork for ads and marketing, and helping to create assets for a promotional web site, install graphics, and countless more elements of 2D art.

The interface designer usually is an expert 2D artist with a strong sense of functional aesthetics. This artist will make just navigating your game's menus an exciting and fun activity. The interface designer is a key team member; be sure you have one, or don't make your game. Sometimes designers and programmers with strong visual design skills can successfully fill this role. This area of art is the most closely tied to your game—the game design, the game mechanics, and the look of the game. And these areas see the most change of any art asset. For these reasons, I strongly recommend against outsourcing your interface design art assets—get the best person you can and work with him full time.

3D Modeler

The 3D modeler was the highlight of the show around 1994-1997. At this time artists with experience in the industry were almost invariably 2D artists who were clever or stubborn enough to get their 2D visions articulated into a painfully small set of pixels using tools such as Deluxe Paint on the Amiga and later the PC. These artists on the whole were not prepared to handle the technical requirements of operating a 3D modeling package. Instead, a strange hybrid programmer-artist with a fascination for things 3D was required to operate the early arcane 3D packages. These artists were also in prime demand in the movie industry, and the scale of wages paid there made it very difficult for the game companies to recruit them over to games. In these years game projects had to train their 2D Deluxe Paint artists slowly to use early versions of LightWave and other technical 3D packages.

Over time the packages got much stronger and easier to use. College courses now teach 3D Studio Max, and in general people have had time to learn how to use the 3D modeling packages. 3D modelers are still highly respected members of any game team, but it is more balanced now with the other key art positions.

Character Modeler

The character modeler is a specialized breed of 3D modeler. Some strong 3D artists are competent at making mechanical things such as spaceships, tanks, and architecture, while others seem to lean towards the organics of characters. Low-poly character modelers have a special understanding of how the detail of the character will come to life in the texture stage to make the most economical use of their polygon budget.

Texture Artist

The texture artist, like the concept artist, is now a highly visible element of your art team. Games are almost always constructed out of polygons with textures on them. The sophistication of the modeling packages is so strong now, the texture phase of creating a 3D object is usually estimated at three to four times longer than the actual building of the model. The texture artist is a 2D artist who can "skin" an object in his mind and create a compelling set of textures to "paint" that skin on the 3D model.

Animator/Motion Capture Studio

Animation comes in two broadly different categories: character/animal/monster animation and everything else. Rotating antennas, windmills, and radar dishes are good examples of the everything else category. Animating a windmill is an almost trivial task for an artist on your team, while animating the snarl on a goblin's face is an entirely different task.

> **JARGON**: *Key framing* is the technique of using a 3D modeling package to set key frames to have the engine interpolate between.

> **JARGON**: *Motion capture* is using a special matrix camera to record the movements of a real human actor wearing a motion capture suit that has funny reflective balls attached to it. Most projects that use motion capture also use key framing for part of their animation duties.

To animate a character, two different solutions are at your disposal: key framing and motion capture. Key framing is the older, more established method of animating your characters. Key framing excels at animating cartoon characters and monsters and for extreme movements—motions that are impossible to capture with a human actor. Animating by key framing is an entirely different skill set from 3D modeling, texturing, or sketching. If your project will involve characters that need to be animated, be sure your team has enough competent animators to get the job done; animation can be a slow art.

Motion capture is the buzzword—this is the state of the art. Humans move with very subtle grace; studying a motion-captured movement will reveal how much the whole body moves during the walk or the swing of a bat. Motion capture's largest drawback would have to be cost in both dollars and time spent massaging the data into usable form. This field is constantly improving, and there are half a dozen competitors in the field. In Chapter 33 I will show you in depth what you need to know about motion capture including how to get a successful bid.

There is quite a bit of technical drudgery involved in smoothing out all of the details of the character's model and animations—dealing with the skeleton, motion capture data, prop bones, and a host of tiny, necessary details. Some studios divide this work between the modelers and the animators depending on the nature of the task, and other studios like BioWare have dedicated folks called character riggers who handle these types of tasks.

Storyboarder

If your game is to have any movies or cinematic sequences, it is important that your team have a storyboard artist. The storyboard artist will be able to design and articulate the scenes in a sequence for internal and external review before committing to costly live action or resource-intensive computer-generated sequences. Show the movies to the publisher, show them to the team, and work it all out ahead of time through simple boxes and captions. Most storyboarders are accomplished concept artists but not necessarily.

Audio Parts

Audio assets come in three main flavors: sound effects, music, and voice-over. In the beginning there were only crude sound effects performing buzzes, beeps, and whistles. We now have full Dolby 5.1 3D sound. Music has come a long way from clever timing of beeps to compositions by film composers performed by 50-piece live orchestras. And voice acting is now an art form performed by stars like Patrick Stewart and contracted under the authority of the Screen Actors Guild.

Voice-Overs

Voices in a game really bring it to life. Compelling voice acting reinforces every other element of interactivity by having the actors speak to your character. The tutorials for Starfleet Command went from being a dry introduction to our gameplay to being the most compelling *Star Trek* moment I ever experienced with George Takei performing Admiral Sulu teaching me to command a starship. I remember when Origin's Strike Commander was released for $50, but an additional speech pack was available for $20 more. That is a testament to wacky product strategies as well as a testament to the compelling depth voice adds to a game.

The only way to get good voice work done is to work with an experienced voice-over director. A good director will know immediately where to secure the talent, the studio time, and the engineer, and get you the post-processed audio in a format you need. In Chapter 29 I will guide you through the process of getting high-quality voice into your game. The pleasant surprise of voice work is that it is probably the coolest element you can add to your game for the money, and it is essential in many role-playing games, which are dialog and VO intensive.

Sound Effects

Sound effect engineers are wizards at listening to one sound and finding clever ways to stretch it, compress it, twist it, and come up with precisely the sound you need. Sometimes they will Foley—that is, record your sound effect from the actual object generating the sound. Sometimes the sound engineer will record some other sound and then twist it around just for your game.

Sound effects are an excellent target for outsourcing as only the larger developers with three or more concurrent projects can keep a sound effects crew productively working. Chapter 30 contains an interview with a sound engineer so you can see what it will take to get strong sounds into your game.

‹ ‹

Music

Some games spend a lot of effort on music, and it really gets the emotional hooks into the player when the music is first-rate. Music is probably the most popular and oldest art form worldwide. Nearly any emotion can be invoked with compelling music. There are two options: synthesized music and music that is performed live. We spent nearly $100,000 on the score and 30-piece orchestra performance for Starfleet Command 2. The music was very special; all of the sounds are richer and fuller bodied when performed by humans versus a synthesized chip. That being said, a single musician can create extremely strong music with a professional synthesizer and software. Chapter 28 will discuss outsourcing music in detail and give you plenty of leads to be sure your game has the emotional impact of high-quality music.

Management Parts

Management of a game project is the most critical component in my experience. In recent private email with other studio heads in the industry, the consensus was that a developer is limited in number of teams not by programmers or artists, but by quality producers/project managers. That being said, the management of a game project is often shared by a group of individuals with different responsibility sets.

Line Producer

The line producer coordinates countless small tasks that one by one are not very challenging, but taken as a whole is a daunting amount of work that needs to get done every day. If a project lacks a line producer, the efficacy of every team member will be compromised by a little distraction at a time. The line producer will often supply the team with food when the hours are forced and late; will get design documents printed and sent overnight; and will often coordinate getting builds out to the publisher and to beta testers. The line is a critical function that should be filled by a line producer, instead of your art director on Mondays, your 3D graphics programmer on Tuesdays, and so on.

> **JARGON**: *Builds* and *revs* refer to interim functional versions of the game distributed for testing to internal and external testers.

Associate Producer

The associate producer is found on larger projects in a single team company, and all ompanies with multiple teams need an associate producer. Publishers also structure themselves with an executive producer managing a group of titles and an associate producer on each title performing day-to-day management. The associate producers have an interesting combination of a lot of responsibility and little authority. The associate producer is the understudy of the executive producer. The business negotiations, contracting, and human resource decisions will be carried out by the executive producer, but in almost every other aspect of the game project the associate producer will have a strong contribution to make. The associate producers are often burdened with the dreary task of updating the schedule and reporting on task tracking. The associate also helps communication between all team members and is usually the strongest advocate

> >

for the game. In truth, each studio has its own name for the hierarchy of managers in the organization such as assistant producers, senior group producers, and project planners.

Studio Head/Executive Producer

The studio head at a game developer and the executive producer at the publisher each have the same fundamental job on a game project: be responsible for planning and executing the project in a profit-producing manner.

Studio heads are almost always the founders of their own companies, those who have risen through the ranks and are industry veterans and who have paid their dues and made money for their publishers in the past. In the case of Valve, Gabe Newell brought lots of project management experience from 13 years of creating software such as Microsoft Windows. Studio heads run small companies—game development shops—and have to simultaneously be game designers who are passionate about their games, software managers who respect technology, and businessmen who are savvy enough to get a good publishing deal. Some developers such as id and Epic have divided the role of the studio head into a more practical split of one person running the business and another acting as the project leader for the game.

The business development executive at the publisher often supplies the executive producer on the publishing side with a game project and game developer lead. The executive producer's job is to then complete the evaluation of the developer and project to determine its suitability for production. If the executive producer is confident the project should go forward, he will negotiate the key terms with the developer and work to help the project meet its first internal green-light or assessment milestone. If the project passes, then the executive producer's job is to oversee the project's progress through the reports generated by the associate producers and by looking over builds of the project in progress. The executive producer is often called upon to maintain the relationship with any licenses and is sometimes involved in contracting external vendors. The executive producer is the person most visible inside the publishing company for the game's success, while the press and the fans tend to focus on the game developer.

Producer

As a game development studio grows into two teams or larger, the role of the producer becomes critical to the effective execution of the studio's projects. The producer is the person who will manage the project at a larger development studio, allowing the studio head/executive producer to concentrate on strategic company issues.

‹ ‹

Quality Assurance Parts

Quality assurance (QA) is another critical component of game development. The single best way to test your game is of course to play it and play it until it is solid and as much fun as you know how to make it. The problem with this method is that it will take a very long time for a single person to play through a game in its entirety (which may not even be possible), and a single person will make errors and have a bias.

The industry has yet to come up with a unified testing method that is known as the best practice employed widely. Instead each developer and publisher and indeed each game project tends to have its own QA process. Microsoft appears to be the organization that exerts the most effort in a rigorous QA process.

Most small developers do not have a full-time QA staff, as they would only see useful work roughly half of a project's lifetime. Larger, multiteam development companies can often gainfully employ a full-time QA staff. For example, BioWare employs a full-time QA department of over ten people, which supplements the even larger QA teams at their publishers, reducing the errors sent to the publishers to speed up development and saving the developers themselves from having to test their own stuff, instead allowing them to focus on finishing new content/features. Smaller developers often cross-train the line producer and associate producer to be the first line of QA with a backup of team-wide testing days.

Publisher QA Parts

All high-profile commercial games receive a considerable amount of professional testing by the publisher's internal QA department. This department follows the guidelines set by the publisher's management and works as efficiently as possible to report defects in content and quality to the developer prior to commercial release. Most commercially released games have anticipated release dates that are difficult to postpone in the case of a late project or a particularly buggy one. These internal QA teams are trained to report the severity of the defect and generally create high-quality bug reports that have items prioritized for the development team's attention.

QA Lead

The QA lead is the person who leads the efforts of the QA staff. The QA lead is always a former tester who showed promise of superior skill in organization and communication. The QA lead coordinates getting new builds or revs of the game in progress.

The QA lead also proofreads all reported defects from her team and discards duplicate and erroneous reports and often rejects reports back to the reporting tester, requesting clarification and/or testing. The QA lead is almost always an aspiring game designer or producer and often includes extensive commentary on the game's content in order to gain visibility for possible promotion. This is because most publishers have an outdated, poor concept

> >

of the QA staff and treat them as low-skilled, low-paid workers, leaving those workers with little choice for a career in QA. Instead they are actively trying to strike out into development or some other role in the game industry. A notable exception to this is Microsoft, which seeks out folks with college degrees and pays well for its QA positions.

Main Team

The main QA team is the team that will monitor the game's progress from the time the game is initially submitted to QA through release and often into post-release. The main QA team will go through stages of varying productivity in direct relation to the development team's ability to respond to the bug reports in a timely fashion. This team is generally referred to as the QA team even though there are many other potential testers of the game. The main QA team will often rotate in fresh team members as a natural process of other games finishing and employee turnover.

Multiplayer Team

Games with significant multiplayer gameplay often have a QA team dedicated to testing this functionality. This is more common with PC games, as console games tend to have much more limited multiplayer gameplay. The multiplayer team is used to be sure all of the modem, LAN, Internet, and matching options are thoroughly tested. Bugs associated with multiplayer code are often more difficult to track down and report; this allows testing of the single-player campaigns and missions to continue on in parallel. In the same manner, individual members of both the

multiplayer team and main team are specialists in a particular portion of the game such as a chapter or character class or playable race.

Fresh Teams

The problem with having dedicated main teams and multiplayer teams who look at the same game from three months to a year is that their ability to discern fundamental problems with gameplay and usability are compromised fairly quickly as they learn the game and lose the critical insight of a new player. It is still important to have efficient teams who know what the game is and what the last reported set of bugs were so they can quickly turn around a bug report to the development team. However, fresh teams are often introduced to a game the closer it comes to shipping, depending on QA resources available internally to the publisher.

Compatibility Team

The compatibility team is often a dedicated team of QA members who happily rebuild computers all day while testing the major functionality of your game. These guys have very little work to do on a console! The compatibility team usually has a standardized checklist of hardware and operating systems the publisher considers commercially important to support.

Localization Team

Also, all big games are localized into various markets, and native speakers of these languages will be employed to QA both the accuracy and the quality of the localization of the game.

Beta Testing

Beta testing is testing performed by unpaid volunteer fans who want a first peek at an upcoming title and who are excited by the opportunity to improve a game before its release. At first many publishers were apprehensive that a beta version of the game would become widely pirated and steal sales from the release version of the game. Or in the case of weaker titles, many publishers consider it a shrewd strategy to avoid the beta testing stage. Perhaps the most successful beta testing programs are run by id; examples of these are Doom and Quake Test. These first-person shooters had multiplayer gameplay and no single-player missions. Even with only three or so maps to play test, these "tests" by id produced more hours of fun and gameplay than most games ever achieve in their final release. I personally played several hundred hours of Quake Test before Quake was released—sniff—thank you, id!

Bottom line, if you want to make a great game, run a beta test and fix your game until beta testing proves you are ready for release. In recent years the advent of the massively multiplayer game has required extensive beta testing. These massively multiplayer games require hundreds if not thousands of concurrent players to analyze how the server will respond to the stresses of full release. These thousands of beta testers are also required to smooth out the authentication, account management, and game balance to avoid having paying subscribers complete the beta testing period. The sheer costs of these games and the limited rigor employed to date on beta testing programs still results in the pressure to release these games to the public and endure two to six months of painful post-release beta testing that strains the faith of your hardcore, early-adopting fans.

Beta Testers

The beta testers are almost always the fans who showed up on your message board when you first opened up shop. They often have beta testing experience or have heard about beta programs and will sometimes be quite proactive in their effort to secure a seat in your beta testing program. The number one rule with beta testers is to communicate with them; failure to do so only creates an expectation in the beta tester's heart that they are part of the development team, only to find out that their voices are unheard.

Beta Testing Program Manager

To facilitate this communication with the beta testers, one of the development team members—often the associate or line producer—takes on the role of beta testing program manager. This is a very stressful job. The time period that beta testing takes place is during the final months of a project when everything must come together. The beta testers are anxious to see their reported defects fixed in the very next version of the game and are quite vocal about new features they want and how they want the game to be balanced. In Chapter 23 I will discuss the mechanisms and techniques the beta testing program director should employ for a successful beta test.

> >

Business Parts

Making games is big business. Depending on how you look at the numbers, the console game market (hardware and software) along with the PC game market generates more revenue than the box-office receipts of all of Hollywood's films annually.

There are a lot of different business executives who are involved in a game project; here I will present the major roles.

Business Development Parts

Business Development Executive

The business development executive is casually called the "biz dev."

> **JARGON**: "Biz dev" is the short name given to the business development executive at a publishing company.

When developers go around pitching games to publishers, they first need to get the approval of the publisher's business development executive before the game is sent to a green-light committee.

The biz dev person keeps a close eye on what is going on in the industry and is the first to know about games in development that are looking for a publishing deal. The biz dev person often negotiates the key terms of a game publishing contract.

Publisher CEO and President

A chief executive is responsible for all aspects of the game publishing corporation. Very often this individual has ten to twenty years in the game industry and has a well-developed instinct for making great games (not infallible

though). Making sure that your game is visible and impressive to this key executive at green-light meetings ensures the highest level of support the organization can bring to bear for your game.

Studio Heads

Founders, lead programmers, visionaries, game makers, CEOs, presidents, head coaches—whatever you call them, studio heads are the chief decision makers at a game development house. Studio heads generally have five to fifteen years of experience in the game industry and at least one hit title under their belt where they held a strong lead role. Studio heads most commonly come from programming and design backgrounds, although there are some medical doctors of considerable renown running BioWare. Artists are the majority shareowner at id, and Gabe Newell of Valve had an extensive background of software development at Microsoft.

Studio heads decide the fundamental structure and working environment for their studios based on past experience. The studio head is intimately involved when a game project is starting up and is usually the salesperson pitching the game to the publishers. Studio heads are generally the most qualified team leaders in their organization and spend a lot of their time training new producers to run teams and subteams.

Lawyers

Both the publisher and the developer need the best lawyers they can afford. Each contract is unique, and while a publisher's contract is the fruit of many painful relationships, the developer should be patient and exercise great care in negotiating terms. This is something you do not want to try on your own.

> **WARNING:** Do not negotiate a publishing contract without the aid of a lawyer who has strong experience in electronic entertainment publishing contracts.

Lawyers are actually good people who help you understand clearly what a contract is and is not saying. Understanding what you are agreeing to before you sign a contract is a fundamental safety mechanism for both the developer and the publisher. In Chapter 27 I provide a list of law firms who are used by different studios.

Licensing Parts

Many games are based on licenses such as comic books, novels, movies, and sports stars. In turn, games themselves are licensed to create strategy guides, action figures, T-shirts, and movies. Publishers may have their biz dev executive manage the licensing of a game, or they may have a full-time staff member for routine licenses such as strategy guides.

Promoting, Buying, and Selling Parts

Sales? Is that not the job of the teenage clerk at the local Electronics Boutique? Well, yes of course, but well before a gamer walks into a computer game store, a sales force has made the larger sale of the game to the buyer agent of the retailer.

The decision on the retail buyer's part of how many units of the game title to order on release depends on how hot the title appears to be, the wholesale price, and the influence of any number of incentive programs that have been negotiated between the publisher's sales force and the retailer's buying force well before the game's release.

Sales Executive

Each publisher has a top executive in charge of sales. This person has a lot of influence on the ultimate sales of a game. The executive in charge of sales has a budget that goes by several different euphemistic phrases such as "marketing development funds"; this budget is spent to buy shelf space at retail. This is a pretty strange concept to people who are unfamiliar with the industry—that the publisher not only needs to absorb the risk of funding the development of the game and its packaging and marketing, but also must completely absolve the retailer from any risk. Selling games is a consignment business.

The retailer will put the product up on the shelves, and if it does not sell quickly enough, the retailer simply sends the product back and gets its money back. Retailers take maximum advantage of this relationship when a highly anticipated game is released by ordering as many units as the publisher will deliver. It sounds great when you have an order of 200,000 units from CompUSA for your game, but if your game fails to meet expectations, CompUSA will not hesitate a moment to send 160,000 units back to you—all marked up with their price tags—and simply order more later. Those 40,000 units you sold at CompUSA effectively had the packaging and shipping costs of 200,000 units, which wipes out much of

> >

the margin from those 40,000 units that did sell.

A careful study of some publishers' financial reports to the SEC will show periodic "write-offs" and "one-time charges." There can be a whole variety of reasons why a business is forced to report a loss on their books, but in the case of game publishers it is often massive quantities of returned games that they have accumulated for as many quarters as they could get away with. It is not unheard of to see six to ten quarters of accumulated returned product discharged as a write-off. Keep in mind that during those six to ten quarters this product was accounted for as revenue. This practice is not sustainable, and the stronger publishers do not do this. A strong sales executive should work closely with the publisher's chief financial officer to manage what is called "sell-in" to the retailers with the goal of having the highest "sell-through" to "sell-in" ratio.

> **JARGON**: *Sell-in* is the number of units the retailers order or buy.
> *Sell-through* is the good stuff; this is the measure of how many units of your game were sold through to consumers —a true sale.

Sales Force and Retail Purchasing Agents

Under the direction of the sales executive, the publisher's sales staff meets periodically with the retail purchasing agents, each of whom represents a different retail chain. Prior to calling on the buying agents, a publisher will often host an internal sales meeting to communicate their product's selling points to the sales force. These meetings can sometimes be fairly lavish with, for example, large ice sculptures

and Klingon impersonators to get the sales staff pumped up and primed to handle the buying agents.

Press Relations Manager

The press relations manager will oversee how the game is communicated to the press. For large titles, this is a nearly full-time job, and a quality PR manager should be split across as few titles as possible—one to three titles at most. The PR manager will field all press inquiries, as well as inquiries by those claiming to be press. The PR manager will strategize and plan how the details of your game will be released to the press.

> **JARGON**: *Buzz*—what the press, fans, and industry are saying about a particular title.

If PR has a solid date on when the game will ship, then PR can create a solid plan for ramping up the buzz in a steady, ever-increasing volume to peak just as the title is released. Releasing too many of your game's goodies too early will provide you with little to say later in the project, and interest in your title will sputter and fade before it is released. On the other hand, if you do not release enough information on your game to grab press and fan attention, it may be difficult to maintain the support of the executives at the publisher and other project stakeholders.

Trade Shows

The Electronic Entertainment Expo, or E3, is the largest show in North America for publishers to get their products implanted in the agents' minds. E3 is a vast show with tens of thousands of attendees strolling through hundreds of displays ranging from mini amusement parks from the likes of Nintendo to a folding desk and some business cards from discount CD duplicators. Thousands of products will be on display and scores of tricks are used to try to get your attention, from the obligatory booth babes to breath mints that are rolled out like cellophane. E3 is a cacophony of sound effects, lights, noise, and people. For all of this energy E3 is the largest news reporting event in the game industry and next to the retail buyers, the game press is the second most important contingent of VIPs to grace the floor. These folks have conspicuous press ribbons dangling from their badge so you know when not to speak candidly (handy).

Like anything competitive, the press at E3 is out to get more viewers and readers. The larger the market share, the more their business will grow. Years ago the press were trying to figure out how to arrange their time more efficiently for those precious three days of E3; they wanted to be sure they looked at every hot game. It would be a minor tragedy if a competing magazine or site were to report on a major title that you failed to see at the show. So the publishers and the press put together a schedule of viewings and demonstrations for all of the large press. That might sound innocent enough, but if you think about it for a moment, you will realize that all of the major press walks into the show with a schedule of titles filling all of the required genres and platforms prioritized in order of importance. Of course this journalist will still walk the floor, but it will be between appointments or at the end of the show. This makes it really tough for the little games trying

to break out, as they are not even on the list to be seen.

The Internet game sites have another pressure—real-time reporting. To keep up, all of the major game sites need to have nearly live coverage of the show in an effort to bring the show to the fans and of course to gain more viewers. Real-time reporting is hard for several reasons, not the least of which is that you need to have something to say. Here again, publishers and the press will work together to give the press an E3 package a couple of weeks before the show. This package always contains the best screen shots, plenty of quotable material, and occasionally a playable preview build of the game. The better journalists look at this material as just more information; the less rigorous journalists (or those with very little time) have been known to lift the majority of the quotable material and publish that in lieu of an original opinion on the game.

Other Trade Shows and Events

E3 is important and dominant no doubt; however, it is hard to get your message across to the buyers, press, and fans when there are 3,000 other titles. Publishers have been creative about how to handle this problem; they hold their own shows in one form or another. For example, Activision hosts its own show in Europe between E3 and ECTS (the major show in Europe) to be sure awareness is implanted before and more effectively than the ECTS show.

Interplay hosted a very cool event for three of the Star Trek games (one of which was Starfleet Command) on the Paramount Studios lot. Press from around the world came to view three games hosted by George Takei. The trailers for all three games were shown in the posh Paramount screening theater, and a fine lunch was served where the press mingled with the developers for an extended Q&A period after the press had a couple of hours to play the games. It was a relaxed but focused event that gave those three games ample time with the press.

The Marketing of a Game

As you can see there is a lot of sales and promoting of a game behind the curtains, but what about the ads—the traditional form of selling a product? Of course games have ads; take a look at your favorite game magazine and it seems like half of the pages are full-page ads. And the online sites have banners, navigational bar headings, and a myriad of advertising terms for the various bits of electronic click-mes.

Like the press relations manager, the marketing director for a game should not be spread too thin across many different games. The marketing manager will work with the producer and development team to craft the game's image in all of its various forms: print ads, banner ads, and the all-important box.

Just like press coverage, it is important not to create too much hype for the game and then fail to deliver on time. Publishers are getting much more savvy and are scheduling their marketing campaigns to kick off only when the ship date is known with confidence.

The marketing manager will also be responsible for getting your game shown at smaller venues such as the GenCon game convention held in Milwaukee. The marketing manager will

coordinate strongly with the press manager and sometimes supervises the press activities. Sometimes it is considered a peer position, and in some places the same person is overloaded with both jobs. In particular, the marketing and press managers will be working closely with any playable demos that are to be released, making sure they are cover-mounted on the game magazine CDs and that the retail stores carry a supply of demos in a display.

Hardcore Fans

It is commonly known that hardcore fans and the word-of-mouth sales they generate is the largest factor in the number of games you will sell. Hardcore fans are eager to check up on the progress of their favorite game at the developer's web site, interact in the forums, and beta test. If they like the game, they can be responsible for not just the sale of the box they buy for themselves, but for the six or eight boxes that they have convinced their LAN party to play with. Or in the case of console games, the hardcore early adopters get the game first and invite people over to play. I have met fans who have sold ten, twenty, and more titles just for their passion of the game. Hardcore fans are always looking for the best in games; they also have a bunch of friends the industry calls casual gamers and mass-market gamers. These casual and mass-market gamers ask for recommendations from the hardcore gamers. The hardcore gamers will in turn recommend the titles they feel comfortable with. This is just common sense, but what it means is that Blizzard's Diablo was perfectly poised to capitalize on the streamlined interpretation of the computer role-playing game genre where just light taps on the left mouse button looted catacombs and vanquished elemental evil. Valve's Half-Life laid a heavy story on top of the first-person shooter genre dominated by id (in fact they licensed id's Quake engine) to produce a mega-hit. And depending on how you measure it, Half-Life and its free, fan-created mods Counter-Strike and Day of Defeat are the most popular online games. These games are simply the most approachable, solid, and just plain fun games you can buy. If you want your game to sell, study how narrow the feature sets of Mario64, Half-Life, and Diablo really are, and how well and deep these few features are executed.

Manuals and Strategy Guides

Games need to have a manual, and if the game is considered a potential hit, then no doubt a strategy guide will be produced for the title.

Manual

How the manual gets written varies from publisher to publisher and from game to game. The most common method is to use an experienced contract manual writer. This person receives a copy of the game about four to six months before release and interacts with a member of the development team while writing to create the most accurate manual possible before a game ships. Another common method is for developers to create the manual given that they are the most familiar with the game's functionality. The biggest challenge in creating a manual is that rarely does one have the luxury of waiting

until all features have been frozen and all stats in the game have been balanced. This results in almost all manuals being vague in some areas and fairly narrow in the scope of just providing use of the controls of the game, rather than how to play the game. Now enters the strategy guide.

Strategy Guide

The strategy guide fills a niche role in the game industry, providing detailed stats, walk-throughs, strategy, and tactics to complete a game. Writers of strategy guides have various stories, but it is not as simple a job as playing your favorite game and writing up all the nifty hints and secrets. What really happens is that the publisher of the game and the publisher of the guide work together to get builds of the game to the strategy guide author as early as practical in the project. Essentially, the guide author is a beta tester too; this makes the job of writing the definitive guide more challenging as the stats, missions, puzzles, and various parts of the game are still in flux. For instance, even the ultra-high-profile game Gran Turismo 3 (GT3) for the PS2 contains many discrepancies in the pricing of various upgrades between the U.S. version of the game and the U.S. strategy guide. GT3 shipped in Japan well ahead of the U.S. version and as such there was a little more time to produce an accurate guide. Despite this there were still discrepancies.

For our own Starfleet Command: Orion Pirates, the strategy guide writer of SFC2, Dennis Green, returned to write the most thorough guide possible. His project came under stress when we at Taldren overlooked some of his

> >

requests for information during the final push. Unfortunately, after we were able to catch up and provide him with the information he needed, several strong chapters of the book had to be cut to reduce paper costs for the guide. It is a tough market to make money when work already created has to be cut.

Manufacturing Parts

I am astonished at how quickly a PC game can reach the store shelves. Do you know how fast a publisher can take the final gold master from the hands of the QA lead and deliver a shrink-wrapped retail box in an Electronics Boutique shop in the local mall? Five days. That is right, in five days a 30-cent recordable CD from the local OfficeMax can be turned into $70 million of merchandise on store shelves in the form of Diablo II. This is perhaps the quickest a game can reach the store shelves and usually only occurs at a fiscal quarter end for the publisher—most especially Q4 for the holiday shopping season!

To accomplish this a publisher has an operations manager who keeps his eyes peeled looking for the strongest vendors for CD duplication, manual printing, box printing, and assembly. This is quite a job, and normally they would like to see about 20 to 30 days to get the job done, so as to not have to pay for express drop shipments between the vendors. But when the end of the quarter is rearing its ugly face, the operations manager saves the day. Toward the two-thirds mark of your schedule, meet with the operations manager to nail down the firm dates for when they need everything—final box,

final manual, and final posters and other goodies in the box. This is definitely an area of the project where it repays you in spades to be proactive and find out the due dates for these deliverables ahead of time.

Hardware Manufacturer Parts

Console Manufacturers

The console manufacturers assign a producer to oversee the development of each of the titles for the platform. The console manufacturer retains broad editorial approval rights for the game, and it is very important to follow their feedback to receive your ultimate approval for the gold master.

Hardware Representatives

Some of the coolest people to work with in the industry are the hardware vendors like SoundBlaster and NVIDIA. These folks are motivated to be sure that not only does your game work on their hardware but also that your game takes advantage of all of the features of their latest cards. What that means to a PC developer is a bunch of free hardware such as sound cards, video cards, joysticks, and speakers for use of the development team to test the hardware. These folks are best approached at their booths at the Game Developers Conference (www.gdconf.com). Tell them your story, where you are working, and what game you are working on, and if they feel that you are for real, you can get test hardware. Please do not abuse this if you are not making a commercial game and will not be making a genuine test of the hardware, as it will only make those resources harder to come by for the rest of us.

< < < < < < < < < < < < < < < < < < < < < < < < < < < < <

Post-Release Parts

Releasing a successful game to retail will be one of the most difficult things you accomplish in your professional career. After all of the cleverness it will take to get your project funded, staffed, and real; after all of the dedication to the craft during production; and after all of the blood, sweat, and tears it will take to drive a game through the final candidate cycle, you will find the day after you signed off on the gold master one of the most pure days in your career with no task that must be done now. Instead, you and the rest of the team will most likely disappear and rediscover what your family looks like and decide to talk with them—and sleep. After this much-needed rest is completed, is it time to dream up a new game? No, it is time for post-release.

Post-release involves patches, updates, answering questions on the forums, helping customer service field questions on the phone support lines, and combating cheating. For massively multiplayer games, these issues are much more serious as you are billing for a monthly service instead of a one-time purchase of a product. In fact massively multiplayer games have whole development teams called the "live teams" to maintain the software, add new content, act as gamemasters, and in general keep the product fresh and alive in the hands of gamers.

Having a bunch of fans is a very good thing; that is the whole reason for your work. However, a bunch of fans require a substantial amount of interaction and communication. At Taldren about six of the employees have taken the initiative to read our forums on a regular basis to field questions and moderate the forums.

Chapter 24 discusses the issues of post-release in detail with guidance from several studios on how to most effectively support the fans of your game.

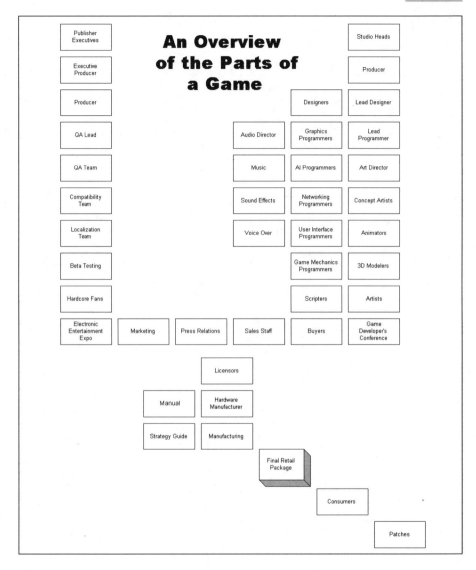

Chapter 6 > > > > > > > > > > > > > > >

Business Context First

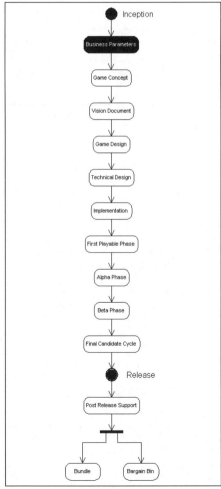

Inception

Business Parameters

Game Concept

Vision Document

Game Design

Technical Design

Implementation

First Playable Phase

Alpha Phase

Beta Phase

Final Candidate Cycle

Release

Post Release Support

Bundle

Bargain Bin

Where the business parameters lie on the project life cycle

The first project sin that people commit is to dive right in and start designing their game, or worse, to start programming. Every project, from the largest massively multiplayer games with development budgets over $8 million to total conversions done by some hardcore fans, needs to be positioned within an appropriate business context. Even if you have no plan to make money off the game, or it is not a business venture, it is still critically important to identify why you are making the game and what the goals are for your game.

The Project Triangle

A useful device for analyzing the goals of your project is to create a triangle and label the points of the triangle as follows: (1) On Budget, (2) On Time, and (3) High-Quality/Feature Rich. It is a business law of software development projects (and just about any other type of project) that you can achieve two out of three of these goals on any project, but you cannot achieve all three. Failure to understand that you can only have two out of three of these properties will result in a game that misses not just one goal, but also two or three of these goals! See the diagram below for a visual aid to this example:

The Project Triangle—pick two out of three goals

Implications of the Project Triangle

Each line on the triangle is a relationship between two of the goals. Each line should be responsibly labeled with the negative consequence of your decision. This triangle states that every well-managed project will exhibit one of three negative behaviors: being late, being over budget, or sacrificing quality. This sounds pessimistic, but it is true. Once again for impact: Well-managed projects will be late, cost too much, or be of low quality; less well-managed projects will exhibit two negatives; poorly managed projects will feature all three failures.

There are many different software development strategies on the market such as Iterative, Waterfall, Extreme, Unified, and others. None of these development methodologies are a magic potion. You will still be faced with the question of how to best manage your particular project and its challenges. Instead, each of these methodologies will have strategies and suggestions for managing costs, time, and features. However, it will come down to the business context of the game and how you manage your project to decide which two goals you will meet and which one you work to control and manage.

■ On Budget and On Time—means you must accept sacrifice of quality

■ High Quality and On Budget—means you must accept a late game

■ High Quality and On Time—means you must accept extra spending

A project where being on budget and on time is more important than quality

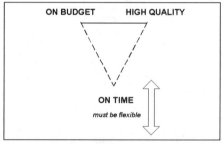

A project where being on budget and having high quality is more important than timeliness

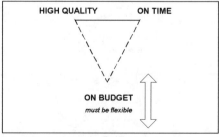

A project where being on time and having high quality is more important than cost

> >

Various Games and the Project Triangle

1. The Sims series: High Quality
2. Diablo series: High Quality and On Budget
3. Quake series: High Quality and On Budget
4. Ultima Online series: High Quality
5. Starfleet Command series: On Budget and On Time
6. Baldur's Gate: High Quality and On Budget
7. Klingon Academy: no goals satisfactorily achieved

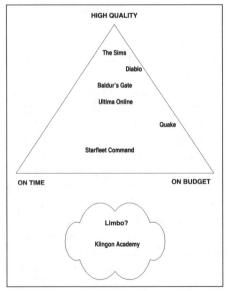

Various games and where they fit on the Project Triangle

How is the triangle related to success? The Sims is probably the highest grossing PC game in history, being at #1 in the charts for close to two years punctuated by a few brief weeks off to allow a major release to have its day. The Sims was notoriously late at over five years and also over budget. Why did The Sims succeed when it achieved only one goal instead of two goals? The Sims met a huge unfulfilled demand to play god to simulated people doing ordinary things; this has enormous appeal to consumers and gamers of all ages, especially women. The designers of The Sims knew that above all they had to get the simulation right. If The Sims was boring or lame, people would be turned off and not play. So they crafted and crafted the behavior of The Sims almost to exclusion of any other features, considering the relatively modest effort spent on the graphics. No one had modeled *people* before quite like this, and in the early days of the project there was only modest support for it, as other games at Electronic Arts were given more resources. Thus the designers of The Sims did the right thing and recognized the business parameters of their project and focused on what would really matter—the behavior in The Sims. Sure, if they'd had stronger corporate backing early on, they could have staffed up and perhaps sped up the research and development phase to under a year and then just another year to create the whole game. This would have been ultimately more lucrative for Electronic Arts, as they would have made this ungodly amount of money earlier and would have had made the team available to do the expansions to The Sims that much quicker. Looking back at game projects from afar, it is easy to be an armchair executive producer and say what you would have done better, but truthfully in the early developmental stages of The Sims there probably was not all that much to see, and so it would be difficult for executive management to understand this game and get behind it.

The Diablo series has been a fantastic hit for Blizzard and is the standard and envy of the PC game industry to measure against. Blizzard first achieved outstanding financial success with Warcraft II, which built upon the classic real-time strategy gameplay of Warcraft I and polished it to a tight and smooth production that is the earmark of a Blizzard production. Blizzard's model for making mega-hits is to set aside a large budget of money, have a large staff (Blizzard reportedly has about 200 full-time staff for a publisher of two concurrent titles), and take as long as it takes to make the game perfect. Blizzard knows they have a reputation for the highest quality games available, and each release they produce is an opportunity to damage that hard-earned reputation. The Blizzard label is probably the single most lucrative publisher brand in the industry. It is a common joke in the industry that if Blizzard ever needed cash in a hurry, they could print a box called StarCraft II or Diablo III and just ship a million empty boxes just for the pre-orders! This total focus on quality has of course repaid Blizzard (and its owners) handsomely. So Blizzard's answer to the triangle is to bypass being on time and focus on quality and, to a lesser extent, budget. I just took a peek at Blizzard's web site and noticed that in their description of one of the programming positions is a willingness to work long hours; apparently Blizzard games take as long as they need to as long as everyone is pushing hard.

The statement of working overtime as a requirement of the job at Blizzard is a pretty clear indication that they too are worried about getting their games done in some sort of timely fashion. The point of this triangle is not to figure out which one of the triangle goals you are going to abandon wildly and throw out the window; the point is to identify in what part of the triangle you enjoy the most *flexibility*. Knowing where you are flexible will keep your project from breaking.

Starfleet Command (SFC) is shown in the figure as on time and on budget. What this means is that quality was the most flexible aspect of the project whereas on time and on budget were not flexible. SFC was produced internally at Interplay during a time of great expectations with the impact of going public and the beginnings of tight fiscal policy. Interplay had many games in production at that time including *three other Star Trek games*—Klingon Academy, New Worlds, and the Secret of Vulcan Fury. Of all the Star Trek games in production, SFC was considered the underdog as our game focused on the real-time tactical simulation of naval starships based on the gameplay of a 20-year-old board game called Star Fleet Battles. Klingon Academy was a sexy 3D space shooter featuring over 110 minutes of live footage with star talent like Christopher Plummer. The Secret of Vulcan Fury amounted to taking the player back to the original series with fully digitized and animated faces of Kirk, Spock, and Bones. New Worlds focused on capitalizing on the real-time strategy genre and impressing the eye with ground troops of the Star Trek universe rendered in breathtaking 3D detail.

We had a trick up our sleeve with Starfleet Command—a completely unfair advantage really. Our game, as I said, was based on simulating naval combat in space between majestic

> >

starships of the Star Trek universe. That is practically half of what the show is about if you think about it—photons and disrupters—just watch *Star Trek II: The Wrath of Khan*. We knew what we had and decided to make the best real-time tactical starship simulation we could. Along the way we broke new ground with real-time tactical warfare, and after we released SFC other titles like Dominion Wars and Bridge Commander attempted to find their own path down the naval starship simulation. With the fixed budget and the requirement to ship on time, our attention was focused on what would make the game: the real-time tactical combat.

To create a foundation for our gameplay we licensed the mechanics of the hit board game Star Fleet Battles. Here we had a coherent set of gameplay mechanics that were play tested and improved over the years. However, these were gameplay mechanics for a hex grid, pen and paper game, not the game mechanics for a commercial game of the late 1990s. Glossing over the hours and hours of design discussions, we settled on an interface where the player sees a third-person 3D view of his starship traveling on an invisible plane, battling with an astonishing array of controls for the operation of the whole warship—the electronic warfare, the shuttles, tractors, transporters, marines, heavy weapons, engineering—bringing all of these systems to bear against the enemy starship in dark skies. This purity of concept was a godsend. I listed SFC as on time and on budget. Yes we were a little buggy when released, but we made a quiet hit game in a market where so many have failed—we made SFC.

Quake and Diablo have a lot in common; both games are produced by development houses with the strongest reputations, both companies have a "when it is ready" policy for shipping their games, and finally both companies have paid their dues.

The real interesting question is not when Blizzard and id ship their games, but how they got where they are today. How did they arrange to make their first hit game so that they could have a pile of money to use for their future games? Blizzard was kind enough to produce a recounting of their first ten years in the business in early 2001. The page is no longer posted at their site, and that is a shame. However, the history of Blizzard started with the name Silicone and Synapse. They, like all developers, started out doing work under contract for other publishers. It is ironic that Blizzard is now eclipsing Interplay, the publisher it worked for when it started in the industry. Blizzard was able to create Warcraft with the help of the Davidsons, who had an uncanny amount of wisdom to invest in a pre-Warcraft Blizzard.

The history of id Software is also about ten years long, where John Carmack and crew developed the platform game Commander Keen featuring a football helmet-wearing child protagonist. It was Castle Wolfenstein 3-D published by Apogee that blew everyone away with its riveting 3D action and launched id into stardom to go on to create Doom I and II, Quake I, II, and III, and to be the engine behind dozens of other hit titles.

These folks did not get lucky; they are creatively brilliant, have considerable business savvy, and have worked hard consistently for the last ten years

< < < < < < < < < < < < < < < < < < < < < < < < < <

through an ever-changing set of param-eters involved in making games. What you need to do as the producer of your game is to think hard, very hard, and articulate on paper what the business parameters are for the game you are making. These parameters—these restrictions and requirements—are not sources of angst to rebel fruitlessly against. Rather they should act as foci for your game's creation; they should act as genuine opportunities to shape a successful vision for your game project.

Questions for You to Answer

Here are some straightforward ques-tions; your mission is to take some time, grab a piece of paper, and write down the answers.

- What are you trying to accomplish with this game?
- When must you complete this game project?
- How much money do you have to produce it?
- Who do you have to get the job done?

What to Do with These Answers

An Ultra-Low Budget Game

If you are funding the project yourself with your free time and hobby money, you have a very distinct limit on how much money you can afford to spend on this project. The goals for your project should be correspondingly low. After performing your preproduction as out-lined in Chapters 6 through 10 with detailed information in Chapters 14 through 20, your project should amount to no more than 500 to 1,000 hours of work per person to finish your project in a year. A way to partially solve your budget problem is to share your project with others: friends, family, and even folks across the Internet. Coordinating a group of volunteers to work together on a game project is very challenging, and their creators abandon the

overwhelming majority of these pro-jects. However, id Software used essentially this method to escape their stay at Softdisk. Chapter 25 contains an interview with one of the founders of Sliver Creek Entertainment, whose first game began as a weekend project.

The goal for this type of project for the creators is most often to do the pro-ject for fun and to act as a compelling demonstration of their abilities to land a full-time position in the game industry. There are two principal paths to take: Make a small game or produce a modifi-cation to an existing commercial game (called a mod).

> **JARGON**: *Mod* is the name for a game that is made from the engine and assets of another game.

Ambitious mods that offer extensive changes are often called total conver-sions. Making a small game and making a mod are two different sorts of pro-jects; each has its own challenges, and you will learn different things by accomplishing them.

Many people might think that cre-ating a demo of a simple real-time strategy (RTS) game that has incom-plete AI, poor art, and no sound could still represent your passion for creating a large, commercial RTS. Yes, you might get your passion across, but in my opinion it would not be the best demonstration. Just like consumers of games, we do not want to have ten features shoddily executed. Instead we would rather see just three or four polished features that are shippable. It is not interesting to know how long it will take you to implement feature X, rather it is much more compelling to know how long it will take you to drive feature X to shipping quality. The folks at Silver Creek Entertainment have taken this to heart and have produced the most excellent card games: Hardwood Spades, Hardwood Hearts, and Hardwood Solitaire. These folks have taken the very simple feature sets of these classic card games and have added gorgeous 2D graphics, flawless online multiplayer format, and clever added features such as customizing your avatar's look and tossing fireballs at your opponents. Silver Creek started with an artist passionate about quality for his card games and two other developers; they now are running their own development company and are hosting their own online games without funding from a publisher. This is a significant accomplishment, for these folks have achieved what many developers aspire to—self-funded games; and they have done it in an area of high risk—online games.

This is such an excellent model— driving a few features to perfection— that the folks at Silver Creek are not sending out their resumes and seeking a job working for someone else in the industry; instead, their hobby project was developed in a product with real value to thousands of players.

To be successful with this model you need to find a game concept that is simple but playable and would require a minimum of engineering to get it functional. This would leave the balance of your time to create lush polish to that feature set.

Creating a mod of a commercial game is another way to work with an ultra-low budget. Principally, two guys, Cliffe and Minh Le, created the phenomenally successful mod to Half-Life called Counter-Strike (CS) with some textures created by three other guys. They started with the Half-Life engine, which is in turn a variation of the Quake engine. Half-Life itself is a mega-hit from Valve Software that taps into the underserved market of players looking for a compelling story to engross them as they enjoy the action of the first-person shooter genre. Starting with a commercial hit game has the same compelling marketing potential for your mod as it does for a publisher's sequel to a hit game. The Half-Life engine was eminently amendable to user modification, to the point where even the menus of the game support choosing a custom game type. The CS project was created by an experienced team that had worked together on Action Quake 2 and other mod projects before, so a single mod project was just the first step for these guys. It was their third project that really blew everyone away including Valve. This team, due to its experience and reputation on previous mod projects, received unprecedented support from Valve including design feedback, technical support, and even project financing.

Counter-Strike perfectly illustrates a project that is on budget and is of very high quality, but the time side of the triangle had to be as flexible as they come. CS was released in the summer of 1999 as beta 1, and it took nearly two years for it to proceed through four more major releases and ship as an expansion to Half-Life in retail.

Fixed Budget, Fixed Deadline

I am most familiar with projects with these sorts of parameters, as all of my shipping titles have had these parameters. I have worked on one professional title that had a ridiculously low budget, PlanetNET, that never shipped. At Taldren we are now working on several game concepts that have a variety of business parameters to fulfill different roles for the future of Taldren. But fixed budget, fixed deadline games are what my reputation is built on. To make these projects work you must walk backwards from your shipping date and determine your beta and alpha dates. This will give you a gross amount of time available for your production and preproduction phases. I am a strong supporter of preproduction and feel that any project worth doing should spend about 15 to 35 percent of the total development time in preproduction. This will give you a crude estimate of the man-months you have available for production. This is your budget for man-months.

Now with your man-month budget in hand it is time to sketch out the feature set of your project. Break down your list of features into three piles: primary features, secondary features, and tertiary features. This section discusses how to identify your core features and put the secondary and tertiary features into other piles. You must then create a project plan that clears away all of the dependencies and risks and supports the primary features. Chapter 10 outlines the project plan, while Chapter 20 drills down to details.

During production on these titles you will find yourself shifting secondary tasks to tertiary and primary to secondary when you are low on time and popping the secondary and tertiary tasks up when you have available time. It is vitally important to your production team that you do not make all features must-do items that you reluctantly cross off as reality presents itself. People perform badly when under the cloud of being failures; for the sake of your team and your game, set them up to succeed by prioritizing your features into these three different categories. In fact, your team members will cruise through their primary tasks so much more confidently that they will develop their features at the fastest rate possible. Feeling like winners and making progress only enables them to get excited and want to knock off the secondary and tertiary items. Perhaps the most compelling reason to separate your features into these three piles is that all features inherently have a priority, and you will make choices during production. But it is only through formally acknowledging these priorities and writing them up in your plan that you will derive all of the planning benefits of knowing what you really must get done.

> **AXIOM**: All games inherently have primary, secondary, and tertiary features; the wise developer will embrace these prioritized features lists and turn them into an asset.

Chapters 11 and 21 discuss specific techniques for measuring progress and task completion that enable the highest quality workflows.

> >

High-Profile/High-Quality Projects

For the high-profile, mega-hit titles from well-established houses like Blizzard, id, Verant, and BioWare, a different set of challenges present themselves—all of them revolving around an industry and fan base with a high set of expectations for these great developers' next titles. This means that quality must be so high that each release sets new high water marks for the industry to try to achieve.

To understand better what goes into a mega-hit game, it is a great idea to look under the hood of a mega-hit and start pulling on the hoses and unbolting the pieces and looking to see how things fit together. I call this process creating a reverse design document after the technique of reverse engineering. Chapter 8 gives you an idea of the steps you should take when writing a reverse design document. For myself I wanted to see what went into the construction of Diablo, so I spent 27 pages of text detailing to myself how characters grew, how big the isometric tiles were, how the palette was laid out, how the inventory system worked, the user-interface, and all of the other parts that went into the production of Diablo, including the manual and box design. What I discovered astonished me: Diablo is actually a very simple game with a small set of features. This hit me like an epiphany. Now when I walk through E3 or flip through a game magazine I quickly project a mini-reverse design document in my mind for these games to get an idea of how complex they are. This led me to formulate Erik's Axiom 13 of Game Design.

AXIOM 13: As the complexity of a game increases, its likelihood of commercial success decreases at a geometrical rate.

I highly encourage you to create a reverse design document for your favorite mega-hit whether it be Quake, The Sims, Total Annihilation, or another title. What you will find is that these games all have a clean, tightened feature set that is polished to a degree that their competitors have not been able to achieve. In fact, Michael Abrash decided to join id Software for many good reasons, but one of the reasons he chose to join the Quake team was because early in the project John Carmack wanted to put in a portal technology that would allow players to seamlessly jump from one Quake map to another in an extremely compelling version of action cyberspace. This feature was cut from production and in fact has yet to ship in a Quake game. This again is a reflection of the theme of concentrating on executing your features well.

But without knowing better I would have thought these very successful developers would give no thought to adding features to their projects—heck, they don't even have to be late. They could just hire teams and subteams to get these features done, right? No is the simple answer. The difference between a strong developer and a weak developer on your team is not just a linear difference in work output; it can literally be a tenfold, hundred-fold, or more difference in productivity. In fact for the networking code in Quake, John Carmack hired a programmer whose whole career was in creating networking code. For some reason this did not work out well for Quake, and the programmer moved on. In two months time John Carmack came up to speed on the issues involved in networked games and produced a solid networking layer that was only 2,000 lines long and, as usual for John Carmack, set a new standard for multiplayer Internet gaming performance. From the time *The Mythical Man-Month* was written by Frederick Brooks, the idea that you could simply add up programmers like cantaloupe in your grocery cart has been under attack. Surprisingly, many people will attempt to add pressure to your project by asking you to hire more folks and get more done—or much more commonly get it done for a specified quarter. You certainly can get useful work

done by hiring crack independent contractors and extra staff, but it is not a magic bullet. You need to organize and manage this extra talent. Adding additional staff requires more administrative overhead, and there is a critical threshold of number of staff in an area on a project beyond which you get diminishing and ultimately negative returns on work, even if the people on the project are competent. This is probably due to the increasingly complex communication required between a large number of people on a project as it grows in team size.

These mega-hit developers have learned they cannot grow their teams to indefinite sizes and still produce clean, compelling hits. For this reason the features in these games are limited to roughly what their current team can produce.

Walk Away

Ultra-low budget projects should be simple games polished to a high degree or perhaps a port of an existing game engine into a new and compelling format.

Fixed budget, fixed deadline projects should organize their features into primary, secondary, and tertiary piles and create their project plan in a manner that most supports the completion of the primary feature sets.

High-profile/high-quality projects concentrate their best development team on a clean, tight set of features that they will execute to a quality level everyone else in the industry will then struggle to match. This will usually result in creating a barrier of entry that will place your organization ahead of the competition, and like compound interest you should be able to reap the result for years to come.

Chapter 7

Key Design Elements

All games start as an idea, something like "Wouldn't it be cool to be a space marine and blow up zombies on Phobos" or "Wouldn't it be cool to be a pilot in a starfighter involved in an epic struggle to overcome the oppression of a star empire gone bad" or "Wouldn't it be cool to drive modified street cars on Tokyo streets at night." These idea sparks are often the source of long conversations between developers late into the night at the studio. Another potential starting point for a game is a licensed property; i.e., "make a RPG/RTS/action game using XXX license." (Fans may want to play that license specifically. Major licenses include Star Trek, Star Wars, D&D, WWF, Lord of the Rings, and Harry Potter.)

Chapter 6 discussed getting your business goals and parameters settled for your project before you start formal design and development of your game. This chapter discusses how to use the structure your business context and your game ideas provide and how to turn them into a game concept worthy of fleshing out into a game design document.

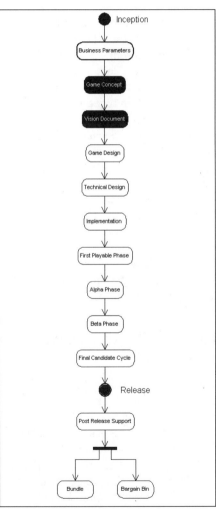

Where the key design elements lie in the project's lifetime

< < < < < < < < < < < < < < < < < < < < < < < < < < < < <

Business Context Shapes Design, or Does Design Shape the Business Context?

First of all, I am not asserting that having your business context in hand will act as a magical tool that will turn any game idea into a well-thought-out game concept. It is only an important aid to assess the *requirements* that your game idea is implying. Some game ideas (such as the faithful recreation of Middle Earth where the whole world is modeled with strong AI, 3D graphics capable of great indoor and terrain rendering, where an unlimited number of players can join in together on both sides of epic conflict between good and evil) cannot be reconciled with the business parameters of two artists and a programmer looking to break into the industry, who have six months of living expenses available to them on their collective credit cards. That Middle Earth concept is an example of a game that will dictate the business parameters. If we take the business parameters of two artists and a programmer, they might want to recreate an arcade classic on

the Nintendo Game Boy Color or Advance, use it to secure their first deal, and then move on to more ambitious projects.

For many game projects there is a middle ground where the business parameters and the game idea go back and forth and refine each other. Perhaps the developer pitches a massively multiplayer game to a publisher who is wary of the costs and risks behind massively multiplayer. From these talks it is quite possible the developer will end up creating a game that exploits a license the publisher has rights to and features a much more modest multiplayer feature set. This is not an acceptance of a mediocre plan; rather it is a mature development of the idea into a viable concept. A viable concept is a game that people with capital believe will be seen through to completion, with a high probability of favorable reception in the market to overcome the inherit risk in game making.

Reconcile the Business Context and Game Idea Early

This process of refining the game idea and business context is the earliest stage of a game project. All projects reconcile their business contexts and the game idea at some point. Tragically, for too many projects this reconciliation only occurs after the project manifests itself by underperforming, usually by missing milestone dates. Some projects have a painful reassessment where senior management allocates more funds and grins and bears it. For other

projects, senior management interprets this late reconciliation as an unpleasant surprise presented by an immature development team and consequently cancels the project.

Allocating more funds and time to a project is a common occurrence, and because it is commonplace, too many developers think it does no harm to themselves and no significant harm to the publisher. That is fallacy; when a publisher is forced to spend additional dollars and push back the release of the title, there are many negative impacts.

First of all, the publisher must extend additional money to the developer. This is an obvious point, but it means that these funds are unavailable towards the development of another title with another developer or (worse for this title) funds may be drawn from the marketing budget to pay for this overage.

The second impact is that the publisher has to delay when they will be able to start recouping their investment and see a profit that they can put to work in future games.

The third problem is that the marketing effort is deflated as the awareness for the game is now ill-timed, and it will be difficult for the game cover that marketing was able to secure for your game last quarter to have real value 18 months later. Right or wrong, the developer is the vendor and the publisher is the customer, and the adage that the customer is always right holds firm in this case, with the developer being tarnished by the reputation of poor estimating capability.

Another reason to avoid going back for extra money and time from your publisher is that the business deal will never improve. A loss of royalty points is common; sometimes you will see a shifting of intellectual property rights. In the extreme sometimes the developer agrees to an assignment of equity in the project to the publisher. In the case of shifting equity to the publisher, the developer is strongly advised to get full value for that equity; no matter how small an equity stake the publisher takes, it will make all other publishers avoid doing business with the compromised developer for fear of a conflict of interest and confidentiality concerns.

The developer is also losing time by going over his time budget, and spending more time on a project with the business deal worsening is not a good goal.

The final reason to avoid a late reconciliation of the business context and game idea is to prevent team members from becoming disillusioned and moving on to another company.

At Taldren we have released Starfleet Command, Starfleet Command: Gold, Starfleet Command: Neutral Zone, Starfleet Command 2: Empires at War, and Starfleet Command: Orion Pirates in less than two years. At the same time we gathered more fans and have always produced a profit for our publisher. Many of our employees are loyal to Taldren because of the steady pace of release; they know their work will be released and not wasted.

The Effects of a Slipped Game

1. Less working capital for the publisher.
2. The total advance is tied up longer than expected.
3. Marketing dollars are often wasted as the hype bugle is blown too soon.
4. The developer's reputation almost always suffers.
5. The business deal never improves for the developer.
6. The developer loses the opportunity to work on other titles.
7. Team members are in danger of becoming disillusioned, and the team may suffer uncomfortable turnover.

‹ ‹

Ion Storm has to be the most infamous example of the consequences for late reconciliation of the business context and the game idea. Ion Storm was founded around John Romero, who is credited with the design of Doom—perhaps the greatest PC game ever. The UK-based Eidos was flush with cash, and John Romero left id just as Quake was entering its final stages towards release. Eidos needed to put the surplus capital from the Tomb Raider series to work, as all businesses must do. Tomb Raider was so successful that Eidos needed to get into a number of games, but established top developers were already booked, so Eidos would need to go with a less established development house. The idea of taking advantage of the designer behind Doom and creating a new development house is not a bad idea; in fact it is a good idea. Experience, a built-in fan base, and a great story for the media would create an environment that would be conducive to game development, one would think.

Ion Storm was founded with the vision statement that design is king. Even this is not a bad idea; treated properly this would mean that Ion Storm would capitalize on its core strength—game design embodied by John Romero—and take advantage of existing game engines. Looking at how Ion Storm interpreted their vision statement would reveal where Eidos made their mistake. Ion Storm used the vision statement, design is king, to treat game development as a pure art form and lost respect for a strong development process. Ion Storm's marquee project Daikatana suffered all of the ills described above. Whole engine retooling caused massive delays and

required Eidos to double the already overgenerous advance of $13 million to $26 million to keep Ion Storm's three projects rolling.

Daikatana did not just lose face in the game press, it became the material for much derision, and even the local Texas newspapers saw the poor management at Ion Storm as a good story for a series of columns. Ion Storm not only suffered crippling turnover, but some employees helped feed the negative press storm by leaking to the press ugly internal email. John Romero was forced to hand over the company to Eidos, and their games shipped to little success. Ion Storm's Dallas office has been closed by Eidos to what amounts to a large write-off of Lara Croft earnings and a reputation for Eidos to overcome. In fact the quieter Ion Storm Austin studio run by Warren Spector, which shipped the critically acclaimed Deus Ex, is now looking for a shiny new name to operate under to distance that studio from the ill-fated Dallas studio.

The sad thing is that John Romero really can design games; just play Doom any day and you will see how amazing a game it was and still is. And Eidos turned on the cash to set up the game for greatness. It is just heartbreaking, really, to think about the potential of Ion Storm and to see it fall for lack of rigorous development methods.

What can be worse than either pumping more money into a late project or canceling a project? *Shipping it.* It should never be done, but almost every large publisher has shipped a game well before it was finished. I don't mean just with bugs; I mean before critical parts of the game were complete.

Descent to Undermountain from Interplay is a classic example of a game that was shipped too early. The idea behind Descent to Undermountain was to take advantage of two key assets of Interplay: the Advanced Dungeons and Dragons license and the mega-hit Descent. Management at Interplay decided it would be a snap to plop down some fantasy environments, characters, and monsters to bash. Management decided the Descent game engine would be ready for immediate development into another title. Most publishers do not have a strong technical director available for code review. Yet at the same time many publishers also negotiate the terms of the publishing deals to either own the software engine behind the game or have a license to the software engine. Descent to Undermountain was a case where the revenue opportunity was so large as to prevent an objective review of what it would take to get the game done. The original business parameters for this title called for a budget of only six months of four developers' time. No established development house was chosen to do the job; rather an ambitious independent contractor programmer stepped up, and various artists at Interplay contributed to the project. No project manager was allocated. Let me share with you what Gamespot thought of the results of this game after it slipped to three years and *six times the original budget*:

From Gamespot review of Descent to Undermountain:

But somewhere along the line something went horribly wrong, and now gamers are asking themselves two questions. The first arose merely out of befuddlement: How could the company that produced Fallout also be responsible for one of the lousiest games to come down the pike in quite a while? The second, though, addresses a much more serious issue: Why did Interplay ship the thing when it wasn't even close to being the sort of cutting-edge product the hype machine had led us to believe it would be? …There's probably no way to learn the answer to the first question, but—thanks to some very frank members of the Descent to Undermountain team—the answer to the second is now common knowledge. The game went out when it was scheduled to go out (in time for a Christmas release) even though it wasn't ready. That's not just me speculating; that's precisely what a member of the DTU team stated in a recent post on Usenet.

When a project is three years in the making and six times the original budget, there is tremendous pressure to just ship the game. At the time, Interplay was receiving a huge amount of attention for Descent to Undermountain; everyone wanted a truly 3D dungeon romp. (Dungeon Siege, the first really 3D dungeon romping game, and BioWare's Neverwinter Nights, which is a more detailed 3D implementation of D&D, weren't released until 2002.) Interplay thought at the time that with all the hype, maybe, just maybe, the early sales in the first few weeks would be large enough to recoup a significant portion of the costs. It was also Christmas time when 40 percent or more of our sales as an industry happen. Interplay had three choices:

< < < < < < < < < < < < < < < < < < < < < < < < < < < <

1. Ship it now.
2. Cancel the project altogether. (Remember lost money really is lost, and it is best not to chase it.)
3. Find a real AAA development house and start over with a new large budget and two years more of development time. (Really the same thing as canceling the project.)

Unfortunately for Interplay at the time, canceling the project or starting over with a new developer appeared to be more expensive than shipping the title. Let us see what Gamespot thought of this decision to ship the game:

From Gamespot review of Descent to Undermountain:

The lesson to be learned should be obvious: If you're gonna ride the hype machine, you'd better deliver the goods. Sadly, DTU doesn't even come close—and the worst part is that sometime over the next year or so we'll probably see this same story played out all over again.

So what have we learned today? That pushing a product out the door before it's ready makes loyal customers angry; that game developers should keep at least one eye on what's going on in terms of technology when working on a new game; and that if you buy Descent to Undermountain after reading this, you get what you deserve.

Descent to Undermountain shipped in a condition that was far below the industry standards of the time, Diablo and Quake II. The hype behind this game also crushed it. It is just possible that if Interplay had developed this title quietly, hard-core fans of AD&D and/or Descent might have bought 20,000 copies and been patient for a patch or two. I am not saying this is a great idea, but it is better than a hype storm. This is a poor way of doing business; the game industry shows time and time again that the mega-hits are just games that offer straightforward gameplay with strong production values. Wacky or niche games or poor craftsmanship are not rewarded. Just make a few quality titles and you will spend a lot less money in development, and your individual titles will have more capital to work with.

Descent to Undermountain was a perfect case where the game idea and the business parameters were in conflict. If Interplay wanted a title in six months and had only a modest budget to accomplish it with, then Interplay should have commissioned the developers of Descent, Parallax, to create a cool expansion pack for Descent and they should have contented themselves with the sales of an expansion pack. Perhaps it was perceived that with Descent II already in development at the time, it would have been competing for sales. The other option was for Interplay to allocate the funds they were to later plow into Stonekeep II and hire a top developer to create a 3D dungeon romp of quality. Stonekeep II would later go into production for five years and then be cancelled. You must create a game that is compatible with your business context or fail.

> >

Methods and the Unified Development Process

Microsoft, the most successful software development organization on the planet, sells a lot of games. Microsoft is perhaps best known for its Flight Simulator franchise, but MS now owns Ensemble (Age of Empires franchise), Bungie (Halo and Myth, formerly the premier Macintosh development house), FASA Interactive, and Digital Anvil (the former Chris Roberts company working on Freelancer), as well as being the publisher for a host of externally developed titles such as Dungeon Siege. Microsoft is a large organization with many layers of development procedures that other publishers do not employ. The first thing Microsoft does when evaluating a developer is to send a small team of game development leads comprised of production, design, programming, and art to evaluate the strength of the team. A large part of this evaluation is to also evaluate the developer's methods to determine if they are compatible with Microsoft's and if these methods give Microsoft confidence that the developer has thought through their project and will deliver a great game, on budget and on time. Development methods must be good things judging by Microsoft's success.

What Is a Development Method?

meth·od *noun*—A means or manner of procedure, especially a regular and systematic way of accomplishing something.

We do want systematic game development; this whole book is dedicated to the presentation of various game development methods. Systematic and repeatable methods allow us to retain what worked and improve upon what did not work well. The alternative to using a method is employing ad hoc techniques over and over again and being successful only by good fortune. I rather like to make my own luck, thank you very much. The first method we need to nail down is how to reconcile your game idea and business parameters. I advocate using a comfortable subset of the Unified Software Development Process developed by the three amigos Ivar Jacobson, Grady Booch, and James Rumbaugh.

Why Use the Unified Software Development Process?

The simple reason is that the Unified Process is quickly becoming the software industry standard. The Unified Process has a long legacy dating back to at least 1967; at this time Ivar Jacobson worked for the telecom giant Ericsson. Jacobson had a radical idea for the design of the next generation telephone switching equipment at the time, a method we would now call *component-based development.* For this project Ericsson modeled the whole switch system and subsystems as interconnected blocks. The relationships between these blocks was then articulated and revised. The dynamic processes of the switch were identified and modeled. Every message passing back and forth from each object was included in this model. This software architecture and object message compilation was probably the best technical design document of the time. This was a radical concept because software customers at the time were not accustomed to seeing a blueprint of the software before the software engineering began. This method was not chosen on a whim; rather it met the demand that the software be robust enough for the telephone switching equipment to remain operating while receiving upgrades and patches to the software components of the switch in real-time.

I will skip the middle part of the history behind the Unified Process; the point is that 35 years ago a repeatable method of creating great software was developed, and despite this, most software organizations have weak methodology.

The Unified Modeling Language is the standardized text and visual language for the articulation of software design supporting the Unified Process. Beyond the development of Ivar Jacobson, Grady Booch, and James Rumbaugh, UML enjoyed broad support and major companies such as IBM, HP, and Microsoft joined in the development and standardization of UML.

Requirements Capture

The purpose of a software development process is to take the user's requirements and transform them into a functional software system. That transform stage is what we game developers are doing when we make games. We take the vision of the gameplay—how it should play—and turn that into a finished game.

> **JARGON**: *Requirements capture*—articulating the requirements the functional software must satisfy, such as to be fun or to run at 30 frames per second.

What is the first step in the development process? Figuring out what we are supposed to do. There is a neat formalized term for this: requirements capture. Requirements capture is something you have already started. Those business constraints from Chapter 6 are some of the requirements the software must satisfy. How do we methodically discover the rest of our game's requirements? The short answer is that there is no quick, magical method to sit down and write up in a single sitting all of the requirements your game must fulfill. Wait, don't go away, I am still going to show you how to do it; it just involves several iterative steps.

Use Cases

First, if you have not already done this, write down your game idea on a single sheet of paper. Write two or three sentences that describe your game in the center of the piece of paper. Now in no particular order write down the major functionality of the game in an outward, radial manner from the game idea in the center. The larger, chunkier aspects of the game should be close to the center and the detailed ideas farther away. For example if you are designing a role-

The role of a development process

playing game, you have characters; write that down. Characters have stats; write that down. Characters have names; creating the characters' names is a feature. What you are doing is brainstorming the gross feature set of your game. This particular method of putting the game idea down at the center of the page is good to get you started if you have not put a lot of effort into your game design document yet. The immediate goal is to identify all of the core activities the player can perform in your game. Each of these core activities is composed of many individual actions the player performs. Each of these actions is called a use case in the Unified Modeling Language.

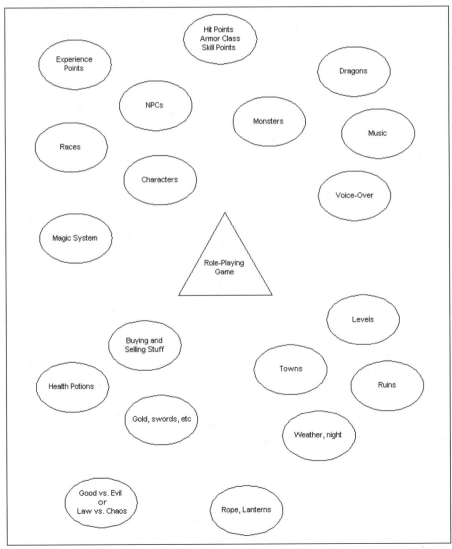

Brainstorming features

< < < < < < < < < < < < < < < < < < < < < < < < < < < < < < < <

> **JARGON**: *Use case*—an interaction between an actor and the software system. A fully articulated use case is composed of both text describing a sequence of actions and a graphical diagram showing the relationship of this particular use case with others in the system.

Collecting these use cases and writing them down will drive our process to identify the requirements of our software. The software requirements will then help us develop the architecture for our software. The use cases represent function, and the architecture represents form. The Unified Process is called use case driven because it is the effort to capture our use cases that drives the development. All of our future efforts in the construction of our software are to further the realization of these use cases into a functioning software system. Now, what exactly does a use case look like?

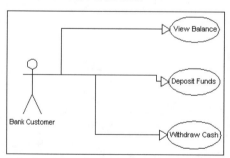

A simple use case diagram featuring the use of an automatic teller machine

It turns out one of the fundamental tenants of UML is that the language shall be extensible, flexible, and ultimately serve only to aid the process of distilling and communicating the system requirements. This ATM transaction diagram uses only three UML symbols: the oval use case, the stick figure actor,

and the relationship line. The stick figure is called an *actor*. Actors represented by a stick figure are most often users of your software, or players of your game, who are interacting with the game. It is better to use the abstract term "actor" so you will see all of the external users of your game system such as the single-player player, the multiplayer player, the system administrator, and the database server of your online component. After identifying your actors, the use cases will flow rapidly. The use cases are the unique interactions between the actors and the software system (game). The use cases are represented by a simple oval with an active verb phrase such as "withdraw cash" or "analyze risk."

> **JARGON**: An *actor* is a user, either human or another external system, that is interacting with the system under analysis.

> **JARGON**: A *relationship* is a line drawn between actors and use cases, sometimes with extra notation that further describes the type of relationship, such as <<extends>> and <<uses>>.

The level of articulated rigor in a diagram should be reasonably proportional to your needs. For example, if it is important to describe the relationship line in better detail, use a one-word descriptor between the less than and greater than symbols. Common examples are the relationship descriptor of <<extends>>, <<uses>>, where *extends* would communicate that a particular use case is really a special case of a simpler base use case, and *uses* would indicate that a particular use case employs another use case as part of its action.

> >

I shall now plop Pac-Man down on the cold steel of our examining table. Cutting the skin of a clean, tight, mega-hit game, let us take a look at the innards of Pac-Man and see some of these use cases in action:

Display System
Display maze
Display characters and their animation
Display score
Display high score
Display credits
View movie (Ms. Pac-Man)

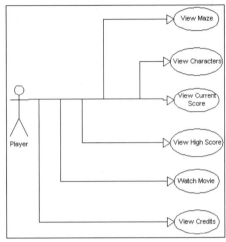

The use cases of Pac-Man that are related to displaying and viewing

Player Input
Insert coin
Push coin return
Choose single player or multiplayer
Move up, down, left, or right

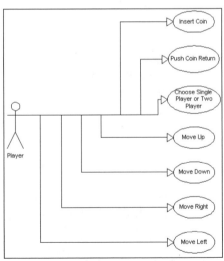

The use cases of Pac-Man related to player input

< < < < < < < < < < < < < < < < < < < < < < < < < < < < < < <

Game Object Interaction
Wall collision
Eat dot
Eat power-up dot
Eat fruit
Eat ghost, send ghost to center of box
Pac-Man dies

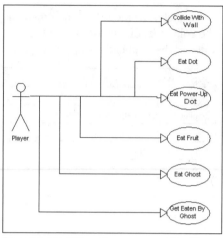

The game object interaction use cases of Pac-Man

Miscellaneous
Receive extra man
Enter initials

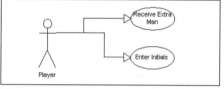

Miscellaneous use cases for Pac-Man

We can also take a higher-level view of Pac-Man and combine these low-level use case diagrams into a generalized use case view of the software package as a whole. See the diagram to the right.

Now you have a good tool for breaking your game idea down into visual parts that describe the required functionality. This is very important, because when your game exists only as an idea expressed in a half-dozen sentences, it is difficult to see the complexity of your proposed game and reconcile it with your business constraints. Looking at the UML diagrams for Pac-Man, we confirm our understanding that this is a very simple game. Looking over the diagrams I can

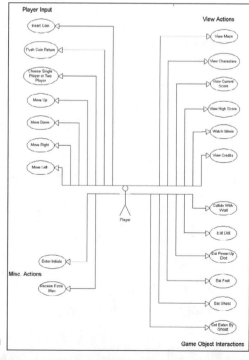

The combined use cases of Pac-Man

> >

see only four roles: a programmer for the 2D display system, a programmer for the game mechanics, an artist, and some audio. This of course is a very small game, and a solid Pac-Man clone could happen inside a weekend for a two- to four-person team.

This process of understanding how something else was put together has a fancy name—*reverse engineering*. I highly encourage you to perform some reverse engineering on other games that you are familiar with. We continue with some sketches from other games.

Case Studies

It is now time to apply these tools to modern games that are of greater complexity than Pac-Man. Each of the following two games, Diablo and Gran Turismo 3, has enjoyed legendary marketplace success, and each has spawned a lucrative franchise of sequels, expansions, and licensed products. Is there a common thread between these games? Did the developers in each case just get lucky, or were the developers just extraordinarily brilliant? I honestly do not know how much luck was involved, but someone with a lot of intelligence, skill, and time honed these two game concepts into production plans that have succeeded far beyond the industry standard. I can show you the elegance in the design of these games, illustrating how, looking back, these were mega-hits from their conception.

Case Study I—Diablo

Diablo is a computer role-playing game for the PC developed by Blizzard North, originally an independent developer of another name bought by Blizzard during the development of Diablo. Diablo featured the killing of hordes of monsters like skeletons, wandering around in a dungeon, gathering gold, and collecting magic items all in the quest to vanquish ultimate evil—all straightforward fun stuff. The key

concept behind Diablo was to make the user interface priority #1, not the story, not the size of the game, not the number of different character types, not customized character appearance, not a rich role-playing game mechanics set; no, the focus was the user interface. Indeed, the mouse controls were a stunning left-click on monsters to attack, left-click on chests to open, and right-click to cast a spell. The interface itself was appealing to look at with large glass spheres that held blue and red liquids representing remaining life and mana (energy to cast spells).

Shortly I will more carefully break down the use cases of Diablo; but there is a tremendous amount of courage and insight behind the user interface design of Diablo. In the summer of 1995 I was up late one night with a bunch of other game developers talking about games we could make. I remember we suggested just a simple variant of Gauntlet, the arcade classic where you just went around bashing monsters, collecting gold, and powering up. I remember how we all laughed at the time and said there was no way it could be viable. No publisher would see the game as feature-rich enough to fund. Perhaps as a bit of forgotten shareware, but no way it could be a commercial game. At that time RPGs such as Bethesda's Elder

Scrolls series were vast worlds with hundreds of NPCs, dozens of cities, hundreds of locations, actual weather, and time of day. Imagine making a game that left out all of these features and just concentrated on a tight interface and high production values—that was Diablo.

Use Cases of Diablo

Diablo is a simple game, a polished game with strong production values such as superb voice-overs and movies, but we will see that Diablo is a simple game behind the features. I will cover the major features and elements of the game; I do not propose to create an exhaustive reverse design document in this chapter.

Display System
Terrain: Draw floors.
Terrain: Draw isometric walls.
Terrain: Color cycling special effects for water and lava (tiles do not animate).
Terrain: Ghost walls when a character is located behind the wall.
Characters: Render and animate characters (2D sprites composed from 3D rendered models).
Game Objects: Colored outlines for interactive objects such as treasure chests, magical rings, monsters, and non-player characters in the town center.
Spell Effects: Display any one of a couple of dozen spell effects with dazzling animations and cool sound effects.
Menus: Display menu choices.
Movies: Display the intro and exit movies to the player.
Audio: Hear sound effects.
Audio: Hear music.
Audio: Hear voice-overs.

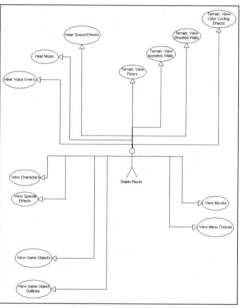

The view related use cases of Diablo

Game Object Interaction
Move Player Character: Left-click to move the player character.
Left-click Object Interaction: Interpret the left-click on an object automatically by object type to mean open a chest, attack an enemy, or move the player to a location as above.
Load Level: When the player directs their character into special trigger areas on a map level, load the target map level.

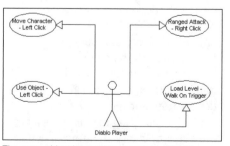

The game object interaction use cases of Diablo

> >

Right-click Object Interaction: If the character has a spell bound to their ranged action, cast a spell at this location on the map or on this character (this could be either an offensive spell on an enemy or an aid spell on an ally). Otherwise if this character has a bow, fire an arrow at the character indicated.

Character Management
Name Character: Small feature for user customization to allow the player to bond with their character.
View Character Stats: View attributes, health, experience points.
Allocate Character Attribute Growth Points: When the character achieves the next experience allow the player to choose where they want the growth points to be allocated, choosing from strength, dexterity, intelligence, and constitution.
Inventory: Display the character's inventory in a "paper-doll" fashion with sockets for the backpack, belt, helmet, hands, pants, boots, and tunic locations.
Inventory: Allow the player to shuffle objects about in their backpack to "make room" for new treasure and to abandon lesser treasure in favor of higher prized treasure. Validate the placement of inventory items based on their type. For example, healing potions can be carried in the backpack or in the belt pouch but not in the helmet slot.

The character transaction use cases of Diablo

Quick Analysis of the Use Cases of Diablo

Looking over the use cases of Diablo you will notice that I have partitioned Diablo into three subsystems: Display System, Game Objects, and Character Management. Below is a short discussion of these systems.

The display system is just a 2D isometric engine that is capable of rendering animating 2D sprites (quite probably used for both the characters and the spell effects). This graphics technology was hardly groundbreaking in 1997; isometric engines have been around since Q-bert in the arcade. The

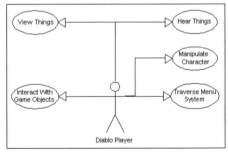

The aggregate use cases of Diablo

game also uses a 256-color palette incidentally. There is no question that the graphics in Diablo look strong; the art direction was strong and led to a consistent look that was foreboding and well supported the theme of the game.

Touching on character management for a moment, the display system is called upon to also render menus such as the menus of the town shopkeepers who have stayed behind after the arrival of demonic forces to make a profit selling adventuring gear to the player's character and the inventory, spell, and character management menus. These again are just menus, displaying customized fonts, buttons, icons, and cool negative space textures.

The characters in the game animate well due to the aggressive use of 3D rendering to produce the 2D frames from which to composite the 2D sprites. This technology is not new either; our example Pac-Man uses just a few frames from open mouth to closed mouth to animate our hero, and the Wing Commander series used an array of images (about eight to sixteen individual images) from all angles around the starfighter to produce its "3D" starfighter game. The plan for Diablo was to again use established technology but take it to a quality level never before seen in games by using over 5,000 frames of animation for just the three main protagonist characters. This dedication to visual fidelity represents a lot of confidence in staying with established technology but taking it to a very high level of quality. I know of another game I will not mention by name that became severely distracted with the pursuit of volumetrically projected pixels, known as voxels, for the rendering and animation of their characters. This distraction helped to cripple this title.

The game object interaction system runs the heart of the game. This is a game of hack and slash and loot gathering. The context of this hack-and-slash has something to do with a crystal in somebody's head, demons from hell, a butcher, and dead townsfolk—plenty of motivation to keep our player character hacking away at the monsters in the game. The game object interaction handles the combat, spell casting, opening doors and chests, triggering traps, and level changes. Notice that my use cases above do not have any detail on how combat, spell casting, or the opening of doors and chests works. Those are detailed use cases that would be covered in the design document; this chapter is focusing on the key design elements of the game in the effort to be sure we have the correct scope for our game.

My use of UML's use case notation has been purposely slim with the use of just the simple table format of major user interactions and a few diagrams to show the relationship of these interactions with each other. In later chapters I will discuss more advanced use cases as we progress through the game design and head into technical design.

Case Study II—Gran Turismo

The Gran Turismo series for the PlayStation and PlayStation 2 platforms published by Sony is all about racing cars. Every conceivable subgenre of racing has been explored over the years as well as many sequels offering the latest technical wizardry for themes already visited. Racing cars have been a staple of video games since the days of the Atari 2600 with Night Driver, where the road and terrain are a solid field of black demarked thoughtfully with some magenta lane markers. Nighttime racing has continued to evolve to Tokyo Street Racer on the PS2 and Project Gotham on the Xbox. Racing games

> >

deliver an experience that almost everyone wants to do—race cars. Some want to race at night, some off road, some want to race taxis, some want to run over pedestrians, but hey, there is a racing game for everyone.

What is it about Gran Turismo that makes it a mega-hit? Was it luck? Was it a large budget? Or was there some sort of planning and direction behind Gran Turismo? I am presenting a case for thoughtful planning.

Gran Turismo's (GT) vision statement was most likely something like "The best racing simulator on any platform." To back up that vision statement we need to look into what it would mean to be the "best racing simulator." The best is so encompassing in its superlative that Sony set out to dominate all other racing games. Hmm, that is a tall order. The first step is to pick the type of racing Sony would model. In the end, Sony chose to model a variety of racing from raw amateur racing of minivans to world-class events featuring million-dollar racing machines achieving the highest form of automotive engineering.

So, at first glance it would appear that Sony violated the design guideline of focusing on one game and a tight set of features and doing them well. However, if we take a look at how they presented these various classes of racing to the player, we will see that it was a seamless presentation of gameplay from the lowliest of minivans to the Suzuki Escudo.

When you load up the simulation mode of Gran Turismo for the first time (it doesn't matter which version), you are given a small amount of credits to purchase your first racecar. Taking a look at the various car manufacturers,

the player has only a couple of choices in the beginning of the game. After spending all his cash, the player then sets out to race some beginner races to build up a supply of cash so he can modify his car. The car modification gameplay is the hidden weapon of Gran Turismo. Here players can ogle new tires, polished ports, oversized turbos, and a host of other modifications to their car. The exhaust improvement conveniently enough has the highest bang for the buck and will most likely be the first purchase for any player. Here the player bonds with his car, and all the cool parts available drive the player to go back to the track and keep racing. This context for the racing is compelling. It is the same inventory/party growth dynamic from a role-playing game like Diablo—a most compelling feature.

This racing around a track and modifying the car goes on and on throughout the whole game. What changes are the events, the tracks, the competition, and most importantly, the car the player is racing. Gran Turismo features hundreds of cars, dozens of tracks, and scores of events. The events are classified into licenses from Beginner to International A. Players can always find a race and almost always can earn some cash to make forward progress on acquiring new goodies for their car. This car modification meta-game is what ties all of Gran Turismo together and presents to the player a world where they can start with a modest real-world car, and through racing, modifications, and licensing they too can be an international racecar driver. This is the brilliant vision behind Gran Turismo— it slowly builds up to the super cars, and all along the way the player is hooked and believes in the world and knows why he is playing this game.

Later in the series Gran Turismo added rally racing. This additional mode of racing was also seamlessly integrated into the core game. Indeed, the player's rally racing cars just need to change the tires to racing slicks and they would often do well in the pavement events. In classic arcade fashion, new tracks would only be revealed to the player after completing a racing series or a licensing program. The rally events in the later GT series upheld that tradition with their own set of rally tracks to unveil. The Gran Turismo series is the greatest of the racing games because it fully delivered on the gameplay that is central to racing and takes players from knowing nothing

about racing cars to being able to carry on an extended conversation about gear ratios and coil-overs.

I justified Gran Turismo's success without ever mentioning that the game has always boasted the most realistic physics model for its racing, the most gorgeous graphics, and a complete aural experience second to none. All of these technical features are of course critically important to an electronic game; however, it is the key features of a game that will lead to success and enable the project to fully realize the efforts of the whole game development team.

Use Cases of Gran Turismo

Here are the key features of Gran Turismo 3 distilled into some use cases for review:

Car Driving Controls
Press the Gas Pedal
Use the Normal Brakes
Turn the Car Left or Right
Shift the Gears Up or Down
Use the Emergency Brakes

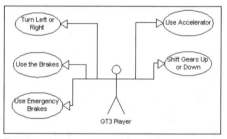

The player input use cases of Gran Turismo 3

Display and Audio System
Render the Track, Terrain, and Sky
Render the Cars
Render the Special Effects
Play Sound Effects and Music

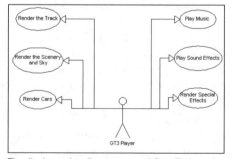

The display and audio use cases of Gran Turismo 3

> >

Shell Activity Menus
Access Buy Car
Access Garage
Access Wash Car/Oil Change
Access Race Car
Access Modify Car
Access Licensing Tests

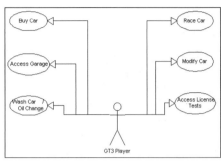

The shell menu use cases of Gran Turismo 3

Modify Car
Browse Major Systems: Engine, Transmission, Aerodynamics, etc.
Review Individual Item: Read the stats of this item and see how it would look on the car if it is an external add-on or what the change to weight and power would be if it is a performance item.
Purchase Item: Buy the specified upgrade part.
Install Item: Have the newly purchased item. This especially makes sense for the purchase of tires; it is useful to the player to be able to choose from a suite of tires.

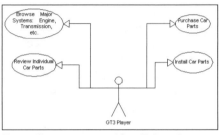

The modify car use cases of Gran Turismo 3

Quick Analysis of the Use Cases of Gran Turismo

Again, this chapter is not discussing how to complete a detailed design document, so I have only covered the higher-level functions of Gran Turismo. But in two areas, driving the car and modifying the car, I drilled down to the individual interactive activities the player has to play with. Driving the car and modifying the car is the game; everything else is in context of these two activities.

Gran Turismo is successful largely due to a clear vision and plan for the game. It was perfectly designed to capture the largest segment of the market who would enjoy racing games. In fact my father and his best friend went out and purchased PlayStations after playing Gran Turismo 1 at my house and went on to compete with actual cash prizes for virtual driving seasons. These two men in the over-50 demographic were not hard-core gamers; they were mass-market consumers who bought the PlayStation just to play Gran Turismo. That is a true hit.

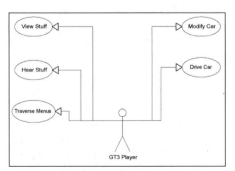

The use cases of Gran Turismo from five miles up

The Key Design Elements of Your Game

I am sure you are now comfortable with this light introduction to UML use cases. They are hardly more than a table of actions and a simple diagram composed of a stick figure and bubbles of action. Now I want you to think about the interactions of your game and write down its use cases.

The methodical way of discovering your use cases is to focus on the core activity of your game and write down all the things the player *does* in the core of your game. Work your way outward, writing down the other activities you have planned for your game, such as buying gear, building a house, researching flame throwers, learning a new spell. Keep working outward until you can't think of anything you missed. At this stage we are looking for the major activities, so don't think about how many buttons the save menu will have, just what are the big interactions between the player and the game.

Then sort these activities into groups based on similar functionality as I have done with Diablo and Gran Turismo. Finally sketch out the use case diagram complete with the player actor and your use cases. It is useful to create diagrams for each group of activity. You have now articulated your gameplay in both an easy-to-read text format and graphical format. These use cases will be the basis of refinement for the game design and technical design stages. However, in this chapter we are looking for *key design elements*. Examine your groups of activities and look hard for a set of activities that stand out as potentially unnecessary to the core of your game. Are there parts of your

game design that are distracting in complexity? Are these parts only fun to a hard-core set of fans? Are these features hidden from the novice player? Can they be cut altogether?

Take a look at your design; are you sure you are only making one game? I think a lot of the projects that slip by years make the mistake of trying to fold more than one game into a single game project. You do not need to make more than one game to be competitive. Just make a small set of features that are inherently fun, make those tight, and take the production values as high as possible. This is how a hit is made.

The Battle of the Counterterrorists Games

There are two games that neatly make the point I am discussing in this chapter, nailing the right key design elements. These two games are Rainbow Six and Counter-Strike. Both of these games feature special operations type protagonists working as a team to defeat terrorists and other modern day bad guys. An experienced development team produced one of these games with a full development staff for an established publisher. The other game was developed principally by two fans who have had experience making mods with modest financial backing of a development house.

Both of these games are successes and I would be proud to have been a team member in any capacity on either of these two projects. That being said, Counter-Strike clobbered Rainbow Six. Counter-Strike is the mod produced by a small staff of fans working part-time, while Rainbow Six is a full game with many man-years of effort. If game development is so hard, how could

> >

these fans have done so well compared to the pros?

While poor technical execution will never make a hit game, the answer to this question lies again in the key design elements of Counter-Strike versus Rainbow Six.

The Key Design Elements of Rainbow Six

Rainbow Six was the earlier of the two games; to some degree this can never be a fair comparison, as the Counter-Strike mod team had Rainbow Six available to experiment with and to refine. Rainbow Six was designed for single-player play, and while it did have multi-player mode, the game was much more playable in its single-player mode. Rainbow Six featured an extensive campaign structure where you managed the team members of your elite special forces. This team management would appear to be at first glance quite fun and supportive of the context of playing the missions of Rainbow Six, much like Gran Turismo, and that might be true. However, the Rainbow Six team added another context layer to the game: mission planning. Here the player planned out the mission to such a degree that they could tell their team members when to throw the flash grenades and which doors to break down and which to sneak through. After the planning stage was complete, the game acted somewhat like the blend of a movie and a game experience. The movie experience came in where your AI teammates, whom you gave instructions to prior to mission start, would follow your orders and have whatever success might befall them; the game part was that you still had interactive control over your character.

Are We Playing a Mission or Planning a Mission?

I think the preplanning of the missions is what prevented Rainbow Six from taking off to a higher level of success. The problem with such a detailed modeling of the preplanning stage is that it was cumbersome in three ways: First, the player already had context for the missions through the campaign structure and the team management feature sets; second, it was cumbersome due to the user interface of the preplanning. It was like having to act as some kind of game scripter, programming your teammates. And finally it was cumbersome; each time you died or otherwise failed on your mission, the player would break out of the cool, immersive action of the mission and be forced to calculate new scripting paths for their AI teammates. All of these awkward bits leaked out throughout the game-playing experience, leaving me wondering if the designers of the game ever came to agreement about whether the game was about playing the mission or playing the premission planning.

RAY SPEAKS: I totally agree. I recall being very irritated with how difficult it was to equip your party, choose your party, plan out your party's actions etc. There was no learning curve; instead you were dumped into an equipping-your-character simulation, which, fundamentally, was not the game I had thought I was purchasing. This created a perception/reality gap for the consumer that made people not want to play the game.

< < < < < < < < < < < < < < < < < < < < < < < < < < < < < <

The Key Design Elements of Counter-Strike

Counter-Strike was designed to have only a multiplayer mode; not even a training simulation against bots like Quake III was available. Counter-Strike's brilliance is much like Diablo's in its courage to strip away game features and polish the core game until it is humming with game shine. For years in first-person shooters, when you died you instantly respawned to frag again. This is of course a load of fun, as one could easily spend a few hundred hours blowing away your friends before you get bored. But eventually people did get a little burnt out on straight death match, and a desire for something more manifested itself. These explorations for more came in the way of mods for Quake and Unreal that had different victory conditions for winning such as capture the flag. The team that produced Counter-Strike took the idea of a mod with context to the next level (that, by the way, is an overly worn phrase in the industry, but it sure is handy).

The next level of gameplay in a first-person shooter was to wrap an economy about the fragging of the game through credits one earned by winning missions and getting frags. This economy would enable the player to buy larger and more capable weapons, armor, and grenades, which in turn would enable him to perform even better and potentially get even cooler equipment. This feature combined with the idea of a death where the player had to sit out the rest of the turn really helped to focus the player on the harshness of the Counter-Strike world and put some good tension back into the game. Players would carry their credit balance forward each time the mission was over, and the frag counting would continue. Thus, Counter-Strike was designed in the beginning to be a replacement for the endless multiplayer fragging and instead be a much more compelling way of playing extended multiplayer first-person shooter action. All of this was accomplished by the thinnest of user interfaces, on top of Half-Life's version of the Quake engine.

In my opinion the Counter-Strike team really understood the gameplay experience they wanted to deliver—the most visceral counterterrorist gameplay experience, period. In the case of the Rainbow Six team, I think they were handicapped by the source material from Tom Clancy's *Rainbow Six* in choosing to model the extensive preplanning stage of a mission. That stage is no doubt realistic and the larger portion of the job in a real counterterrorist mission, but it just gets in the way of having fun hunting terrorists. And we are in the profession of delivering fun, not realism. Realism should only be used to create fun, not detract from it.

Most Popular Multiplayer Game

It is interesting to see that Counter-Strike is the most popular multiplayer gameplayed online, with anywhere from 25,000 to 60,000 simultaneous players. One could say that Half-Life itself was a mega-hit with over two million copies sold, whereas Rainbow Six was a more modest success, and use that argument to explain why Counter-Strike is the more popular counterterrorist game. However, that argument fails when you realize people do not play games they do not want to play. Sure, marketing can help a game get off the ground to some extent, but the games business is still dominated by word-of-mouth sales where one fan recommends the title to another. The big titles that receive large marketing budgets are also fun and playable games that enjoy strong word-of-mouth sales. Unlike the movie business, an aggressive marketing campaign cannot save your bacon. There is a long-standing tradition of going to bad movies just to see how bad they are; this does not happen with games. Games are too expensive at about $50; no one is inclined to buy a game just to see how bad it is. However, a bad movie has a couple of chances. First of all, just seeing what mischief with toddlers Arnold Schwarzenegger has gotten himself into complete with some buttered popcorn, a fountain soda, your friend's company, and a walk about the mall is a good entertainment value. This movie will go onto DVD, VHS, rental, cable, then prime-time TV, and eventually the USA channel—plenty of ways for a non-hit movie to recoup and make a small amount of money for the studio.

The 50,000 people playing Counter-Strike online is even more impressive when you think about the ratio of people playing the multiplayer portion of a game relative to the single-player portion. It has been casually measured across a number of games, excluding the massively multiplayer online role-playing games, that only about 5 to 15 percent of the purchasers of a game will go on to play it in its multiplayer format. Thus Counter-Strike was much more successful than Rainbow Six, and it was working with only 5 to 15 percent of the counterterrorist market.

Of Intersecting Sets and Elite Forces

A second-tier game will sell its most copies in the first few weeks when the early adopters who have kept on top of all the previews will buy the game. During this time period the online reviews are written up. To my surprise it appears that strong reviews cannot sell a game either. The most excellent Elite Force (not anywhere close to being a second-tier game) developed by Raven received the most stellar press reviews one could ask for, including game of the year from most publications. Built on the Quake engine and developed by a top developer, it had lavish press coverage generating plenty of awareness before the release of the title. The title was reasonably on time and reasonably bug-free. The team behind the game was so into the game, they produced a free expansion pack. Elite Force was firmly expected to be a major hit inside of Activision. I do not know the actual numbers on the internal return-on-investment worksheets, but I have heard they were expecting 700,000 to 1,000,000 units in the first year worldwide. Elite Force went on to do about one-third of those numbers. Why? Why did Elite Force not succeed when not a single person at Raven, Activision, or the press could have set the game up better for success? Is it bad luck? Is the gaming public so fickle?

I have a theory why Elite Force failed to meet Activision's expectations. First of all, the game *did* sell well at approximately 300,000 units generating a gross revenue of $15 million. That is enough money to make a living for all involved and keep at it. However, I think it is the expectations that were at

< < < < < < < < < < < < < < < < < < < < < < < < < < < < < < < <

fault; I don't think the game could ever hope to sell more units than it did. Sure a truly immense advertising campaign with television commercials played 20 times a day on all channels and appearances of the game on all of the late-night talk shows would have sold maybe 100,000 to 200,000 more copies, but Activision would have had to pay for each copy they were selling. My theory is that when you are experimenting with genre crossing and blending, be sure you are creating a union between the two or more sets of players you are marketing to, and not creating the intersection between these markets.

> RAY SPEAKS: This certainly is an art form, but I think it can be done; it's just difficult. Creating the correct impression on the fans of both genres and making the parts that don't appeal to the other genre's fans at all times accessible is probably the hardest thing to implement, but this is critical to achieving mainstream success through selling to a few hard-core genres in a cross-genre game.

The two markets for Elite Force were the Star Trek gamers and the first-person shooter gamers. Activision has been working hard for years trying to find a breakaway hit for the Star Trek license they paid so dearly for, and teaming up with world class developer Raven and using the fabulous Quake engine should produce a lavish 3D-game with production values far and above any that a Star Trek gamer has seen before. And for the first-person shooters who are tired of blowing monsters up in worlds freshly created with little or no backstory, Elite Force offered the Star Trek universe, which consumers have had exposure to for

over 25 years. Sounds wonderful, so why did this game not sell a million copies or more? Warcraft II was just a sequel to a game of orcs and humans gathering rocks and trees and banging on each other. That sold millions of copies; why shouldn't Elite Force sell a million? The reason is in the key design elements themselves; the very strategy used to make a hit—a cross between Star Trek and first-person shooters—is what held Elite Force back.

Let us first take a look at Elite Force from the perspective of a Star Trek gamer. *Star Trek* is about a starship named *Enterprise* exploring the galaxy on romantic adventures that are solved through cleverness, diplomacy, or the gunboat diplomacy that the *Enterprise* can deliver with photons and phasers. The Star Trek gamer is looking to live the experience depicted in the television episodes and movies. These episodes feature fantastic science, starship combat, and exploring various social themes in a futuristic context. Star Trek does feature combat between individuals in the form of the hand-held phaser, a device that you just point and shoot to disable or to disintegrate. This weapon reveals an utter disdain for prowess of personal martial skill; this hand phaser is almost a nerd fantasy where they can get back at every childhood bully by just pointing their garage door opener—and bzzt!—no more enemies. The Star Trek gamer is not looking for a first-person shooter; there is nothing in the Star Trek universe backstory that leaves the player wanting to explore a shooter. The most successful Star Trek games have been the adventure games 25th Anniversary and Judgment Rites, as well as the

> >

starship games of Starfleet Command, Starfleet Academy, and Armada.

From the first-person shooter perspective, an FPS player traditionally looked for the technically impressive and challenging games such as the Quake and Unreal series. However, after the release of the story-rich Half-Life, the industry realized that the FPS crowd would love to have a good reason to exercise their martial prowess. The creepy world of Half-Life is a good reason, the pulse-pounding excitement of World War II through Day of Defeat is a great reason, and hunting terrorists with a submachine is always great fun. But again the Star Trek universe lacks any compelling imagery of personal combat. Sure, Kirk would slug it out with the occasional alien, and Spock could put someone to sleep by pinching them; either way, *Star Trek* lacks that visceral appeal.

Star Wars, on the other hand, has a glorious tradition of martial combat on the personal scale through the use of light sabers. This style of combat was indeed a strong success with the Jedi Knight series from LucasArts. Finally, let me repeat, Elite Force was not an unsuccessful game; it was a great game, very well produced. And missing the expectations set for it is not a reflection on the execution of Elite Force, but rather a reflection on the key design concepts of the game.

Some Straight Questions to Ask Yourself

The case studies I presented introduced use cases from the Unified Modeling Language and illustrated what I mean by determining the key design elements of your game.

I ask you to pause just a moment before you wield your scalpel and slice off the most extraneous bits of your game design. I would like you to first get a bit more material down on a second sheet of paper to consider while you review your key design elements.

What Genre or Genres Does Your Game Feature?

First, what is your game's genre, such as adventure, role-playing game (RPG), real-time strategy (RTS), real-time tactical (RTT), action, first-person shooter (FPS), puzzle, sports, or some other genre?

Or is it a blend of genres?

Write down your game's genre or genre blend, and why.

Will the Game Be Single-Player, Multiplayer, or Both?

Does your game play well as a single-player game but perhaps not make much sense as a multiplayer game? Or is it the other way around where it takes real humans to play against to make it fun? Or is it reasonably fun either way?

Write down single-player, multiplayer, or both, and why.

What Is the Platform?

Which platform are you targeting: PC, handheld, Xbox, PlayStation 2, or GameCube?

Write down the platform or platforms you are targeting, and why.

< < < < < < < < < < < < < < < < < < < < < < < < < < < < < <

What Is Your Target Market?

Is this a game anyone could enjoy? Or is it targeted for the core game market of males 18 to 45 years of age? Are you targeting women as well as men? Children? What is the violence level in your game? The language? Sexual content?

Write down your target market, and why.

What Major Technologies Are You Using?

Is your game to be 2D or 3D in its fundamental presentation? Will it use a commercial engine? Is there something special about the physics? Perhaps you envision cell-shaded rendering of characters or the scene.

Write down the major bits of technology you will employ in your game, and why.

Now What?

Notice I did not give any opinions or suggestions on how to answer those questions or which answers I thought you might choose. It is not my place to tell you that a cell-shaded 3D RPG would be the next big thing on the Game Boy Advance. No, the answer to the questions above need to come from your heart, that place of inner vision where you can see and play your game in your mind's eye. That gameplay in your mind—I want you to write that down. This is your game. If you told me your game concept, I could offer suggestions and opinions, but they would be just that—opinions and suggestions. For this game of yours to be a success you must be able to have a strong vision for how your game will play.

Now find a table someplace comfortable and put in front of you the notes you have taken on game concept, business context, and the feature questions asked above. Then I want you to put this book aside and just keep visualizing your game. Get up and take a walk, get something to eat, and come back to your table of notes. Now, start slicing out the parts of your game feature brainstorm that are not actually central to your game design. Before you invest in creating a hundred-page game design document and develop a total technical design, you should figure out what you are making. The game design and technical design stages are a lot of work; be courageous and kill the features that are superfluous before you spend any more effort on them.

All of the great games have a small feature set that is well polished. Make your game great.

Chapter 8

> > > > > > > > > > > > > > > >

Game Design Document

What Is a Game Design Document and What Does It Do?

When one says "Look it up in the design document," folks are generally referring to the game design document. This is the fun document that details all of the characters, the levels, the game mechanics, the views, the menus, and so on—in short, the game. The game design document for most designers is great fun; here they get to flesh out their vision with muscles and sinew on top of the skeleton of the game concept that it was before. By no means am I saying it is easy to create a complete design document. Creating a finished design document is so difficult I have never been able to finish one of my own, nor have I seen anyone else finish his or her design documents. With my two latest projects, Starfleet Command: The Next Generation for Activision and Black9, I am certainly taking the design efforts to our highest levels, and I see the results paying off with faster and stronger production.

The game design document is part of a suite of documents that specify the game you are creating. All of these

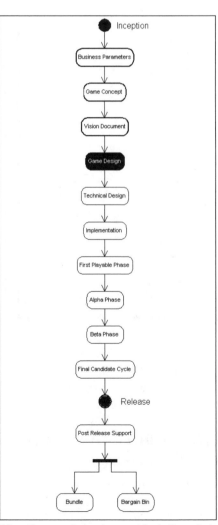

Where the game design document lies in the project life cycle

< < < < < < < < < < < < < < < < < < < < < < < < < <

documents I collectively call the production plan:

- Concept/Vision/Proposal Document
- Game Design Document
- Art Design Document
- Technical Design Document
- Project Schedule
- Software Testing Plan
- Risk Mitigation Plan

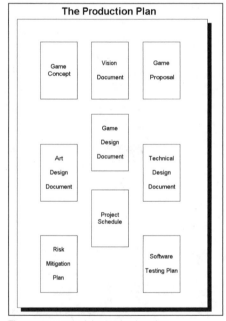

The components of the production plan

The purpose of creating all of these documents is to know what we are *going to do*. To figure out what we are going to do, we need to do a bunch of thinking. Writing down what we have thought about in the form of diagrams and notes forces us to drive the quality and quantity of thinking to the required level for making a production plan. Knowing what we are going to do will help us answer a great deal more planning questions: Who is going to do them? How long will it take? What needs to be done prior to getting that done? What features do we need to cut to give us time to do that? What are the risks in this project? This is all the most basic stuff to kick off a software development project to reassure each other we know what we are doing, and incidentally most good publishers require this planning. This chapter will focus on the game design portion of the production plan.

There are several good books on the market that discuss game design in particular. This book aims to cover new ground by discussing game production and development as a whole of which game design is a subtask in this greater effort. What I will not do is design your game for you. I will not be offering opinions on whether your game should be multiplayer or 3D or online or all three. I have neither the inclination nor the hubris to make a book offering such suggestions. I am merely presenting a rigorous and systematic approach to game design you might apply to your own creative vision.

What About the Proposal Document?

An observant reader will notice that I have omitted a formal discussion of what should go into your proposal document, which you would show publishers in order to receive funding. A few years ago established developers could write up five to ten pages of game vision and accompany it with some sketches and likely receive funding if a publisher believed in the concept. As time passes, the competition gets stronger and the games themselves are larger in scope and require deeper talent and skill to execute competitively. The publishers are now expecting to see a playable prototype of your game demonstrating all the talents your team is bringing to the table from programming, art, and design to sound and animation.

I am not suggesting that you will not need a vision document or a proposal to pass around; you will need one to sell your game after you have a playable prototype to demonstrate. The downside of this trend is that the development house has to shoulder a larger portion of the financial risk of the project by performing the early financing for the project. This in turn leads to

only the stronger, more willful developers being able to develop original content—the holy grail of all developers across the land.

I am suggesting specifically that you go ahead and create the first draft of your game design document *before* you create your proposal. There are a few reasons for this: First you still don't really *know your game*, so if you take the time to create a first draft of your game design document, you will create a much stronger vision document and proposal. When you take the game concept in your mind and first try to lay out a proposal, you will find a need to use vague language in parts (or just outright guesses) to describe your game. But if you have your game design document in your hands, you will be able to write a tight proposal.

When Do You Write the Game Design Document?

You should write your first draft of the game design document immediately after narrowing down your key design concepts from the preceding chapter. However, as I will show you, the game design document is a large undertaking itself in the breadth of topics to be detailed.

You might be reading this book from a variety of different perspectives: as a producer or project leader or holding some other position in the industry or looking to get into the industry. If you already have a team of folks to work on this game with you, I encourage you to distribute and delegate portions of the game design document to your team. This is somewhat controversial, and I am sure a good many of my peers would disagree and feel more

comfortable with a strong designer at the helm of the ship articulating the game's design from a single, focused mind. I do agree that you need to have a visionary who has ultimate ownership of the game's design and who holds executive control, but I advocate judiciously distributing some of the more modular, more straightforward tasks to other team members. Or at least provide textual or visual sketches and allow others to elaborate on your designs. The reason for this delegation is twofold: One, creating a game design document is so much work that it is natural to break the job up across multiple people to get the work done more rapidly and with higher quality. My other justification for this delegation is that this is one of the effective ways

< < < < < < < < < < < < < < < < < < < < < < < < < < < < <

you can build a strongly bound, effective team for your project. They will not be able to disengage from the project easily if it is their ideas and plans that make up the project.

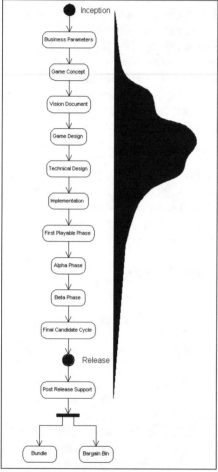

Game design activity is always happening.

To delegate design tasks well, be sure to take the time to clearly describe to your teammates what topics you need them to design and provide a style guide or template that you require the work delivered under. This is important because many of your team members may be new to game design or lack the creative initiative that your designer self has. After all, that is why you are leading the production plan. If you lay out what they need to write up, specify what diagrams they need to create and what their text needs to discuss, and provide a template, they will not feel frustrated but will feel empowered in contributing to the project in the early stages. This will help them understand that their role is important and create a feeling of project stakeholder in the team member.

Again, I have never seen a completed design document, and one of the reasons is that game design documents need to be maintained through the course of production. With every game developer wishing they had just another few weeks to add this bit of polish to their games, it would be logical to think that every game design document could have added a bit more detail here or clarification there. In the end, you should measure the completeness of your game design document by how well the team was led by the game design. How much confusion or lost work was created by a lack of detail or clarity in the document? How much reworking of the gameplay had to be performed in the course of production due to ill-thought-out designs? These are the questions you should ask yourself in the postpartum stage of your game's cycle.

Take the time to review your game design document at the beginning of each milestone to be sure your developers have ready the most accurate and up-to-date reflection of the game's design before they commence that

> >

milestone's work. Also look farther into the future to document design changes so that your developers do not lay the groundwork for elements of the game no longer needed even if they are beyond the current milestone.

What Should Go into a Game Design Document?

Game design documents are more akin to business plans than blueprints for a building or a mechanical engineering diagram in that the industry has developed no standardized formal requirements for a game design document. This is part of the lack of development discipline and rigor that is pervasive throughout the software industry. Games used to be so much smaller in scope and complexity that it was much simpler to document the game design, so no great amount of formalism was required. The movie industry has settled down to such a degree that there are hundreds of universities and colleges that offer specific courses on how to write a movie script. The game industry grosses more revenue than Hollywood does at the box office, yet just a few pioneering universities and colleges are offering classes on game programming and art for new media. I know of no class that teaches game design. Thus, we are just too young an industry and our technology is changing too rapidly for us to settle on the requirements of a game design document. Another complication is that all of us get our starts on smaller projects or conversion work where the demand for a detailed design document is substantially lower, robbing us of an opportunity to grow our game design skills before we reach the Big Project.

What am I going to do about this lack of a game design document

standard? I am sharing my game design requirements as well as providing information from other development houses illustrating what we are doing in the field and what we are looking for in a game design document.

A happy, productive game developer backed up with strong designs

The game design document should describe to all the team members the functional requirements of the features they are implementing for the project. The ideal game design document is complete and has seen revisions to fix gameplay and add clarity. In theory the game developers should be able to take their copy of the game design document and run with it. In practice it is very difficult to create a document that strong.

‹ ‹

Section One: Defining the Game

I will discuss the content of the game design document by using sections; the order of the sections was chosen to lead the reader from general information concerning the project at large towards the details of the project that are specific to only certain members of the development team.

Articulate What the Game Is as Clearly as Possible

I remember reading the postmortem of Tropico in *Game Developer* magazine. I really appreciate reading postmortems of game projects, and I am always grateful to the developers who have the courage to document what they did wrong and what they did right. The most amazing thing I read in the Tropico design document is that after a year of development the team came to the shocking realization that there were about half a dozen different visions of Tropico being developed by various team members. Each team member was implementing his or her own version of the project! I was first shocked to hear that something like that could happen; I was then shocked to read that the team had the courage to document it and share it with the industry. Then I thought about it more carefully, and I realized that every game project has the potential to splinter off into separate projects and that many other projects have suffered from the same lack of central vision. I believe this is why so many developers advocate a strong lead designer who dictates all decisions from art to dialogue to placement of buttons on the screen. Experienced developers have been burned by design-by-committee too

many times to tolerate their time being frittered away, and they demand a strong and clear vision for the game.

Every game design document should have a section at the front that clearly describes to the reader what the game is. It should be written so clearly and succinctly that it does not leave any vagueness in the reader's mind what the game is about. It should describe the world, the gameplay, and what motivates the player. Following are a couple of examples.

Pac-Man: An arcade game featuring a single joystick for controls where the player directs the protagonist, Pac-Man, to clear levels of mazes of dots by eating these dots. The enemies of our hero are four cute pastel-colored ghosts that will eat our hero unless our hero is under the influence of the big power-up dot.

Doom: A first-person shooter played on the PC platform, where the player controls a space marine in a 3D environment against a horde of bizarre monsters. The player has a configurable set of controls taking advantage of the keyboard, mouse, or joystick. The gameplay is action based with no strategic or role-playing elements; instead the game depends on bleeding edge technology providing a rush of adrenaline through its aggressive attention to carnage. Single-player mode will provide three episodes of missions against an increasingly horrible cast of monsters and scary settings; the multiplayer mode will feature an unprecedented level of player-to-player combat.

From my own experience I know there are many personalities in the game business; some personalities belong to wonderful human beings you want to spend a bunch of time with; other personalities are less inviting. I think a lot of projects suffer when the leaders of the projects choose to practice conflict avoidance. I would hazard a bet that members of the Tropico team sensed they were working towards different goals yet decided not to rock the boat either in an effort to create a more pleasant workplace or to selfishly give their own version of the game more time to grow (perhaps to a level of commitment where it could not be cut back). This is an area I find particularly hard to manage. I think my teammates would be surprised to hear me say that. They would probably say I lead the team well and with strength. However, I must confess there are only a few things in life I like to do less than to cut off the design direction of one of my team members. This is because while I believe a game project needs executive direction, I also believe the best games are made when everyone's energies are woven into a stronger whole than any individual can deliver. Therefore my advice is to take the time to write up exactly what your game is and present it to your team members as early as possible. If you know one of your team members despises real-time strategy games, but you are committed to creating a real-time strategy game, no good can come out of misleading him—tell the truth straight up. He will either do his best to create the best real-time strategy game he can or move on to another project that fits his interest. But by no means would it be a good idea to keep investing in a team member making role-playing features that you cannot use. When it comes time to cut those features out, you will have a

genuinely pissed off person and a confused team.

Set the Mood

When the game is so clinically described as I advocate above, often the soul of the game is lost in the translation. Many games are role-playing games set in a fantasy world. This does not mean that Ultima, Bard's Tale, Baldur's Gate, and Pool Radiance are the same game. I like to see a short piece of fiction at the opening of a game design document to quickly give me the feel for this world, to put me in the mood. The intro movie in a released game has the same function: to introduce the player to what sort of challenges the game holds.

Some games do not lend themselves well to a fiction treatment, such as the abstract puzzle and classic arcade games of Pac-Man, Frogger, and Tetris. Even so, a snippet of words from an auto-racing television commentary intermixed with entries in a racecar drivers' journal discussing the upgrades he has performed on his car and how desperately he needs to win this race to pay his debts would quickly draw me into the world of Gran Turismo.

Section Two: Core Gameplay

Now we move quickly from general statements about the game to direct comments about the core gameplay. We want to fix in the reader's mind the vision and feel for the gameplay early on so that when he digests the rest of the document it will be in relation to the core gameplay and create a tighter understanding of the game design.

<<<<<<<<<<<<<<<<<<<<<<<<<<<<<<<<<<<

The Main Game View

Some games have only one view of the game; others have several view modes or even different levels of gameplay with different views. This chapter in the game design document needs to define the *main* game view of the game. Is it a 3D view? 2D? Isometric? If it is isometric, what is the scale of the tiles and characters? If it is a 3D view, what kind of 3D view? Is it an interior engine type game, or do you require exterior environments? If it is an exterior engine, how far does the view need to extend? Is it primarily rendering hills and trees or is it rendering a racetrack or a city? Make a few sketches of the view, or even better get an artist on your team to make a full-color mockup of the view.

> **MUST DO**!—The main game view of the project must be in every game design document and quickly convey to the reader what the game will look like.

Core Player Activity

What does the player do in this game? What is the key interaction? Pilot a starship? Drive a racecar? Organize an army? Maneuver a character through a 3D space? This is where you detail the key interactions between the player and the game. Together with the main view from above the reader will develop a strong understanding of the game you are creating.

This is an excellent place to use the UML use case diagrams introduced in the previous chapter to document the interactions between the player and the game. Create the UML diagrams that organize these interactions in a graphical manner for easy digestion on the reader's part.

The Controller Diagram

A critical diagram to create is the controller diagram. This diagram shows at a glance how the game inputs are mapped to a game pad controller or a keyboard.

The controller layout for Taldren's upcoming game Black9

In-Game User Interface

Working outward from the view and the core activities, what are the other user interface items visible on the main display? Health? Time? Mana? Distance to target? Radar? Map? Now is the time to detail the rest of these user interface items to be found on the main display. Take the time to create a diagram or mockup for each of these display items and update your use case hierarchy to track these interactions (even if they are a non-interactive display, the player uses these items by viewing them).

An early preproduction view of the Black9 main interface

> >

Section Three: Contextual Gameplay

This will be a fairly meaty section. In this part of the game design document you will detail all the rest of the game mechanics that were too deep to discuss in the core gameplay section.

Shell Menus

Most games on both the consoles and the PC have shell menus for creating characters, upgrading cars, reviewing inventory, selecting spells, viewing how many stars or crystals have been collected, and so on. Now is the time to create a mockup of the shell menus complete with all the displays and buttons. We have found it particularly useful to create UML use case text and diagrams for all the shell menu activities the player can go through. It is also important to create a menu flow map showing the relationship between all the menus—how the player may navigate between the activities in the game.

The Nuts and Bolts of Game Mechanics

Now is the time to talk about how much horsepower that engine will develop, how many marines that transporter can transport simultaneously, how many charges are in your magic wands, how fast the characters move. Detail everything you can of the game mechanics. I find it useful to pretend I am creating a pen and paper role-playing game or board game complete with all the details. Of course all these elements will need to be tweaked and balanced in the future; however, every time I drive down to this level of detail I learn more about my game at the higher levels of abstraction and go back and adjust elements of the higher design. This section should be replete with spreadsheets, charts, and diagrams.

Tutorial Mechanics

Almost all big games have integrated interactive tutorials in the game. Some

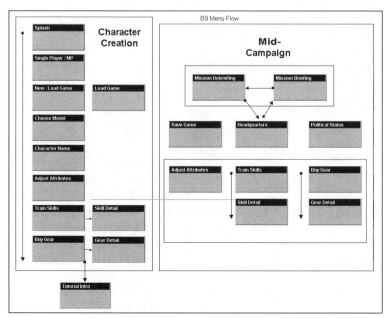

The menu flow for Black9

of these tutorials are explicitly tutorials, others are billed as licenses as in Gran Turismo, and other games simply create very easy levels for the beginning of the game like in Mario64. For Starfleet Command: The Next Generation, we modeled the tutorials around the education an officer in Starfleet would receive while going through Starfleet Academy. Discuss your philosophy when approaching the tutorial content, discuss what you want the player to learn here, and discuss what activities you will employ to reinforce what the player is taught to make for a smooth transition into actual gameplay. In Baldur's Gate, BioWare had the player character start out in a safe town where all of the NPCs acted partly as an interactive in-game manual and also related backstory to the players to get them into the world. How are you going to introduce your player to the game?

Consciously decide what controls and game mechanics you are going to directly cover in your tutorials and what material you are leaving for the player to learn over time as they master the game. Keep in mind the goal of the tutorial is not to teach everything in the game; rather the purpose of the tutorial is to get the player into playing the game successfully and without frustration as quickly as possible.

Multiplayer Mechanics

Will your game have a multiplayer component? If so, what flavor? Will you support LAN play for PC games in the office or home LAN environment? Perhaps you will feature online matching via GameSpy or Microsoft's Gaming Zone. If your game is a massively multiplayer role-playing game, then of course you have a multiplayer feature set to document.

If you did not cover your multiplayer menus in the shell menu section, then this is the perfect place to detail the activity flow between the menus. Write down the functionality of each of the buttons and describe the player's choices. Also detail the technical requirements of the multiplayer feature set that the technical design will need to address. How many players will your game support? Are these players simultaneous, concurrent players as in a Quake game? Or are the players residing in a hybrid system like Starfleet Command's online campaign that is capable of supporting hundreds of simultaneous players where the battles are played out in smaller sessions of up to six players each?

Create diagrams documenting these activity flows. Will your game support the historic modes of multiplayer such as serial, modem-to-modem, or even hot seat?

With the latest generation of consoles starting with SEGA's Dreamcast and on through Sony's PS2 and Microsoft's Xbox, the game designer now needs to consider online multiplayer gaming for their console games. On the console side, multiplayer games have often used multiple controllers. Will your console game have multiplayer gameplay? Will you split the screen? Will you hot seat between players?

Many game designers put off describing their multiplayer gameplay until later in the project. This has led to disastrous delays, poor gameplay and game balance, and outright bugginess. This procrastination in multiplayer game design is fairly widespread and carries down the line, with the

> >

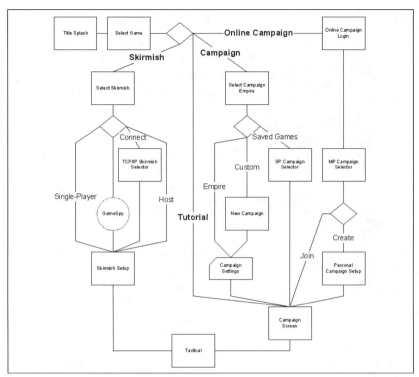

The menu flow diagram for Starfleet Command 3

technical design stage often postponing a serious discussion of the multiplayer engineering requirements. Sometimes these delays are so manifest, games have resorted to the outright outsourcing of the multiplayer project. Examples of this are Interplay's Klingon Academy and id's Return to Castle Wolfenstein, where Grey Matter develops the single-player game and another developer will come along behind and implement the multiplayer aspect of the game. I am highly skeptical of outsourced game creation in a piecemeal fashion. The only reason people delay thinking about their multiplayer feature set is because it is hard. But being hard is not a good enough reason for putting it off!

Section Four: Talk Story

This section of the game design document calls for the game designer to elaborate on the world they have created. Many game developers would really rather work on this part of the game design document than discuss the mundane buttons on the multiplayer screens. The reason I have pushed this section back as far as I did is because I feel the game design document should serve the team rather than the designer. So I started with setting the mood and quickly followed with capturing the key requirements of the game. Now let's roll out the graph paper, character sheets, and scripts for the cut scenes!

< < < < < < < < < < < < < < < < < < < < < < < < < < < < < < <

World Backstory

A fan-made map of Britannia from the Ultima series

Detail your world; what is the relevant history of the world? Draw a map of the world the player will explore. Use cool maps for fantasy games such as Baldur's Gate and Ultima Online, but also include ship blueprints for games like System Shock 2, or the oceans of the world for a naval simulation. The depth of this section is highly dependent on the genre of your game. id Software is very proud that their Doom and Quake series of games have no need for such frills as a backstory! Ultima Online and Baldur's Gate each draw upon decades of development for their world's backstory.

A game such as Gran Turismo would only need the lightest treatment of a backstory where the racing events, the tracks, and the manufacturers of cars would be enumerated to flesh out the scope of the world's backstory.

Character Backgrounds

The character background section is also game dependent. All games have characters; it is just the concept of what a character might be that is stretched a bit in some genres. For example, role-playing games, action-adventure, and platformers would all have a section that is quite straightforward in its representation of characters, with sketches of how they look and text describing their behavior and attitude in the game. Include all of the game mechanics stats that correspond to this character such as attributes and inventory. Include references to where in the game the character will be found and indicate what type of character this is: protagonist, playable, non-player, antagonist, or boss monster.

In the case of Gran Turismo I would argue that the individual cars are the characters, especially unique cars like the Suzuki Escudo. Here the stats behind the cars and the history of the creation serve as the backstory. In a real-time strategy game each of the individual combat units is a character to be detailed. For a real-time tactical game like Starfleet Command: The Next Generation, we actually have three different classes of "characters" that are quite different from each other, but all need to be detailed. These three character types are the classic characters to be found in the story, the ships the player will command or interact with, and the ship officers that the player will recruit and train in the course of their career.

> >

CONCEPT ART
SUBJECT: OBERON
ARTIST: NATE SIMPSON

A character concept for Black9

Level, Mission, and Area Design

This is my favorite part of writing a game design document. I love examining and reading maps! Most likely your game is broken down into levels, missions, areas, tracks, episodes, decks of a ship, or some other manner of location partition. In abstract games like Lemmings, the levels are single screens of challenge for the Lemmings; for Gran Turismo it is the different tracks of course; for Doom it is bizarre and frightening levels that the designers come up with in a backstory after they have made them.

To document a level you have to take into account what sort of game you are making and how it is broken up. For classic role-playing games, large-scale fantasy maps of the countryside with detailed blueprints scaled to ten-foot corridors serve very well. For 3D games, whether platformer, shooter, or

action-adventure, it can be very challenging for the designer to specify the level in detail. The reason is that the designer may be a good designer but terrible in the use of a 3D CAD tool such as UnrealEdit or WorldEdit. Often these types of games employ a lead designer who is good with these tools and can articulate her visions directly in the tools. For the developer without these skills, very detailed writing as found in a narrative supplemented with sketches will often serve to give the level designer a strong description to work with.

Be sure to give good detail: Talk about the colors, the textures, the lighting, what the sky looks like. What are the sounds that are present in this area? What are the characters? Detail each trick, trap, challenge, or feature in your level design. On your first few passes through here, just make notes to yourself to follow up later and add more detail in the next pass.

This is the time to explain your campaign structure; show a flow diagram that relates your areas to each other. Is it linear? That is, can the

A view of a level in production for Black9

player proceed through your levels along only one path like the increasingly challenging levels of Lemmings, or can the player wander about without any direct purpose as in Ultima Online? Be sure to diagram this flow.

Declare the purpose of the area; is it a key hub area that the player will visit often or is it a bonus area or is it a part of the user interface such as the difficulty selection of Quake I? Discuss how this level may be reused like the reversing of tracks in Gran Turismo or going back for six stars in each of the worlds of Mario64.

Cut Scene Descriptions

If your movie will employ cut scenes, then write the scripts for these cut scenes. While the game industry has no standard format for the description of a cut scene, there are two important components: a storyboard and a script.

The storyboard is a key frame-by-frame visual design of the cut scenes that reads much like a comic strip. This is a critical design document for both communicating with the artists who will create the level and for achieving buy-in from the project stakeholders.

The script should follow standard movie script formatting guidelines. See the following script excerpt for an example of how to format your script for voice-over (VO) and off-stage (OS) voice work.

With this section complete, no reader should have any large questions or vagueness about the world and cast of characters in your game design. The reader should also have a strong understanding of what challenges the players will face as they proceed through the game structure.

INT. MISSION BRIEFING ROOM (GENESIS HQ-LAX)
Set in the mission briefing room of the Genesis Operations Headquarters in the LAX spaceport metroplex. The mission briefing is a short cinematic sequence performed in letterbox format using the in-game Matinee feature of the Unreal engine. The briefing room has four characters: the player character, the Genesis Operations Chief, and two other contract Genesis agents, one large, physically powerful male and one slim female.

GENESIS OPERATIONS CHIEF (VO)
We have a very serious development with our secure AI labs on the moon. We have had no communication from the base personnel in 36 hours. While the computer network seems to be functional, we have lost access to the data arrays—somebody has changed the authorization code. Fly-bys show no actual damage to the structures and we have sent two regular patrols from Luna II—they have failed to report in after reaching the lab.
(beat)
It appears that The Tea-Drinking Society is getting desperate now that we are so close to our goal; they must have launched an assault on the lab and taken physical control—now they're busy downloading all of our hard-earned work.

Your mission is to reclaim our labs and eliminate any hostiles that may be present.

You have two support operatives this time.

The Chief gestures towards a slim female in black super-hero spandex

GENESIS OPERATIONS CHIEF (VO)
Cassandra will provide you with infiltration and electronic hacking services. Her job is to get the team in there as quietly as possible. The goal is to catch The Tea-Drinking Society in the act, get it on film, and eliminate the suspected TDS agents before they are able to return to their masters with the fruits of our lab work!

Nodding towards a bulky male human with obviously large guns

> >

GENESIS OPERATIONS CHIEF (VO)
Rojak is a heavy weapons specialist. He'll back you up in a firefight and ensure that anything hostile becomes a detail of history in short order.

The Chief points towards the player character

GENESIS OPERATIONS CHIEF (VO)
As our most celebrated agent, you're in charge. Make contact after you've landed and entered the base.

PLAYER CHARACTER (VO)
"Thank you, sir. We will not let you down."

Cinematic fades to black, the sound of rocket engines throttle up out of the darkness…

A snippet of a design document of Black9 featuring a cinematic sequence

Section Five: Cover Your Assets

This section's format really is particular to your game's genre and method of construction. This last point is so important I would recommend not creating asset lists until you are mostly through the technical design stage. You should certainly jot down the assets that come to mind in each section at the end of your first pass on the game design document; however, your technical design document might reveal that on the platform of your choice and with your particular set of requirements, you are limited to the creation of just 20 character models rather than the 100 your initial design called for. Or you might find that the technical format and specification of your assets goes through some bit of exploration during the elaboration of your game in the technical design stage. Nevertheless, here are some categories of assets you should list in your game design document. These lists will come in handy when creating the production plan, which should be created after the technical design stage has been mostly completed.

2D Sprites or 3D Models

Whatever your technology, no doubt your game features moving bits of eye-pleasing pixels. Write up the list of such assets in a spreadsheet and include columns for attributes that are specific to your game's design and technical requirements.

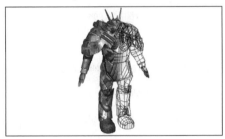

A character model in production from Black9

Missions, Levels, or Areas

List the missions, levels, or areas to be created for your game. Indicate game-specific parameters such as size, priority, or placement in a hierarchy of locales.

The city of Baldur's Gate

Voice

It will be way too early to document this section in the early phases of game design; however, strong description of the voice actors required can certainly be detailed early in the project. As production rolls along, maintain this section to prevent a panic workload when it comes time to record the voice.

Command 190: Basic Controls
Setting: The Neversail NCC-0001 at Treasure Island, San Francisco, Earth

- Helm
- Target
- Phaser Fire (somehow have plenty of phasers to fire)
- Destroy Cargo Boxes

Title: Command 190: Basic Controls
Briefing: This simulation will cover the basic controls of a starship.
Setting Text 1: Aboard the Neversail NCC-0001
Setting Text 2: Starfleet Academy, Home Fleet
Setting Text 3: Treasure Island, San Francisco, Earth

{The Neversail NCC-0001 is a police frigate armed with only Phaser-3s}

{The screen is already set in full screen mode}

{There is no terrain, only a beautiful backdrop}

{The player's ship is already in motion at a speed of 10}

{The player's ship is already at Red Alert}

{VOICE TALENT: FED-INSTRUCTOR-EARTH: Scotty? Not Sulu – we will save him for later tutorials.}

FED-INSTRUCTOR-EARTH: "Lieutenant, welcome to Starfleet Command school. To earn the rank of Lieutenant Commander, you must pass both Command 190: Basic Controls and Command 290: Intermediate Helm Controls. Let's get started."

FED-INSTRUCTOR-EARTH: "The basics of starship control are very simple, yet require a lot of training and practice to master. Let's begin with basic helm control aboard a small police vessel, the USS Neversail."

FED-INSTRUCTOR-EARTH: "To turn the Neversail, use the mouse and left-click on the 3D tactical display. This will issue a helm command to port or starboard."

FED-INSTRUCTOR-EARTH: "Left-click on the 3D tactical display in the direction you wish to turn. Your helmsman will choose the appropriate turn, port or starboard."

{Wait for the user to turn the ship. Add sarcastic/encouraging comments to the player to hurry them along.}

Sarcastic Comments
FED-INSTRUCTOR-EARTH: "Well Lieutenant, what are you waiting for? A Klingon invasion?"

FED-INSTRUCTOR-EARTH: "Lieutenant, when I give an order I expect it to be obeyed."
FED-INSTRUCTOR-EARTH: "I don't have all day, Lieutenant."
FED-INSTRUCTOR-EARTH: "[Sigh]. We are all waiting."
FED-INSTRUCTOR-EARTH: "Lieutenant, make up your mind before I make it up for you – and give you a failing grade."

Positive Remarks
FED-INSTRUCTOR-EARTH: "Very good, Lieutenant."

{Add 1 prestige point for each helm command up to 3 points}

FED-INSTRUCTOR-EARTH: "The farther you wish to go from your current heading, the tighter your turn will be. Starships are massive vessels, even one such as this quaint police cutter. It takes time to maneuver them. Plan your turns in advance for maximum advantage."

FED-INSTRUCTOR-EARTH: "Now let's talk about phasers. I knew that would pique your interest. To familiarize you with the trustworthy phasers, I have created replicas of standard Federation cargo containers for you to target and destroy."

FED-INSTRUCTOR-EARTH: "To target a container, point the mouse at the container that you wish to target and right-click. This will set the cargo container as your current target. Alternatively you may tap the T key to cycle through all targets in sensor range."

{Add 1 prestige point for each targeting command up to 3 points}

{Wait for the user to target a container. Add sarcastic/encouraging comments to the player to hurry them along.}

Sarcastic Comments
FED-INSTRUCTOR-EARTH: "C'mon, Lieutenant. It doesn't take that long to target a container."

{Default the weapons to 1 at a time firing}

FED-INSTRUCTOR-EARTH: "To fire a Phaser-3 at the selected cargo container, left-click your mouse on the fire button in the lower left corner of the display. Alternatively, you can tap the Z key to issue a fire command. Either one will direct gigawatts of ionized superheated particles at your target. Sounds impressive."
FED-INSTRUCTOR-EARTH: "Now destroy all three targets."

{Wait for the user to fire upon a container. Add sarcastic/encouraging comments to the player to hurry them along.}

Sarcastic Comments
FED-INSTRUCTOR-EARTH: "What's keeping you? Most midshipmen enjoy this part of the tutorial."

Encouraging Comments (when container destroyed)
FED-INSTRUCTOR-EARTH: "There she goes!"

FED-INSTRUCTOR-EARTH: "Good! Starfleet doesn't approve of mindless destruction, but phasers do have their uses."

{Add 2 prestige points for each container destroyed up to 6 points}

FED-INSTRUCTOR-EARTH: "Excellent, Lieutenant, you are coming along very well. Perhaps Command 290 will provide a greater challenge for your abilities."

A shooting script for Starfleet Command 3

Key Framing and Motion Capture

If your game features human characters moving about, then you might require motion capture or you can use key framing to animate your characters.

List your characters and the required moves for each character. Maintain this list during production. See the following example.

< < < < < < < < < < < < < < < < < < < < < < < < < <

Sample Shot List
Confidential

Scene#	filename	performer	character	concatenated capture description	client moves description	Loop	TrackProp
1	"A1-walk-idle"		"assassin"	(we place a formula here which "concatenates" all your detailed info into one item)	"Assassin looks around, standing in place."	to be shot for looping (blending) in post	"rifle"
2	"A1-walk-idle-fire"		"assassin"		"Assassin fires assault rifle straight ahead from standing position."	to be shot for looping (blending) in post	"rifle"
3	"A1-walk-forward"		"assassin"		"Assassin walks forward carrying assault rifle."	to be shot for looping (blending) in post	"rifle"
4	"A1-walk-forward-fire"		"assassin"		"Assassin walks forward firing assault rifle."	to be shot for looping (blending) in post	"rifle"
5	"A1-walk-backward"		"assassin"		"Assassin walks backward carrying assault rifle."	to be shot for looping (blending) in post	"rifle"
6	"A1-walk-backward-fire"		"assassin"		"Assassin walks backward firing assault rifle."	to be shot for looping (blending) in post	"rifle"
7	"A1-walk-step-left"		"assassin"		"Assassin sidesteps to the left carrying assault rifle."	to be shot for looping (blending) in post	"rifle"
8	"A1-walk-step-left-fire"		"assassin"		"Assassin sidesteps to the left firing assault rifle straight ahead."	to be shot for looping (blending) in post	"rifle"
9	"A1-walk-step-right"		"assassin"		"Assassin sidesteps to the right carrying assault rifle."	to be shot for looping (blending) in post	"rifle"
10	"A1-walk-step-right-fire"		"assassin"		"Assassin sidesteps to the right firing assault rifle straight ahead."	to be shot for looping (blending) in post	"rifle"
11	"A1-walk-turn"		"assassin"		"Assassin turns in place carrying rifle."	to be shot for looping (blending) in post	"rifle"
12	"A1-walk-turn-fire"		"assassin"		"Assassin turns in place firing rifle."	to be shot for looping (blending) in post	"rifle"
13	"A1-run-idle"		"assassin"		"Assassin looks around, standing in place, heavy breathing, excited."	to be shot for looping (blending) in post	"rifle"
14	"A1-run-idle-fire"		"assassin"		"Assassin fires assault rifle straight ahead from standing position, heavy breathing, excited."	to be shot for looping (blending) in post	"rifle"
15	"A1-run-forward"		"assassin"		"Assassin runs forward carrying assault rifle."	to be shot for looping (blending) in post	"rifle"
16	"A1-run-forward-fire"		"assassin"		"Assassin runs forward firing assault rifle."	to be shot for looping (blending) in post	"rifle"
17	"A1-run-forward-hurdle"		"assassin"		"Assassin runs forward carrying assault rifle, hurdling low obstacle."	to be shot for looping (blending) in post	"rifle"
18	"A1-run-forward-hurdle-fire"		"assassin"		"Assassin runs forward firing assault rifle, hurdling low obstacle."	to be shot for looping (blending) in post	"rifle"
19	"A1-run-backward"		"assassin"		"Assassin runs backward carrying assault rifle."	to be shot for looping (blending) in post	"rifle"
20	"A1-run-backward-fire"		"assassin"		"Assassin runs backward firing assault rifle."	to be shot for looping (blending) in post	"rifle"
21	"A1-run-step-left"		"assassin"		"Assassin sidesteps quickly to the left carrying assault rifle."	to be shot for looping (blending) in post	"rifle"
22	"A1-run-step-left-fire"		"assassin"		"Assassin sidesteps quickly to the left firing assault rifle straight ahead."	to be shot for looping (blending) in post	"rifle"
23	"A1-run-step-right"		"assassin"		"Assassin sidesteps quickly to the right carrying assault rifle."	to be shot for looping (blending) in post	"rifle"
24	"A1-run-step-right-fire"		"assassin"		"Assassin sidesteps quickly to the right firing assault rifle straight ahead."	to be shot for looping (blending) in post	"rifle"
25	"A1-sneak-idle"		"assassin"		"Assassin looks around cautiously on balls of feet, standing in place."	to be shot for looping (blending) in post	"rifle"
26	"A1-sneak-idle-fire"		"assassin"		"Assassin fires assault rifle straight ahead from standing position."	to be shot for looping (blending) in post	"rifle"
27	"A1-sneak-forward"		"assassin"		"Assassin sneaks forward carrying assault rifle."	to be shot for looping (blending) in post	"rifle"
28	"A1-sneak-forward-fire"		"assassin"		"Assassin sneaks forward firing assault rifle."	to be shot for looping (blending) in post	"rifle"

29	"A1-sneak-backward"	"assassin"		"Assassin sneaks backward carrying assault rifle."	to be shot for looping (blending) in post	"rifle"
30	"A1-sneak-backward-fire"	"assassin"		"Assassin sneaks backward firing assault rifle."	to be shot for looping (blending) in post	"rifle"
31	"A1-sneak-step-left"	"assassin"		"Assassin gingerly sidesteps to the left carrying assault rifle."	to be shot for looping (blending) in post	"rifle"
32	"A1-sneak-step-left-fire"	"assassin"		"Assassin gingerly sidesteps to the left firing assault rifle straight ahead."	to be shot for looping (blending) in post	"rifle"
33	"A1-sneak-step-right"	"assassin"		"Assassin gingerly sidesteps to the right carrying assault rifle."	to be shot for looping (blending) in post	"rifle"
34	"A1-sneak-step-right-fire"	"assassin"		"Assassin gingerly sidesteps to the right firing assault rifle straight ahead."	to be shot for looping (blending) in post	"rifle"
35	"A1-sneak-turn"	"assassin"		"Assassin turns in place with soft steps carrying rifle."	to be shot for looping (blending) in post	"rifle"
36	"A1-sneak-turn-fire"	"assassin"		"Assassin turns in place with soft steps firing rifle."	to be shot for looping (blending) in post	"rifle"
37	"A1-crouch-idle"	"assassin"		"Assassin looks around, crouching in place."	to be shot for looping (blending) in post	"rifle"
38	"A1-crouch-idle-fire"	"assassin"		"Assassin fires assault rifle straight ahead from crouching position."	to be shot for looping (blending) in post	"rifle"
39	"A1-crouch-forward"	"assassin"		"Assassin walks forward crouching and carrying assault rifle."	to be shot for looping (blending) in post	"rifle"
40	"A1-crouch-forward-fire"	"assassin"		"Assassin walks forward crouching and firing assault rifle."	to be shot for looping (blending) in post	"rifle"
41	"A1-crouch-backward"	"assassin"		"Assassin walks backward crouching and carrying assault rifle."	to be shot for looping (blending) in post	"rifle"
42	"A1-crouch-backward-fire"	"assassin"		"Assassin walks backward crouching and firing assault rifle."	to be shot for looping (blending) in post	"rifle"
43	"A1-crouch-step-left"	"assassin"		"Assassin sidesteps to the left crouching and carrying assault rifle."	to be shot for looping (blending) in post	"rifle"
44	"A1-crouch-step-left-fire"	"assassin"		"Assassin sidesteps to the left crouching and firing assault rifle straight ahead."	to be shot for looping (blending) in post	"rifle"
45	"A1-crouch-step-right"	"assassin"		"Assassin sidesteps to the right crouching and carrying assault rifle."	to be shot for looping (blending) in post	"rifle"
46	"A1-crouch-step-right-fire"	"assassin"		"Assassin sidesteps to the right crouching and firing assault rifle straight ahead."	to be shot for looping (blending) in post	"rifle"
47	"A1-crouch-turn"	"assassin"		"Assassin turns in place crouching and carrying rifle."	to be shot for looping (blending) in post	"rifle"
48	"A1-crouch-turn-fire"	"assassin"		"Assassin turns in place crouching and firing rifle."	to be shot for looping (blending) in post	"rifle"
49	"A1-jump-standing"	"assassin"		"Assassin jumps straight up, carrying rifle."	to be shot for looping (blending) in post	"rifle"
50	"A1-jump-standing-fire"	"assassin"		"Assassin jumps straight up, firing rifle."	to be shot for looping (blending) in post	"rifle"
51	"A1-jump-forward"	"assassin"		"Assassin leaps forward carrying assault rifle."	to be shot for looping (blending) in post	"rifle"
52	"A1-jump-forward-fire"	"assassin"		"Assassin leaps forward firing assault rifle."	to be shot for looping (blending) in post	"rifle"
53	"A1-jump-backward"	"assassin"		"Assassin jumps backward carrying assault rifle."	to be shot for looping (blending) in post	"rifle"
54	"A1-jump-backward-fire"	"assassin"		"Assassin jumps backward firing assault rifle."	to be shot for looping (blending) in post	"rifle"
55	"A1-jump-left"	"assassin"		"Assassin lunges to the left carrying assault rifle."	to be shot for looping (blending) in post	"rifle"
56	"A1-jump-left-fire"	"assassin"		"Assassin lunges to the left firing assault rifle straight ahead."	to be shot for looping (blending) in post	"rifle"
57	"A1-jump-right"	"assassin"		"Assassin lunges to the right carrying assault rifle."	to be shot for looping (blending) in post	"rifle"
58	"A1-jump-right-fire"	"assassin"		"Assassin lunges to the right firing assault rifle straight ahead."	to be shot for looping (blending) in post	"rifle"

< < < < < < < < < < < < < < < < < < < < < < < < < <

59	"A1-chest-hit"	"assassin"	"Assassin flinches from shot in chest while carrying assault rifle."	to be shot for looping (blending) in post	"rifle"
60	"A1-chest-hit-fire"	"assassin"	"Assassin flinches from shot in chest while firing."	to be shot for looping (blending) in post	"rifle"
61	"A1-gut-hit"	"assassin"	"Assassin flinches from shot in stomach while carrying assault rifle."	to be shot for looping (blending) in post	"rifle"
62	"A1-gut-hit-fire"	"assassin"	"Assassin flinches from shot in stomach while firing."	to be shot for looping (blending) in post	"rifle"
63	"A1-left-hit"	"assassin"	"Assassin flinches from being shot from the left while carrying assault rifle."	to be shot for looping (blending) in post	"rifle"
64	"A1-left-hit-fire"	"assassin"	"Assassin flinches from being shot from the left while firing."	to be shot for looping (blending) in post	"rifle"
65	"A1-right-hit"	"assassin"	"Assassin flinches from being shot from the right while carrying assault rifle."	to be shot for looping (blending) in post	"rifle"
66	"A1-right-hit-fire"	"assassin"	"Assassin flinches from being shot from the right while firing."	to be shot for looping (blending) in post	"rifle"
67	"A1-knockdown-front"	"assassin"	"Assassin is knocked down by force from the front while carrying assault rifle."	to be shot for looping (blending) in post	"rifle"
68	"A1-knockdown-front-fire"	"assassin"	"Assassin is knocked down by force from the front while firing."	to be shot for looping (blending) in post	"rifle"
69	"A1-knockdown-back"	"assassin"	"Assassin is knocked down by force from the back while carrying assault rifle."	to be shot for looping (blending) in post	"rifle"
70	"A1-knockdown-back-fire"	"assassin"	"Assassin is knocked down by force from the back while firing."	to be shot for looping (blending) in post	"rifle"
71	"A1-roll-stand-front"	"assassin"	"From knocked down from front position, assassin rolls up and stands carrying rifle."	blends from "A1-knockdown-front"	"rifle"
72	"A1-roll-stand-back"	"assassin"	"From knocked down from back position, assassin rolls up and stands carrying rifle."	blends from "A1-knockdown-back"	"rifle"
73	"A1-activate"	"assassin"	"Assassin activates a wall switch."		"rifle"
74	"A1-crouch-tinker-start"	"assassin"	"Assassin crouches and begins tinkering with gadgetry."	blends into "A1-tinker"	"rifle"
75	"A1-tinker"	"assassin"	"Assassin tinkers with gadgetry."	to be shot for looping (blending) in post	"rifle"
76	"A1-crouch-tinker-stop"	"assassin"	"Assassin stops tinkering and stands."	blends from "A1-tinker"	"rifle"
77	"A1-use-medkit"	"assassin"	"Assassin presses small object to neck, injecting healing serum."		"rifle"
78	"A1-pickup-table"	"assassin"	"Assassin picks up an object from table height."		"rifle"
79	"A1-pickup-floor"	"assassin"	"Assassin crouches, picks up an object from the ground, and stands."		"rifle"
80	"A1-stunned-flash"	"assassin"	"Assassin covers face with arm and cowers for 3 - 5 seconds before returning to a normal stance."		"rifle"
81	"A1-death-falling"	"assassin"	"Assassin collapses to ground with some impact."		"rifle"
82	"A1-death-slump"	"assassin"	"Assassin folds up and slumps to ground."		"rifle"
83	"A1-death-spasms"	"assassin"	"Assassin has several violent spasms before collapsing to ground."		"rifle"

NOTE

Please refrain from punctuation in your moves description and be as specific and brief as possible.

The list of moves to be motion captured for Black9

> >

Sound Effects

Sound effects are elusive critters to nail down early in the game design document. My best advice is to mentally walk through the mission/level/area section of your game design document and listen to what you hear as you walk through these areas.

Music

Almost all games feature music; the only exception I can think of is Quake III, which opted to allow the player to play his or her own favorite music. In this section, list the various tracks you will require to help set the mood of your game. Some games employ sophisticated track blending routines to go smoothly from tense battle music to celebratory victory tunes. See the Black9 audio bid on the following page for an example.

Asset Reference	Description	Maya Slot Reference	Animation Name	Animation Notes	Sound Name(keyframe)	SFX Notes	Attribute	Volume	Status
								5	1
Nevin Combat	Custom	14: Time Dilation Slash 1	timeDilationSlash1		SlashSquishDelay1 (5)			5	1
		15: Time Dilation Slash 2	timeDilationSlash2		SlashSquishDelay1 (5)			5	1
		16: Time Dilation3_ Fierce Slash	timeDilationSlash2		SlashSquishDelay1 (5)			5	1
		17: Time DilationVictory	timeDilationVictory	E3 Victory1	SpinSwirl4(3), Landing (17)			5	1
		18: TimeDilationTraverse	timeDilationTraverse	Return Move					
		19: TimeDilationNormalSpinSlash	TimeDilationNewSpinSlash	E3 Attack	SpinSwirl3 (2), SlashSquishDelay1(5)	Flangy swipe		5	1
		20: TimeDilationNormalSpinSlash2	TimeDilationNewSpinSlash	E3 Attack	SpinSwirl3 (2), SlashSquishDelay1(5)			5	1
		21: TimeDilationThrustySlash	timeDilationThrustySlash	E3 Attack	SpinSwirl3 (2), SlashSquishDelay1(5)			5	1
		22: TimeDilationChoppyFlipslash	timeDilationChoppyFlipSlash	Final Attack					
		23: TimeDilationTransPos2toPos3	TimeDilationTrans_Pos2_to_Pos3	Start	Stretch4b (1),			5	1
		24: TimeDilationTransPos2toPos1	timeDilation_Pos2_to_Pos1	Start	Stretch4b (1),			5	1
		25: TimeDilationTransPos4toPos1	timeDilationTrans_Pos4_to_Pos1	Start	Stretch4b (1),			5	1
		26: TimeDilationTransPos4toPos3	timeDilationTrans_Pos4_to_Pos3	Start	Stretch4b (1),			5	2
		27: TimeDilationVictory Flip	timeDilationVictoryFlip		SpinSwirl3 (6), Landing (19)			5	2
		28: TimeDilationVictory Spin	TimeDilationVictory2		SpinSwirl3 (3), SpinSwirl2 (5), HardKnock2 (15)			5	
	Attack	0: fastSlashCombo1	basicFast1	1 thru 8 *	SlashChop (2)	Leopard Roar 4, WB03	Combat	5	3
		1: fastSlashCombo2	basicFast1	9 thru 18 *	SlashChop (2)			5	3
		2: fastSlashCombo3	basicFast1	19 thru 27 *	SlashChop (2)			5	3
		3: slowSlashCombo1	basicPower1		SlashHard (1)	ComboLibrary, SwipesSwingV6		5	3
		4: slowSlashCombo2	basicPower2		SlashHard (1)			5	3
		5: slowSlashCombo3	basicPower3		SlashHard (1)			5	Bad Export

The combat sound effects list for the character Nevin from Outrage's game Alter Echo

< < < < < < < < < < < < < < < < < < < < < < < < < < < < < <

Black9 Audio Bid

IMPORTANT: PLEASE READ ENTIRE DOCUMENT IN ORDER!

Note: The goal of the budget is to come as close to the final product as possible. In a game of this scope it is impossible to know the exact amount of minutes of music. Both parties understand that these figures could change slightly either way but that the figures given should be a very good representation of the budget needed.

MUSIC

In-Game Music: There are 3 different "worlds" in Black9. The music styles would be representative of those worlds but would follow a sci-fi ambient based vibe (refer to CD). Analog pads, percussion, arpeggiatted synth lines and Enya themed instrumentation will all be used to accomplish our goal. For certain worlds and levels such as China we can incorporate ethnic Asian instruments such as Tibetan Bowls, Java Gamelans, Korean Gongs, Chinese Cymbals, Japanese Kotos and Taiko Drums to give it a certain environmental flavor. Music does not need to be triggered at all times during the game. In fact a lot of the game should be sci-fi environmental location based ambience. "Sci-fi analog action style" music can be triggered when certain key events in each level happen (i.e., Canyon Chase sled escape). Refer to last 2 songs on audio CD called "Wild 9" and "Hover Bikes". The use of short (3-5 second) musical stings can also be used when certain events happen (i.e., pulls important lever to open important door). There are 3 different "worlds" in Black9. The music styles would be representative of those worlds but would follow an ambient sci-fi feel/vibe.

Mars World:
6 search/ambient songs (@ 1:30 minutes = 9 minutes)
4 chase/battle/vehicle songs (@ 1:30 minutes = 6 minutes)
5 stings (@ 5 seconds = 25 seconds)

Hong Kong World:
6 search/ambient songs (@ 1:30 minutes = 9 minutes)
4 chase/battle songs (@ 1:30 minutes = 6 minutes)
5 stings (@ 5 seconds = 25 seconds)

Moon/Luna World:
4 search/ambient songs (@ 1:30 minutes = 6 minutes)
2 chase/battle songs (@ 1:30 minutes = 3 minutes)
4 stings (@ 5 seconds = 20 seconds)

Total In-Game music: Approximately 40 minutes

Cinematic Music: Story and cinematics play an important role in Black9. The music for the cinematics should be extremely subtle so that it adds a layer to the dialogue but does not get in its way. There doesn't have to be music playing during every cinematic and some of the in-game music could be used as well.

Mars World:	3 songs @ 1 minute = 3 minutes
Hong Kong World:	3 songs @ 1 minute = 3 minutes
Moon/Luna World:	2 songs @ 1 minute = 2 minutes

Total Cinematic music: 8 minutes

Menu Music: There will need to be menu, sub-menu, and credits music. These can be based off of popular motifs we would be creating for the game. Until actual screen interfaces are created it is hard to visualize the style and tempo.

> >

Menu/Sub-Menu theme: 2 minutes
Credits music (variation of menu?): 3 minutes

Total Menu music: 5 minutes

Music Totals
In-Game: 40 minutes
Cinematics:8 minutes
Menus: 5 minutes
TOTAL: 53 minutes (approx.)

53 minutes x $1,000 per minute = $53,000

SOUND DESIGN
Sound design will be the most important audio element in the game.

In-Game SFX: Big and beefy reverbs, amazing weapons, huge deep doors, frightening alarms, etc. Think of the best sci-fi movie you've ever heard… then double it!
    The main character will have common sounds that will always need to be loaded in memory (footsteps, weapons, getting hit, landing from a jump, etc.). There will be other common sounds as well (pause menu, text messaging, pick-ups, health, etc.) Each of the 16 levels in the game will have unique sound effects for the enemies, vehicles, objects, surfaces, elements, etc. I would average about 50 unique sounds per level considering some of the enemies and weapons will be reused throughout the game.

Common sfx: 100
Level sfx: 50 X 16 levels = 800 sfx

Environmental/Ambient SFX: Strange room tones, machinery, equipment, and generators no one has ever heard before, airy and cosmic tones, deep analog sweeps, dark dramatic atmospheres. Each area may have a different "tone" which when mixed properly gives the sense of travel and exploration. These ambiences should be looping, streamed and about 1 minute each in length. In some areas you would only hear the ambiences with no music. These are very important! The player will hear these more than they will the music! Ambiences can be reused for multiple areas. If we budget 3 looping ambiences per level we could mix and match just fine.

16 levels X 3 looping 1 minute ambiences = 48 minutes of ambience

Cinematic Sound Design/FX: The cinematics will be in-game based (not FMV) so technically they will be handled the same as the in-game sfx (SPU based). I would estimate another 10 unique sfx per level to be used in the cinematics.

Cinematic SFX: 10 sfx X 16 levels = 160 sfx

Menu/Sub Menu SFX: Would depend on the look and style of the menus.

Menu SFX = 10 sfx

Sound Design Totals
In-Game: 800 sfx
Environmental: 48 minutes/sfx
Cinematics: 160 sfx
Menus: 10 sfx
TOTAL: 1000 sfx (approx.)

Sound Design = $30,000

DIALOGUE/V.O.

Because of the sci-fi nature of the game, effects will play an important role in the creation of the voices. All sorts of robotic, helmet gear, radio, flange/phaser, strange and unique effects will be used in pre- and post-production. Think Star Wars.

Cinematic Character voices:

Genesis Contact, Player, Aegis, NPC Buyer, First Guard, Genesis Man, Oberon, Black Dragon Master, Genesis Operations Officer, Fire Elder, Fire Elemental, Piwan, Dr. Tan, Agent Cassandra, Protagonist, Babbage Entity, Elder, Tea-Drinking Society Operations Officer, TDS Ops, Hashi, Dr. Kellon, Tran, Automated Receptionist, TDS Shuttle Captain, Charles, TDS Man, Gardener, Zubrin Marine, Zubrin Operations Officer, Lao, Zubrin Man, Zubrin Merc, Civilian, Zubrin Ops, Ambassador. (35 total)

Enemy voices: There would also have to be enemy character voices recorded. Screams, yells, hits, jumps, dies, etc.

We would need about 15 actors to record 35 characters. Each professional non-sag actor's price would vary depending on experience, how many characters, versatility, etc.

    These are not one-liners (like Boxing), this is more serious acting. SAG rate for a 4-hour block-out (3 characters max.) is $612.00. To get non-SAG actors (who are really in SAG) for a buyout usually costs about $750. Some actors will charge $1000 and others will cost only $500. $750 I feel is a good average for a non-SAG buyout. It should take 3 studio days to complete the script. In a script of this nature (characters, acting, size, etc.) it is always smart to put a 10% contingency in the budget for call-backs.

Actors:	15 X $750 = $11,250
Studio:	3 days X $1000 = $3,000
Casting Agent:	$1,000
Editing,Mastering:	$5,000
Contingency (10%):	$2,000
Total:	**$22,250**

This is my **recommended** buget.

GRAND TOTALS:

Music:	$53,000
Sound Design:	$30,000
V.O.:	$22,000
Total:	**$105,000**

Breathe, David… breeeeeathe….. Now count to 10.
    Okay good!
    Please realize that this is a huge game and there is a ton of audio here. I have given my $1,000 per minute of music rate (usually $1,200-$1,500) because there is quantity. Same for the sound design; normally for the amount of sounds required it would be much higher. If you were to go to any company in the industry and ask them for this amount of work you'll get prices that are a little lower and some that are much higher.
    The prices I cannot come down on. I cannot go lower than $1,000 per minute and I can't do 1000 sfx for under 30K. If we needed the budget to be lower we could do the following…

Music:

Please keep in mind that the recommended budget was NOT a wish list. I had to struggle to get the minutes of music to where it currently is. Notice that each tune is only approximately 1:30. 2 to 3 minutes is usually the norm, but I feel that because of the ambient style of music we will be using that if I'm tricky with my loops I can get away with 1:30. We could easily just take the music figure down to about 40 minutes and just deal with it. It does start to take a quality hit as far as repetitiveness goes (which I am already assuming in the 53 minutes), but it's not the complete end of the world. New total: 40 minutes of music.

> >

Sound Design:
The sound design is a tough one because there is no getting around it! The game is big and there are tons of SFX. If worse came to worst and we really had to squeeze it all together we could unhappily shave an extra 5K off the 30K figure and use less looping ambiences and reuse in-game sfx for the cinematics. Once again, quality would go down because of repetitiveness. New total: Approximately 800 sfx.

Dialogue/V.O.:
This one is a little easier but the consequences are greater! We could easily get a bunch of actors @ $500 but I can guarantee you that the quality WILL NOT be great. Acceptable, but not great. We could also take out the 10% contingency and just live with what we get in the sessions. New V.O. total with those changes = $16,500

New Grand Totals:

Music:	$40,000
SFX:	$25,000
V.O.:	$16,500
Total:	$81,000

If you are thinking of making this game an A or AAA title, the 100K budget is absolutely necessary. For a B title you can easily get away with the 80K figure. Anything less and you're headed for the C title blues.

Let's discuss once you've had a chance to digest it all and talk it over with some people.

Thanks,

Tommy

The music requirements for Black9

Special Effects

This is a sort of catchall category that is specific to your game's genre and technical implementation. For example, in Starfleet Command a list of the weapon effects, astronomical features, and other system effects like tractor beams will need to be created. For a first-person shooter, enumerate the weapon effects and explosions. For a platformer, write down the magical effects when the character picks up a power-up or gathers another star or crystal.

< < < < < < < < < < < < < < < < < < < < < < < < < < < < < <

WEAPONS AND AMMO

WEAPON	Cost	AMMO	Range	Damage	R-O-F	Magazine Size	Magazine Cost	Categorization	Weapon Type	Illuminati Specialty?	Threat Level	Mission First Available	Comments
9mm Pistol	$1,000	Bullets	21	10	5	15	$15	Firearms	pistol	no (global)		1	
Shotgun (sawed off)	$800	Shells	10	15	3	5	$20	Firearms	rifle	no (global)		1	
Shotgun	$700	Shells	25	10	3	5	$20	Firearms	rifle	no (global)		1	
Sub-Machine Gun	$5,000	Bullets	45	8	9	30	$5	Firearms	pistol	no (global)		1	
Sniper Rifle	$20,000	high-caliber rounds	300	25	1	1	$10	Firearms	rifle	no (global)		4	
Silenced Pistol	$15,000	Bullets	15	5	5	5	$10	Firearms	pistol	no (global)		4	
Crossbow	$5,000	Bolts	60	10	1	1	$5	Special	rifle	Tea-Drinking Society		7	
Crossbow	$5,000	Poison-Tipped Bolts	60	3	1	1	$25	Special	rifle	Tea-Drinking Society		7	
Crossbow	$5,000	Explosive-Tipped Bolts	60	25	1	1	$20	Special	rifle	Tea-Drinking Society		7	
Grappling-Hook Crossbow								Special	rifle	Genesis		1	grapple across open spaces, but vulnerable to attack as it becomes the equipped weapon
Magnum Pistol	$1,500	high-caliber rounds	24	15	5	5	$10	Firearms	pistol	no (global)		4	
Suitcase Gun	$2,000	Bullets	12	5	1	3	$25	Firearms	pistol	no (global)		8	
Grenade	$25	N/A	8	30	1	1	$25	Explosives	thrown explosive	no (global)		1	
Flashbang	$10	N/A	8	5	1	1	$10	Explosives	thrown explosive	no (global)		4	
Mine	$50	N/A	n/a	50	1	1	$50	Explosives	dropped explosive	no (global)		4	
Tripbomb	$80	N/A	n/a	20	1	1	$80	Explosives	mounted explosive	Zubrin		12	
Motion-Sensor Bomb	$120	N/A	n/a	40	1	1	$120	Explosives	mounted explosive	Zubrin		12	
Satchel Charge	$75	N/A	n/a	75	1	1	$75	Explosives	dropped explosive	no (global)		5	
MIRV Grenade	$150	N/A	8	15 ea	1	6	$150	Explosives	thrown explosive	Zubrin		12	explodes into smaller grenades
Detonation Pack	$100	N/A	n/a	100	1	1	$100	Explosives	mounted explosive	Zubrin		12	
Flare Grenade	$30	N/A	8	3	1	1	$30	Explosives	thrown explosive	Genesis		4	blindness lasts longer than flashbang
Rocket Launcher	$30,000	Rockets, MIRV Rockets, Guided Missiles	200	50	2	5	$180	Heavy Weapons	launcher	Zubrin		12	
Rail Gun	$75,000	high-caliber rounds	200	60	3	10	$250	Heavy Weapons	armature	Genesis		5	
Flamethrower	$6,000	fuel	10	40	1	5	$50	Heavy Weapons	rifle	no (global)		5	
Grenade Launcher	$4,000	Grenade Shells, MIRV Grenade Shells, Remote Detonation Grenade Shells (aka Pipe Bombs)	100	30, 15 ea, 30	1	8	$200	Heavy Weapons	launcher	Zubrin		12	
Rad Flux Rifle	$100,000	none (recharges)	80	25	5	n/a	n/a	Heavy Weapons	rifle	Genesis		5	
Assault Rifle	$10,000	Bullets	90	20	8	30	$50	Firearms	rifle	no (global)		1	
Heavy Machine Gun	$25,000	Bullets	200	20	10	100	$75	Heavy Weapons	armature	no (global)		5	
Katana/ Wakizashi pair	$5,000	N/A	0	30	3	n/a	n/a	Melee Weapons	two-handed melee	no (global)		1	
Blit Sword	$9,000	N/A	0	40	4	n/a	n/a	Melee Weapons	one-handed melee	Tea-Drinking Society		7	curved blade conducts energy from tip to base
Stun Gun (Tazer)	$500	N/A	0	5	1	n/a	n/a	Melee Weapons	one-handed melee	no (global)		1	
Blackjack	$100	N/A	0	2	1	n/a	n/a	Melee Weapons	one-handed melee	no (global)		1	
Dagger	$150	N/A	0	5	1	n/a	n/a	Melee Weapons	one-handed melee	no (global)		1	
Blit Dagger	$250	N/A	0	6	1	n/a	n/a	Melee Weapons	one-handed melee	Tea-Drinking Society		7	curved blade conducts energy from tip to base

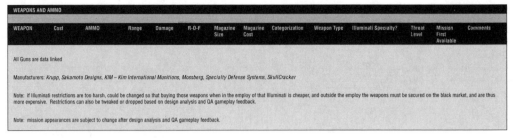

The weapons and ammo list for Black9

Stepping Back a Bit

Looks like a bunch of work, huh? Good, that is why it is a *job* being a game designer and not a hobby. If it seems a bit daunting to undertake this effort in writing up your game, I have a suggestion. Practice the *skill* of game design by writing up the game design of an existing game. Go through this entire rigor on a game that is already successful! It is perfectly reasonable in any other profession—medicine, engineering, automotive repair—to practice the skills involved before moving on to practicing the profession. Even novelists can take creative writing courses and budding scriptwriters can take scriptwriting courses. So I think it is perfectly logical that a game designer should practice writing detailed game design documents by analyzing another game designer's game.

> >

Chapter 9 > > > > > > > > > > > > > > >

The Technical Design Document

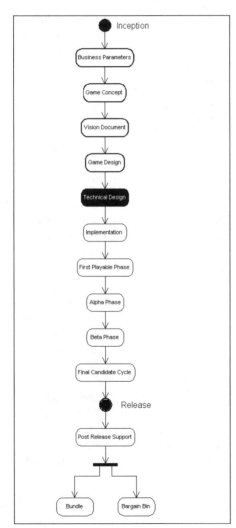

Where the technical design document lies in the project life cycle

This chapter introduces the technical design document and the work involved in putting together the technical plans for creating your game. As an introduction, this chapter includes the concepts in a light overview designed to kick-start your technical design process; however, it is Chapter 18 that discusses the technical design stage in detail.

Object-Oriented Design

Modern electronic games are large software projects that run from hundreds of thousands of lines of code to millions of lines of code. Object-oriented design (OOD) was invented to cope with large software projects. I am not going to fill up this book with pages discussing the pros and cons of object-oriented design versus procedurally designed software; there are countless good books discussing object-oriented design at your favorite bookstore. I am already sold on OOD, and I approach the technical design document using OOD; I am only concerned here with the application of OOD and UML to game construction. There is also a bias towards C++ as the language for implementation of the game code.

< < < < < < < < < < < < < < < < < < < < < < < < < < < < <

There are a few other important languages for creating games such as C and Java. I will not evangelize for C++ here either. If you are using Java, then you are probably creating a game without significant performance requirements for graphics and are interested in cross-platform distribution. If you are using C, then you have probably made the determination that C++ is not yet right for your team or have some other requirement keeping you with C. Assembly language is of course used when hand optimizing critical sections of code and is not relevant from an architectural or design point of view.

Purpose of the Technical Design Document

The technical design document is the blueprint for the software engineers on your team to use in the creation of the game. The ideal technical design document will specify to your developers not only what needs to be created but also how it will be implemented. I was introduced to strong software architecture for the first time in the game industry when I worked under Jay Lee at Interna (a game company that has since joined the mound of defunct game companies). When I signed up for the job as a developer at Interna, I was looking to learn more about C++ and artificial intelligence.

What Jay Lee did was to use strong encapsulation of the implementation details by creating a detailed set of interfaces for the classes of the whole game (a massively multiplayer casino game). Jay labored for two months writing header files. There was not a bit of working code at the end of his two months, just header files. I remember that the members of the team were a bit skeptical about this; we thought while leadership was great and architecture was probably a good thing, would it not be better if our best programmer were writing some code? Well

it turned out that it took three junior developers just three months to flesh out the source files as indicated by Jay's headers to implement the software Jay described. It was the fastest any of us saw software come together.

> **JARGON**: A *header file* or a .H file is a file in C or C++ that describes the interface to the software module defined in a corresponding source file (.C or .CPP file).

Jay Lee demonstrated very strong software architecture; ever since that experience I have been learning more about creating software better. The relationship between software architecture and the technical design document is that the technical design document is broader in scope and less detailed than a software architecture plan. The technical design document must synthesize the requirements of the game, develop a software design, serve as a testing plan, and also supply the project manager with critical information such as the required developer roles, dependencies between tasks and developers, and an estimate of how long it will take to perform each of the tasks assigned to the developers.

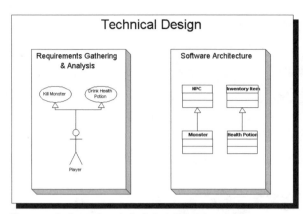

The conceptual overview of a technical design document

The technical design document has other customers besides the developers on your team: The game publishers are becoming savvier in their technical evaluation of game developers as the scope of the projects grows and the associated risks with the projects increase. Most likely you will need to deliver a technical design document as an early milestone to your publisher. The problem with a technical design document is that while most of the strong publishers are now asking for them, there are few senior game developers with the requisite technical expertise to perform an adequate review of the developer's technical preparations. This lack of technical review means the technical design document will be poorly reviewed and as such is not a very visible deliverable. This creates another problem; early in the project the executive management is almost always eager to see progress in a game's development. Often they cannot visualize the game the way the game designers are able to and are forced to green-light a project based on feelings of trust in the developer. All executive management teams would rather replace this trust with seeing some cool eye candy on the screen showing that the game is happily in development and looks fun. This creates an unholy tension when the developer is pressured to not think about the technical design of the game much in the early stages and must instead play catch-up all project long. It is widely known in the software engineering field that you would much rather identify and fix a defect in your software at the design stage than at the end of the project. Estimates vary, but the consensus appears to be that it is *fifty* times more expensive to fix a bug at the end of the implementation stage than at the design stage. Thus, I encourage you, by whatever means you can, to take your time on the technical design phase of your project and work closely with your publisher or executive management to make the work of the technical design stage visible and reviewed to assure that progress is occurring on the project. Email me if you come up with tips on how to get publishers more excited about the technical design document.

< < < < < < < < < < < < < < < < < < < < < < < < < <

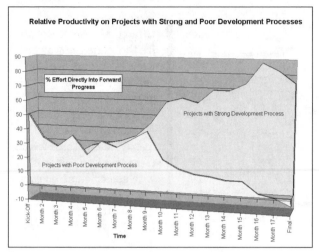

Strong process, poor process—relative efficiencies

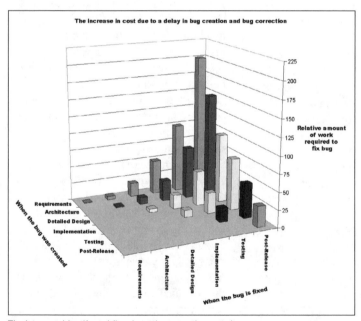

The later you identify and fix a bug, the more the cost rises.

Why Have a Software Development Process?

All development houses have a development process even if they do not consciously go about creating one. A development process is the method your team uses to take the game specifications and turn them into a game. Even the solitary game developer working on her own private game, iterating each night after working the day

> >

job, still has a development process. This lone developer's process could be as informal as writing up a sketch of the main game interface on a piece of graph paper and then incrementally building the game, a new feature every night, until the game is playable. Some high-profile game development companies also use this method.

Steve McConnell's seminal book *Code Complete* is one of the most accessible works discussing in detail software development methods and why organizations resist learning new development processes. The problem with learning a process is that it *takes time*, and most organizations are in short supply of time. They are under great pressure to get something visible and running as quickly as possible to reassure management that the project is well under way (a recurrent theme in this book, I know). A strong software development process will emphasize thinking at the beginning of a project where a weak development process will create an even larger burden of wasted time at the end of the project. In the most extreme cases of poor process, the projects find themselves in such a hole of despair due to poor decisions made at the beginning of the project that the project itself is cancelled rather than throwing everything out and trying again. I am firmly convinced that all of the games in the industry that are taking 30 to 60 months to complete are being performed at development houses with a poor development process, which results in a poor preproduction.

It is understandable why game development companies are generally poor at enforcing a strong software development process. First of all, most *software companies* are poor at the development process by all accounts; second, the industry holds creativity sacred (a good thing, but it can be used as an excuse to avoid professionalism); and third, the games themselves are always becoming larger, faster, and more complex—about at the rate of Moore's Law. The result is that studio heads or publisher executives who might have had hands-on experience in creating a game five years ago now have a misguided interpretation of the scope of the project they are responsible for. Interpreting Moore's Law liberally, it would suggest that over five years a game would be *eight* times larger in complexity and scope than an equivalent title five years before. This last point I think is significant and rarely discussed; managers are often walking around with an impression of the work to be completed as much smaller, like when they were creating games hands-on. They were successful then, or they would most likely not have achieved their leadership position. That means they must have been successful with *their* software development process and that the penalties back then were *correspondingly smaller*. I think this is a great source of subtle evil in the game industry.

> **JARGON**: *Moore's Law*—computing power will double every 18 months.

So are you ready to hear about a better software development process?

The Unified Software Development Process

We at Taldren use a modified, light version of the Unified Software Development Process. I will, however, present an overview of the full Unified

< < < < < < < < < < < < < < < < < < < < < < < < < <

Software Development Process and then go back and explain what we do.

The core workflows of the Unified Process are *requirements*, *analysis*, *design*, *implementation*, and *test*. Looking over this list of five activities, I would imagine most people in game development would be surprised to see the three preproduction activities: requirements, analysis, and design. If I were to interview game development houses to ask them what core workflows (after explaining what I meant by the term) they are using in their development, they would probably say design, implement, and test. This is one of the key features of the Unified Process; it formally recognizes that gathering your requirements is a different activity than analyzing the requirements, which is in turn a wholly different activity than designing your software to meet your game's requirements. If you think back towards an earlier chapter on gathering your key business parameters before creating your game design document, you will notice that I added a bit of material from the game development domain to the requirements capture stage.

Core Workflows of the Unified Process

1. Requirements
2. Analysis
3. Design
4. Implementation
5. Test

The Unified Process recognizes that a real-world project cannot crisply complete one workflow and then move to another workflow. To address this, the Unified Process is an iterative and incremental workflow method, where each stage of the project is driven through *inception*, *elaboration*, *construction*, and *transition*.

Phases of a Workflow in the Unified Process

1. Inception
2. Elaboration
3. Construction
4. Transition

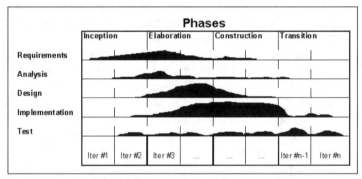

The work flow of the Unified Software Development Process

In the real world you will find yourself late in the project, perhaps near alpha, when you realize that your game inventory system is broken and not fun (it turns out tracking the adventuring gear to the nearest gram was not a great idea), so now you need to go back and design a new inventory system. The Unified Process would have you stop and think about your new inventory system, review your requirements, analyze what impact the new inventory system requirements will impose on the existing game, design the new

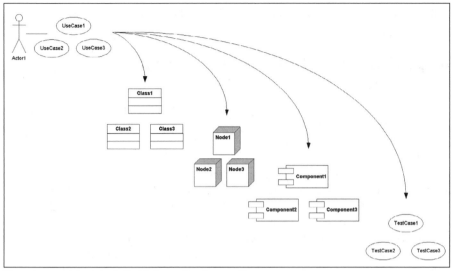

The various models of the Unified Software Development Process

inventory system, implement it, and test the inventory system.

Perhaps at this point you may be getting bored and rolling your eyes and thinking to yourself, "This is just a bunch of fancy multisyllabic names; of course I think about my stuff before I code it." While it is true that these terms are just a bunch of jargon, if you actually consciously name what activity you are performing, you will have a much greater awareness of what you are doing. This awareness will translate directly into being more purposeful about collecting your requirements when the sign over your head says you are in requirements capture; you will be a far more effective analyzer of the requirements when you are not obligated to think about how you are going to code the rasterizer. Your designs will be much stronger when you have all of the requirements and their impact laid out in front of you.

When Should the Technical Design Document Be Written?

The technical design document should be developed in preproduction along with the game design document but perhaps staggered back a bit to allow the game design document time to form up. The technical design document needs to be developed with a thorough set of plans and time estimates before the schedule and the project plan (discussed in the next chapter) can be completed.

During production it sometimes becomes necessary to change the direction of some features in response to technical research, focus group testing, market research, or an awareness of a lack of thorough design in the preproduction stage. In response to any change in the game, a fast response mini-technical design stage should be initiated before any new development of these changes is undertaken. In other words, don't allow your deeply thought-out technical designs to be

< < < < < < < < < < < < < < < < < < < < < < < < < < < < < <

held up like stone tablets that must be followed. By all means, change your design during implementation if you identify a better design.

What Goes into the Technical Design Document?

Now that I have established that a technical design and architecture are good things to have, it is time to define what goes into the technical design document. The technical design document acts as a plan of attack on the requirements of the game: a plan for whom, when, and how these requirements will be accomplished. This technical design document is a miniature project itself going through several stages: *requirements capture, requirements analysis, high-level architecture, mid-level software design, deployment design,* a *testing plan,* and a *transition plan.* Each of these stages will be chock full of documents, diagrams, and time estimates to complete the tasks described within.

being part of the engine development. The goal is to write down every single expectation the team, the executive manager, the designers, and the fans have for the game. Note that this stage is named simply requirements capture; there should be no efforts to cull, prioritize, or otherwise analyze the requirements and make any decisions. The goal is to just cast the net as wide and as far as possible and be very thorough in collecting all of the fine details. Any premature efforts to analyze the incoming requirements will bog down the process and create decisions that are made on less than the full set of information available to make these decisions.

Requirements Capture

Requirements capture is the process of identifying all the requirements the game as a piece of software must satisfy to meet the goals and expectations for the game. Requirements can take a myriad of forms from a frame rate requirement of 60 frames per second, to fitting on a single CD, to not taking more than 80 programmer-months to complete, to having very few defects, to having 3D sound or 10,000 polygon characters, to

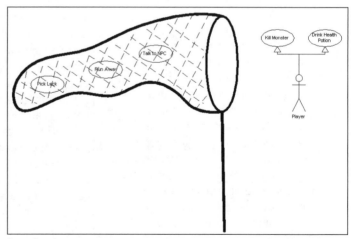

Capturing use cases

The requirements capture stage is the most critical to a successful project and in many ways is the most difficult. It is

> >

difficult to decide when you have identified all your requirements, and it is also sometimes difficult to describe them clearly, such as when you are trying to push your graphics to the "next level," whatever that might be.

Let us tackle it in order of easiest to most difficult. The easiest requirements to capture are the requirements described in the game design document! This document should have a design for the main game interface, the shell screens, the game mechanics, the art design, and the content such as missions, levels, and puzzles.

The Unified Modeling Language has the use case diagram, which is most helpful in the requirements capture stage. The idea behind the use case diagram is to note the actors (users and other discrete systems such as a CD authentication server) and the interactions these actors have with the software system.

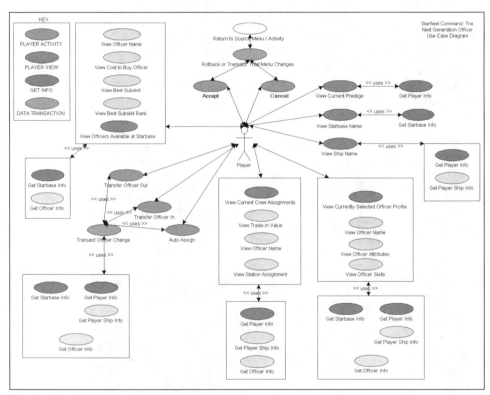

The use cases of the officer menu in Starfleet Command 3

<<<<<<<<<<<<<<<<<<<<<<<<<<<<<<<<<<

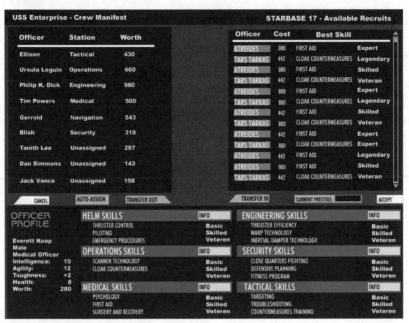

The mocked-up officer screen early in production

The nearly final officer screen

The above use case diagram is from Starfleet Command: The Next Generation. The function of this menu is to act as a vending machine, "selling" new officers for the players to use on their starship and allowing the players to "sell" back the officers they already have. The purpose of this diagram was to collect every single action the player would have with this menu and arrange it graphically to aid in the technical analysis of what needs to be done. Accompanying this diagram is a regular document detailing these individual interactions or use cases.

Officer Menu Use Cases

Displays or Player Views

These are just views; there are no player interactions in these use cases.

View Ship Name
This is a simple text display of the player's ship's name.

View Current Prestige
This is a simple text displayer of the player's current display. Display these prestige points in normal text output color if they have enough prestige to buy the least expensive officer in the base; if not display this prestige as red text.

View Starbase Name
This is a simple text display of the name of the starbase or location that the player is performing officer selection. In the case of multiplayer or skirmish games, display the name of the mission type.

View Current Officer Assignments
This is a complex display combining the following elements:

- Officer Name
- Station Name and/or Station Icon
- Officer Trade-In Value

This display displays six such officers; there is no scroll bar.

At all times there is to be an officer displayed here; even when the player transfers out an officer, a flunky ensign with basic skills throughout will be displayed. We need a long list of potential officer names that is race specific and easy to add to.

View Officer Profile
This is a complex display combining the following elements A and B:

A. Officer Attributes
- Officer Name
- Officer Intelligence
- Officer Toughness
- Officer Health
- Officer Cost to Buy / Officer Trade-In Value

B. Officer Skills
Each of the skills is broken down into three sub-skills and a display of skill rank. The skill rank should have a header of skill rank rather than the vague info as depicted in the current interface diagram. The skill rank should be a word description:

- **Basic [Green Text]**: A basic understanding of the skill category. The officer can perform the skills in this category, but with a negative impact on ship performance.
- **Trained [Blue Text]**: Trained. The officer's performance has no effect on gameplay and is altogether neutral.

- **Skilled [White Text]**: Skilled. The officer will impart some slight improvements in game effects to the performance of ship operations in this skill category.
- **Veteran [Yellow Text]**: Veteran. The officer will bestow modest improvements to ship performance in this skill category.
- **Expert [Orange Text]**: The officer has attained a skill that few others can compare; the gameplay effects are fairly strong as an officer effect.
- **Legendary [Red Text]**: The officer has attained a level of skill that is unearthly. They are miracle workers.

Helm Skills

- **Thruster Control**: Improve acceleration
- **Piloting**: Turn radius
- **Emergency Procedures**: High energy turns (HET) breakdown adjustment

Engineering

- **Thruster Efficiency**: Improves maximum speed
- **Warp Technology**: Reduces vulnerability time before and after warp
- **Inertial Dampener Technology**: Reduces the effects (recovery time and regeneration) of breakdown

OPS

- **Scanner Technology**: Improves the range and effectiveness of the scanner systems
- **Cloak Counter Measures**: Decreases enemy cloaking effectiveness
- **Find Weakness**: Finds weak spots in the enemy's defenses, which in turn increases weapon effectiveness against targeted ships

Security

- **Close Quarters Combat**: Increases combat effectiveness of Marines
- **Defensive Planning**: Increases ships' natural resistance to raids and boarding
- **Fitness Program**: Decreases likelihood of officers getting injured, including damage from any assassins

Medical

- **Psychology**: Sustains crew morale across missions
- **First Aid**: Increases the likelihood that an officer who is stunned recovers quickly
- **Surgery and Recovery**: Increases the likelihood severely injured officers survive

Tactical

- **Targeting**: Increases weapon efficacy
- **Troubleshooting**: Reduces the effects of weapon degradation due to damage
- **Counter Measures Training**: Reduces the effectiveness of both natural and artificial ECM

View Available Officers

This is a complex display combining the following elements:

- Officer Name
- Officer Cost to Buy
- Best Officer Sub-Skill
- The Skill Rank in this Sub-Skill

If there are no officers available at this starbase, display this text:

- "No officers available"

- This display is a scrolling display with no limit to the number of entries.

- The cost of the officer should be displayed in red if the player does not have enough prestige to buy the officer.

- The skill rank of the best sub-skill for the officer should be colored by the schedule of colors from the previous section.

> >

Player Activities

Cancel

All transfers in and out and auto-assignments of the player's officers are thrown out and the officers the player had in place when entering the menu are restored as well as the prestige the player had at the start. The player is then returned to the source menu or activity from where they came from.

An "Are you sure?" modal dialog might be a good addition to this choice.

Accept

All transfers of officers in and out of the ship and auto-assignment of officer stations are committed as well as the prestige changes. The shadow copy of the officer assignments from the beginning is thrown out. The player is then returned to the source menu or activity from where they came from.

An "Are you sure?" modal dialog might be a good addition to this choice.

Transfer Out

The officer that is currently selected on the side of the player's ship—the crew manifest—is transferred off of the player's ship and is placed in the starbase (and is viewable there). When the player transfers an officer out they only receive a K constant on the trade-in value for the officer. I would like to initially set this value to 1.0 so that the player has no inhibition on transferring their officers from station to station. However, I would like to be able to change this value later, for balance or difficulty settings.

It should always be successful to transfer an officer out.

The transfer out button is always available.

If the player selects one of those basic ensigns with no skill, it just disappears into the ether and cannot be effectively transferred to a new station. This is to prevent the player from transferring out their infinite supply of ensigns and filling up the starbase.

Transfer In

The transfer in button will take the officer currently selected on the starbase side and swap places with the officer currently selected on the player's ship side (effectively performing a transfer out of this officer at the same time).

If the player does not have enough prestige to transfer in the selected officer from the starbase, then the color of the cost of that officer is red and the transfer in button is not enabled.

Auto Assign

By a simple algorithm the officers on the player's ship will shuffle about to have the officer with the best skill for each station. The algorithm should be something like this:

Take an officer and average the officer's Medical sub-skills to compute an average Medical skill rank; repeat this with all major skills and all six officers.

Now sort the officers in order of who has the highest major-skill value from largest to smallest.

Whomever is at the top, assign them to the station that corresponds to the skill that has the highest major-skill rank.

Keep going down the list until all six stations are filled.

The use cases of the officer screen

A fundamental tenet of the Unified Modeling Language (UML) is that you should never create documents and diagrams just for documentation's sake. You should use your own judgment on how much rigor you should apply to the problem. That is because beyond the use case diagram, UML offers *eight* more diagrams such as the *test case*, the *activity diagram*, the *sequence diagram*, the *class diagram*, the *package diagram*, and the *deployment diagram*. This could be a bewildering array of diagrams if you went about every menu with nine different diagrams and 50 pages of supplemental text. You would quite clearly never make a game, but you might make a bureaucrat proud.

With that cautionary statement about not going overboard, I think it is well worth your time to collect all the use cases that directly involve the player. Unlike most business applications, we game makers have the player perform many interactions, and some are quite complex. Take the time to create a use case diagram for each shell screen. Most of these you will not need to document much, just some notes here and there about how many characters that text entry should take, how many digits that display should produce, and so on. It is absolutely required that you create a menu flow (my term) diagram to chart the flow between your shell screens.

The main display of your game, whether it is an isometric role-playing game, a starfighter game, or a racing game, should be where you put in most of your use case analysis time. Take the time to mock up the display in Adobe Photoshop or some other layout tool. Then carefully hunt and peck for every interaction and requirement you have for the main display. I would recommend using a whiteboard or a piece of graph paper to collect this first pass of interactions and use cases.

Next, rearrange your use cases to factor out common functionality or behavior from your various interactions and create your use case diagram in a tool such as Visio. As a last step, adorn

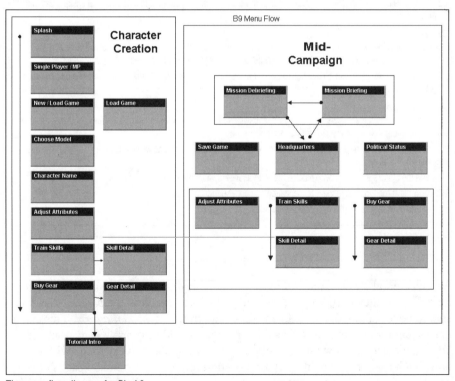

The menu flow diagram for Black9

> >

your use cases that have certain requirements, like a frame rate of 60 seconds, that are not direct interactions. This can be articulated as a note on the view main display use case.

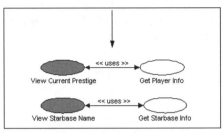

An example of adornment

To be productive with interactions, do not attempt to analyze the use cases into anything that resembles implementation. At this point you do not care *how* the interactions will be handled; rather you just want to know *what* the interactions are.

Reverse Engineering

Now all this is just fine when you are working from a clean slate, but in this world of licenses and franchises you will often find yourself working on a sequel or port of a previously released game. Use case diagrams are a valuable tool for performing *reverse engineering,* that is, taking a system that is already built and working backward to understand how it works. Understanding how the existing system works is a key step to successfully taking over someone else's code base. Here all of the use cases are already functional in an existing game. Your job is to play the game and take note of every interaction the player is having with the game and every requirement expressed in the previous game and produce use case diagrams and use case documents to

describe the existing engine. Last year at Taldren, when I hired Ken Yeast to take over maintenance programming for my area of SFC: Empires at War, he had a little trouble wrapping his mind around the sequence of events and interactions involved in the matching of humans and AIs in the online gameplay for SFC: EAW. Ken not only came up to speed with my code in an efficient manner, but was actually fixing subtle and complex bugs with the ability to "see" what is expected of the system.

No matter how hard you look, you will never uncover all the use cases and system requirements for your game project during the technical design portion of preproduction. Don't worry about it; anytime you discover a new use case, just figure out where it is factored into existing behaviors, if any, and update the use case diagram and supplemental text.

Nonobvious Requirements

Here are some other nonobvious requirements that your game may have:

Design requirements—you want the game to support user extensibility, such as a map editor or a scripting language, or use an existing code base.

Interface requirements—similar to a design requirement but closer to the code, such as using OpenGL over DirectX for portability.

Implementation requirements— these are unusual coding standards such as the commerce level of transactions and database storage when implementing your own billing system for an online massively multiplayer game. A simple example is the platform for your game—PS2, PC, GBA, etc.

< < < < < < < < < < < < < < < < < < < < < < < <

Performance requirements—examples of these requirements are the all-important high frame rate or a tolerance to a specified level Internet latency.

Requirements Analysis

The purpose of the requirements analysis stage of the technical design document is to take the use case model of the game, which describes the game in terms of player interaction, and create an analysis model of the game in the highest level of technical design for the developer. The following table enumerates the purpose of the analysis model.

Use Case Model	Analysis Model
Described using the language of the player	Described using the language of the game developer
External view of the game	Internal view of the game
External structure by use cases	Internal structure by use of stereotypical classes and packages
Used primarily to build a contract between the development team and the publisher (executive management, i.e., customer) to articulate what requirements the game must fulfill	Used by the game developers to understand how the game should be designed and implemented
Captures the functionality of the game including nonobvious requirements	Outlines how to create the game including a high-level architecture; this is the first pass at formal design
Defines use cases that are further analyzed during the rest of the design through to the test cases	Defines use case realizations, each one the result of the analysis of a use case

The analysis model is not the name of a diagram, rather it is the name given to the collection of diagrams, text, and designs that lie between the requirements capture stage and the deeper design stage. It will be in the design stage that you make your final plans for the construction of the software. In short, the analysis model is perhaps a fancy name for your first pass at the rest of your technical design. You can create a package diagram recast in the analysis model, a sequence diagram, or a collaboration diagram. What you are seeking to do is iteratively move towards the deeper, more specific constructs. The goal is to avoid creating bugs and defects in the game's design and architecture that could be fixed now just by rearranging some symbols in Visio rather than rewriting a tree of classes near the shipping of your game due to a subtle bug. You must use your judgment here to decide how far to push the analysis model. Getting the client-server interactions of a massively multiplayer game is a place I would feel comfortable taking my time.

Looking over the previous table, it is clear that no matter what software development process or lack of one is employed, you will always end up analyzing your requirements and implementing the requirements. What is to be accomplished in the requirements analysis stage is to pause and take stock of the use case model and "parse" it into developer language by taking the use cases that have been grouped together by factoring common behavior and come up with proto-classes and basic sequences of events. The idea is to start jelling the technical design without committing to final class diagrams; this will prevent you from following what may be the wrong path

> >

of implementation. In other words, if you start producing final class diagrams in response to the first use case you see, then you will produce a system that best answers that first use case. In any area of the game where you have a complexity of use cases, all of them vying for your attention, you should probably take the time to stop and produce an analysis model of the aggregate use cases.

As always, use your judgment; there will be many times parts of your game will not require the rigor of an interim analysis model to be developed before going ahead and creating your final technical design. For example, the menu presenting two buttons to the players requesting them to choose between single player and multiplayer game mode will not require deep thought, and you should just go ahead and take the use case diagrams as the analysis model—with a mockup of the screen and its place in the menu flow, I would call it a final design!

Class Diagram

The class diagram describes the static relationships and roles of the classes that comprise your game's software. The class diagram can be exhaustive and detail every class and relationship and be printed out on several hundred sheets of paper and pasted to a wall (we have a couple of walls at Taldren serving this purpose for fun), or your class diagram could be focused on a narrow portion of the game such as the classes driving the AI of the starships in your game.

The class diagram is the workhorse of technical design. Most programmers along the road of object-

oriented design will discover the class diagram on their own. Either they were faced with a tangled set of code in a maintenance job and started scratching sense out on a graph pad, or perhaps they are facing a complex new system they have been tasked to create, and they want to nail it so they reach for the whiteboard to consider a few different class hierarchies.

As the following diagram shows, the class diagram is a simple collection of boxes, each representing a class, and lines between the boxes showing how the classes are related to each other. There are many bits of detail and formal notation we could add to the class diagram such as descriptors declaring a method to be public, private, or protected, and whether a class is a template class or whether we are referring to an instance of a class—an object. These additional bits of notation are a part of the UML I will introduce later, but for the moment let us just consider the essence of the class diagram: classes and relationships.

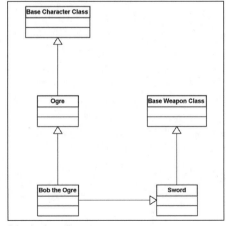

A basic class diagram

< < < < < < < < < < < < < < < < < < < < < < < < <

Relationships

The class diagram models the static relationships between the classes. It does not model any dynamic behavior of the classes such as when they are instantiated or destroyed, and it does not describe the message flow between the classes. It is the relationships between the classes that make a class diagram a picture of value rather than just a collection of boxes on a piece of paper. These relationship lines describe the dependencies between the classes, and these dependencies define the architecture of your game. There are several vocabulary words that are employed in formal OOD to describe the relations between classes, however they are all variations of three possible relationships. The "is a" relationship is used when one class is derived from another class. An example of this is: a textbook is a child class that "is a" book. The "has a" relationship denotes the relationship between a class that uses another class in its composition. The textbook class could have a "has a" relationship with the page class. Very neat and tidy, eh? Well, I have a loose end. There is one more relationship that occurs between classes; it is the compile time dependency in which one class uses another class in the implementation of a method (also known as a function). Any module that manipulates strings is quite likely to include the header file string.h from the Standard Library. Each type used as a parameter in a function creates a dependency between that class and the invoked type. Drawing every single dependency relationship between a class and all of the other types that are employed in methods of our class under study would only create a very hairy diagram sporting way too many lines to be useful. That is why the dependency relationship is a kind of third cousin to the more important "is a" and "has a" relationships.

Drawing "is a" and "has a" Relationships and Ordinalities

The "is a" relationship is denoted by a line between two classes with an arrow on one side pointing to the parent class. The "has a" relationship is just a line. The "has a" relationship line is often adorned with the cardinality of the relationship on either or both sides. An example: The "has a" relationship between the **textbook** and the **page** class would have the Arabic numeral "1" on the side of the **textbook** and an asterisk "*" on the side of the **page** class. This shows an indeterminate number of **pages** contained in the **textbook**. It is also quite possible to be more specific. The relationship between the **die** class and the **face** class could be adorned with a "1" on the side of the **die** class and a "6" on the side of a **face** class unless you are playing third edition Dungeons and Dragons as I like to do from time to time; in that case the relationship between **die** and **face** would need that asterisk back again to account for your pile of 20-sided, 12-sided, 10-sided, 8-sided, and 4-sided dice.

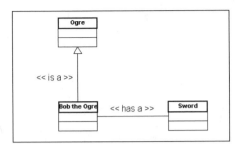

Focusing on the difference between "is a" and "has a" relationships

Adding Annotation

Quite often you will want to add important information and details to a class diagram that is not a class or a relationship but a note. To add a note to your diagram, simply draw a rectangle and dog-ear a corner, then draw a line to the class, object, or relationship that you want to clarify. Adding performance requirements such as "must render a steady 30 frames per second to the 3D view class" is a good example of a relevant notation.

Other UML Diagram Types

The Unified Modeling Language provides a number of diagrams that support different areas of technical design and software architecture. In a later section I will cover in greater detail the diagrams I find useful. Here I will present the briefest of introductions to the rest of the UML diagram family.

The class diagram is one of the diagrams used to perform *structural modeling*. Two other UML diagrams for structural modeling are the object diagram and the package diagram. The object diagram is a variation of the class diagram where the instanced objects and the relationships between these instanced objects are the focus of the diagram. The class that the object is an instance of is semantically designated by naming the object box like this: Goblin: Monster. Important attributes and values of the object are listed below a dividing line in the box as seen in the accompanying diagram.

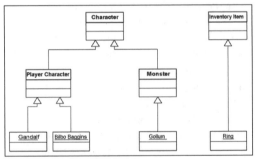

An example of an object diagram

Package diagrams are used to organize your class diagrams. Once you have about a dozen or so classes on a sheet of paper, they will start to blur together and lose their meaning. A package diagram looks a lot like a collection of file folders where the interesting bits of class are listed inside the file.

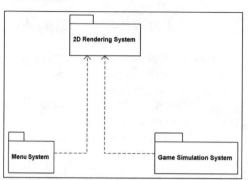

An example of a package diagram

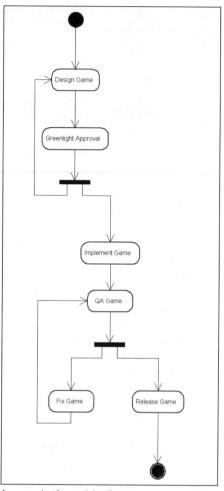

An example of an activity diagram

Dynamic Modeling

Structural modeling is the modeling of how the software will be constructed from a static point of view—in short, the activity you would imagine when setting out to architect your game. However, your game also has dynamic functionality, and UML has diagrams to handle this activity. Remember flow charts? UML has polished up the flow chart and now calls it the activity diagram. The activity diagram models the logic flow from start states to end states.

Sometimes a simple state diagram cannot model the complex message flow between various objects performing interesting tasks in your game. For example, in a client-server game there is often a complex flow of data going back and forth from the clients initiating requests and providing user input and the server taking all of this information in, resolving the game actions, and sending out packets to cause the clients to correctly update their displays. A very useful diagram to model this detailed, complex behavior is the UML sequence diagram.

A few more esoteric elements of dynamic modeling remain behind the curtains, and I will leave them there for the time being; see me again in Part III.

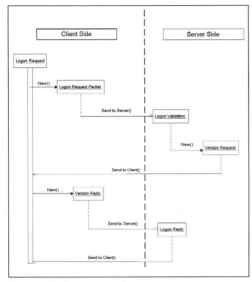

An example of a sequence diagram

Architectural Diagrams

Modern games are becoming large pieces of software that need to be designed and orchestrated on a macro scale. The UML provides component diagrams to illustrate the relationships between modules, libraries, dynamically linked libraries, databases, and other significant chunks of your whole game's software composition.

UML also provides a deployment diagram that appears to be useful only for massively multiplayer client-server games. The deployment diagram describes where all the pieces of the software are going to reside at run time.

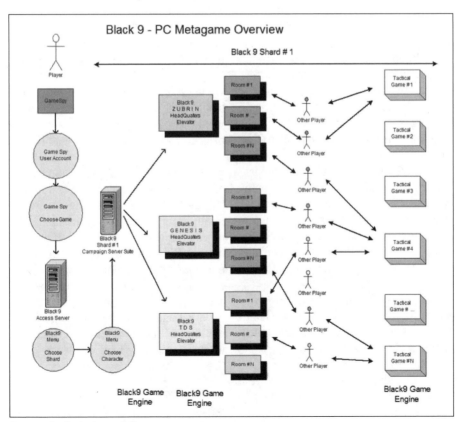

An example of a deployment diagram

< < < < < < < < < < < < < < < < < < < < < < < < < < < <

For most games, especially console games, the deployment of the game software is well understood and a deployment diagram would only be another diagram in your technical design document suitable only for impressing Dilbert's boss.

Large-Scale Planning and the Evil of a Long Build Time

There are a few tricky parts of building large software projects that all of this solid planning aims to keep in check. The largest bugaboo of large projects is large build times. With computers already amazingly fast and only getting faster every month, it is easy to not care about build times. When your project builds and runs in five to fifteen seconds after making a change to your code, you never break your concentration. When the build times grow to about a minute or two in duration, the build time might be just long enough for you to reflect on what you are doing and perhaps be able to perform useful thinking. Once build times grow to five minutes or more, you have a serious productivity leak. When build times reach twenty minutes or more, people will naturally take a walk down the hall to chat with neighbors, hit the restroom, gulp some water, or get invited out for lunch, and two hours may elapse before they settle down again at their workstation.

A full rebuild of any large project will take a long time, but a small change to the implementation of a single function in a file will be a snap for the compiler to change and the linker to come up with a new executable for you. However, the gray area is where you realize you must change the interface to one of your classes and a header file

must be touched. If only a couple of files include this header file, no worries, but if dozens and dozens of files include this header file, look out—you might as well just do a rebuild all.

The trick to good large-scale project making is to consistently practice good OO and keep your code modularized. Very crudely speaking, do not get in the habit of copying the include directives from one file to another like a huge fishing net, hoping to catch the right file. Take the time to verify that each and every include directive needs to be at the top of the file you are working on. This has been a constant struggle with our Starfleet Command series. When I took over the project in 1998 it was my largest project to date and I had a lot of challenges. (I will skip boring whining comments.) Too far down the list of priorities was writing code with a fast build time. At the time we were under heavy pressure to make a date, and all of us thought this game would be it and we would be on to other projects. We had no idea our game would be such a success as to merit working with the same code four years later. Our project builds slowly due to its size, but it is a crime that relatively minor architectural changes cause significant build times (30 minutes or more!). We would love to rewrite the entire Starfleet Command code base from the ground up—that would be the way to go! However, with tight budgets we must use as much of the animal as possible with each release. In this real-world example we have chosen to go the route of incremental refactoring.

Refactoring

Refactoring is the art and science of making the code *better* without adding

> >

new features. A smart maintenance programmer will take time to not only understand the code but also to clean up OO foulings and other architectural errors in the code.

Refactoring can be applied to cleaning up *any* aspect of how your code is created. For the latest version of Starfleet Command we have separated the 3D rendering engine into a separate DLL, and we have vastly decreased the labor involved in sending messages back and forth between the client and server. The multiplayer code base both at the application level and the UI level were refactored. And the disappointing UI engine that we inherited from 1998—Quill—we have wrapped a safe and sane coding condom around that performs as advertised while leaving the underlying Quill alone. Refactoring is a pragmatic practice, and I am a practical person. So we are rewriting and polishing up significant chunks of the code as we go, creating better software as we maintain a regular release schedule.

Please see the excellent book on refactoring, *Refactoring: Improving the Design of Existing Code* by Martin Fowler, Kent Beck, John Brant, William Opdyke, and Don Roberts for a full discussion on techniques of refactoring.

Insulation

I fear I may be straying a little off the path of the technical design document. However, I defend myself by wanting to convey to you not only passion for reducing build times, but also some practical advice on achieving faster build times. I also argue that a section in your technical design document

discussing your coding practices and software design approaches, including a section on build times, could only earn you a nod of approval from the folks who are to review your technical design document as well as acting as the most clear piece of communication to your team about how you intend for build times to be managed.

Besides just practicing good OO there is another technique your programmers can employ tactically to sections of the game to dramatically insulate portions of the code from each other. It goes by different names such as Interface-Impl and Insulation. The basic idea is to create an interface class that contains an implementation class. The role of the implementation class is the traditional role of getting the job done, and the role of the interface class is to be the only public access to the rest of the project. This permits the developer of the implementation class to change the attributes and members of the implementation class all day long without needing any other modules to be recompiled!

A classic example of the use of insulation is a class that is a *stack*. The stack could be written using an array or a linked list (or quite a few other data structures) to push and pop data onto the stack. You write this class as clean as you want, but you will always give away your implementation details in the header file. Sure, that information is privately declared, but it is still publicly viewable and, more germane to this point, any changes to the stack classes implementation, say from an array to an STL list, will cause a rebuild of all modules that ever used your stack class.

< < < < < < < < < < < < < < < < < < < < < < < < < < <

```
// stack.h - implented as an array
#if ! defined ( stack.h )
#define stack.h


class cStack
{
    private:
        int*  pStack;
        int       size;
        int       length;

    public:
        cStack();
        cStack( const cStack &stack );
        ~cStack();

        Stack& operator= (const Stack &stack );
        void mPush( int value );
        int       mPop();
        int       mTop() const;
        bool      mIsEmpty();
}
#endif
```

A stack written as an array

```
// stack.h - implented as a linked list
#if ! defined ( stack.h )
#define stack.h

class cStackLink;

class cStack
{
    private:
        cStackLink*      pStack;

    public:
        cStack();
        cStack( const cStack &stack );
        ~cStack();

        Stack& operator= (const Stack &stack );
        void      mPush( int value );
        int       mPop();
        int       mTop() const;
        bool  mIsEmpty();
}
#endif
```

A stack written as a linked list

> >

```
// stack.h - fully insulated we do not need to know the implementation
#if ! defined ( stack.h )
#define stack.h

class cStackIter;
class cStackImpl;

class cStack
{
    private:
        cStackImpl*pStackImpl;
        friend          cStackIter;

    public:
        cStack();
        cStack( const cStack &stack );
        ~cStack();

        Stack& operator= (const cStack &stack );
        void        mPush( int value );
        int         mPop();
        int         mTop() const;
        bool  mIsEmpty();
};

bool operator== ( const cStack& left, const cStack& right );
bool operator!= ( const cStack& left, const cStack& right );

class cStackIterImpl;

class cStackIter
{
    private:
        cStackIterImpl* pStackIterImpl;
        cStackIter( const cStackIter& );
        cStackIter& operator= ( const cStackIter& );

    public:
        cStackIter( const cStackIter& stack );
        ~cStackIter();
        void operator++();
        operator const void* () const;
        int operator()() const;
};
#endif
```

A stack fully insulated from implementation details

In practice there are many variations you can take to elide your implementation details, with the wholesale privatization of the implementation class being the most aggressive and achieving the highest degree of insulation. I have worked on a project that used this method of insulation aggressively throughout the project, and after discussing it in depth with my teammates, in the end we disagreed with the widespread use of insulation. In particular it makes inheriting a class a pain, and while it does save a lot of mind space by hiding the implementation details from the rest of the team, it also places an extra duty upon the developers who have to write the interface and implementation classes. In the end, we decided it is most useful in larger classes like game manager classes, which are likely to undergo a lot of revision in development while at the same time are unlikely to ever have anything derived from them.

Please read the detailed and well-written book on a relatively unexciting topic, *Large-Scale C++ Software Design* by John Lakos.

Forward and Backward Code Generation with a Modeling Tool

So why do I advocate UML's particular set of boxes and lines for describing software? Well, any set of lines and boxes will do, as long as you think through the stuff you need to think through and communicate it well to your teammates and project stakeholders. That being said, UML is making rapid progress in being accepted as the industry standard for describing and documenting software.

By becoming an industry standard we are now seeing several products on the market that will perform both forward code generation from your diagrams and reverse engineering on existing code. I should let that settle with you for a moment.

Think about it; your programmers can link a bunch of boxes together in a class diagram describing the relationships between the classes, attributes, members, parameters, public, private, protected—quite a few details—hit a button, and bam—the files are created and the skeleton code is written! All that is left for the programmers to do is program. That makes UML cool.

The reverse engineering part can come in handy when you need to digest a whole mess of code. It really is quite fun and educational to generate large class diagrams and spend an afternoon pasting them to a wall and reading over them to get a feel for the lay of the land.

There are several tools to choose from for the creation of UML diagrams, including Rational's Rose and Together from Together Soft. We have even been teased by Microsoft that Visual Studio 7 will come with a new version of Rose bundled into the development environment.

So yes, you can use your own boxes and lines, but why not use the boxes and lines that have software out there that can help you?

Testing Plan

Towards the end of your technical design document you must have a section on your testing plan. How will you test your game? Toss it to the publisher and fix what they ask? Beta testing, unit testing, black box testing, or white box testing—which will you employ?

Unit Testing and White Box Testing

Unit testing is the most straightforward of testing procedures. As you finish a piece of your software, write a testing suite to exercise your new piece across all ranges of valid and invalid input and see what breaks. This is the sort of activity developers of the piece of code should implement as a matter of course in the development of their work.

Also note that unit testing will not work with poorly architected code as you will have few truly modular parts of your game that can be tested independently from the rest of the game.

> >

The best kind of unit and white box testing is automated. For example, some developers of 3D games have a test where a computer constantly generates random locations and directions for the camera to look at to see if any positions and/or views cause a crash. In the development of Excel, Microsoft employs three or more redundant, independent algorithms for the calculation of the worksheets and compares the values across them all to identify errors in the algorithm that is being optimized for shipping with Excel.

Black Box Testing

This is the type of testing most publishers will perform on your game. They may have organized checklists to follow, but in the end it will be a bunch of young folks early in their careers playing your game in a relatively unstructured manner, looking for things that are broken. The advantage black box testing has over white box testing is that since the testing is performed from the user's perspective with no knowledge of the implementation details, black box testing will often find bugs that a white box testing plan was not even looking for. The flip side is that since the testing is not based on any knowledge of the implementation of the game, the testing can become rather unfocused and can consume quite a lot of man-hours in the pursuit of bugs.

Beta Testing

Beta testing is great; it is putting the game in the hands of people who will buy your game. Fix all of the bugs they identify and you know for sure you are spending your time on bugs that need to be fixed. The problem with beta testing is that it is an exaggerated form of black box testing, where you have fans just playing the game and reporting what they feel like reporting. Beta testers also consume great amounts of the development team's attention, as they are real people who will express their feelings and need continuous feedback and direction to keep them happy and productive. However, every game (and product for that matter) should undergo beta testing, as it is the only way to determine if you really are making something people will enjoy.

From Use Cases to Test Cases

How do you organize your black box and beta testing? Again, UML offers an aid, the test case diagram. The great thing about this diagram is that it is just the use case diagrams from the start of our project being dusted off and getting a shiny new label. Remember all of the use cases you worked up to describe all the interactions between the player and the game? Those interactions are precisely what you want to test during your black box and beta testing efforts. Just collect all of your use cases and convert them into a checklist of a testing plan for the black box testing team and the beta testers to test.

> >

Chapter 10 > > > > > > > > > > > > > > >

The Project Plan

What Is the Project Plan?

The project plan is the culmination of the planning articulated in the game design, technical design, and other design documents such as an art style guide. The heart of the project plan is a schedule that describes what will be accomplished, how long the tasks will take, and who will perform these tasks. The project plan contains other information such as milestone dates, task dependencies, and a risk management plan. The information in the project plan is published to both the executive management for progress reports and to team members in the form of tasking. It is also used by the project manager to level tasks between resources, identify critical paths, and develop contingency plans. A good project plan will act as a major tool to avoid surprises. All this seems like good stuff, so let us get on with making a project plan.

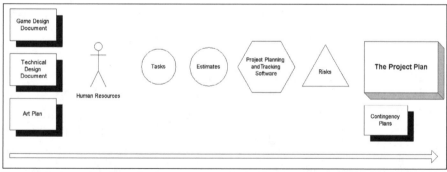

Components of a project plan: estimates, resources, tools, tracking, dependencies, risks, and alternate plans

How Do We Create the Project Plan?

To create the project plan we will need a list of tasks to be completed, who is available to perform those tasks, when the critical project dates are such as milestones, and what the relationships are between the tasks. The list of tasks, the estimates of how long it will take to perform these tasks, and their dependencies will come directly out of the game design document and technical design documents.

Critical project dates such as milestone and release dates should be iteratively arrived at with the executive management team as the project plan is compiled. Many projects are schedule driven; however, the most common for the game industry is the holiday shopping season from Thanksgiving to Christmas every year. Often projects will be planned by walking backwards in time from November to discover the critical dates like beta, alpha feature lock, first playable. With these projects it will be the project plan that adapts to the critical dates. This is discussed later in this chapter.

Developers Conference I discovered there was a fairly wide range of project management rigor applied to game development. Some shops considered themselves too small to plan their work; they just worked on whatever was the most pressing task at the time. Many developers just used simple spreadsheets in Excel to plan their projects; some folks used Microsoft Project to plan their tasks and then followed up in Excel to perform their task tracking; the more determined developers used Project for both planning and tracking; and one large French developer that was part of a construction firm used Project to plan and Microsoft Team Manager for task tracking.

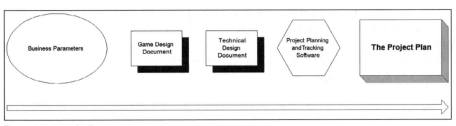

The project plan pipeline

All of this project information will need to be compiled into a usable format for project analysis and report generation. With tools such as Microsoft Project or Primavera's SureTrak products, a myriad of reports and graphs can be generated to review the workload across team members, understand what the critical path is, measure project progress, and a whole host of other views of your project status. Many people are intimidated by project planning, or they have seen project planning only partially implemented that failed to work. From my roundtables on game production at the Game

Gantt and PERT Charts for Organizing Project Tasks

There are many reports, graphs, and charts used in project planning and tracking. The two most commonly used charts are the PERT and Gantt charts. The acronym PERT stands for *Program Evaluation Review Technique*, a methodology developed by the U.S. Navy in the 1950s to manage the Polaris submarine missile program. The PERT chart places each task in a rectangular box with a line drawn to the predecessor task and a line to the next task; thus the whole diagram looks like some sort of tree. The PERT chart's key feature

> >

is the visual ease in identifying the relationship between tasks and the critical path of the project as a whole. The drawback of a PERT chart is that its utility is limited to just the higher-level view of a project. When individual tasks of any nontrivial project are displayed, the resulting chart is crisscrossed with lines and is too unwieldy for the viewer to absorb.

excels in data entry, as there is no end to fussing about where to put the boxes as in a PERT chart. The project manager usually just needs to enter the task name, estimated time to complete, and a resource to complete the job. A tool like Microsoft Project will automate the graph side of the chart. The Gantt chart will also accept task dependency information like the PERT

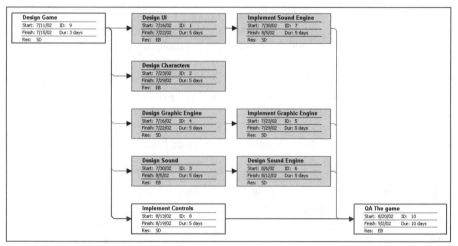

A PERT chart from Microsoft Project

The Gantt chart turns out to be the most generally useful of the project planning and tasking charts. It features a spreadsheet-like data entry on the left-hand side of the chart with any number of columns, the minimum being task name, task start date, task duration, and resource name. On the right-hand side of the chart is a modified bar graph where each task is a horizontal bar organized in a cascading hierarchy as time progress. The Gantt chart

chart and draw arrows between tasks to show what order the tasks must be created in; however, the Gantt chart produces a more flat graph that does not show off the dependencies of tasks as well as the PERT chart. The visual clutter of a Gantt chart can be minimized to a great extent by nesting the tasks into a hierarchy of task, subtask, sub-subtask, etc. Microsoft Project allows for a total of nine levels of task nesting.

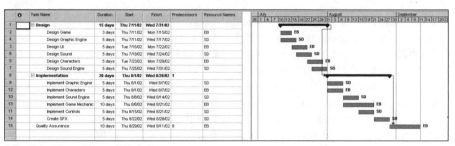

A Gantt chart from Microsoft Project

In my experience in game production I have found the Gantt chart to be crucial and the PERT chart fun. By fun I mean that the PERT chart is so easy to digest visually that seeing the key tasks getting completed and checked off as the project heads towards completion is a visual treat. The problem with the PERT chart is again you must reduce the task resolution to just the highest level tasks. This results in relatively chunky task descriptions like "implement 3D engine," "script campaign one," and "alpha test," and these relatively chunky tasks are actually composed of many tasks spread over a great deal of time. The PERT chart becomes dissatisfying when you want to mark off a PERT box when something is 90 percent complete even though the final 10 percent will not be completed for some time. For this reason I do not use PERT charts for my own projects.

> **NOTE**: Please see Chapter 20 for a quick survival guide to Microsoft Project.

Focusing on the Gantt Chart

So how exactly do we create a Gantt chart? Obviously we need to know what the tasks are, who is going to do them, and how long they will take. The ideal Gantt chart entry is a single, clear, discrete task with a short duration

(debate rages but aim for between .25 day to 3 days in your task resolution). An example of a poor entry would be *3D engine, 4 months, Bob.* This task is poorly described for two reasons: The first is the name itself, *3D engine.* What does that mean? Test it? Design it? Debug it? Implement it? Review it? Break it? Fix it? Vague project task names must be attacked ruthlessly and reduced to a lean, aggressive name like *Create static design of the core 3D engine.* The second thing wrong with this task is that *it is four months long!* Good grief, why are we even putting together a schedule? How will it serve to measure progress when we can only look Bob up after 15 weeks and ask if he thinks he will make it next week? With such coarse resolution we are simply not getting enough incremental task progression data to have a meaningful analysis of whether the project is tracking. For if we are not tracking, maybe we should cut features in the 3D engine, or maybe we need to add another programmer to work on the custom shaders, or maybe we should kill the new 3D engine altogether and make do with the previous engine or integrate a commercial 3D engine. All of these tough choices can be uncomfortable or even impractical for you and your project, but these choices are certainly not more comfortable when Bob has been working for 15 weeks and then admits that the 3D engine turned out to be tougher than he thought and that in four more weeks he will know more!

There is a time and place for coarsely defined Gantt charts—very early in the project when you are defining your business parameters. At this time it is useful to block out your project with these coarse task granularities to get an idea of how many people you will need and about how long it will take to get the job done. This proto-Gantt chart can then be used iteratively to help define the costs of the project while they are still fairly malleable in the early project negotiation phase. In the ideal world a publisher would sign up a project and pay for three months of preproduction to determine the detailed project schedule; this rarely happens. Instead, you often work on the rough size and scope of a project and then use the early milestones to refine your schedule and kill features to make the project fit into the negotiated costs. I have to warn you, creating these proto-schedules is not a substitute for going through with your full preproduction phases and determining your task estimates in detail! You should also avoid creating a proto-schedule if you have little experience in project planning, or where the game has not yet jelled into a clear vision, or where there are a lot of associated technical risks because you or your team have not developed a similar game.

> **WARNING!**—Creating proto-schedules should only be done by experienced project planners who have managed similar projects and where the game scope is well understood.

Using the Technical Design Document

The technical design document is supposed to have the information for the technical tasks. Depending on how you organize your team members, the game design document, the technical design document, or a stand-alone art asset document will describe the art tasks. Wherever the information is coming from, as you sit down to enter these tasks and time estimates into Project, you will discover that these tasks are not ready for immediate entry. For instance, the 30 luminosity maps needed for your starships will be listed as 45 man-days from your art director. Should you enter that as a single task named *luminosity mapping, 45 days, artists*? No you should not; that would be creating a vague task entry like the previous 3D engine example. Will you have all of your artists working on this for 45 days? Will you burn one of your artists on this tedious task? Do you need all of the luminosity maps done at the same time? These are the questions you need to ask yourself as you translate the task estimates from your leads into your schedule. For a task like this I would write up 30 1.5-day tasks and distribute them evenly across the artists I had available to perform these tasks (in my management style, if there is something boring and repetitive, I generally distribute the tasks evenly, perhaps a bit heavier on the junior team member). Getting ahead of myself into a discussion of risk management and task dependencies, I would schedule these repetitive, low-risk tasks towards the end of the project with perhaps some sample luminosity maps done early on to verify we understood the production path and time estimate to create the maps. These 30 1.5-day tasks would be an eyesore to look at if we were to enter them flat into the schedule. To handle that bit of dust, sweep these 30 entries into a super-task named *create luminosity maps*. This way we can view this individual information easily by expanding the super task *create luminosity maps* and hide it when it is not of immediate interest. Each of the 30 subtasks should also refer to the specific starship that the map is for or at the very least be uniquely identified as in *create luminosity map for Federation Enterprise-E, 1.5 days, Ed.*

It will be difficult to always break down tasks into their proper subtasks. For example many times you will get a reasonable-sounding task like *investigate pixel shaders, 3 days, Tom.* It has a fairly clear verb—investigate—right? Well, does it mean Tom will spend three days on learning what is going on with pixel shaders and then move on? What is the deliverable for this task? Will Tom merely know more about pixel shaders or are you expecting to implement pixel shaders? Will the artists need to perform additional work to support the pixel shaders if Tom gets them done? I recommend this task be broken down into the following tasks: *Investigate the*

A poorly broken down task—too long

The previous task broken down into 30 bite-sized 1.5-day tasks distributed to two artists, with an early phase to determine the validity of the task estimate for both artists, rolled up under a super-task.

> >

feasibility of pixel shaders, 1 day, Tom; Implement core support for shaders, 1 day, Tom; Implement simple shader for ripple effect, 1 day, Tom; Determine what additional work the Artists must perform, .25 day, Tom; and then wrap up all of these tasks under a super-task named *implement ripple shader.* Picture in your mind that it is your job to view each and every incoming task as a crystalline rock that you examine closely, looking for the fissures that represent the subtasks inside of the project. Then you grasp the task firmly in your hands and break it up along these fissures.

Breakin' down tasks

Task Granularity and Task Leveling

Task leveling is the act of distributing the workload across your developers so that no one developer is stuck holding up the show while the rest kick back at the beach. Task leveling is a difficult and imprecise business. No two developers on your team will produce code, art, or other game development bits at the same rate and with the same level of initiative and independence. Task tracking is such a central activity of game production that the next chapter is dedicated to its discussion. However, here in the planning stage we can set ourselves up for success later by planning our task leveling now. In the

previous section I stressed breaking down large, vague tasks into clear, crisp, small tasks; it turns out that breaking tasks up into crisp bite-size chunks is also critical for effective task leveling. By breaking up the tasks into their smaller pieces you will not only see more clearly just how much work you have to do, but you will also be able to better analyze how to distribute your tasks across your company.

How Long Will That Task Take?

As you enter the data you will not only need to break up the tasks into smaller tasks, but you will also need to spend a moment chewing on the time estimates being reported by your team members. There is a lot of debate in the community about padding tasks by two times or three times to count for the chronic underestimation that developers are prone to make. I fundamentally disagree. I think it is a very bad thing for the development team to think in terms of "programmer-hours" and feel assured that their management lead will take responsibility for padding the schedule to accommodate their optimism. If you think about this for a moment, it does seem ludicrous to take the developer's estimate and institutionally lie and come up with another number. I believe the reason organizations do this multiplying technique is they have found that taking the developers estimates has resulted in previous projects slipping and going over budget. The answer is the development process is flawed, and that is why the project is late, not because a developer makes poor estimates. How can a project succeed when such arbitrary estimates are tossed around?

So how do you get good time estimates? First of all I do not make creating the time estimates *my responsibility* as the project manager; I make that the *developers' responsibility*. Is this just a semantic nuance? No, the way to success is to push down to them the *responsibility*, the *authority*, and the *accountability* to create their own time estimates. I will not be performing the work; they will. Your team members are not just coders or pixel pushers; they are game developers. Grow your organization so they understand that creating quality estimates is part of their job and that they need to make an estimate they can live with.

Will pushing estimating down to the team members work? What about the new artist; does he know how long it will take to texture the level? How about the AI programmer; now that he has been tasked to create the networking code, how will he come up with a quality estimate? I am not saying that the senior team members such as the art director and the lead programmer as well as the project manager should not participate and help develop the estimates. What I am saying is that my team performs best when they are working under a schedule they drafted. It may look like I have not solved the time estimate problem; it may look like I just moved it down to the developer, but that is too casual a statement. When you walk up to Sally and ask her how long it will take to create a mission editor for the game, she might reply with a shrug and a soul-searching glance at the ceiling and come back with an estimate of two months. This is a low-quality estimate. Much better is to walk up to Sally and say to her, "I

want you to think about what it is going to take to get the mission editor done; specifically, I want you to review the technical and game designs for the mission editor and break it down into a task resolution of one to three days each and enter your tasks into Microsoft Project. Would Friday be okay with you to review your schedule?" This is much stronger because you gave a clear task of getting her area estimated and put into a schedule, and you told her how to get it down with the comments on the time resolution and Project. You also gave a firm date and gave every indication that it is her responsibility.

So what do you do when developer estimates are too short or too long? You are the project manager, and you have responsibility for running the project. While the buck stops with you, your job is to get the right people matched to the right tasks with the proper tools and resources to get the job done. It is the artists and the art director who are responsible for the art estimates. You said that before, Erik, but what do I do with a time estimate that is clearly too short? I want you to review every time estimate for a reality check, a second opinion, and for your own benefit to build up a better mental map of how long the myriad of development tasks take. What I suggest you do with a short time estimate is interview the developer and/or lead for that section and ask them why they thought they could accomplish it so quickly. Maybe you will find out something you did not know; that would be a good thing. Maybe they will shrug and admit they didn't give it enough thought. Or maybe it is a feature they very much want to see get done and do not want to see it cut so they are "selling you" the feature.

Short Time Estimate Possibilities

If the developer did not give the estimate enough thought, then simply kick it back for a revision. If you simply were not aware of something that will make the task quicker to complete— no problem, accept the estimate. However, when it turns out they are selling you on a feature, this could be a problem. First of all, this means you have a flaw in your schedule that needs to be corrected or the rest of your schedule will be affected. The hard part is that your developer is selling you this feature because she really wants to see it get in the schedule and she felt she needed to underestimate the task to get it on the schedule. You have three choices: Kill the feature, allow the feature, or allow a fixed amount of time to work on the feature. Each situation is unique, but I tend to ask the developer why she thought it was so important to implement the feature. If she does a reasonable job convincing me it is a desirable feature but I cannot afford to rearrange the schedule to fit in the true time for this task, then I will encourage the developer to drop the feature. Many times the developers will be passionate about getting it done and will propose to keep the time estimate to what the schedule can afford, and they will work hard to squeeze it in. This I feel is fair; the manager should not create schedules that require overtime, but I do feel comfortable with developers working as many hours as they like to create the highest quality game they can.

Estimating Research Tasks

How do you estimate how long it will take to get something done that no one has done before, or no one in your organization has done before? Perhaps there is little in the way of journal articles or books to give direction. How do you estimate how long one of these tasks will take? The first step is to break down the research task into as many small, discrete tasks as possible as we discussed previously. An example: Elaborate on a task named *research pixel shaders* and modify the task to a series of tasks like the following:

1. Install video card with pixel shader support
2. Install DirectX 8.0
3. Review DirectX 8.0 sample shader code
4. Create stand-alone test bed to explore pixel shaders
5. Create water effect through pixel shaders
6. Create fire effect through pixel shaders
7. Design architecture for the 3D engine to utilize pixel shaders
8. Implement pixel shader architecture
9. Unit test the pixel shader code
10. Implement fire effect—attach to fireball spell
11. Implement water effect—attach to water blast spell
12. Test the fireball spell
13. Test the water blast spell

By breaking down *research pixel shaders* into 13 subtasks, we can put good estimates on most of the tasks. Only task number four, *Create stand-alone test bed to explore pixel shaders*, looks like a type of research that resists being nailed to a firm time. The solution here is to set a *time box,* a fixed period of time you will allocate to the task. At the end of the time box you will either be done with the research or it will have turned out to be too expensive to continue. Mm, yes, what is that? How can you walk away from something not done? Well you might have to. Say you have 15 months to get your game done with ten developers, five of them programmers. Allowing three months for preproduction and three more months for testing and transition leaves nine production months or a total of 45 programmer months. This is your time budget; if the rest of your project is looking like 44 programmer months, then you have just one month left over to play around with your pixel shader. Put a time box of one month around the pixel shader work. These are the types of hard decisions you will have to make if you are going to run your project on budget.

Oh, so the pixel shaded spell effects were a core feature? Everyone thinks that is what it will take for your Diablo killer to make it over the top? After the one month passes and you are still not done, would you feel it is still so important a task that you would allocate more time to get it done? If so, then your original time box was not honest by taking into account your priorities. Time boxes only work if you stick to them. If the feature is really that important, then you should have allocated two months or three months. When setting a time box, set the maximum amount of time you are willing to spend on a feature of that priority level. Too many times when we are deciding whether or not to implement a feature, we just ask how cool it will be or

whether the competition has it, in the end deciding to implement the feature for a number of compelling reasons. Remind yourself that the great games all have a slim feature set that was executed with excellence. Think about that cool research-intense feature; do you really need it? Only a project with unlimited financing and no requirement for shipping can afford to implement features without asking the cost. Think of time boxes as stones in a stream where the rest of the tasks flow around these blocks of time; a few rocks are cool, many rocks is a stretch of rapids, and a wall of rocks is a dam. Determining a task's priority deserves its own subsection.

Task Prioritization

Assuming you and your team are creative folks and that you are making a game with a budget of time and money, you will always face a situation where you have too many ideas for cool features and not enough time to implement them. You are then faced with the job of prioritizing your features to be sure you get the critical features accomplished at the right expense of the less important features.

I have a reliable method for task prioritization: First discover all the absolutely required overhead tasks your team must accomplish or you will not even have a shipping game. These tasks include preproduction, beta testing, getting hardware manufacturer approval, getting licensor approval, creating milestones, and responding to milestone feedback. These are what I call zero-level tasks. Also do not forget to estimate the number of holidays, vacation, and sick time your team members will take, and make a

> >

reasonable provision for turnover (I use one developer for every ten developers per year). Subtract all of this nonproduction time from your overall schedule; this will leave you with the real production time you have to work with. Enter all of the zero-level tasks into your Microsoft Project Gantt chart. (See Chapter 20 for a quick overview of Project and such tips as customizing your team's calendar.)

The next step is to take your design documents and toss every task into one of three buckets: core tasks, secondary tasks, and tertiary tasks. Take your time with this. I highly suggest discussing the relative priority of the tasks with various team members to build consensus and to have some solid feedback.

Now that you have your three buckets, lay out all your core tasks in Microsoft Project using good task articulation techniques, and assign the tasks to the resources on your team. Now that you have your zero-level tasks and your core tasks entered into your Project file, use the project-leveling tool to see how the zero-level and core-level tasks will lay out over time. If you were conservative with what you labeled as a core task, then you should have some extra time left over to start plugging in your secondary tasks. However, if the buckets ended up with too much to do for even your core tasks on the first pass through, then you have to prioritize your core tasks and convert enough of them to secondary to make up the difference. This means that the secondary and certainly the tertiary tasks are unlikely to be completed if you are having trouble accommodating even the core tasks.

> **JARGON**: *Leveling* is the term in project management for the related tasks of seeing how the tasks will lay out over time and how loaded each of your resources are, and the process of distributing tasks across your team to achieve a more even workload.

How do you prioritize the core tasks when you already consider them core? First realize they cannot all be core. A rigorous development process requires developing good time estimates, and you have done that; now you are looking at a body of tasks that are core and *features you really want but do not have the budget for.* Perhaps you can make a strong enough case for these features to get approval to expand your project's budget. If you can do that, great—problem solved. If you are still holding to your original budget, then let me show you how I do low-level task prioritization. It's a crude method really, but it is effective: Take all your core tasks and enter them into a spreadsheet (use Excel) with a column labeled priority next to each task and a task time estimate. Now quickly run down your tasks, reading the task names and saying out loud the first gut-level priority that occurs to you for that task such as 7 or 3 or 10 if it is really critical. Go down your whole column of tasks whether it is ten core tasks or 200. Do this first pass quickly; taking longer will only make it harder. Now you will have a first pass priority for all of your core tasks. Have the spreadsheet software sort the core tasks from most important descending to least important. If you are like me, then you will see that you have stubbornly labeled too many tasks with a 10 or 9, and too few tasks have earned the label of 3 or 2. The way to solve this is to allow yourself only three level 10 tasks, three level 9 tasks, and so on. Start at the first item labeled 10 and take your time thinking deeply about the feature, discuss it with your team if you have to, but one by one you are going to demote your 10s to 9s until you are left with just three must-do 10s. Repeat this process all the way down your list. The mathematically astute will notice that this specific labeling system will fail if you have over 30 tasks. The exact labeling scheme is not important; it is just important to force yourself to make these prioritization choices. You could use the numbers 999 to 0, you could use the alphabet, or you could use a three-letter alphabetic core like AAA to DDD; whatever you use just leave yourself a set of three tasks at each prioritization level. The size of your task set should be roughly one-tenth of the overall numbers of tasks to be prioritized. Now just draw a line where you run out of time for core tasks, and toss the lower priority tasks in with your secondary tasks.

Bug ID	Bug Title	Priority
2929	CD-Key	
2953	SP - Klingon Campaign - Beginning Stardate is 112400.1, twice what it should be	
2979	Dynaverse - Fleets do not have accept / forfeit options in mission panel	
2987	Dynaverse - Hex changed color to red when Fed was leader and Kling was member	
3031	Dynaverse - Romulans can transfer in Borg officers	
2561	Global - Freighter Convoys do not have escorts	
2607	Campaign Screen - Player's ship gets stuck in Hex	
2609	Tactical Sim - Fed vs Fed fights	
2617	Dynaverse - Jumped from Lt. Commander ranking to a Fleet Admiral ranking	
3110	Dynaverse - Ten turn countdown results in stuck in Hexes	
2624	Dynaverse Campaign Screen - Fleet leader is not clear	
2632	Dynaverse - Can make movement bar disappear when leaving a Hex with refit	
2633	Dynaverse - While being attacked, attacking another will teleport player	
2637	DYNA - Map Screen not refreshing on completion of Mission	
2641	Campaign Screen - Ships inconsistent for Convoy between Attacking or Defending	
609	SP - Campaign Screen - States we are partners with the Contested Sector	
2058	Dynaverse - Cause of numbers appearing after player names in the chat box	
2119	New Conquest - Music stutters and pointer freezes loading new Conquest	
2701	Global - When AI forfeits it stays in the Hex	
2763	Dynaverse - Role of convoys	
2765	Access Server not using list of IP addresses	
2780	SP - General - Player can initiate a battle then auto move kicks in	
2784	SP - General - Player can be attacked when auto move kicks in	
2797	Hex information should appear in game display	
2799	SP - General - There needs to be a message when auto move is enacted	
2817	Dynaverse - "Stand by for mission briefing" panel repeats text	
2826	Dynaverse - Spectate does not work	
2841	Campaign Screen - All races should begin equally allied to Neutral Hexes	
2868	Dynaverse - Able to access buttons (campaign screen) anywhere on Hex map	
2869	Dynaverse - Enemy AI kills fleet member AI - Defeat with prestige	
2880	Dynaverse - Borg cubes appear very infrequently in Shipyard	
2309	Dynaverse - Destroyed enemy ship reappears on Hex map immediately	

2318	Tactical Sim - Visioneer opinion on buying Starbases
1681	Dynaverse - Officer advancement text cut off in message board
2452	AI doesn't know to go back to a repair station to repair hull
2981	Dynaverse - Severely damaged AI attacks healthy players
951	Dynaverse - AI does not team up properly in a Hex
2023	Dynaverse - Able to join missions in old Hex after leaving for new Hex
1790	SP - Tactical Sim - Able to click on map behind "Campaign Over" screen

The list of bugs and issues unprioritized

Bug ID	Bug Title	Priority
2929	CD-Key	A
2953	SP - Klingon Campaign - Beginning Stardate is 112400.1, twice what it should be	C
2979	Dynaverse - Fleets do not have accept / forfeit options in mission panel	B
2987	Dynaverse - Hex changed color to red when Fed was leader and Kling was member	C
3031	Dynaverse - Romulans can transfer in Borg officers	B
2561	Global - Freighter Convoys do not have escorts	B
2607	Campaign Screen - Player's ship gets stuck in Hex	A
2609	Tactical Sim - Fed vs Fed fights	B
2617	Dynaverse - Jumped from Lt. Commander ranking to a Fleet Admiral ranking	C
3110	Dynaverse - Ten turn countdown results in stuck in Hexes	A
2624	Dynaverse Campaign Screen - Fleet leader is not clear	C
2632	Dynaverse - Can make movement bar disappear when leaving a Hex with refit	C
2633	Dynaverse - While being attacked, attacking another will teleport player	
2637	DYNA - Map Screen not refreshing on completion of Mission	
2641	Campaign Screen - Ships inconsistent for Convoy between Attacking or Defending	
609	SP - Campaign Screen - States we are partners with the Contested Sector	
2058	Dynaverse - Cause of numbers appearing after player names in the chat box	
2119	New Conquest - Music stutters and pointer freezes loading new Conquest	
2701	Global - When AI forfeits it stays in the Hex	
2763	Dynaverse - Role of convoys	
2765	Access Server not using list of IP addresses	
2780	SP - General - Player can initiate a battle then auto move kicks in	
2784	SP - General - Player can be attacked when auto move kicks in	
2797	Hex information should appear in game display	
2799	SP - General - There needs to be a message when auto move is enacted	
2817	Dynaverse - "Stand by for mission briefing" panel repeats text	
2826	Dynaverse - Spectate does not work	
2841	Campaign Screen - All races should begin equally allied to Neutral Hexes	
2868	Dynaverse - Able to access buttons (campaign screen) anywhere on Hex map	
2869	Dynaverse - Enemy AI kills fleet member AI - Defeat with prestige	
2880	Dynaverse - Borg cubes appear very infrequently in Shipyard	
2309	Dynaverse - Destroyed enemy ship reappears on Hex map immediately	
2318	Tactical Sim - Visioneer opinion on buying Starbases	
1681	Dynaverse - Officer advancement text cut off in message board	
2452	AI doesn't know to go back to a repair station to repair hull	
2981	Dynaverse - Severely damaged AI attacks healthy players	
951	Dynaverse - AI does not team up properly in a Hex	
2023	Dynaverse - Able to join missions in old Hex after leaving for new Hex	
1790	SP - Tactical Sim - Able to click on map behind "Campaign Over" screen	

Prioritization starting (use A, B, C or 1, 2, 3)

< < < < < < < < < < < < < < < < < < < < < < < < < < < < <

Bug ID	Bug Title	Priority
2929	CD-Key	A
2953	SP - Klingon Campaign: Beginning Stardate is 112400.1, twice what it should be	C
2979	Dynaverse - Fleets do not have accept / forfeit options in mission panel	B
2987	Dynaverse - Hex changed color to red when Fed was leader and Kling was member	C
3031	Dynaverse - Romulans can transfer in Borg officers	B
2561	Global - Freighter Convoys do not have escorts	B
2607	Campaign Screen - Player's ship gets stuck in Hex	A
2609	Tactical Sim - Fed vs Fed fights	B
2617	Dynaverse - Jumped from Lt. Commander ranking to a Fleet Admiral ranking	C
3110	Dynaverse - Ten turn countdown results in stuck in Hexes	A
2624	Dynaverse Campaign Screen - Fleet leader is not clear	C
2632	Dynaverse - Can make movement bar disappear when leaving a Hex with refit	C
2633	Dynaverse - While being attacked, attacking another will teleport player	B
2637	DYNA - Map Screen not refreshing on completion of Mission	A
2641	Campaign Screen - Ships inconsistent for Convoy between Attacking or Defending	A
609	SP - Campaign Screen - States we are partners with the Contested Sector	B
2058	Dynaverse - Cause of numbers appearing after player names in the chat box	C
2119	New Conquest - Music stutters and pointer freezes loading new Conquest	C
2701	Global - When AI forfeits it stays in the Hex	C
2763	Dynaverse - Role of convoys	B
2765	Access Server not using list of IP addresses	A
2780	SP - General - Player can initiate a battle then auto move kicks in	A
2784	SP - General - Player can be attacked when auto move kicks in	A
2797	Hex information should appear in game display	C
2799	SP - General - There needs to be a message when auto move is enacted	B
2817	Dynaverse - "Stand by for mission briefing" panel repeats text	A
2826	Dynaverse - Spectate does not work	B
2841	Campaign Screen - All races should begin equally allied to Neutral Hexes	B
2868	Dynaverse - Able to access buttons (campaign screen) anywhere on Hex map	B
2869	Dynaverse - Enemy AI kills fleet member AI - Defeat with prestige	B
2880	Dynaverse - Borg cubes appear very infrequently in Shipyard	C
2309	Dynaverse - Destroyed enemy ship reappears on Hex map immediately	A
2318	Tactical Sim - Visioneer opinion on buying Starbases	C
1681	Dynaverse - Officer advancement text cut off in message board	C
2452	AI doesn't know to go back to a repair station to repair hull	C
2981	Dynaverse - Severely damaged AI attacks healthy players	C
951	Dynaverse - AI does not team up properly in a Hex	B
2023	Dynaverse - Able to join missions in old Hex after leaving for new Hex	B
1790	SP - Tactical Sim - Able to click on map behind "Campaign Over" screen	C

All tasks have received a priority.

Bug ID	Bug Title	Priority
2929	CD-Key	A
2607	Campaign Screen - Player's ship gets stuck in Hex	A
3110	Dynaverse - Ten turn countdown results in stuck in Hexes	A
2637	DYNA - Map Screen not refreshing on completion of Mission	A
2641	Campaign Screen - Ships inconsistent for Convoy between Attacking or Defending	A
2765	Access Server not using list of IP addresses	A
2780	SP - General - Player can initiate a battle then auto move kicks in	A
2784	SP - General - Player can be attacked when auto move kicks in	A
2817	Dynaverse - "Stand by for mission briefing" panel repeats text	A
2309	Dynaverse - Destroyed enemy ship reappears on Hex map immediately	A
2979	Dynaverse - Fleets do not have accept / forfeit options in mission panel	B
3031	Dynaverse - Romulans can transfer in Borg officers	B
2561	Global - Freighter Convoys do not have escorts	B
2609	Tactical Sim - Fed vs Fed fights	B
2633	Dynaverse - While being attacked, attacking another will teleport player	B
609	SP - Campaign Screen - States we are partners with the Contested Sector	B
2763	Dynaverse - Role of convoys	B
2799	SP - General - There needs to be a message when auto move is enacted	B
2826	Dynaverse - Spectate does not work	B
2841	Campaign Screen - All races should begin equally allied to Neutral Hexes	B
2868	Dynaverse - Able to access buttons (campaign screen) anywhere on Hex map	B
2869	Dynaverse - Enemy AI kills fleet member AI - Defeat with prestige	B
951	Dynaverse - AI does not team up properly in a Hex	B
2023	Dynaverse - Able to join missions in old Hex after leaving for new Hex	B
2953	SP - Klingon Campaign - Beginning Stardate is 112400.1, twice what it should be	C
2987	Dynaverse - Hex changed color to red when Fed was leader and Kling was member	C
2617	Dynaverse - Jumped from Lt. Commander ranking to a Fleet Admiral ranking	C
2624	Dynaverse Campaign Screen - Fleet leader is not clear	C
2632	Dynaverse - Can make movement bar disappear when leaving a Hex with refit	C
2058	Dynaverse - Cause of numbers appearing after player names in the chat box	C
2119	New Conquest - Music stutters and pointer freezes loading new Conquest	C
2701	Global - When AI forfeits it stays in the Hex	C
2797	Hex information should appear in game display	C
2880	Dynaverse - Borg cubes appear very infrequently in Shipyard	C
2318	Tactical Sim - Visioneer opinion on buying Starbases	C
1681	Dynaverse - Officer advancement text cut off in message board	C
2452	AI doesn't know to go back to a repair station to repair hull	C
2981	Dynaverse - Severely damaged AI attacks healthy players	C
1790	SP - Tactical Sim - Able to click on map behind "Campaign Over" screen	C

And now they are sorted.

Resource Leveling

In a real schedule it will be much more likely that the bulk of your core tasks will fit in your schedule but one or two of your developers have been overscheduled.

If at the end you have leveled the tasks the best you can and you are still left with an overloaded resource, then you will have to take their tasks and run them through a rigorous task prioritization session with the spreadsheet as I described above. Find the true core tasks and relegate the rest to a secondary phase.

Hold on to your secondary and tertiary task lists. When you create schedules that your developers can accomplish, they will appreciate it and respond with timely execution. It is common for them to be excited and push themselves to see how many of the secondary and tertiary tasks they can pick up. See the next chapter on task tracking for more tips on how to keep your team humming along.

If you were conservative with your original labeling of core and secondary tasks and you did have a surplus of time, or if you had a surplus of time with part of your development team, then now is the fun time of piling on your secondary tasks until you are out of time with your resources. Use the detailed task prioritization method on the secondary tasks if you are having trouble deciding which of the secondary features you will implement.

Task Dependencies

Creating the schedule is not too bad so far, is it? Painful decisions about what will be a core task and what will be a secondary task is about the only

difficult job. A rather tedious job, I admit, entering tasks into Project, but mechanical and straightforward. Project planning enters a new level of complexity when task dependencies are taken into account. Task dependencies develop when one task depends on the completion of another task. A great example is all of your production tasks should be dependent on the completion of the preproduction milestone. After you have entered all your zero-level and core-level tasks (as well as any secondary tasks you found time for) you will now need to draw dependency lines between tasks that are *truly dependent* on each other. In Microsoft Project there are two easy ways to link tasks: One is to draw a link between two tasks by simply left-clicking on one task and dragging the pointer to another task and letting go. The other method is to simply type in the task ID number in the Predecessors column.

> **JARGON**: *Dependent tasks* are two tasks that are linked such that work on task B cannot start without the completion of task A. This makes task and resource leveling more complicated.

	❶	Task Name	Duration	Predecessors	Resource Names	Fri Sep 13
						12 AM / 2 AM / 4 AM / 6 AM / 8 AM / 10 AM / 12 PM / 2 PM / 4 PM / 6
1						
2						
3						
4		Buy Food at Grocery Store	1.5 hrs		Erik	Erik
5						
6		Make Lunch	2 hrs	4	Erik	Erik
7						
8		Eat Lunch	1 hr	6	Erik	Erik

An example of linking tasks

> >

Try not to link too many tasks; specifically, link only tasks that are dependent on each other. Some people, out of frustration with Project's leveling algorithm, start linking all kinds of unrelated tasks to get their project to flow in time the way they plan for production to follow. In other words, do not use the task dependency links to establish task priorities. Microsoft Project has a field for task priority for every task entry. Now run the Project leveling tool; if you are very lucky, all of your tasks will politely level out and none of your developers will be overscheduled due to the task dependencies you entered.

The resource usage screen; the red numbers indicate an overallocated resource.

Setting the priority level of a task from 0 to 999

Most of the time, however, entering task dependencies will cause one or more of your developers to go over schedule. Now you will earn some of your salt; this is an area where it is difficult to give general advice that will

apply to your specific overallocations due to dependencies.

You first need to study the Gantt chart and the resource usage charts to understand what your dependency problem is all about. In all cases your developer was okay before the dependencies were drawn in from the earlier stage where you determined the zero-level and core tasks. So looking back up the chain of tasks you will see one or more tasks that are holding up the show for your overscheduled developer. This will create a pocket of free time for this same developer earlier in the schedule as he is stalled waiting for work. Now the most elegant solution would be if the work he is waiting for is something he could do himself; then you can simply assign it to him and fix the dependency problem. And in turn you will need to take some other work off this developer and exchange it with the original developer who was the bottleneck before.

The resource usage report shows holes and gaps indicating a problem of one resource waiting on another.

The gaps filled by task reassignment

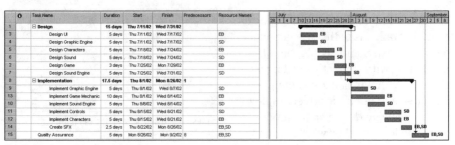

The Gantt chart of the fixed schedule

If exchanging and rearranging tasks still leaves you with a pocket of dead time and a later overallocation of one of your developers, then you will have to trim off the overallocation and bring up a secondary task to fill the void. That will be the best you can do if all other efforts to exchange, rearrange, and distribute the overallocated tasks fails.

The Top Ten Risks Document

By far the schedule is the major deliverable of the project plan, but there is one more document that is critical: the top ten risks document. For this document enumerate the ten most significant risks to the project. Choose only ten items; a longer list will lose its focus. With each of the risk items also list what actions you have taken or will take to contain or address the risk. Hopefully you will be able to create a positive solution to each of your risks; however, that is not a requirement. The important thing is to create a short, focused document with one through ten of your risks that you can share with your executive management and with your development team.

This document should be maintained with delivery of each of your development milestones from preproduction to the game's release. You will then see a much greater awareness from your executive management of the risks, and you should be able to address these risks with more energy. In fact, these short top ten risk documents are the most effective way I have found to communicate to my executive management just how much I need something: another programmer, two more artists, or timely audio asset delivery.

DATE: 3/1/02

Rank	Risk	Effect	Solution
1	Mission design slips	slip	Finalize Missions ASAP
2	User interface design slips	slip	Finalize UI ASAP
3	QA resources added late to the project	low quality, slip	More QA Resources earlier
4	Voice-over assets delivered late	slip	Finalize dialogue ASAP
5	Feature creep	slip	Stop adding features
6	Late solicitation to beta testers	slip	Submit to beta testers earlier
7	Server stability	low quality	Create testing tools
8	Design process overly distributed	washed out quality	Reduce number of authorized designers
9	Overextended use of overtime	slip, low quality	Address slip issues
10	UI overcorrected for mass appeal	lack of distinction	Fewer designers

A top ten risks document

> >

The Non-Zero Chance of Delivery

At the end of the day your job as the project planner is to create a plan for how long it will take to get the job done, *not the earliest possible date with a non-zero chance of delivery.*

>>>>>>>>>>>>>>>>>>>>>>>>>>>>>>>

Chapter 11 > > > > > > > > > > > > > >

Task Tracking

Production Begins—Now What?

Congratulations! You have made it through preproduction, your project is approved and funded, now all you have to do is follow your plans and make your killer game! This is a short chapter on how to track the completion of tasks and how to get the most productivity out of your team.

Task Visibility

You cannot just print out copies of your Gantt chart then surf the web for a year while your people make the game. *This will not work*. Even if you made the most professional Gantt chart ever, printed out in color and spiral bound. Passing out these project binders to everyone is an excellent idea, but if that is all you do to make your developers aware of their tasks and their team's tasks, then you will fail to get anywhere near your team's full production potential. I am not saying people are inherently slothful, no, quite the opposite— almost everyone I have met in the industry prides himself on his ability to work hard under a crunch to produce a hit game. It is just that left to their own devices, your folks will probably work on what tasks are most interesting to them unless they are reminded of where they are on the schedule and where everyone else is on the schedule.

The key is to make the tasks visible. Team members need to know in detail what they should be doing, and they need to know how the work they are doing correlates with others on the team. They need to feel a part of the team and share a sense of urgency to get the job done. As tasks are completed it should be communicated as quickly as possible to the rest of the team to give them a sense of the pulse of the project. I have some specific techniques to share with you to achieve strong task visibility.

The Wall

I have an effective, low-tech way of getting task visibility out to the team members: I print out the Gantt chart and/or task lists and pin them up on a central wall in our workspace. Software solutions such as Microsoft Team Manager and intranets to publish your schedules and tasks are distinctly unsatisfactory for two reasons: One, your developers need to remember to even open up the document or visit the site, and two, monitors are too small to show a whole Gantt chart, denying your team the appreciation of the project progress as a whole.

It is easy to print out your schedule and pin it up. I recommend just displaying task name and ID, start time, end time, who is assigned to it, and any predecessor tasks on the left-hand side and the Gantt chart on the right-hand side. You should use the widest time setting you have wall space for; when a schedule is scrunched up into just displaying quarters or months on the Gantt window, you are not getting any real-time information.

Now I make a requirement to my developers that they come out to the Gantt chart and mark the tasks off themselves. I do not mark them off even if I know they have been completed. This is to get the developers to come out and find their place in the schedule, mark off with a bit of pride what they have finished, and then look ahead to see what is coming up. Developers will almost always take the time to then look over the whole schedule to gauge how are they doing compared to other team members.

When I first started using this method of task tracking it was considered somewhat controversial. Some people asked me privately if this was a good idea. If someone were not accomplishing his tasks on time, would it not be demoralizing for him if this were made public knowledge? Would not that developer feel more comfortable staying in his office and explaining privately why he is behind in the schedule? Bah! My first assumption is that everyone

on my team is a professional, and even on an off day all would want to be treated as professionals. Why would protecting their comfort be of higher importance than getting our tasks done in a timely manner? If people are tasking late, they must have a reason. Was it illness? Jury duty? Task underestimation? Were they distracted helping another team member on another problem? All of these are legitimate reasons for being late and certainly nothing to cause embarrassment or discomfort. On the other hand, if they are late because they were just goofing off, then I feel comfortable making them squirm in front of their other team members and letting them know they have let the team down. Knowing that the whole team is aware of what they are and are not getting done goes a long way to inhibit goofing off.

A healthy bit of competition develops with a good wall. Assuming your schedule was a sane schedule and manifestly fair in the time allocated to the tasks to be completed, your team will be in a high morale state to begin with. I use brightly colored highlighting markers to mark off the tasks. Your developers will come out at the end of the day to mark off what they got done then look ahead for something simple to do before they go home—bam! Another task is taken care of! This competition effect will give extra momentum to your whole project. It will give your developers a meta-game to push themselves, and they will enjoy it.

Another benefit of the wall is that it makes a great piece of visual feedback to the executive management team. They look over the wall and see all the marked-off tasks spanning 25 square feet of wall space and nod to themselves and move along. Do not under-estimate the importance of reassuring your management that you are respecting their time and money and are making measurable, steady progress. If you are working in a large studio or in a publishing house, the other teams will see what you are doing and think you are obviously trying to get attention. So what—you are trying to grab management's attention. There is no glory in obscurity.

Encourage your team members to go ahead and write any unanticipated tasks they had to complete onto the wall's task lists. This will help team members who might be falling behind in tracking due to being sidetracked by tasks that were not originally on the schedule. While it may seem crude to scrawl new tasks on the list, it is legitimate. You are after the maximum visibility for all tasks, not just the ones you were smart enough to think of earlier.

When the time comes to update the schedule, the wall charts with the new tasks written on it and the completed tasks marked off will come in handy. Just tear it off the wall and bring it to your workstation where you have Microsoft Project.

Journals

I have a background in engineering, and while in school we were introduced to the value of a journal to record actions, observations, and data from the lab. The idea is that no effort you make should be unworthy of record. While I admit that when we make a game we are not building a skyscraper or a transorbital spaceship, we are still creating something important and we should take every care we can on the execution of our game projects.

The Cult of the Yellow Notebook

For the last seven years I have been using yellow notebooks that are about 5" by 8" inches and feature lined paper on one side and quad-ruled paper on the reverse. This format allows me to track micro-tasks and thoughts on the lined side, and use the graph paper for game designs, user interface layouts, and technical designs. I have this notebook open as I work, taking notes whether I am working at my workstation in Photoshop, MS VC++, Project, Visio, Excel, or simply Word. I also take my journal with me to every meeting to record what I need to do and what I need to follow up with. On a shelf in my office are the 40 or so notebooks I have filled so far in my career. These yellow notebooks are a staple that we purchase for all of the employees at Taldren, and we have an ample stock for when people fill theirs up.

I am passionate about these notebooks because I have seen countless small tasks fall through the cracks in our overburdened minds—such a waste that the simple act of note taking can fix! About once every two to four weeks I go back through my pages to search for tasks I might have failed to address, and I pull them forward into a new checklist.

Walk Around

There is no older and simpler method of task tracking than simply walking around and seeing how people are doing. I try to carve out an hour or two every day to walk around and meet with the individual team members to see how things are going. At this pace I would visit everyone in the company two to four times a month. This lets people know their work is important, and the human connection really shows you care about getting a great game done. When the project hits a tough spot you will find that you want to stay in your office and focus on the burning fires. But it is when the times are smoky that you should make the extra special effort of visiting with your team members. Also be aware that no matter how much you like everyone on your team, there will naturally be some personalities that you enjoy spending more time with than others. Some people might feel slighted so be sure to visit all of your team members, not just the ones you like to talk to.

Often it is by walking around that you discover that tasks you thought were the clear responsibility of one developer have been conveniently relegated to the no-man's land between two developers and have dropped to the floor. This is a great time to clear up such misunderstandings and get these tasks properly assigned. If you ask the right questions and remain approachable, these walkabouts will also turn up the deeper concerns your team members might have felt too uncomfortable bringing up in some other forum or method. Keep your ears and eyes open and *talk* to your team members.

Milestone Orientation Meetings

Another useful technique I have found is to kick off each milestone iteration with a milestone meeting to review what everyone is tasked with and what the associated expectations are for their work. I did not start this ceremony until just this year; however, each time I run the meeting I am amazed at how many misunderstandings we are actually carrying around, and this is on a project that has received our most detailed preproduction to date!

At these meetings I simply keep everyone in the room as I go through the features and tasks one by one and get a verbal discourse back from the responsible developer to be sure they understand what they need to do and to give them a chance to request clarification. They will also get full visibility for what they need to accomplish in front of the whole team; this goes a long way to fight the impression that so and so does not have much work to do.

Praise People Publicly

I also take the time to praise individual team members at each of these meetings—not necessarily everyone—but I do try to keep a running tab of who is due for some recognition. While no one I know would admit it, I think receiving praise and recognition from your team and supervisor is a great morale boost, and the lack of praise and recognition can be a significant drain on morale.

There are good books devoted to how best to reward your employees with all sorts of clever ideas from silver nameplates to holiday turkeys, but I think the best is a public thank you.

Maintain the Gantt Chart

By far the least fun part of project management is updating the Gantt chart. As you sit in front of Microsoft Project, none of the tasks will seem to have been completed on the days you planned. And so if you simply check off tasks as they are completed, you will be left with a schedule that is full of hard-to-move completed tasks that indicate they were completed on the wrong day. These blocked off dates will not be used in subsequent leveling operations, and soon your schedule will look like a mess.

No matter how tedious it is, do not put off maintaining your schedule for longer than a month. I have slacked myself and have regretted it every time. It just takes too much time to repair a badly out-of-date schedule. When a schedule is really in bad shape I sometimes just start a fresh Project file.

The latest version of Microsoft Project does have one simple new feature: It lets you move completed tasks back and forth in time! A minor miracle, I tell you. In the older versions you would have to unmark a completed task, move it to the time it was completed (or at least out of the way of the current task leveling concern), and then remark it as complete. This only made a tedious job twice as hard as it needed to be.

Take the time to enter in completely new tasks that your developers have taken the time to write on the wall. Also take a close look at any open tasks that are refusing to complete despite one of your developers working hard on the task. My bet is that if you look under the hood of that task, you will discover it is composed of multiple tasks, some of which have been completed. Take the time to break up this task into its component parts and give your developer credit for what has been accomplished. Quite often your developers will tell you that this or that feature is 90 percent done and that they clearly had to move on to more pressing tasks for fear of causing stalls in the project. Their judgment is almost always correct in that there was little profit in having them polish up some feature to true shipping quality when there are others waiting for them to finish something else. This is the same as a task that is really composed of subtasks. In this case the subtask is that final 10 percent of polish on the radar, which is unimportant to solve now. Take that 10 percent polish task and enter it into the schedule; just put it further down in time to when you really will take care of the polish task.

For larger projects I strongly suggest you delegate to your section leads the input and maintenance of their part of the schedule. This will help them grow a valuable task, and it will help you keep your job sane. To facilitate this I favor using a tree of inserted Microsoft Project files so that each developer can work on his section of the schedule. I discuss this in detail in Chapter 20.

< < < < < < < < < < < < < < < < < < < < < < < < < < < < < <

Update the Risks Chart

Rounding out the task tracking set of duties is to update the risks chart: Take the time to review your Gantt chart; is it indicating a new problem down the road? Are the artificial intelligence tasks tracking? How is the mission editor? How are the art assets coming along? How is the testing of the multi-player code coming along? Ask yourself these types of questions as you review the Gantt chart to see if a new risk has developed or perhaps an older risk has risen in priority. Also take a look at the old risks; have some of then lessened in importance or have they faded away altogether? Some new risks may be introduced from your walks around the team or from a daily journal type mechanism or simple email from your team members. Also take the time to review what you are expecting from your third-party vendors. Are they on time? The true impact of a risks document only comes into play when it is maintained like the project schedule. Be sure to visit with your executive management and apprise them of the latest risks. Post these risks in a public place so that all of your team can review them and have an opportunity to respond to them. After all, taking the time to discover your risks is a good idea, but sharing your risks with the rest of the team and management is key to getting focus on the problems. Of course occasionally you may develop a risk that is personal in nature and is not fit for wide dissemination. Use your common sense and discretion when choosing what to post on a wall.

> >

Chapter 12 > > > > > > > > > > > > > > >

Outsourcing
Strategies

Why Outsource?

Many talented folks can be involved in medium to large game projects from the obvious artists and programmers to writers dedicated to dialogue, to motion capture actors, to voice-over directors, to quality assurance leads. Artists and programmers perform the bulk of the labor on a game project, with these other specialized tasks occurring for relatively short blocks of time in midproduction.

Layers of game production—games are software with toppings.

As can be seen readily in this diagram, a single game project team requires full-time work from the artists, programmers, design, and management; however, the audio, dialogue, voice-over, motion capture, and other

specialized tasks do not occur as a steady task across the whole project. This means that to be efficient in the employment of these folks with specialized game development talents, we need to either be a large development house with many game projects in simultaneous production, or we need to *outsource* this work to third-party vendors who will execute these production tasks under our direction. Otherwise, audio and other specialists who cannot be gainfully employed across the duration of a single project would cause a financial burden on our projects.

Most game developers would much prefer to have generous budgets in order to hire in-house all of these experts and be able to work more closely with them to achieve the highest level of quality possible. There are a couple of problems with this approach: First of all you are burning prodigious cash whenever you cannot task them directly to your game project; when they are independent contractors you only pay for the work you need to get done. Second, it is difficult to find excellent people to fill these positions. The higher the quality you are looking for, the more likely the individuals would have risen to a key position at another developer or third-party production house or may even be the owners of their own production house. In short, it will take your organization a long time to build up the financial strength to employ multiple teams and find and retain excellent people for the non-core tasks.

Almost all organizations outsource to some degree; most publishers outsource *game development* to developers, and even those that internally produce their own titles outsource a multitude of tasks such as disk manufacturing and payroll management. Now, what are some good strategies and tasks to keep in mind when weighing outsourcing?

When to Think About Outsourcing

Your outsourcing plan, which describes what work will be outsourced, by what contractor, by what date, and for how much money, should be determined in the earliest parts of preproduction, ideally before the final budget of the project is decided. There is a natural tension here. The project needs an honest preproduction phase to figure out what tasks need to be performed and who can perform them. Many times we are creating new technology, and it will take a bit of experimentation to figure out how a particular kind of asset will need to be created. All of this planning will take a few people a couple of months—varying widely depending on the size of the project—which means this will take money. However, the way game projects work is that the publisher and developer have to come to agreement on what the final budget will be before any money is spent on the project. This requires an unpleasant choice for the developer: Either work without compensation during the preproduction phase to be able to rigorously determine the costs or enter into a fixed bid agreement with the publisher *and then* figure out how much the

project will cost. It is this tension that is a major source of business frustration in the industry and is the root of a considerable lack of profit for all concerned.

That is why I have dedicated such a large portion of this book to introducing outsourcing in all of its various forms. Experienced game developers make better educated guesses on the costs of various features and assets due to having been there before. Too often a project manager will arbitrarily budget X dollars for voice-over work and Y dollars for music, only to find that music requires more money and that the voice-over could get by with less money. This is fine if you catch this discrepancy before you approach either the music contractor or the voice-over director, but it is awkward indeed if you have already signed a contract with the voice-over director! This chapter only introduces outsourcing; several chapters in Part IV are each devoted to a particular type of asset for outsourcing. I hope to provide material for you to take advantage of so that you can begin planning your music needs as soon as possible on your project—before the entire budget parameters are fixed.

> >

What to Outsource

In short, you should outsource tasks that are not your core competency and/or are needed for a short period of time in your project. In other words, if your organization is weak at something, hire someone good to do it for you.

Do Not Outsource Programming— Exceptions Noted

A big exception to this rule is the programming. You should never outsource your programming tasks on a game project. A game is *software* and if you do not have the expertise to create the software, then you should hire the programmers for in-house production. If you do not have programmers on staff, you should not be making a game; make what you are good at. This is why a lot of publishers have outsourced game development; it is the most difficult and risky part of publishing games, and so they have externalized those risks to game developers. Almost all organizations can find a bucket of useful work for programmers to perform year round.

Occasionally I have heard of projects where the map editor, the video compressor, or some other modular tool-like portion of the project was outsourced to an independent programmer. This may work and is more likely to succeed the closer this task is to being modular and having few interdependencies with the game's development. This works especially well when you are not prepared to staff up and increase head count to perform this minor amount of programming.

Much more controversial is the outsourcing of the multiplayer portion of a game project. The several exam-ples I can think of where the multi-player was outsourced all ended with abysmal failure due to a lack of communication between the core team and the multiplayer team, as there are just too many interdependencies between multiplayer and single player to successfully outsource this area. The only exception that comes to mind is the case of Return to Castle Wolfenstein, an amazing game produced by id Software and developed by Grey Matter with the multiplayer portion of the project developed by Nerve Software. This worked well because Grey Matter was working with id Software's solid Quake III engine and could focus on the content creation. Likewise, Nerve had the same solid engine to work with and could work on multiplayer parts of the game without needing constant communication with Grey Matter. Thus, the work was modular and there were no awkward dependencies between the two projects.

Taldren has outsourced a couple of programming projects: We have had external folks create missions for Starfleet Command II, and we have had folks create a ship editor for SFC II. For the missions, it did not work out well because the scripting API was still being developed internally when we had to get started making scripts (a dependency). For internal teams this is not that big an inconvenience and happens on most projects; the engine development and content creation stages are often overlapping (it is, of course, much better to complete your engine before content creation starts). In the case of missions, we had to have more communication with the external mission programmers than was efficient, and we had to perform significant maintenance on the scripts later in the development cycle. The ship editor project worked out better because the folks came forward with a functional prototype of what they wanted to do and just wanted an okay to move forward on what was essentially their own independent project.

On Outsourcing Art

Art would have to be the next area I would be reluctant to outsource from my core development team. The outsourcing of art is probably the oldest and most well understood of the tasks to outsource. In the days when a single programmer was all that was needed to challenge the modest hardware, it was common to find an artist buddy and buy a month or two of art from him. Now most games have their own internal art teams to produce the required art for the game. There are, however, common exceptions.

Movies, Cut Scenes, or Full Motion Video

The most commonly outsourced art tasks are movies in a game. These movies are sometimes called cut scenes, in-game cinematics, or full motion video (FMV), depending on the technique used to create the movies and the role they play in the game. The reason movies are most commonly outsourced is that movies are a labor-intensive process that generally requires building assets in a format and of a higher quality than the game's engine and using tools and techniques that are not applied in the production of assets for the game itself. Large

development houses such as Blizzard and Square have developed very large and internationally recognized movie making teams.

> **Sideways Comment on Large Movie Teams**
>
> Again, you should outsource when you are contemplating work that is beyond your core competency or it would be an overall financial burden to staff up for this work. In the case of Blizzard and Square, both organizations have enjoyed so much historical success that they could easily afford to employ in-house movie teams. This allowed them to create movies that the rest of the game industry can only envy. There is a significant drawback to having a killer in-house movie team of such power—it needs something to do.

How do you outsource a movie? This is discussed in detail in Chapter 32. I will merely outline the process here. To prepare for outsourcing a movie it is best if your team has a competent storyboard artist who can communicate all of the scenes, actions, and assets that will be required in making the movie. If you lack a sketched storyboard, create one with just words.

Take your storyboard to a number of movie houses and ask them to respond with a fixed bid to perform the work. Be sure to define clearly what work you want them to perform. For example, if you want them to create a silent movie that you will later take to an audio house, specify that, or they might include audio in the quote. Also explicitly indicate if you will supply any of the models or other assets featured in the storyboard; otherwise they will assume they are to create these models.

> >

As the movie houses are responding to your bid request, follow up with their supplied references and ask people who have worked with them before if they are satisfied with the work performed.

In the end you will need to choose the movie house based on your own business parameters: fast, cheap, or high quality (which two of the three do you want?). Maybe one of the movie houses can do the work for you in a rush as you need, but at a steep price. Perhaps another has a key art director that *you know* will nail the movie and you are willing to pay her fee. Or perhaps there is a movie house with a substantial hole in their revenue stream and they are willing to offer a deep discount to keep things flowing. In the end, never grind so hard that you only force them to come back and ask for more money or to underperform the work to get by.

3D Models—Modeling

Almost all modern AAA games are 3D games: shooters, strategy games, role-playing games, and adventure games. The hardware is just so capable that it is pretty much uncompetitive not to be a 3D game. Most game development companies will have their own internal staff of 3D modeling artists. However, your project may be particularly 3D model intensive and you prefer to outsource than staff up, or you may simply be late and you need some extra modeling bandwidth to accomplish your project's goals. Or perhaps your development organization is relatively young and does not yet have 3D modelers in house; in any of these cases outsourcing your models would be a good idea.

How do you outsource a model? Models tend to outsource well because it is relatively easy to specify what you are looking for by way of a sketch and some technical details like poly count, and models are modular and largely have no dependencies on any other aspect of the project. Finally, it is fairly painless to inspect a model for completeness.

Approach several art houses with concept sketches of your model— spaceship, racecar, or whatever you need modeled—and provide a complete technical description of the format you need your model delivered in. Consult your own art director and graphics lead to determine if your models can have only triangles or if quads are okay. Determine poly count, and in addition to being textured, specify any other assets such as a damage layer, luminosity, or specularity. What file format— 3D Studio Max or other? Write all of this up and include other parameters such as required delivery date and send it out to the art houses you have prescreened based on the portfolios and references they have sent you.

Finally, as stated above, you must select your modeling team based on who is the best fit to your business parameters: fast, cheap, or high quality.

In Chapter 32 I will go over this in detail and provide a list of modeling houses for you to contact.

Animation and Motion Capture

What good would having a fleet of static character models be? Not much—that is why we invented character animation. Roughly speaking, characters can either be animated by hand, using what is called key framing, or the motion can be captured from the movements of a live human, called motion capture. In practice, almost all motion capture involves manual animation techniques to smooth out the noise in the data capture to achieve final quality motion as well as to create secondary motions such as facial expressions and hand gestures.

A key decision to make is whether you are exclusively key framing or are using motion capture. Motion capture will tend to produce more natural looking, realistic movement, usually also at a greater cost than key framing. Key framing, on the other hand, may be better for your game if you are *looking* for unrealistic movements such as a game featuring cartoon characters or a game about non-human animating characters. I provide a deeper discussion on the pros and cons of outsourcing motion capture in Chapter 33.

User Interface Art

How about outsourcing your user interface art? I have strong feelings about outsourcing your UI art. In short, don't do it! UI art is one of the most intimate bits of your game's art. It is the UI art that will need to be tweaked many times all the way through alpha and beta to get it just right and to accommodate new features and changes to existing features. There is almost no way I can see a contract to outsource this work; it is simply unfair to keep asking an artist contractor to revise over and over again the UI as the game progresses. Also, the changes in UI tend to be small and incremental and require an inordinate amount of communication between the programmers, designers, and artists to get right. An out-of-house artist would have to make far too many visits onsite to make this

work practical. It takes game programmers, game artists, a designer, and a producer to call yourself a game development team. Without someone representing all four of these key positions, you should not make games.

All of these warnings aside, I did successfully outsource the UI art on a gambling game that I ran back in 1997 when our game development house lacked art bandwidth. To address this we created what is fondly referred to as "programmer art" throughout the industry and kept on tweaking that art until we had exactly the functionality we needed. Then I turned that over to a great guy, Bradley W. Schenck, who I am happy to say is now one of my employees.

Audio

Audio assets, on the other hand, are an excellent and time-honored set of assets to be outsourced. Audio does not take as long as programming and art to complete. Each of the three major types of audio assets—music, sound effects, and voice-over work—require considerable talent, experience, a specialized toolset, and often contacts with other talented folk such as cello players that the rest of us do not regularly maintain (or at least I do not).

Music

Music is almost always outsourced, and only the largest of studios choose to keep a staff composer on hand. Keeping a composer year round would take an extraordinarily versatile composer as well as at least six major concurrent projects. Highly talented and skilled composers are readily available, and all the composers I have met are rather technical people quite interested in

> >

game work and willing to deliver their best to make the gaming experience the strongest possible.

The first step is to contact a few reputable composers and discuss the vision for the game project with them. Usually, people look into music for their game after a lot of work for the game has been completed. When that is true, it is useful to provide a tape of the game to the composer for review. You have to outline to the composer your total budget for music including post (unless you are taking care of postproduction yourself). Detail how many minutes of music you are looking for and how you would like to break down the music in terms of themes. For example, in Star Trek games we often create a Federation theme for when the player is playing as the Federation as well as themes for the other playable empires such as Klingon and Romulan. Themes are also broken into victory, defeat, battle, and suspense music. If you can, supply your candidate composers with some CDs of music that illustrate what you are looking for; this is as effective as providing a storyboard to illustrate a proposed movie.

Your candidate composers should then go away for a week or two and give your project some deep thought. They should then come back to you and give you their proposal of how they will approach the project: number of minutes and whether or not they will perform the music electronically or have live players. If they will have live players, they should articulate how many, the instruments, and the proposed venue for the live performance. As for providing a demonstration of the work, it could go two ways: First, the composer could deliver a small snippet in

electronic form; second, he might propose that a palette of new sounds be created before any actual composition work is performed.

Review the proposals and go with the composer you feel has been most responsive to your game. This is all discussed in detail in Chapter 28.

Sound Effects

Sound effects are another excellent set of assets to outsource. To effectively outsource this work, you must have a very good idea of the number of sound effects you are looking for and a strong description of each sound. The game developer creates a cue list of all of the sounds, indicating which ones loop and which do not, stereo or mono, bit-depth, and sample frequency.

Ideally, all of the in-game animation that corresponds to the sound effects should be complete (or complete as far as timing) with videotape of each of these animations available for the sound effects engineer to review while making the sounds. If you do not have the animations, then there will be a needless amount of revisions and the sounds will ultimately never quite fit the animation.

With your cue list and animation clippings in hand, select three different sounds that should test the range and versatility of the sound engineers. Send out the business parameters, time of delivery, budget, and delivery format as well as the entire cue list, and highlight the three sample test sounds you would like to hear from the sound engineers. If you send it out to half a dozen folks, you will probably end up with one or two who perform two of the sounds well and two or so who perform one of the sounds really well, and the rest just miss. Now comes judgment time. After getting it down to three or so choices, I go with professionalism: Which engineer made the best impression to work with? And finally, I get whomever I select to listen to the sounds another engineer might have done better in a particular case to better illustrate what I was looking for. The process of acquiring sound effects is detailed in Chapter 30.

Voice-Over

Almost all voice-over work is outsourced to some degree as very few of us make strong voice actors. Most top games these days employ SAG talent, and often quite high-profile stars are used. Voice-over work involves six roles: the talent, the director, the studio, postproduction, the producer of the voice-over work, and the game designers who specify what lines are needed in the game.

I recommend using a full-service voice-over house. The game designer wants to focus on designing the game, not filling out SAG union paperwork, finding studio time, and organizing the VO sessions.

Your job, in my opinion, is to design the game and come up with a VO script for all the actors in your game, not handle all of the mundane tasks associated with VO production. However, there could be the odd case where you have

the right facilities or the job you need done is so small that it makes sense to do it yourself. (I just have not seen a job too small to have it done right.) Chapter 29 discusses voice-over production in detail.

What Else to Outsource

Of course there are a few other types of work that could be outsourced. For example, if you are self-publishing something and want to sell direct to consumers, you should look into electronic software distributors and outsourcing your credit-card-taking activities.

Outsourcing web site design makes sense only if your team lacks both art and web skills; however, a web site design is usually well within the grasp of a game development team. Outsourcing the web site hosting makes good sense, and there is a wide variety of vendors available; the services are so standardized that it has become a commodity.

I have seen a few businesses advertise themselves as software testing labs. While I do believe they will perform very rigorous testing, I do not believe there is a good market for these folks to exist in—the ones I know of have failed. I believe you as a developer will need the facilities to test your own game, and any strong publisher will be sure to test your game.

> >

Chapter 13   > > > > > > > > > > > > > >

Shipping Your Game

Shipping Is a Phase

Shipping a game is not a point in time where the game goes instantly from production to a shrink-wrapped product on a shelf at Electronics Boutique; rather it is a process and a phase of the project. Arguably all of the game development process is in support of shipping the game, so shipping starts at the achievement of alpha with the team taking a feature-complete game and trying to make it the most polished game they can before the last final candidate is burned and turned into a glass master.

Great games truly become great in the shipping phase, and the masses of mediocre and almost-great games settle into mediocrity in the shipping phase. Sometimes the challenges are just too great to save a mediocre game in the shipping phase: too many bugs, development overran its time budget, the game's vision has been misplaced. Indeed all of the previous material in this book was set down in the earnest hopes of setting your game up for the greatest degree of success.

How Do You Ship a Great Game?

There is one way I know to guarantee shipping a great game: Simply play your game (and have others play your game) and keep fixing bugs, correcting flaws, tweaking balance, and performing wholesale changes to your game until it is the most fun, addicting game available. You will see your total dedication to gameplay and quality well rewarded with appreciation from your fans, critical acclaim, and probably strong sales. There is a large downside to this method though: You have no way of anticipating how long it will take to finish your game. Without that knowledge, marketing will not be able to put together a marketing plan, the sales-

people will not be able to sell your game into stores with early strength, fans will become frustrated waiting for the game, the game magazine cover that was so precious a year earlier is forgotten, the publisher may choose not to have an open checkbook, and finally, the ultimate sales of the late but great game may not support the additional time and money spent on the project.

In short, working on a game incrementally and without a plan until it is well done is a risky method of development, and only the top developers in the industry are such bankable game makers that they can routinely get away with this strategy.

‹ ‹

The solution to the dilemma of quality versus timeliness can be solved by continuously focusing your whole team's efforts and all of the resources available to you to achieving the widest bandwidth of play testing, balancing, bug detection and correction, and being as organized as possible in utilizing the time you have to make a great game. While a game is a work of art, the testing and tweaking part of the project can be successfully engineered. I do not claim that you will be able to fix all your bugs, correct all the flaws in your user interface, or actually be brilliant in your game design and balance. I just claim that I have some good suggestions for using your shipping phase time to maximum effect. This chapter acts as an introduction to QA on game projects while Chapter 18 discusses QA methods in depth.

Alpha—Feature Complete

The industry standards for alpha, beta, final candidate, first playable, and demo vary from publisher to publisher, year to year, and project to project. My definition of when a game achieves alpha is when it is feature complete.

What Is Feature Complete?

It can often be painstakingly difficult to decide if a game is feature complete. It is easy to say that a first-person shooter is not complete when the characters are not yet taking damage, but I would argue that if the texture artists want to keep improving the look of a level but the level is otherwise complete and playable, then you have a feature-complete level.

Additional Content

The gray area in my mind is what to do when you have the game feature complete, but you have some folks with extra time on their hands who could be used to make additional levels, models, or missions for your game—pure content. Do you go ahead and create this work after alpha, cut this content from the final game, or delay alpha? After all, alpha means that this is the first time the complete game is together in one place and is available to be played; should we not feel comfortable adding content to make the game fuller between alpha and beta? I think the answer to this question is feature specific; however, I have my own rule of thumb: If the potential post-alpha content feature is very modular with no dependencies on other members of the development team, if the game could ship without the additional content, and this additional content will have only a minimal need for testing, then I feel comfortable allowing this content after alpha. If this additional content would require significant testing or creates dependencies with other tasks, I then have to determine whether it is a core feature or should be cut.

Feature Trimming

If you are not quite done with your feature list but the anticipated date of alpha is looming close at hand, you should seriously consider changing the rules and cutting features. How much do you cut and how much do you move your alpha date out? Answering this question is why you are in charge. This

> >

is an exquisite balancing act where you measure input and influence from your executive management, your team, your fans, and most importantly your inner voice and choose a path to alpha. It is easy to say cut the features that are secondary and trivial and push for the features that are primary. How you make these choices is the hard part. For myself I line up all of the open features in Excel (I seem to take comfort in lining up features for the cutting block when they are neatly laid out in Excel) and just start calling out loud to myself "core" or "kill." After I have made my list of cut features, I print it out and take it to a team meeting. There I announce the fate of the features one by one with a stony, poker

face. My team has worked with me long enough to speak up for a feature that I have killed and attempt to make a resurrection. If they can make compelling enough arguments to me and the team to resurrect a dead feature, then they must identify a feature I have designated to live as a lesser priority than the feature they are arguing for and I swap them. By coming to the meeting well prepared, I am making an uncomfortable meeting—a meeting where the topic is a group failure to realize features—as comfortable as possible with strength and direction. This is tempered with the purpose of the meeting where the team members review my decisions and ratify the feature-cut plan.

Testing Plan

Now that alpha has been achieved and we have all of our features, it is time to test the game. At the beginning of the project we created a set of test cases from our use cases and requirements; now is the time to finalize the testing plan.

Publisher QA

For almost all major releases the publishers assume formal responsibility for the quality assurance of a game before it is released. Some very small projects have just a single tester, others have a team of six testers led by a lead tester, and some larger projects have dedicated single-player and multiplayer testing teams. Occasionally close to the final push new testers will be rotated in on a project to give the game some fresh minds. Other significant milestones such as alpha and beta may

enjoy the attention of a dozen or so testers for a week or two to verify the readiness of the game.

These dedicated QA teams are usually the only folks who are employed full-time to test the game. They should be the major source for bug detection and sometimes are invaluable in getting deep coverage on an elusive problem. These publisher QA teams will develop their own feature checklist for your game, and they will move around the feature list, testing as they receive builds, and perform full verification sweeps at a lesser frequency. The list that this QA team compiles will be considered the bug list that the other sources of bugs and flaws are added to. This bug list will be maintained in a database. Some publishers roll their own solutions, and others such as Activision employ a web-based bug tracking solution called PVCS Tracker. This QA team or a dedicated team will also perform compatibility testing for PC games to ensure that the game runs well across the spectrum of PCs from the minimum requirements to the latest hardware.

These QA teams sometimes do a great job, and sometimes they are uninspired in their testing of the game for a variety of reasons. My complaint with publisher QA is that as an industry, the publishers consider the testing positions to be low skilled and low paying. Of course, I understand how the executives at a publishing house would be hard-pressed to have a more enlightened view of their QA when a casual analysis would show that you are looking at people who are very young, at the beginning of their careers, who are getting paid to sit around all day playing the latest games and occasionally writing down their observations on the game. What skills could be involved in playing a game that you are selling to the masses? Why should you pay a premium wage for a position that has endless applicants?

If you were the manager of a professional baseball team, I doubt the thought to fill some open positions on the team's roster from the pick of Krispy Kreme's employee softball team would ever cross your mind. Hey, there are millions of softball players who would love to play ball professionally, and you could get them cheap too, but then they would not be *professional* ball players, would they?

Team Testing

Team testing is critical to the polish and balance of a game, and it is also one of the most difficult tasks to schedule.

The idea is to get everybody on the team to stop implementing new features and fixing bugs and take a fresh and hard look at what they have created. The development team will be the game's harshest critics; no one outside of the team knows the full potential of the team and the game, and the game's shortcomings will stand out sharply in their own eyes.

It is commonly advocated to play the game for 30 to 60 minutes two or three times a week. In my opinion it is costly to ask people to switch tasks, no matter the task, and to ask them to play the game for such a short period. I don't think you get a lot of quality information from that effort. Instead, I advocate a full four hours spent on gameplaying as often as your project can tolerate the distraction—once every 10 to 20 business days at the longest interval. With these longer play sessions your team will be able to really wrap their minds around the game and dig deep to get real feedback. Some of these sessions can be aborted after a relatively quick hour or two if you come across a fatal flaw that prevents the rest of the game from being appreciated. Also, it is not critical that every single team member participates in every play session; it is just important that the whole team feels a sense of ownership and pride in the game through direct play experience.

Often great leaps of inspiration will come out of these sessions, especially in the areas of usability and user interface. This is when the team is most likely to have an objective eye and look at a feature and say, "That sucks, let's do this instead." Having a festive atmosphere at these times, such as ordering pizza, will go a long way to making

> >

these sessions a loose, fun, and productive method of testing.

Project Leader Testing

Following the trend inward, from publisher QA through team testing, we arrive at project leader testing. The project leader, lead designer, project visionary, or whatever name you choose, is the one who is ultimately accountable to the gamers for the overall quality of the game—whether it is fun. The project leader should play the game thoroughly and often—more thoroughly than often. In a game such as Starfleet Command, I don't necessarily play every mission in depth before release; rather I play with all of the user interface and a lot of multiplayer, and I spend a lot of time thinking about how the game could be made better.

The project leader is the person who has to simultaneously decide what goes in and what is cut in the quest for fun. All the while the project leader must maintain the schedule. Only by playing the game directly will the project leader have a proper appreciation for relative importance of the change requests being showered at the game from all directions. It is also the project leader who must bear the responsibility for acknowledging critical weaknesses in the game that can only be corrected by large efforts. These weaknesses must be confirmed through the project leader's own experience with the game and must not fall into a trap of just responding to the latest cry for change.

Automated Testing

Almost all games would lend themselves to automated testing for at least a portion of the game. For example, many 3D shooters employ an automated camera test routine by randomly placing the camera in any valid point in the 3D level pointed in a random direction. Any resulting crashes, assert, or any other detectable fault can be trapped, and all of the relevant conditions such as the stack are saved off for a programmer to follow up with. Thinking of portions of your game that lend themselves to automated review is a great task for the programming staff to brainstorm about. For example, in Starfleet Command we have a mode I call Popcorn where we have AI controlled ships fighting each other in a random free-for-all, and when a ship is destroyed another is created to fill its place. Over time, most of the tactical game space is covered by these AIs smashing each other, automatically uncovering bugs in the tactical game as we go.

Focus Group Testing

Focus group testing is a quasi-science unto itself. Anyone can perform focus group testing; however, there is a growing industry of professional focus group testing folks. The idea is to put the prospective consumers in front of your software and watch everything they do. Observe every difficulty, every missed click, every indication of being lost through the use of cameras and direct observation. The idea is that anyone who is on the team or on the publisher's QA team is too familiar with the game to give true objective feedback. The focus group testing can result in your strongest ego-busting feedback (as in "this game sucks" or "this is stupid"). However much your pride might be damaged by the experience (many publishers do not let the development team observe the focus group testing), you must look hard and deep past their initial complaint and get to the root of their difficulties and address them.

We must remember we are making consumer software that people do not need to buy. Consumer software must work well right out of the box, and thus it is the first 15 minutes of use of your software that you want to nail. Recent mega-hits are known to craft the opening 30 to 120 minutes of gameplay to a much higher level than the rest of the game. This is where focus group testing shines; this is the best method to discover the flaws that your game is presenting to the new user right out of the box.

The most important task involved in a focus group test is to sort out all of the comments and throw away those that are purely frivolous, outrageous, or impossible to accommodate and then carefully review the more reasonable comments and develop a strong set of new directives to fix the user interface, usability, or other first-impression problems the focus group testers experienced. A large danger exists, however, of overreacting to the input from the focus group testers and creating flaws that will be apparent to the players of your game who are hooked.

Beta Testing

Beta testing should be a big part of the QA process on a strong PC title; it is probably the most rigorous way to identify design flaws, compatibility problems, and outright bugs. With a beta test, the developer or publisher distributes either the full game or more commonly a portion of the game via CD or electronically to either a closed or open set of beta testers. Mailing CDs

out to a few hundred beta testers is now a fairly reasonable cost as there has been tremendous competition among CD duplication houses. Last I checked, you could deliver a master CD-R to a duplication house and get them duplicated with four-color silk-screening for less than 40 cents each.

Unfortunately for console titles, beta testing is impractical as currently it would be far too expensive to get your beta test build duplicated by the hardware manufacturers to send out to the beta testers. With duplication fees at $10 and more per unit this could quickly get out of hand. Also, I am unaware of any console game that has ever had a beta test, and it may prove impractical to obtain the permission of the hardware manufacturer. I believe with the advent of the hard drive and built-in broadband access in the Xbox, we will see an electronically distributed beta test of the online games for the Xbox in 2003.

Open or Closed Beta Test?

The decision of whether your beta test should be open or closed is somewhat project specific. For example, if your game is a tightly scripted narrative game that may only be played once, such as Myst, I suggest that you do not employ an open beta test, as too many potential customers would see how to win the game and would not perceive the released version as having significant value.

Any kind of multiplayer game lends itself to open beta testing, with perhaps the Quake tests and Counter-Strike being the two strongest examples of an open beta test. In the Quake tests, id Software releases a demonstration/beta test of the game well before actual release, often longer than six months before release. These tests may have content that will not ship in the final game, and most certainly the game balance will change. What id is primarily looking for is feedback from the hundreds of thousands of users of their Quake tests for compatibility reports. As id games are creating the bleeding edge of games, id is very careful to have robust and reliable software so as to not alienate consumers. So despite having arguably the most advanced graphic engines in the game industry, id games run well on machines that meet the minimum specification with very few complaints at the final release. Also it acts as an early adopter, word-of-mouth marketing mechanism by appealing to the hardcore gamer's sense of being "elite" by getting in on the ground floor of a new game.

Of course another reason not to perform an open beta test is because your game is not up to widespread scrutiny. You are showing the world what your game is made of, and if it is not compelling, it would probably be better not to do an open beta test. Consider holding a closed beta test before an open test. The closed beta test may be performed with as few players as you like (I suggest between 50 and 500 people). This way you will receive reports on your most egregious flaws before the rest of the world sees them. The best way to conduct a beta test is to go in stages from 50 to 150 to 500 and then open. Then, at each stage you have fresh people looking at the game (and fresh systems to run your game on) while each time fixing the largest bugs before going forward.

In Chapter 23 I present methods for organizing your beta testers, soliciting and collecting bug reports, and communication strategies not only from development to beta testers but also between beta testers.

Manufacturer Testing

In the console world, the manufacturer will test your game thoroughly against their quality standards before allowing the game to be duplicated. This is probably the single strongest reason why console games generally ship in better condition than PC games. The hardware manufacturers are not nearly as motivated as the developer and the publisher to ship a game and thus can afford to be much more critical about the quality of the game. The reason for this is two-fold: There are at any given time scores to hundreds of games being produced for their platforms, so sending any one game in particular back to development is unlikely to materially affect their short-term cash position; and two, it is in their best interest to maintain the quality levels of games on their platform; otherwise the consumer could quickly become disillusioned and wander off to another game console.

The manufacturer's quality standards are typically written up at an early stage of the platform's life cycle and updated from time to time, with a certain amount of the rules being an oral history. Also note that between large territories such as Japan and North America, the standards on something as basic as the common accept button on the controller differs from the X button and the O button.

The great thing about a console of course is that compatibility testing is not a large task. Rather, the game must be eminently playable, with short load times, high frame rates, and very forgiving gameplay relative to a PC game. In Chapter 23 I discuss how to better prepare your game for the hardware manufacturer's testing process.

Licensor Testing

When you create a game based on a licensed property such as our Starfleet Command series based upon *Star Trek*, the licensor (the folks who own the intellectual property) will usually enjoy some sort of signoff authority on the game's look, feel, and content to be sure your work supports the license and does not infringe upon other properties.

Typically the licensor will be involved at the game's conception and take deeper looks from time to time during the project, especially paying attention to the finished game design document, the first playable build, the beta build, and the final release candidate.

Occasionally you will work with licensed material where the licensor does not have any approval rights over your work. That was the case also in Starfleet Command for the Star Fleet Battles material developed by Armadillo Design Bureau, which we used to base our core game mechanics upon. It was critical in the case of Starfleet Command that we have *only one* licensor with final design approval (I shudder at the nightmare of having two!). It is very important to maintain a great relationship with your licensor as most often they are not in the game business and they may not immediately appreciate what you are trying to achieve with their property. You do not want them to be close minded about the liberties you will likely need to take to create a great game.

How Do You Balance a Game?

Game balance is the finest art in game making. It is painstakingly difficult to analytically describe what a balanced game is or present a method for developing balance in your own games.

The simpler the game and its game mechanics, the closer to perfection your balance will need to be. For example, the game chess has had its rules tweaked and refined over the centuries. Many years ago, the rules changed from the queen being able to move only a single square of distance like the king to her present powers of destruction. Later, pawns were given the ability to move one or two squares on their first move. In response, the move en passant was created to rebalance the game after the pawn was given this two-square option for first move. With the advent of powerful computers, previous end games that were thought to be theoretical draws have been won by computers that found winning sequences—some after more than 200 non-capture moves! The purpose of these rule changes has been to achieve a perfectly balanced game. At the professional level, there are scores of rules involving adjournment, time controls, and a host of other details that are adjusted as we strive to create the perfect game of chess. This refinement is also occurring in professional sports where many minor rules are made or adjusted that are not apparent to mainstream viewers.

The general idea with game balance is to start with the most dominant rules and balance those first and work your way out slowly to refine the secondary and tertiary rules. The following diagram illustrates how we prioritized game balance in Starfleet Command 3.

For example, in a first-person shooter, first determine how fast you want the characters to run, turn, and jump before you determine the damage and rate of fire of the plasma rifle. In a real-time strategy game, determine how much the basic grunt units will cost to build in time and resources before you determine what the zeppelin brigade will cost. Work your way outward.

For PC games, the beta testing cycle will provide you with plenty of feedback about game balance, especially if there is a multiplayer option to your game. I believe it is between

humans, not against the computer, that you will have a strong enough opponent to develop true balance.

I have discussed how to achieve balance but not what balance is. I regard a well-balanced game as one that delays as long as possible the point at which it is apparent to the loser that he will lose the game. As soon as the loser is certain of his doom, the game becomes uninteresting and the loser will want to quit. You want this realization to be as close as possible to the last moment in a game. Storytellers know this intuitively, as every time a chess game is used as a prop in a movie or a book, the winner cleverly checkmates his opponent in some surprising manner that the loser was not anticipating.

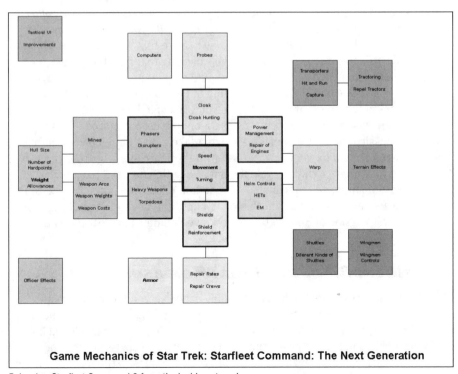

Game Mechanics of Star Trek: Starfleet Command: The Next Generation

Balancing Starfleet Command 3 from the inside outward

For many games there is not a clear winner or loser. In games such as SimCity, you play as you do with a toy rather than play a game. It is still important to balance these games though. Here again, the goal is to prolong the moment of manifest ending. Instead of losing the game, a play-oriented game must provide a lot of simple game mechanics that interrelate with each other, like Play-Doh and Legos building upon each other. The goal is to create an apparent endless amount of replay through different scenarios. In SimCity a friend of mine wanted to find out what it took to map the entire city with Arcologies, and I would build my cities up into greatness only to wreak devastation and let the simulation run overnight to see if the city would recover without my guidance.

Final Candidate Cycle

The final candidate cycle is where *everything* comes together to make a game. The final candidate cycle produces many war stories of not going home, missing FedEx deadlines, and finding obvious bugs that have somehow escaped every form of testing to date. Strong development teams bond even closer during the final candidate cycle, and unhealthy teams sometimes turn on each other with team members scattering to the four corners of the globe as soon as the game ships.

It is extremely important in your final candidate cycle to make as few changes as possible to your game. This means that you should fix very few bugs during your final candidate cycle if you have a fixed ship date that cannot move. I learned just how important this is with the first version of Starfleet Command. During the final two weeks before we shipped we fixed probably 100 bugs. As soon as the final candidate was off to duplication we began to find more bugs in the game. The bugs we found in the first week after having the game sent off to duplication were all bugs that were created *by fixing other bugs late in the final candidate cycle*. I now believe that when you are approaching that final two weeks, you should document all of the bugs you find in the second to last week and not change a single line of code (maybe data-only fixes, but no code fixes). Then take a long hard look at that bug list. If there are any bugs that you cannot live with, you need to alter the schedule to provide not only time to fix the bugs, but also time to have a clear two-week buffer to retest the entire game.

Transition, Ship, and Point Release

This chapter illustrates that shipping a game is not a single event in time where the gold master is handed over for duplication; rather it is a phase that starts as far back as first playable, through alpha and beta testing, through final candidate, and on into commercial release. For PC games there is often the compelling need to patch and balance your game post-release. The largest PC games in the industry, the massively multiplayer games, perform

> >

the greatest amounts of post-release work. That is why they have not only what are called transition plans to go from development to release, but they have *transition teams* to hand off the project to a *live team*.

Console games have had to live up to a much higher standard of quality in the late 1990s as compared to PC games, as there was no opportunity to patch a game after release. The strongest PC developers and publishers release games of the same or even higher quality standards of a console game and do not *rely* on post-release patching. Rather, companies like Blizzard and id Software use point releases as an opportunity to offer additional

content, fine-tuned balance based on customer feedback, and the occasional bug fix for a particular piece of hardware incompatibility. Increasingly, as PC games incorporate more multiplayer and online gameplay, the post-release patches are often required to perform critical cheat-prevention measures. Now that consoles such as the Xbox are shipping with hard drives, it will be interesting to see if publishers have the stamina to remain as rigorous as they have in the past or if they start to slip and offer post-release support that starts off with additional content and later degrades into mere patches. In Chapter 24 I discuss how to best manage your point release efforts.

Part III > > > > > > > > > > > > > > > > >

Game Development

> >

Chapter 14 > > > > > > > > > > > > > >

The Vision Document

All games need to be sponsored by some sort of bankroll. It might be Lara Croft's money at Eidos, or it might be some sweat capital from some young guys in Texas. At any rate, all games will need that signoff before they are able to proceed. For modern games capable of competing with the main field this is a tidy sum indeed. Many aspiring game developers have asked me and others in the game industry this question: "Hey, um. So I have this great idea for a game, how do I get it funded?" The truth of the matter is there is no magical formula; each and every game project has had its own path to funding. That being said, all games need some sort of outline or vision document that explains to an executive team why this game, of all of the hundreds of game proposals they have received, needs their support and attention.

The vision document (also known as the concept document) is an executive summary of the game design document that touches upon all the key features of the game in such a manner to grab them and get them to request to see the game demo and move forward with a deal. Despite this rather pragmatic use for the vision document (I know, I know—you are a creative sort and are not really interested in the dirty details of raising money), it does serve

a noble purpose in keeping the game's focus clear to all stakeholders in the game including the development team.

Write the Vision Document Twice

This chapter on creating the vision document has been placed before the main chapter on creating a design document on purpose. The writing of the vision document begins the moment a game is conceived. Lawrence Block, a very successful mystery writer, advises in his book *Telling Lies for Fun and Profit* that inexperienced writers should actually start off writing novels instead of short stories. The reason is that it is much more difficult to find just the right words and say something important in a few words than it is to stumble around and write a few hundred thousand words and hope that your readers will entertain themselves on the way.

Your vision document, you hope, will win the equivalent of the year's best sci-fi short story award and be picked up by a major publisher and help motivate your team to its best efforts.

The only way to make this document tight and strong is to write it, seek out criticism, and revise the vision document. You will learn a ton about the game you are proposing to make as you perform your game design and technical design processes. So I

< < < < < < < < < < < < < < < < < < < < < < < < < < < < < <

advocate revising your vision document again at the end of the design phase.

So Is the Vision Document a Proposal?

A formal proposal would contain the vision document plus a schedule, a budget, the team bio, and the company's history. Some folks put their proposed budget and schedules straight into their vision documents. I think it is better instead to keep the budget as a separate document, the schedule as a separate document, and your team bio/company history as another separate document. The reason for this is that it usually takes a long time to sell a game project, and you will most likely learn important new facts about your game that will materially affect your budget and schedule as you are circulating the vision document. What usually happens is that you mail out or drop off your vision document (possibly with a VHS of gameplay) with a publisher's business development person, and your proposal sits on their desk for a while until they call you up and want to learn more. I have had publishers call me six months to a year after I passed them a proposal, and I have had publishers visit my studio without having yet seen the vision document. Each relationship is unique, and you should hold onto the schedule and budget information until you have firmed up interest from the publisher and your facts are as current as possible.

Thus I recommend you prepare a separate document that features your company, discusses the management team, highlights the strengths of the key employees, and indeed discusses all of your employees and resources. A game company is not about a single star developer, but rather about a team. This document will come in handy to pass out to other potential partners of your team that are not necessarily publishers looking to pick up a new title; for example, you may want to pass it over to your local NVIDIA developer relations representative.

Instead of placing the schedule and budget information with the vision document, focus on getting the publisher to visit your shop and meet your team and firm up interest. When your prospective publisher is ready to know about the budget, don't worry, they will ask.

Only 1 Percent Catch the Eye

When I was working at Interplay as a senior group producer, my boss at the time resigned and was so distracted by his new prospects that he forgot to come back and clean out his office. His office sat that way for two weeks while I wondered what should become of his office. Is there not some sort of standard plan for cleaning up an executive's office? Presumably there are contracts and stuff in there, right? Well, being the temporary senior guy in the division, I shrugged and went in there with a few boxes to start cleaning it out. The most interesting thing about the abandoned office was the more than 200 game proposals/concept documents/vision documents that were lying about in stacks. I boxed these up and took them to my office and looked at them for a while. Then one night Sean Dumas (one of my two partners at Taldren) and I sat down and looked through all of them critically as if it were our own money we were looking to invest and wondering which games we would pick up. After leafing through the more than

200, it came down to just two vision documents; only 1 percent looked like they were potentially worth backing to us. Why these two vision documents?

Both were carefully prepared with oversized paper, liberal use of colorful graphics, and unusual bindings, and from page 1 we understood what the proposed game was about and were compelled to keep leafing through the vision document learning more about the game. We found that we wished we could go and meet the guys who put together these two vision documents. That is what a good vision document will do for you; it will attract people to come and meet you and see what you are all about.

What About the Precious Game Secrets?

Some people might wonder about passing out their game's secrets to people they have never met. Even worse, some big publisher might just steal their idea! I have never seen or heard of this actually happening. The industry is full of game concepts; virtually every developer I know of has his own pet game project, and some have cabinets full of them. Very few people in the industry want to use someone else's idea in place of their own. If your vision document is compelling, they will want to meet your team. Making a great game is far more work then coming up with a strong idea, and all of the publishers know that.

In fact, after a publisher develops interest in your vision document, the most likely game deal will be that they meet the team and place one of *their* ideas in your team's hands to execute.

Visuals

The vision document must be liberally illustrated with images—both concept art and screen shots—to accurately convey the gameplay as well as give the game life in the hands of the reader.

Select one single image, most likely a concept image, to grace the cover of your vision document. This one image alone should convey the game.

Throughout the rest of the vision document be sure to place a striking visual on each page that helps reinforce the topic of the pages. For instance, if you were making an RPG, the section on backstory should feature an outdoor shot giving the reader an impression of what the world is about and another drawing of perhaps a character in full gear on the section on character creation.

The document as a whole should be somewhere between 5 and 20 pages. Most people would suggest keeping it at the lower end of the range, and I would instead say keep it at the longer end of the range if you have strong visuals to carry the extra material.

Another idea for visuals is to use a full page to illustrate the controls in your game proposal. Use a picture of the controller itself with annotations describing the function various controls perform.

Another striking use of visuals is to illustrate your proposal with logos— your company's logo of course, the game title's logo, but also include the PS2, Xbox, or GameCube logo if you are proposing a game for those platforms. If you are licensing an engine such as Unreal, Quake, LithTech, or

< < < < < < < < < < < < < < < < < < < < < < < < < <

NetImmerse, then by all means place their logos on the page where you discuss your approach to developing the game.

Tactile

The actual physical binding of your vision document is very important. At Taldren, each of our proposals has been bound in a unique manner: a wooden and brass screw setup for a horror-western game, an American Indian inspired design featuring beads and feathers (our most impressive), and Black9's metal binding. These bindings do not need to cost a lot; the metal bindings for our Black9 proposal were made from two 90-cent steel joist straps bound together with two 10-cent bolts! Use oversized paper and consider using a landscape format instead of the normal portrait layout for your vision document.

Most of those 200 vision documents that I dismissed were presented in regular report covers that one might use for a freshman English composition class, some were just stapled pages without any formal binding, and one was submitted in a peach folder! You might accuse me of being shallow; however, Sean and I read every single vision document, and there was a rigid one-to-one correlation between the quality of the game concept and the presentation of the game concept. If you do not care enough to make your best impression, why should anyone else care enough to fund your project?

The physical presentation of the Black9 vision document

What About the Words?

Yes, of course your vision document should include a carefully selected set of words to communicate the game's vision. What are these words?

The hook: In just one to three sentences describe the hook of your game. I personally cringe every time I hear a movie-type person say something like "It's *Shrek* meets *Fast and Furious*." Your mission: Say why the world needs your game for its unique offerings, yet simultaneously reassure the funding source that it is substantially derivative in either gameplay or licensed content to assure certain success. Yep, that is why it is unique, compelling, and more of yesterday's hit at the same time. That last bit might sound a little cynical, but I am very sympathetic to the problem; regardless of the size of the risk it is just common sense to make a piece of entertainment software that many people will actually "get." No points are awarded for eclectic artistic expression in the game industry; save that material for the National Endowment for the Arts.

Touch upon every major feature in your game. Think about the back of the box and what the marketing messages will be for this game. You must be the champion for your game at this point and put on your marketer's hat. Don't be modest; now is the time to be the confident showman. Marketing is all about the art and science of getting people to buy what they are told, and you must be the one to start the sales pitch.

After you write up the first pass of the vision document, I recommend taking it down to your local copy shop or coffee shop or anywhere your target audience may be hanging out. Let them casually leaf through the vision document and see if they like it. My favorite is the copy club where we sometimes get stuff copied and bound. I put an extremely deadpan look on my face as if I were an overworked office drone, and I plop the vision document down on the counter and ask for it to be bound. Then I watch the clerk's eyes very

carefully. If he starts leafing through it and comes back to you saying, "Whoa, this is cool, so are you guys making games or what?" then you know you are on the right track. If he could not be bothered to leaf through it, then you should consider taking it back to the conference room table and discussing with your teammates how to spice it up. (You can see that I like to beta test everything!)

I would actually say very little about the development team inside the vision document; that is what the team bio and company history are for, and you would be handing them out simultaneously. Instead, have the vision document focus just on the game.

Contact Information

Always place your contact information on the last page of the proposal. List phone numbers, email, fax, street address, and phone extensions. Don't put any barriers in the way of a prospective nibble on your vision document!

> >

Chapter 15 > > > > > > > > > > > > > > >

Requirements Gathering

The key to successful game development is planning, and you cannot create a good plan without understanding what goals or requirements your plan must fulfill.

Where requirements gathering stops and requirements analysis and game design begins is in reality a bunch of fuzzy borders, and you may certainly consider the requirements capture stage the first step towards creating a game design document.

In traditional software development you have customers that have a need fulfilled, for example, ATM or inventory control software. In games we of course have customers, and when working on sequels there is usually no shortage of customers expressing desired features. But for original games your customers do not yet exist. This makes it a bit more challenging to determine your customers' needs. Instead, as a game development team you will need to look into your creative minds and work with your publisher's executive and marketing teams to develop the requirements for the game.

The Flavors of Requirements

There are many types of requirements that are routinely placed on a game such as creative, functional, technical, fiscal, licensee, and temporal requirements. Perhaps LucasArts has approached your team and has requested a proposal for a *Star Wars Episode I-II* RTS exploiting your game engine to be delivered by Q4 of the following year. This request for a proposal has touched upon a great variety of requirements, and you must build these requirements out before you are able to submit a bid of any confidence.

Creative/License Requirements

With our hypothetical example of a *Star Wars Episode I-II* real-time strategy game, we are able to rapidly understand the creative space to build the proposal around: The ground assault mechanized units should not be the AT-AT walkers from Episode V, the game should not feature Star Trek Enterprise E's floating about, etc. Now this is a fairly easy example to understand; however, take the Star Trek license. In the years that my company has worked on the Starfleet Command series, Viacom has seen fit to license out portions of the Star Trek universe to Interplay, Simon Schuster, Hasbro, and Activision. The licensees of the modern eras like Voyager and Deep Space 9 could and would

< < < < < < < < < < < < < < < < < < < < < < < < < <

sometimes feature material from the original series via some sort of time travel mechanisms. This would of course irritate Interplay, which held the TOS license, as it waters down their "exclusive" license. Even more wild is that the Star Trek universe features forward time travel, and indeed Harry Lang at Paramount's licensing group agreed that it was certainly plausible for Interplay to request to use Next Generation material!

Even more complications arose with the fractured licenses; Interplay was the oldest licensee at the time with the most vaguely written license. For Starfleet Command 2 we proposed to create the online Dynaverse with substantially the gameplay of a massively multiplayer game. Activision at the same time had spent quite a large sum of money to wrap up all of the licenses under their banner and demanded to have the exclusive license on massively multiplayer games. So who had the rights—Activision or Interplay? It looked like Paramount briefly sold the same thing twice inadvertently due to the age of the Interplay contract. The frustrating thing about it was during the development of SFC2 we were required to never refer to SFC2 having any kind of massively multiplayer gameplay. We struggled for months to help Paramount find the language that would best market our game yet at the same time not require Activision to more actively defend their license.

So you can see from the example of Star Trek above, that licensing requirements may sometimes be difficult to understand and document clearly. I understand that the game industry is currently entertaining two entirely

independent Lord of the Rings licenses: one license derived from the book and the other from the movie! Goodness grief! Regular folks like us would not think to cut a cake so cleverly!

Take your time and understand exactly what license you have in your hands. Find out if you are able to kill major characters in your game. This is an important feature for many games as they are not a linear medium; you must allow the player to explore different options whether it is a role-playing, strategy, or action game. Games must almost always allow for alternate possible histories. Determine whether or not you are allowed to create new material for the license, and how the approval process works for adding this new material (forget about owning the new material; no license holder of any property with value would allow the ownership to become fractured).

Technical Requirements

The technical requirements are mundane requirements such as the publisher requiring that the game ship on one CD or one DVD as that will significantly lower the cost of goods sold.

The hardware manufacturers of the consoles have many dozens of individual technical requirements like how long you are allowed to load a mission or level, and what buttons on the controller may be used for what purposes. By and large these console requirements are born from many years of experience that aim to provide the players with the best gaming experiences. The nice thing about these requirements is that you will not be given any opportunity to negotiate these items so you may free yourself from that

> >

responsibility and just get on with designing your game to fulfill these console requirements!

Other technical requirements include minimum frame rates, and for the PC game market you will need to identify your system requirements:

System Requirements for BioWare's Neverwinter Nights:

	Required	**Recommended**
Operating System:	Win 98/ME/2000SP2/XP	Win 98/ME/2000SP2/XP
CPU:	Pentium II 450 MHZ or	Pentium III 800 MHZ or
	AMD K6-450 MHZ	Athlon 800 MHZ
Memory 98/ME:	96 MB	128 MB
Memory 2000/XP:	128 MB	256 MB
Hard Disk Space:	1.2 GB	
CD ROM:		8x
Audio System:		DirectX certified
Video System:	16 MB TNT2-class OpenGL	NVIDIA GeForce 2/ATI Radeon
	1.2 compliant video card	
DirectX:		version 8.1

Of course, the lower your system requirements, the broader the base of consumers' machines your game will run on. However, the broader your requirements, the tougher it will be on the programming team to develop an engine that will simultaneously take full advantage of the higher end of the machines available and not leave behind the machines that just barely meet the minimum spec. The decision on where to set the minimum specification is usually a negotiated discussion involving the marketing and development teams, and both sides need to keep in mind what the targeted market is for the game. First-person shooters from id Software generally push the world's computers into the future, and Sesame Street games for kids need to work on pretty much any machine out there!

Fiscal and Temporal Requirements

Know what your budget of money and time is and be prepared to design your game around these parameters. Much discussion earlier in the book has been devoted to this subject. I feel comfortable sharing with my team members the overall budget numbers we have to work with as I find it empowers them to make stronger contributions to the design and overall production of our games.

Use Case Diagrams

Traditional software development would interview the future customers of the software and create use case diagrams to document these interactions between the user of the system and the software. That would indeed be a requirements gathering activity; however, that is essentially impractical in games. The game designer must step forward and lend his magic to the

‹ ‹

process and design these player (user) and game (system) interactions. As this process is more of a creative design activity rather than a formal requirements gathering process, I have placed the discussion of the use case diagrams in the next chapter on the game design document.

The Design Document

The design document is the soul of the game. Some design documents exist only as visions in their designer's head, and others consist of hundreds of HTML linked pages complete with a version control system tracking the changes to the design document. Most other game design documents lie in between these two extremes.

My goal in this book has always been to focus on sharing what I know about the production and development of games and to shy away from being a book about game design. There are already several of those at your local bookstore, and despite the heavy emphasis on rigor and process throughout this book, I still feel that the true *game design* process is an art form that is difficult to put on paper. How does an artist decide what will be a moving piece before he creates it? I do not know, and I would be very depressed to learn that someone has figured out the emotional magic to art and has developed a formula that someone else could follow.

Thus, I will focus on how best to articulate your game design document and only touch upon some of the creative processes that might be involved in developing the game design ideas.

What Does the Game Design Document Do?

Obviously it communicates what the game should be to the development team, but let's take a closer look and examine what that implies:

1. The programming staff must be able to pick up the game design document and efficiently develop the technical requirements and technical design for the software that is needed to be developed for the game.

2. The art team led by the art director must be able to read through the game design document and understand the look and feel as well as the scope of the art assets involved in creating the game.

3. The game designers on the team must understand what areas of the game require their detailed hand in fleshing out such as 3D levels, dialog, and scripting.

4. The audio designers must understand what sound effects, voiceovers, and music need to be created for the game.

5. The marketing folks should understand what themes and messages they need to use to build the marketing plan around.

6. The producers must understand the various components of the game so they are able to break the game down into a production plan.

7. The executive management team must be able to read through the game design document and develop all of the required warm and fuzzy feelings it would take for funding.

That is certainly a heavy list of customers for this game design document! Not just a sketch of the game world and some descriptions of the monsters, huh? To deliver on all of the above effectively, we should be organized about the task.

The Game Design Document as a Process

The game design document is not something you simply dash off over the weekend. Instead, it is a process that must be carried out over time by a team of game developers for a game of modern complexity and scope.

Game Concept

This is the classic step of imagining a game that you would love to create, a game so compelling that you wish you could play it yourself, *right now!* This is the sort of task you could accomplish over the weekend or just an evening. At Taldren this usually occurs late at night after some milestone has been accomplished through a non-trivial amount of blood and sweat, and we lie there in exhaustion and begin to have glimmerings of what we would love to create next. This magical process I cannot help you with; you either have it in you or one of your team members has this juice. The next step is to document the vision.

Write out just two or three pages that describe the game to your most intimate development team members. Don't take the time to justify anything —just write. After you have nailed the core idea and the excitement behind your game, gather your team into a

conference room with a whiteboard and stacks and stacks of different colored Post-it notes. What, didn't you know that Post-it notes stick well on whiteboards?

Brainstorm

I have designed games by myself and with others. Games that are designed by committee are usually horribly muted game designs and games that are designed by solo individuals often contain spikes of "game design noise." Think of all of the minds churning out game design thoughts as sound sources making sounds of all different shapes, intensities, and durations. And now think of the process of culling these design thoughts down into a design document. It's easy to see each individual will bring his own bias, perspective, wishes, and agenda to the design. If you allow a solitary individual to make the game, you have the purest expression of art in a game, and the game will simply hit or miss upon this one person's vision. The trouble with this approach is that games are now very large projects. The Interplay game Planescape had over one million words of dialogue; that is enough for ten novels! It takes an exceedingly talented, skilled, and

> >

hardworking designer to perform the design solo. On the other hand, think of a committee of designers where each member has the ability to censor an idea. This will act as a low-pass and high-pass filter allowing only the ideas that everyone may agree on to pass through. The result will be insipid, derivative games without any reason for being created.

The game design process requires a lead designer with a team of designers below contributing to the overall design. Let me show you how this would work in the initial brainstorm session:

Open the brainstorm meeting, having already passed out the game design document some 2 to 24 hours beforehand so that the game concept is fresh in everyone's mind. Next, take your stack of colored Post-it notes and create a colored key of topics along one of the lower corners of the whiteboard. (By the way, did I tell you to get a *large* whiteboard? We have found a great deal at the local Home Depot hardware store: 4-foot by 8-foot whiteboards in the raw without a border or frame for $11! Compare this to hundreds of dollars for a whiteboard of comparable size at the local office superstore.) This key of colors should include a color for audio, technical, art, game design, level/mission design, backstory, user interface, controls, marketing, and miscellaneous issues.

Now with your color key on the whiteboard, open the floor. You are now soliciting ideas, concerns, areas of discussion, notes, tasks, *anything* worth noting belonging to any of these categories. If you find there is no appropriate category available, use the miscellaneous category or create a new one.

Anything goes; stand up there with a good fat felt tip pen and dash off the notes with only one concept per sticky and put it on the board. Continually rearrange your stickies for better logical grouping of the ideas. Here is a stream of possible ideas: power-ups, level designers, hire lead animator, 3D engine, user extensibility, new chat system, dark color schemes, transparent menus, Chinatown, Old West, steam locomotives, lip-synching, use Patrick Stewart for voice, finish by Q4 2008, and so on. Litter your whiteboard with concepts.

I have found this whiteboard brainstorm method to be a powerfully effective method for rapidly digging up tons of new issues that I and other members of the development team must follow up on in the course of the design process.

Delegate Design

After about one to two hours of brainstorming, the quality of ideas will start to diminish; watch it carefully, allow some humor of course, but be careful not to allow it to devolve into a sillyfest. When it is time to wrap it up, delegate groupings of stickies to be followed up by individuals and subgroups. Make sure every single sticky has an owner who is responsible for carrying out the idea or issue to resolution.

Be sure each individual understands what specific deliverables he or she must produce for the design document, from staffing plans to memory tests on the PlayStation2. Each of these design tasks must be scheduled and have a due date. It may be useful to lay all of these design tasks out in Microsoft Project or some other project planning software if the number of

< < < < < < < < < < < < < < < < < < < < < < < < < < < < <

design tasks is large or represents more than three to six man-months of effort.

Managing the Design Document

The design document is referred to in the singular as if it were a massive tome only suitable for the largest three-ring binders your office super-store carries. I think it is wrong to keep the design document as one massive document. As such it is much harder to delegate sections to be worked on by various team members. Break the doc-ument up into as many discrete building blocks as possible.

Place your design documents into a version control system such as Per-force or Visual Source Safe from the very first iteration. This of course pre-vents losses and allows you to go back and understand what the changes have been and perhaps revert to an older document if you find yourself in a design cul-de-sac.

Consider connecting all your docu-ments, spreadsheets, diagrams, sketches, and notes into a web of docu-ments using HTML (after all, HTML was designed to assist scientists in con-necting their research papers). It is up to you and your organization to deter-mine what the overhead costs are for connecting all the documents through web links.

For each individual document I rec-ommend listing the controlling author and one-line descriptions of the revi-sion history including dates.

60 Seconds of Gameplay

A defining document of the game detail-ing 60 full seconds of every bit of gameplay and response crystallizes the game experience and leaves no room

for individual interpretations of what the game could be about. I remember reading the postmortem of Tropico in *Game Developer* magazine. The author of the postmortem was courageous enough to admit that after one full year of development on Tropico it became evident that the development team was not working together to create a game of a single shared design, but rather individual members were pursuing their own game design for Tropico and were actively and passively campaign-ing for features and assets that would support their vision of the game! I have never seen this written down in print anywhere else, but I have seen this wholly unproductive behavior in action on several teams. I think of it almost like the quantum description of elec-trons flying about the nucleus of an atom, each electron representing a member of the team and his personal design for the game, and factoring in the Heisenberg uncertainty principle, no one really knows where anyone else is and what their velocity is at the same time. Obviously this is a misunder-standing at best and a dysfunctional team at worst.

With dysfunctional teams, the pro-ducer and management must be merely hoping the team will accidentally come together and produce a commercial game. And for teams suffering from misunderstanding, think of all the wasted effort pursuing bits of games that almost were. The 60 seconds of gameplay document will nip these scat-tered games before they start growing by making the actual gameplay clear. This sort of document is a little difficult to write with certainty from day one, and it may take many iterations before

> >

the 60 seconds of gameplay settles down to its final form.

As a side benefit to the marketing team, console manufacturers and the executive management team will be grateful for (or sometimes demand) the 60 seconds of gameplay, and you will have it on hand to pass out to these stakeholders.

Core Gameplay

Building upon the 60 seconds of gameplay, create a document to flesh out the core gameplay with a complete description of all of the interactions, behaviors, and controls for the game. Take a car racing game for example; describe all of the controls for maneuvering the car, and describe all of the interactions with the environment such as bumping into other cars and walls and traveling across gravel, sand, and wet pavement. Perhaps the game will feature time of day, weather, and glare from the sun. For a role-playing game note melee, ranged, and spell attacks, healing spells, information gathering spells, walking, running, speaking to non-player characters, traveling to new cities, gaining experience, allocating experience points, buying new armor, buying food, and so on. Don't take the time to detail all of these activities to the finest detail; create separate documents for each of these. For example, after listing that the player is able to buy weapons, armor, and magical items in the town in Diablo, create separate documents that list the details for each of these items and the vendors for each of these subtypes of equipment.

Now you have a high-level design document describing all of the core gameplay for the game. This high-level design document will then act as a finding guide to the rest of the subgame design documents.

I highly recommend using UML use case diagrams to document each and every one of these core interactions with the game. These use cases are readily usable by the programming team to flesh out a technical design, and the use cases will also serve as the platform for developing the QA plan for the game.

Note just by looking at the following use case diagrams for the three genres of real-time strategy, role-playing, and first-person shooter, we are able to discern at an analytic level what these genres are about and the gameplay experience delivered by these three genres.

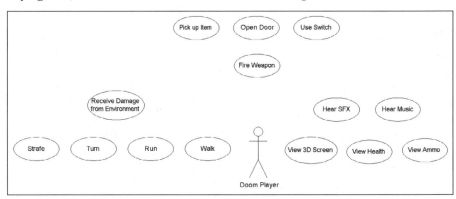

The core use cases of Doom

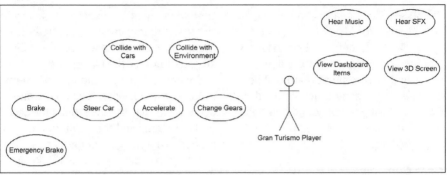

The core use cases of Gran Turismo 3

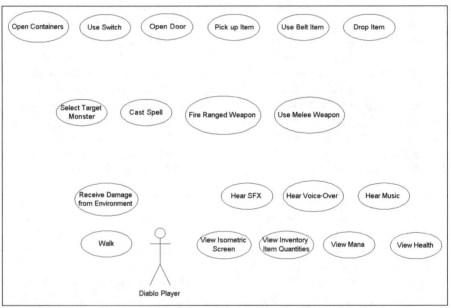

The core use cases of Diablo

The Walkthrough

One of the most valuable parts of the game design document will be the asset lists, which I cover in the next section. However, to create comprehensive asset lists you will need an understanding of the complete gameplay experience. This is the *walkthrough* for the entire game.

The walkthrough covers *all* of the gameplay experience the player would encounter through one pass through the whole game. Commonly this would be the documentation of the single-player campaign for games that feature campaigns. For our Black9 action-RPG game we took the time to detail every line of dialogue and every trap and challenge the player would face during each of the 16 missions that occurred during the single-player game.

> >

> **JARGON**: *Walkthrough*—the complete documentation of the player's experience from the start of the game to the end of the game.

The exact format or type of walkthrough would differ dramatically between different genres of games. For the racing game of Gran Turismo, the walkthrough would consist of describing all the races, race series, championships, and licensing courses. The walkthrough would cover all the enemies encountered during the game: enemy cars, enemy superheroes, enemy goblins, or enemy disasters, such as in your SimCity game.

The completed walkthrough is a major accomplishment deserving of a fine meal! This walkthrough acts as a travel guide for the rest of the team with the very first application of the walkthrough being the asset list compilations.

Asset Lists

Asset lists are the spreadsheet lists of all the little bits that comprise the game such as spell effects, characters, racecars, car parts, crowd cheers, tiles, movies, music, animations, AI behaviors, weapons, and so on. These asset lists are fun to pore over and dream about as the game takes shape. The walkthrough from above makes it easy to produce these asset lists as the AI programmer only needs to read through the walkthrough, highlighting AI behaviors as he comes across them. The lead animator will build the animation matrix from seeing the character list and examining all the moves that each of the characters must come up with. Without a walkthrough you will be limited in your ability to list all of the required assets. This is quite dangerous

to maintaining a tight schedule. Without having all the information in front of you when making the development plan, you will inadvertently allocate too many resources for the creation of some secondary or even tertiary assets and only later find in the schedule that you have run out of time to complete some truly primary assets. This is one way game projects slip.

Here is a short list of some of the asset lists you should have (note that some of these may not be appropriate to the title you are creating):

1. Sound effect list
2. Voice-over list
3. Music theme list
4. Weapon list
5. Gear list
6. Spell list
7. Character model list
8. Environment model list
9. Animation matrix
10. AI behaviors
11. Mission list
12. Cut scene list
13. Physics scripting list
14. Power-ups list
15. Car parts list
16. NPC list

After you compile your asset list, the producers and section leads can start to fill in time estimates and dependency information used later to build the production plan. Remember that so far in the process you have not formally sat down and cut any features or assets yet, and you don't do that on your first pass with the walkthrough and asset lists. Instead of cutting right away, I recommend you get on with other areas of design while the asset lists stew for a bit, gathering flavor. After at least two weeks and preferably four, go back with a fresh eye and start to remove requested assets, both from the asset lists and the walkthrough, that are clearly superfluous and will have no meaningful impact on the game. There is a fine line between detailing a game world and creating asset verbiage that never needed to be created in the first place.

Use of Other Games

Using other games for inspiration and as guidance for the implementation of specific features is a good practice. For example, since Diablo the industry is pretty much settled on red-colored health meters and blue-colored mana meters. Don't make yellow-colored health meters and brown mana meters, not even if you use nanotech, quintessence, spell points, or any other magic system—just use blue. For first-person shooters, default the left mouse button to fire the main weapon in normal mode; no one will appreciate the right mouse button being the default behavior.

If you are designing a role-playing game with an inventory system and you like the paper-doll mechanics of Diablo, take a screen shot from Diablo and annotate what specific features will remain the same and what you are modifying. Referencing other games and taking the game industry forward is not plagiarism; it is just practical use of time. Some other aspects of game mechanics may not lend themselves to a screen shot. In that case, make a written reference in your design document about a feature such as "the player should be able to lasso his units as in Warcraft III."

Plagiarism is copying another game, making a few minor modifica-

tions, and peddling it around town as if it is something new. Many publishers are guilty of opening up their latest copy of *PC Data* or TRST sales data and looking at what the number one selling game is and then promptly setting off to green-light a new game project that is a clone of one that is already a major hit. Think about the poor timing: The hit game was conceived at least 24 months ago, and now the publisher will play catch-up and fund a new title that will take another 24 months to reach the market. Meanwhile, the guys who made the original are wrapping up their sequel and securing their position on the franchise. This seems dumb to me; I would rather be making the hit game that others are chasing.

Menu Design

All games have some sort of menu system, and in general the fewer menus the better. The trend nowadays is to embed as much of the menu system as possible into the actual game. I remember how brilliant it was in Quake I where id had the player choose his difficulty level by running through a small level and jumping through a teleporter. It was interesting to note that the insane difficulty setting was hidden by the use of a traditional secret along the path of choosing hard.

By current tastes the Quake I method of choosing a difficulty level would probably be considered laborious; however, it is even more popular to use the 3D engine of the game to render the menu interfaces. Dungeon Siege from Gas Powered Games featured animating chains and gears pushing and pulling the menus around, and many games now have the player choose their character model only after

> >

seeing the character models on display in their "living" format with sample animations and facial expressions. In Grand Theft Auto 3 the player bought weapons not through a 2D menu like the weapon dealer in Diablo, but rather by entering Amunation in Liberty City and simply walking through and colliding with the object of their choice.

The design of the menu system might be a drag, but it is very important to creating a clean, professional gameplay experience for the player. Creating slick menuing systems is more difficult than one would first think. The process I employ is to enlist my trusty friend the use case diagram and note all of the steps involved in getting the player from startup to all of the various modes of play and options.

Game Mechanics Detail

The game mechanics detail is probably what most people think of when they

hear game design document. This document details all of the itty-bitty mechanics of your combat system, your sell system, or your racing model. All games are a simulation of some sort of activity, and the game mechanics detail is the formal analysis of that simulation and the description of how that model will be realized in your game. The game mechanics are much too specific to a particular game for me to be able to develop a generalized plan or format for its presentation.

Write the Manual?

One interesting suggestion from Steve McConnell that I have yet to try out on a project is to write the manual for the game during the game design process! If I were to try that, I think the best place is after the core gameplay, walkthrough, asset lists, game mechanics, and menu designs have been laid to paper.

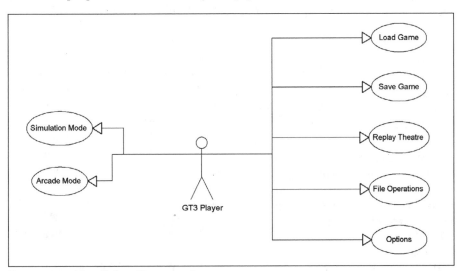

The use cases of Gran Turismo 3's menu system

‹ ‹

Concept Sketches and Art Style Guide

The art director should be leading the art team through a series of sketching, prototyping, and visual design tasks while assisting in the overall production planning process. The sketches will help all involved understand the look and feel of the game. The user-interface prototypes dramatically assist in the communication of the core gameplay.

On Completeness and Uncertainty

As the author of a book on how to go about doing something, I am obliged to assume the role of someone pontificating. As a pontificator on performing a rigorous game design process, I will freely admit here that in my professional career I have yet to create a game design document that lives up to what I have described not only in this chapter, but in the rest of the book. In the real world you will have many competing time pressures. Instead of carrying everything out to full completion, you must use your judgment and determine what areas of the design require the most game design resources. If you are making a sequel to a game that your team has already made, then you should not spend time creating documentation for the parts of the game that are not changing; instead, focus on the creative differences the new version is bringing to play. In areas of the game design document that still need more design effort but that you don't have time to address at the present time, simply note the incompleteness, assign it to a member of the team, and suggest a date for completion.

The twin brother of incomplete work is uncertain work. Games are art forms realized in a piece of engineering brought forth by team effort. There is no way anyone has ever written down at the start of the project every detail about a game without changing his mind on the way to making a great game. It's fine to note straightaway in the game design document areas that you feel need further examination or are dependent on learning new facts that will be unveiled at a later point in the project. As with incomplete work, be sure this area of uncertainty has an owner and a suggested date when the issue will be reexamined.

Cut Features Even Before Considering the Schedule

After laying out all this game design material on paper, most people would go straight to time estimates and project planning without considering cutting features. I hold a fervent conviction that the world's great games do not have an abundance of features, rather they have *just the right amount* of features polished to an uncommonly high standard! To help make your game a great game, rather than just plugging in every single feature you and your team can think of, instead consider your process to be like sculpting the perfect game out of game developer mind-stone. As these extraneous features are cut from the project, the true beauty of a great game will shine. By cutting now, without any pressure from a time resource point of view, your feature cuts will be more pure and objective. Go ahead and cut big features as well as small features. No worries if you cannot bring yourself to make permanent cuts; simply designate truly

> >

great features as primary, the lesser ideas as secondary, and the most obviously weak features as tertiary.

You will no doubt have to repeat this process of prioritizing and cutting features later in the production process, but that task will be much easier with all of this thinking about what *really* needs to be in the game already completed.

Maintain the Game Design Document

Ah, so you are all done; HTML everywhere, no one has ever pushed UML use cases to the limits you have, and you are prepared to have an auditing company review your asset lists. Fantastic! Congratulate your team and have a beer. Now get on with the rest of the production plan and production in general. Oh, wait, there is one thing left to do with the design document: Keep it up to date. This can be difficult, tedious busywork for a team, and you must decide what level of formality and rigor must be applied to maintain your own game design document. However, the moment a game design document is saved and checked into the source control system it starts to diverge. This is due to people finding their own improvements to the design. Perhaps the design was vague, or perhaps the developer learned of a better technique, or perhaps someone ran low on time and cut some features. All of this activity should be documented to assist developers downstream. Think of the QA team that must update the testing plan, the manual writer, the voice director who must plan the dialogue sessions; there are a good many people who need an up-to-date design document.

On Fulfilled Expectations

Great games create expectations in the player's mind, and you should deliver fully on these expectations. Take your time as the game design document is being wrapped up to ask yourself what expectations the game design suggests to the player. Brainstorm a bit and compile a list of these expectations and then go back and review your game design document to determine if you are truly delivering the best gameplay experience for fulfilling these expectations. Also look for features that are listed in the game design document that are not apparently fulfilling any expectations. This would be another clue for some feature trimming. If after searching your soul your game design creates a nice set of expectations and delivers fully with no excess fat, then you may safely declare that the game design document is complete.

> >

Chapter 17 > > > > > > > > > > > > > >

Unified Modeling Language Survival Guide

The Unified Modeling Language (UML) is referenced frequently throughout this book, and the reasons for the use of UML are amply supplied in the text. This chapter aims to provide you, in a single sitting, a quick and dirty guide to UML so that you may focus immediately on the requirements and technical design of your game.

Use Cases Deliver Requirements

The use case in UML is the conveyor of requirements, and it is requirements gathering that is the cornerstone of technical design. The use case is a standardized method of documenting a scenario or an interaction between the user and the software—in short, a use. An interaction could be to withdraw money from an ATM or to send the document to the printer or to cause the player character to jump, pick up an object, or swing a sword. A collection of shapes and notations featuring stick figure actors, ellipsoid uses, and line relationships comprise the visual components of a use case diagram.

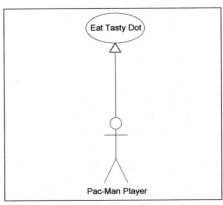

The simplest use case diagram

Collections of interactions may be plotted together in the same diagram to help organize and prepare for the formal design process.

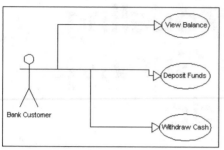

A use case diagram featuring the automatic teller machine

Use case diagrams cannot get too complicated. They are designed to allow the software developer to quickly write down an interaction between the user and the software with a verb-like label, wrap an ellipse around the label, and draw some relationship lines.

For those of you who are curious, formal UML includes varying types of line shapes to describe different types of relationships:

1. Association—the basic relationship representing the communication path between an actor and a use case, drawn as a simple line.

2. Extends—the insertion of additional behavior into a base use case that does not know about it, drawn as a dashed line with an arrowhead with the tag <<extends>> accompanying the line.

3. Generalization—a relationship between a general use case and a more specific use case that inherits and adds features to it, drawn as a solid line with a triangular arrowhead.

4. Inclusion—the insertion of additional behavior into a base use case that explicitly describes the insertion, drawn as a dashed line with an arrowhead with the tag <<include>> accompanying the line.

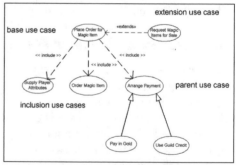

A use case diagram featuring various relationships

Class Diagrams Are the Keystone of Design

A class diagram describes the static design of your software, the associations between your classes, and the subtypes of your classes; it is the workhorse software design.

Taking the lead from Martin Fowler's *UML Distilled* is the concept of design perspectives. When designing software the modeler will be engaged in one of three distinct phases of

design: Conceptual, Specification, and Implementation.

Conceptual design happens as you are starting to sort out the implications from your use cases and are laying out proto-classes to help organize and see the behaviors start to take shape. It is not necessary that all of the conceptual classes map directly at a later stage to classes that will end up being imple-

> >

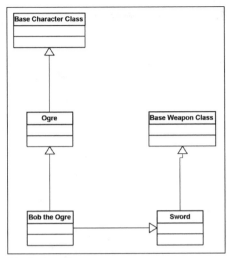

A basic class diagram

bits of your classes are documented and displayed like a dissected frog in a biology class.

Like all aspects of UML, you do not need to doggedly pass through these modeling stages before you write code. If the domain you need to model is something you are familiar with and it is not too complicated, maybe dashing off the implementation model is the most efficient for your task. Perhaps your task is so straightforward that absolutely no design work is required, and you may start tapping out code right off. However, if you are at the start of your project and you are designing a complex system, go ahead and work through the phases.

It is fairly important to identify what specific stage of technical design you are in. For example, you might understand one part of the domain fairly well and start right in at the Implementation design and then wander out of this area of deep understanding and still attempt to design at the Implementation view. This is likely to create bugs in your software at design time. If you need Conceptual or Specification work but you stubbornly try to force an Implementation model on the less well understood parts just out of momentum, you are bound to create errors. A more specific example: Suppose you licensed Epic's Unreal Technology engine and decided to use GameSpy's multiplayer libraries. You already understand the GameSpy libraries from earlier games, so you start dashing out Implementation diagrams but end up creating a poor design because you did not take the time to understand how the Unreal engine handles starting up a multiplayer game.

mented. Rather the purpose is to get all of your class-like thoughts down on paper for study and review before committing to the next phase of construction: Specification.

Specification design occurs after you have used your use case diagrams to describe requirements and have developed your requirements with the use of the Conceptual model. The most important benefit of object-oriented programming is to separate the interface to a class (or package, library, etc.) from the implementation of the class. The goal of Specification is to nail down the interface of the object; the implementation details are kept out of the Specification model, and what is left is a clean view of how that portion of the software you propose to create interacts with the rest of the software.

Implementation design may proceed after the Specification phase has been completed. The Implementation design is what most people think of when they think of object modeling. At this stage all of the glorious detailed

Detailed Syntax of the Class Diagram

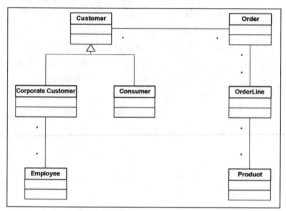

A class diagram with multiplicities marked

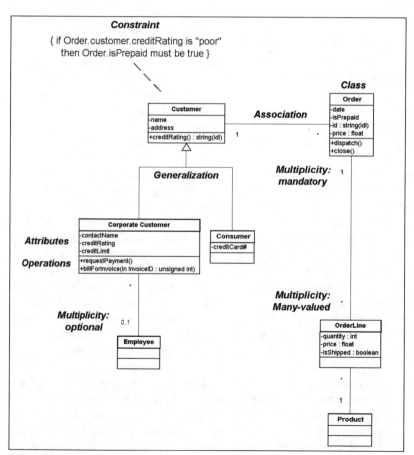

A class diagram with all the fixins'

Associations

Associations are the connections between the classes in your class diagram, represented by lines attaching the classes (boxes) to each other. These associations represent the relationships between the classes: The cPlayerCharacter class may have a cInventory container class. UML decorates these simple association lines with symbols and text to fully describe the nature of the association.

Role names are text labels that are placed at either end of the association line to describe what role this class portrays.

describes how many instances of the targeted class may be connected to the class at the other end of the association. The notation for multiplicity is writen as the number of instances of the class, such as simply a 1 for one instance, 6 for a half dozen, 1..6 for the range of possibilities from one to six, 0..1 when there can be only one or none, and finally an asterisk to represent an infinite quantity, such as 2..* for at least two and upwards to infinity. To describe the number of legs an animal has, use the notation of a comma separating the discrete values the number of instances may take on such as 1, 2, 4, 6, 8, 30, 750 for clams, turkeys, salamanders, lobsters, house centipedes, and the millipede species of Illacme plenipes of California, respectively.

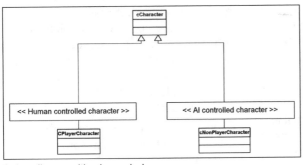

A class diagram with roles marked

Multiplicity is another detail of the association that is described at either end of the association line. Multiplicity

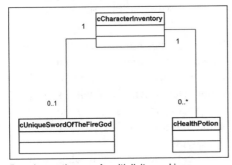

Focusing on the use of multiplicity markings

Navigability and *generalization* are the last bits of adornment that occur at the ends of association lines, drawn simply as open arrows with just lines (navigability) or as arrowheads (generalization). These two arrows depict the two broadest relationships possible between classes: the "has a" and the "is a" relationships. Generalization is the "is a" relationship where one class that is more specialized in function is derived from another class that is more generalized in function. Navigability would then of course be the "has a" relationship; the direction of the arrow in a "has a" relationship illustrates which class is the container class.

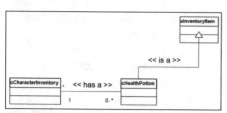

Focusing on the difference between an "is a" and a "has a" relationship

If navigability occurs in only one direction (the usual case), it is called unidirectional; if both objects point to each other, it is called bidirectional. In the case of an association line without arrows, UML says the association is either unknown or bidirectional. We think this ambiguity in the language is a flaw and recommend treating lines without the arrows as unknown rather than imply a bidirectional behavior.

Attributes

Attributes may be thought of as simple fields in a class. At the conceptual level an attribute is just a "has a" association. An example of an attribute is the name of the player in the cPlayerCharacter class. Class boxes are subdivided into three sections: class name, attributes, and operations. The full syntax for an attribute is:

> visibility name: type = defaultValue

For example: + mplayerHealth: int = 100

cPlayerCharacter
+mPlayerName : wstring(idl) = Bob +mPlayerHealth : int = 100 -mCurrentPosition #mBackpack

A class with some attributes indicated

This declares a public member data with the name mplayerHealth on the

cPlayerCharacter that is of type int, which is instantiated with a default value of 100.

Visibility describes how this attribute is seen in the interface: public, protected, or private.

Table 1—UML Symbols for Visibility

public	+
protected	#
private	−

Operations

Operations are the activities defined in individual methods that a class contains. For Specification modeling we are only concerned with the public methods defined in a class; when Implementation modeling, we are of course concerned with all of the member functions: public, private, and protected.

The full UML syntax for describing an operation is:

> visibility name (parameter list): return-type-expression {property-string}

For example: +GetAmbientLightLevel (in timeOfDay: Date) : float

A class with some operations marked

This describes a query operation available on cEnviroment by the name of GetAmbientLightLevel that given the timeOfDay of type Date will return a float that represents the fraction of ambient light to be used for the rendering engine.

There, that is what it takes to produce a class diagram—the keystone of UML and object modeling!

> >

Forward and Reverse Engineering of the Class Diagram

The coolest aspect (not necessarily the most beneficial) of UML in my opinion is the ability to have software applications such as Rational Rose, Together, or even Visio create code from your diagrams (forward engineering) and/or create diagrams from your code (reverse engineering). There are at least 75 UML modeling tools (most of them perform forward engineering and a smaller set perform reverse engineering) for sale as of this writing (summer 2002). One list of these products is maintained at Objects By Design: http://www.objectsbydesign.com/tools/umltools_byCompany.html.

At first thought it may seem like magic that a computer could read a diagram. What these tools do is act like the parser in your compiler to explore the interface and composition of your classes and draw the corresponding UML diagrams with the correct syntax. In the forward engineering direction, these tools generate skeleton code in a number of different programming languages (e.g., C++, Java, SmallTalk, C#, VB, Eiffel) with C++ and Java being the two most commonly supported languages. Common sense would tell you that adding the member function huntForFood() on your Ogre class will not cause any software in the world to be able to figure out what you meant by huntForFood and flesh out the code for you (explanation follows).[1] Rather, it will just create the template

of code for you. Here, let me walk you through a sample with our friend the Ogre:

For this set of examples I decided to try a UML modeling product that I had not tried before, Embarcadero's Describe (http://www.embarcadero.com/products/describe/index.asp). While I have barely scratched the surface, I was able to download the product, install, and start modeling straightaway without using the help system at all. Fairly impressive endorsement if you ask me. Now on with the example:

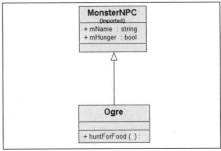

A basic class diagram for Ogre, an NPC derived from MonsterNPC

First we create a basic class diagram with our Ogre derived from the base class MonsterNPC.

MonsterNPC has two public attributes, mName of type string and mHunger of type bool (although I am sure you would not make your attributes public). Ogre has been fleshed out with the public member function huntForFood().

---

1 Of course, that sentence should be read with the connotation of "currently." No doubt computers will continue to grow in power exponentially and someday neural nets, expert systems, and probably a hodge-podge of AI techniques will allow a computer to guess at the implementation for huntForFood(). It is interesting to note that computers and software are already designing integrated circuit chips at the lowest level and performing the majority of stock trades automatically.

Now all I need to do is press the code generation button (while I am using Describe, other tools like Rational Rose and Together also have buttons to generate code). At this point I am given many options in the

Describe UI that are not directly relevant to this overview of UML. One of these options is to proceed with the code making! Here is what Describe generated:

```
//************************************************************
// C++ Class Name : MonsterNPC
// -----------------------------------------------------------
// Filetype: (HEADER)
// Filepath: C:/Program Files/Embarcadero/Describe/GDTemp/MonsterNPC.h
//
//
// Describe Properties
// ----------------------------------------------------
// - Symbol Type : CLD_Class
// - Method : UML ( 5.6.1 )
// - System Name : Ogre
// - Diagram Type : Class Diagram
// - Diagram Name : MonsterNPC
// ----------------------------------------------------
// Author : Administrator
// Creation Date : Sun - Jul 7, 2002
//
// Change Log :
//
//************************************************************
#ifndef MONSTERNPC_H
#define MONSTERNPC_H

class MonsterNPC
{

public:
 string mName;
 bool mHunger;
 MonsterNPC () ;
 virtual ~MonsterNPC () ;
 MonsterNPC (const MonsterNPC &x) ;

};
#endif
```

Code generated for MonsterNPC.h

The first file is MonsterNPC.h, defining the interface to the base class that Ogre is derived from. Notice all the nice comment work supplied by Describe; just think how envious your fellow teammates will be with your diligent code style!

The next file created was MonsterNPC.cpp; notice how it has done a lot of typing drudgery for us, and now all we have to do is fill in the body of the functions. Again, there are many nice bits of commenting that one should really get around to filling out.

> >

```
//***********************************************************
// C++ Class Name : MonsterNPC
// ----------------------------------------------------------
// Filetype: (SOURCE)
// Filepath: C:/Program Files/Embarcadero/Describe/GDTemp/MonsterNPC.cpp
//
//
// Describe Properties
// ----------------------------------------------------
// - Symbol Type : CLD_Class
// - Method : UML ( 5.6.1 )
// - System Name : Ogre
// - Diagram Type : Class Diagram
// - Diagram Name : MonsterNPC
// ----------------------------------------------------
// Author : Administrator
// Creation Date : Sun - Jul 7, 2002
//
// Change Log :
//
//***********************************************************
#include "MonsterNPC.h"
//----------------------------------------------------------
// Constructor/Destructor
//----------------------------------------------------------
MonsterNPC::MonsterNPC ()
{
}
MonsterNPC::MonsterNPC (const MonsterNPC &x)
{
}
MonsterNPC::~MonsterNPC ()
{
}
```

Code generated for MonsterNPC.cpp

Now here is Ogre.h; notice how Describe knows to write the correct syntax for deriving Ogre from MonsterNPC. Neat, huh? I think so.

```
//***********************************************************
// C++ Class Name : Ogre
// ----------------------------------------------------------
// Filetype: (HEADER)
// Filepath: C:/Program Files/Embarcadero/Describe/GDTemp/Ogre.h
//
//
// Describe Properties
// ----------------------------------------------------
// - Symbol Type : CLD_Class
// - Method : UML ( 5.6.1 )
// - System Name : Ogre
// - Diagram Type : Class Diagram
// - Diagram Name : MonsterNPC
// ----------------------------------------------------
// Author : Administrator
// Creation Date : Sun - Jul 7, 2002
//
```

```
// Change Log :
//
//*********************************************************
#ifndef OGRE_H
#define OGRE_H

#include "MonsterNPC.h"

class Ogre : public MonsterNPC
{

public:
 huntForFood () ;
 Ogre () ;
 ~Ogre () ;
 Ogre (const Ogre &x) ;

};
#endif
```

Code generated by Describe for Ogre.h

Finally Ogre.cpp shows the skeleton
constructor, copy constructor, destructor, and huntForFood().

```
//*********************************************************
// C++ Class Name : Ogre
// ------------------------------------------------------------
// Filetype: (SOURCE)
// Filepath: C:/Program Files/Embarcadero/Describe/GDTemp/Ogre.cpp
//
//
// Describe Properties
// ------------------------------------------------------------
// - Symbol Type : CLD_Class
// - Method : UML ( 5.6.1 )
// - System Name : Ogre
// - Diagram Type : Class Diagram
// - Diagram Name : MonsterNPC
// ------------------------------------------------------------
// Author : Administrator
// Creation Date : Sun - Jul 7, 2002
//
// Change Log :
//
//*********************************************************
#include "Ogre.h"
//------------------------------------------------------------
// Constructor/Destructor
//------------------------------------------------------------
Ogre::Ogre ()
{
}
Ogre::Ogre (const Ogre &x)
{
}
Ogre::~Ogre ()
{
```

> >

```
}
//-------------------------------------------------------
// huntForFood
//-------------------------------------------------------
Ogre::huntForFood ()
{

}
```

Code generated for Ogre.cpp

Describe, like all other good forward code generating tools, automatically updates its own diagrams to reflect the additional functions such as the constructor, copy constructor, and destructor that have been added to the classes. This is very neat as well.

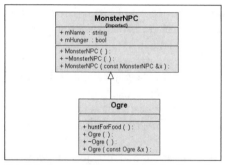

The class diagram has been updated after the code generation.

What just happened might have been reverse generation of the diagram update with the constructor, destructor, and copy constructor by writing the code first and then updating the diagram, or it could have been forward generation by modifying the diagram and then proceeding with the code generation. I could not tell you since it all happened within a blink of the eye.

To test the reverse engineering capabilities of Describe, I added a new member function to Ogre: pickTeeth-WithElfBones(). It seemed like a fun thing for our Ogre to do on occasion.

To accomplish this I opened up the code generated by Describe in a simple editor like Windows Notepad and added the declaration of pickTeethWithElf-Bones() to the public members section of the Ogre class in Ogre.h. (I omit this painfully dull figure illustrating a one-line change to Ogre.h.) I then told Describe to reverse engineer the diagram from the source code:

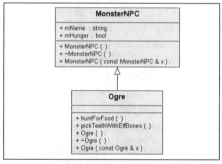

The new function pickTeethWithElfBones() has been automatically generated.

Bam, there is the pickTeethWithElf-Bones() member function in the Ogre box including the + symbol indicating it is a public function. As a final step I then directed Describe to perform some forward engineering magic by again generating code from the diagram. What is there to generate? The skeleton of the function pickTeeth-WithElfBones() in the Ogre.cpp file of course!

This brings me to a very important point to keep in mind about UML. While I have been advocating a methodology that is likely to be a more extensive process than you are currently using, by going with UML and with the flow of the industry standard, not only will your team be creating higher quality software on time through all of these magical benefits of wholesome software engineering, but as a *side effect* or *bonus* your team will save itself from the tedium of making header files and stubbing in their functions. Using UML with a good UML tool such as Describe, Together, or Rational Rose will save your team time.

The Other Seven Diagrams of UML

The use case and class diagrams from UML are the two most useful diagrams for any software engineering project, especially game projects where the technical design phase must often be conducted under constant pressure to get on with it and start some gameplay action. The use case diagram exists to collect behavior and requirements, and the phases of class diagrams (conceptual, specification, and implementation) exist to design the software. That is a whole lot of functionality in just two diagrams; however the UML provides *seven* more diagrams.

Table 2—The Nine Diagrams of the UML

Static Design Diagrams	Dynamic Behavior Diagrams
Class diagram	Use case diagram
Object diagram	Sequence diagram
Component diagram	Collaboration diagram
Deployment diagram	State diagram
	Activity diagram

As you can see, there are four diagram types listed as static design diagrams. Besides the class diagram there are the object, component, and deployment diagrams. Honestly, these types of static design diagrams are merely variations upon the theme of a class diagram.

Static Diagrams

The *object diagram* depicts the static behavior of a set of instantiated objects and the relationships between these objects. This is useful for illustrating tables in a database in relation to specific objects elsewhere in the system. Again, an object diagram is very similar to a class diagram but is instead focused on the perspective of allocated, instantiated, real objects. This diagram is not needed for all modeling jobs; however, it is useful when examining the static relationship behavior of a system of objects that can vary quite a bit under different scenarios.

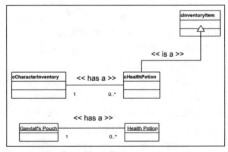

An example of an object diagram

Indicating a function with class scope versus instance scope

The syntax for the object diagram is to declare the name of the object as instance <u>name: class name</u>. Attributes of an object are often shown in an object diagram as it is the varying values of the attributes in a class that compose an instantiated object.

The underline notation for the instance name should not be confused with the underline notation used on attributes and operations. An underlined attribute or operation indicates an attribute or operation that is of class scope rather than limited in scope to the instance.

The *component diagram*, also known as a *package diagram*, is simply building upon the concept of a class diagram but with larger chunks of your software system besides single classes. For example, component diagrams are well suited for depicting the connections between the 3D rendering engine, the AI subsystem, and the network layer. Each component may be drawn as a simple box or more ornately as a file-folder-like icon or a box with two tabs on the left-hand side as if it were to plug into something. Draw simple lined arrows between the components to indicate dependencies.

The component diagram is a great tool for developing a road map for maintaining a body of code and for working with a team of developers in general. Also, if your body of code is becoming tangled and your build times are growing out of control, mapping the

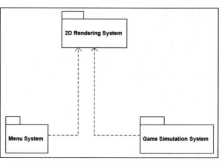

A sample package diagram based on a simple 2D game

dependencies between the classes across your project may guide you to perform some surgical refactoring to bring your builds back under control. A great book on the problem of dependencies and build times is *Large-Scale C++ Software Design* by John Lakos.

Component diagrams do not need to be fancy; however, inside the folder icons for a component, you may list the important parts that comprise the component as well as the UML standard visibility symbols such as +, –, and #. In fact, the class, component, and deployment diagrams share the following UML structures: stereotypes, generalizations, and associations.

The *deployment diagram* acts as the most natural extension of the component diagram, the physical arrangement of your software system and subsystems with a pictorial description of the delivery platform and where the major components live on the delivery platform.

For many games, especially console games, the deployment diagram would be a simple diagram with just a single machine being the platform. However, in the case of very fast hardware video and hardware audio, it may still be useful to depict what subsystems of the hardware the various bits of your game engine are running on.

Deployment diagrams are an excellent opportunity to use all of the Visio stencils that are lying about. You can use a cloud to represent the Internet, different server icons, modems, satellite dishes, whatever you want; the deployment diagram is the diagram that expresses the software in its most physical terms.

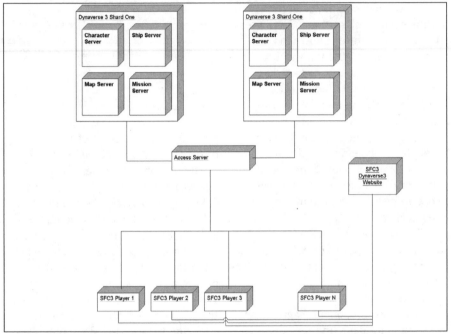

A sample deployment diagram based on SFC3 and D3 with clients, servers, and web site

Dynamic Diagrams

The class, object, component/package, and deployment diagrams comprise the four static design diagrams of the UML. As shown in Table 2, there are five diagrams to assist in describing the dynamic behavior of software. It is an inherently flawed process to render onto a 2D plane the time-dependent dynamic behavior of software. There is no guarantee that the software should not rightly take up more than two dimensions in representation and no guarantee that it will lay its time component out nicely to be read top to bottom or left to right. That may be one reason the UML has defined more (five) diagram types for the dynamic behavior of software compared to the four diagram types of static behavior.

You are already familiar with the handiest of the dynamic behavior diagrams, the use case, but what are the rest of the dynamic diagrams about?

Activity diagrams are useful for documenting the behavior of objects that have complex state-changing behavior. A programmer I knew from my earliest game programming job used to exhort rather menacingly about the lack of appreciation we younger programmers had for the state machine. I have to admit that while I had a general idea what the guy was talking about at the time, I did not understand exactly why state machines are a panacea to programming. Now that I know more, I know the state machine *is not* the panacea to strong programming; instead, the state machine is just another good tool in the programmer's box. I believe what the older programmer was trying to say was that the *failure* of younger pro-grammers to visualize and understand the state machines we were already creating caused a lot of bugs. Thus, the utility of the state diagram to visualize and model objects with complex state behavior.

The first bit of notation you will immediately pick up on is that the boxes in an activity diagram are round edged; these are the states that your object transitions between. Martin Fowler uses the terms "activity" for the round-edged box states and "actions" for the transitional arrows drawn between the states. The idea is that actions would be quick (how quick depends on the nature of the problem you are modeling) and that activities happen "for a while" (how long again depends on your problem).

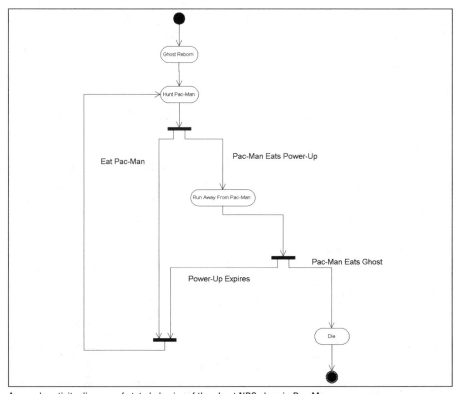

A sample activity diagram of state behavior of the ghost NPC class in Pac-Man

< < < < < < < < < < < < < < < < < < < < < < < < < < < < < <

Each of the transitions in your object should be documented with the *guard condition*, which is a boolean condition that when met allows the object to pass to the new state. For example, when Pac-Man eats the power-up, the Ghosts then start to flee from Pac-Man.

There are also two predefined states for all objects in the UML notation: the start state and the end state, represented by solid filled circles, with start usually placed at the top of the diagram and end at the bottom.

It is common for an object to transition among a set of related activities (states) while at the same time open to being interrupted and transitioning to another state that is connected to all of these related states.

Sequence diagrams are designed to address the need to model the dynamic behavior *between* objects. Again, the state chart tracks the changing of state internally in an object, while the sequence diagram tracks the communication occurring between a number of objects.

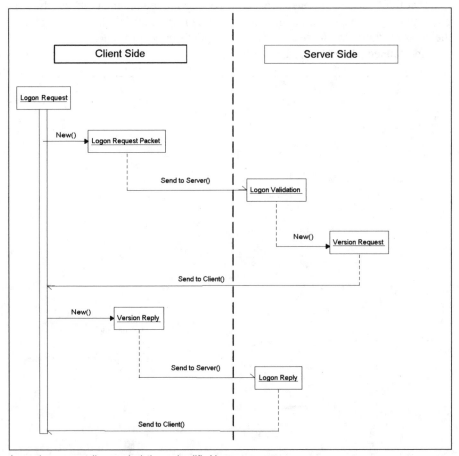

A sample sequence diagram depicting a simplified logon sequence

> >

The sequence diagram is useful for designing how your components and packages will interact at the specification stage and assists you in designing the message traffic in your objects in the implementation design stage. A sequence diagram documents a single scenario or course of events. In fact, a sequence diagram maps well to a use case diagram. You should certainly spend more energy on collecting your requirements into use cases rather than rigorously ensuring that you have a documented sequence diagram for each of your use cases.

The main benefit of sequence diagrams in game development is in multiplayer code technical design. Multiplayer code tends to need a lot of asynchronous callbacks, multi-threading, blocking calls, or combinations of all of these. You also have peer-to-peer or client-server communication. There is usually a lot of complicated messaging going on. Zachary Drummond and I independently developed sequence diagrams on our own while working on a client-server game in 1997. Later we found out there is a standardized language for expressing this messaging behavior!

Now a quick overview of the syntax behind the sequence diagram: First, all of the objects that are part of the scenario to be designed are listed across the diagram from left to right, with the leftmost object being the instigator of all of the action and the rightmost object generally being the last object to be instantiated in the scenario.

Below each object is the object's timeline represented by a vertical dashed line, starting at the bottom of the object's box and extending to the bottom of the diagram. From the time the object is actually created until it is deleted, the timeline has an open rectangle on top of the dashed line. At the bottom of the rectangle, if the object is deleted in this scenario, a large, bold X is placed to clearly indicate when the object was destroyed.

The messages themselves are lines with solid filled arrowheads that lead from the calling object to the called object. This message line is always labeled with the name of the calling object's member function that is making the function call or asynchronous message (or by whatever messaging vehicle you are using). Additional conditions may wrap the message label to document what conditions would have to be met for the message to fire off.

Objects may send messages to themselves; this is documented by having the object point an arrow back to itself. Messages that are simple returns are drawn by using a dashed line with a solid arrow back to the calling object.

Like many bits of the UML, you may choose to use additional symbol types to add clarity to a diagram. For example, UML uses half-filled arrowheads to represent asynchronous messages.

The *collaboration diagram* in my opinion is just not useful or at best can only be useful in odd cases. Maybe I have failed to appreciate the use of a collaboration diagram; like anything I put forth in this book, if you take issue or have a suggestion, please drop me a line at erik@taldren.com.

The basic syntax of the collaboration diagram is to basically smash together a class diagram and a sequence diagram and end up with a diagram that does a worse job at

‹ ‹

modeling dynamic behavior than the sequence diagram and a worse job at static modeling than the class diagram. That is, it uses boxes for objects and message arrows to indicate calls between the objects.

Essentially this diagram is an informal sequence diagram where object lifetime is not required to be drawn and you feel the need to sprawl about your drawing surface. I have so much disdain for these collaboration diagrams that I am not even going to include an example. I highly recommend *UML Distilled* by Fowler and Scott, and if you are morbidly curious, you can check out the collaboration diagram in that book!

Collectively, the sequence and collaboration diagrams are called UML's interaction diagrams. Use the sequence diagrams.

State diagrams are the last bit of the UML to discuss, and as with the collaboration diagram, I do not think the state diagram is useful. The state diagram is essentially a flow chart using UML notational bits. Sure, flow charts are useful and they had their day, but I feel the trio of use case, class, and sequence diagrams are the different views to use, representing requirements, and static and dynamic behaviors. The odd state diagram will also help you out with particularly state-driven complex objects.

Here again, to sabotage the state diagram I omit a diagram for it; see *UML Distilled* if you remain interested. Email me if you're passionate about the state diagram; I see it only useful for the high ceremony shops that would like to make an easy-to-read flow chart.

> >

Chapter 18 > > > > > > > > > > > > > > >

Technical Design

The technical design document is second only to the game design document in importance for a successfully planned project. The technical design document is the reflection of the game design document and a blueprint for your development team.

Every organization has a different format for technical design documents and depending on the size of the organization, its experience, and the size of the game project and the goals for the game, the level of effort that is spent creating this document varies wildly.

First off, it should be noted that even with business software, the design phases and the technical design/architectural phases overlap each other, and no technical design document is 100 percent complete before starting formal production of your game. In fact, attempting to achieve perfection in the technical design phase is *not* keeping your eye on the true goal: creating a great game. Instead your group should achieve a *good* design that meets your requirements and goals for the project. In other words, I will be spelling out a whole bunch of detail that could possibly go into a technical design document, and you will need to use your own judgment of what is appropriate for your team and your project.

Nominate Functional Leads

At Taldren we have found that modern games have grown too large in scope and complexity for a single lead programmer to know everything important across the whole of the project. And even if one programmer could keep it all in his head, that would not be best for your team or the project.

Instead of the lead programmer or technical director designing all software, we nominate functional leads for each subsystem of our games. This has been common practice at other game development houses for some time now. Besides not overwhelming a single developer, we find that we create a lot more energy and buy-in from our programmers if they have specific subsystems that they own. Also, this is a necessary exercise if you want to grow your programmers into stronger programmers. In my opinion, growing your folks into stronger developers should be a goal as important as making a great game, possibly even more important than a solitary game. Your games must be the strongest you can create in order to ensure the success of your business; however, never forget that your games are created by people

< < < < < < < < < < < < < < < < < < < < < < < < < <

thinking, and structuring the challenges in your projects that cause each of your programmers to stretch and grow is how to truly make a great company.

This goal of developing your more junior people into stronger developers and taking your strongest programmers to new levels may find heavy resistance from some who prefer (subconsciously or consciously) to remain a hero programmer who calls all the shots in a given area and feels indispensable. This is negative to the ultimate health and performance of your team. At Taldren we consciously cross-train at least two developers, and ideally three, in each major area of expertise, such as graphics, AI, and networking, to ensure that we do not have any indispensable hero programmers. It sounds like we are callous of people's egos, and in a way we are. I am not interested in protecting an ego that depends on hoarding technical knowledge. Instead, I want to grow healthy egos that discuss their technical challenges and proactively share their knowledge with each other.

After nominating each of your functional leads, it is time to parcel out the game's requirements and game design document to each of the technical leads. Of course the entirety of the game design documents and other documentation should be readily accessible to all developers, but here is where the lead

programmer or technical director makes a conscious decision to parcel out information to his leads. This parceling out ensures that the leads will actually *read* their area of the game design document and not get lost trying to get through the whole pile of documents. I have discovered through experience that some folks enjoy reading whole design documents and others do not. For the latter types you must pull out what you want them to read. (For our latest project, in addition to having all of the design documents in the version control system with easy access to all of the development team, I burned a CD with all of the documents at the end of the game design phase and handed it out to every member of the development team so that they would have the convenience of not having to look for the documents on SourceSafe and could also conveniently take a copy of the game design material home with them. I will let you know how this turns out.)

Some of the leads we have on Black9:

1. Artificial Intelligence
2. Unreal Warfare
3. Xbox
4. PS2
5. Networking
6. Quality Assurance
7. Level Design

> >

Synthesize Use Cases and Nonvisible Requirements

How do your developers actually create a technical design for their areas of responsibility from the design documents?

Start with the Use Cases

Those use case diagrams that illustrate the game design document are excellent collections of the behavior of the various subsystems in the game. The technical leads should take the use case diagram to a whiteboard (or paper or modeling software such as Describe) and start to annotate it with questions that will lead to further refinement of the design and notes suggesting the technical design of the system.

Over time these annotated use case diagrams should be used as the raw material to develop the static design of the software. In some areas it might be appropriate to start right out with class diagrams, and in other areas it might be better to start at a higher level such as a package or component diagram.

Casual, Frequent Design Review

As the functional leads are performing the analysis of the requirements, they should meet with each other at irregular points when they have reached some intermediate stage of design and discuss their proposed design with those who have areas of responsibility that border on the work of the first developer. This is an activity that the lead programmer or technical director should be actively monitoring and pushing to happen. This will help ensure that all of the game is designed as a coherent whole and that there are no

missing tasks that fall between two developers when no one claims responsibility for that area.

Two developers rejecting a task—it falls through the cracks.

This is an amazingly important process, and it is the main reason you co-locate your developers in an office so that they can communicate with each other. Hundreds of minor decisions will be ferreted out with this discussion process that were never identified as needed.

Nonvisible Requirements

Use case diagrams are only able to document the interaction of the game with the player and in some cases between the client and the server or other players. There are a great many requirements that games need to meet that are not interactions with the player. I lump all of these together as nonvisible requirements.

All games have a minimum frame-rate requirement, with strategy and puzzle games being able to get away with as few as 10 or 15 frames per second and most console games using 30 frames per second. The highest performing action games are 60 frames per second. In the requirements gathering document, the designer merely wrote down what his frame rate requirement was. Now the technical leads must work together to develop a technical plan to meet these requirements. The technical design document is not merely an echo of what another guy said earlier when the requirements were identified; now the requirements must be analyzed, and a plan of attack must be articulated. It is fine if the issue is not fully understood yet. For example, if a wholly new 3D engine technology must be created, it would be fine if the technical design discussed a strategy called frame-locking to keep the frame-rate smooth and if the document spelled out various ways that performance will be optimized or met through modifying assets such as polygon and texture map reductions.

Other nonvisible requirements should or may include the following:

- Maximum run-time memory footprint (this is especially important with console games)

- The layout of the data structures on the physical media such as CD, cartridge, or DVD

- The maximum bandwidth allowed per player per second

- The customer support and release quality requirements

- All of the console manufacturer's requirements (there are dozens of them)—I recommend creating a little distilled checklist of requirements that is used to generate specific tasks.

- For PCs, develop a technical plan to meet the specified minimum system requirements such as the memory on video cards.

- Specify what SDKs and APIs the game will use and declare at what point you will lock down these third-party software libraries and what your risk plan is if they fail to deliver on all of their promises.

- Detail how the game will be localized, how the game's strings will be organized, and how the font will be swapped out for other languages' fonts. Make sure your strings are stored as double-byte strings to facilitate worldwide localization.

- Security —what is your strategy to prevent copying? CD-keys or some sort of CD encrypting software?

- Security/cheating—if your game features online gameplay, then you must address cheating or popular games will die a sudden death.

- Portability—is it a goal to move the code over to Linux? Mac? PS2? GameCube? Xbox? Plan ahead to isolate platform-specific code.

- Database usage—you may not have a full-blown use for SQL in your game, but you certainly have art and audio assets that must be efficiently organized and referenced both during production and at run time.

- Concurrency and threads limitations—for example, virtually all consoles do not support the use of threaded programming; your plan must explicitly detail the use or non-use of threads.

> >

These are just some of the nonvisible requirements that your game could be holding on to; your team has the responsibility to look for the rest of these not-so-easy-to-spot requirements.

Measure Twice, Cut Once

As your team prepares the technical design document, it should also be performing tests and experiments to establish reasonable confidence in the performance of the game software. Some concrete examples are in order. Suppose you are licensing the Unreal engine from Epic to make your game (as we are). What are the performance parameters of the engine? If you load in a character model with 5,000 polygons, 20 animations, and one 512 by 512 by 24-bit texture map, how much run-time memory does the geometry require? How much for the texture map? Which compression algorithms are you using for the texture map? How about that animation data? How much memory will that take up? How does key-framed animation data compare to motion captured data from a memory footprint?

It is critical to both measure the actual values observed as well as *predict* what the values ought to be, based on simple calculations of the data involved. For example, we ran a set of tests on Unreal's performance with animation data, and the results we got back from the first test indicated that Unreal used an outrageous amount of memory for each animation. This outrageous value was presented at a team meeting, which I interrupted to do a back-of-the-envelope guesstimate of the order of magnitude the data should require. It turned out to be roughly 12 times less memory. So a deeper test

was called for, and we soon learned that indeed Unreal used the much lower amount of memory as predicted by the calculation and that there was an error in the first estimate.

I remember being taught this lesson when in graduate school at USC's Aerospace department when one of the youngest professors there, Dr. Irwin, challenged a highly respected older graduate student to calculate the orbital velocity of the KH11 spy satellite on the spot. The student said he would need to know how much mass the satellite had before he would be able to proceed with the calculation. Dr. Irwin responded harshly, "Guess!" The student surprised himself by being able to come up with a decent number for the mass. Then the student said he was not familiar with the radius of the orbit the KH11 used. Dr. Irwin responded again harshly, "It is a damn spy satellite—guess!" This of course was a strong clue that the spy satellite orbited at a very low altitude and that the student knew that already. From there it was a simple equation that the student had worked through probably a hundred times before in the regular coursework. The moral of the story is that fragile, worthless engineers are handicapped by documentation and textbooks, and thinking, useful engineers have some idea of what is reasonable (with the accuracy of the guesstimate ranging widely depending on the problem to within an order of magnitude or ± 25 percent). Your developers should know how many bits it should take to represent a 5,000-polygon model and should be ready to interpret the actual results measured. Raw measurements without any thought behind them are even more dangerous than no numbers; at

< < < < < < < < < < < < < < < < < < < < < < < <

least with no numbers you *know* what you don't know.

Another simple example of this is that very quickly your developers should spot the impractical requirement that a PS2 game support 1024x1024x32 texture maps for the characters. It is easy to calculate that this one texture map takes up 4 megabytes of memory—the exact size of the PS2's video buffer!

Another solid example of the usefulness of looking at the whole enchilada and making sense of your numbers occurred in an episode of clever task estimating for a Game Boy Advance project we were considering. The question at the time was how many artists the project required. We knew that GBA teams required very few team members; however, this side-scroller would require the best of our artists and quite a bit of art. This last requirement, quite a bit of art, triggered the question in my mind of "Never mind how many artists do we need for the project, instead how much art can we possibly cram into the GBA?" Taking the largest cartridge size that Nintendo uses for the GBA we were able to quickly calculate that two of our artists working full time on the project for six months would produce more art than the GBA could even handle! Two artists by six months was the upper limit of our budget, and we happily penciled it in on the schedule as one of the rare cases when you know without a doubt that your time estimate is as strong as possible.

Even when the final draft of the technical design document has been completed and the team is ready to move on to production, it is important to keep monitoring your expected

results to actual measured results. This is basic scientific procedure taught in physics labs in all college physics courses. I repeat it here as so many of us in the game programming craft are self-taught.

Specify Tools, Languages, and Processes

Your technical design document should specify what programming languages will be used, such as C++, SQL, UnrealScript. If the language choice is important, then the technical design document should elaborate on why each of the languages are the best choice for their jobs.

SIDEBAR: On scripting languages, I have worked my way up in the game industry from being a scripter on an adventure game, through game programmer, to producer, and now CEO of Taldren. I have a love/hate relationship with scripting languages and it is mostly on the hate side. It is entirely influenced by my first experience with a scripting language (a proprietary language named SAGA II developed by my first game industry employer, The Dreamer's Guild). This language was designed to be C-like yet supposedly made crash-proof by ignorant scripters such as myself. I think the very goal of this scripting language was the flaw: to reduce the amount of serious bugs caused by scripters. Instead of the relatively short time it would have taken to train good scripters to avoid producing array-bounds, memory leaks, and other crash bugs, many man-months were devoted to the creation and the maintenance of a mediocre language with crude debugging tools. Essentially SAGA never fully worked as advertised, and we scripters still created bugs that required the attention of more senior programmers to solve. Recently at

> >

Taldren we have been introduced to the UnrealScript language. This one I highly approve of, as it has a much nobler goal: to be able to be used by consumer end users for user extensibility. With this requirement Epic was forced to push the quality level of UnrealScript far above what most internal tools in the game industry would achieve. Unreal-Script is an object-oriented scripting language somewhat like Java that produces decent code. In the end, I prefer that teams develop APIs in C++ that other team members are able to use to more effectively grow their core programming skill set instead of developing throwaway knowledge in a proprietary scripting language. For the truly robust projects that may benefit from a scripting language, by all means use or develop one. This area of the technical design document should fully articulate the reasons for using or not using a scripting language.

How about if you are using a new process such as taking advantage of Unified Modeling Language as suggested in this book? Or will your team be using a software-modeling tool such as Rational's Rose for the first time? What about on the art side; will you switch from 3D Studio Max to Maya and if so, why?

Decide which components for the game may be reused from existing software or be licensed from third parties. Solid third-party software is almost always less expensive than building your own. However, you may have strategic goals for creating your own software that is a requirement your team is preparing to meet.

When using APIs and SDKs such as the Miles sound libraries or DirectX, it is important to articulate at the technical design stage which version of these APIs the game is going to be made with. Many PC games have been delayed a year or more after switching to the latest version of DirectX due to the overwhelming desire to take advantage of a feature that only the latest DirectX supported. Sometimes teams upgrade their APIs and SDKs late in the development cycle only to find that the new stuff is not fully backwardly compatible with the older stuff—big bummer. Identify as early as possible if there is a likely need to upgrade during the production of the game and if so, take stock of the risks involved early on. If possible commit to rigid cutoff dates where the project will no longer tolerate upgrades and revisions to these APIs and SDKs.

Goals for the Architecture

Besides merely satisfying the immediate needs of this particular game project, many projects have implied requirements that would move much more rapidly towards being realized if these requirements were articulated and planned for during the technical design phase.

Are you building up the code base for your company? Is it intended to build a robust 3D engine that may be reused in a future project? How about portability? Will this reusable 3D engine you are proposing to engineer always run on the PlayStation2 or do you intend to port to the GameCube or Xbox?

How about user extensibility? Do you want your gamers to be able to modify or create new content for your game?

Any and all of the above must be explicitly planned for during the technical design phase, as it will materially

‹ ‹

affect how the technical leads go about designing the game's software.

Identify what sort of code and technical design reviews your team will utilize during the course of production for the game.

Identify Areas of Likely Change

The game design document and/or the technical design document may identify areas of the game that are likely to undergo significant change during the development of the game. An obvious example would be the design of a level in the game. The level designers are likely to make hundreds of adjustments and tweaks to a level. This implies strongly that a robust and easy-to-use level-building tool is a key requirement for the successful production of the game. Something less obvious may be the numbers behind the game mechanics in a game, such as weapon damage tables. Put these tables into easy-to-modify text files so that the designers are able to modify these directly without the aid of a programmer.

The Quality Assurance Plan

Quality assurance on a game project deserves its own book; however, I will use the remainder of this chapter to outline how the quality assurance plan is really a part of the technical design document that your programmers are creating and offer some suggestions for your quality assurance plan.

Your quality assurance plan should discuss a number of topics including the defect tracking system, automated testing sweeps, focus group, and beta testing. One of your programmers should be assigned to develop or help develop the QA plan with the lead QA team member. Often the lead QA guy over at the publisher is unavailable at project green-light and your team is on its own in the planning stages for the QA plan.

Defect Tracking

Tracking bugs is the central activity for the QA plan. If you do not actively identify and record your bugs, not much is going to get fixed. There are quite a number of details you might want to include in your bug reports; listed below is a good set of fields to track in your bug database:

- Bug ID—a unique identifier for a bug; never recycle bug IDs in the course of a project.

- Title—a one-line description of the bug

- Submitter—the name of the tester who entered the bug

- Description—a complete description of the bug including steps required to reproduce. Optionally, attached files such as screen shots or debug dumps may be included to help describe the bug's behavior.

- Date Submitted—the date this bug was born

- Build Number—this is a critical piece of information as you do not want your programmers chasing down bugs that have already been fixed or have been made obsolete in more recent builds or were understood to be nonfunctional with the build identified.

> >

- Production Status—this records the development team's status with the bug—Unassigned, In Work, Request Verify Fixed, Request Not A Bug, Cannot Duplicate, Need More Info, etc. There are a good many potential states that production could be in.

- QA Status—Is the bug open or closed? Perhaps your organization needs more resolution than that such as Closed—Verified Fixed, or Closed—Resolved.

- Platform—if your game is multi-platform, it is critical to state which platform the bug was identified on.

- System Specs—for PC games it might be quite handy to have the submitter's system specs readily accessible straight from the bug database.

- Owner—who is the current owner of the bug? Bugs without owners simply will not be addressed. Assign a bug back to the QA lead after development has fixed it so that it is now QA's job to verify the fixed bug.

- Severity—use numbers or descriptive words such as High, Medium, Low, and Suggestion or Critical, Important, Moderate, and Cosmetic.

- Area—use a field to note in what portion of the game this bug was identified, such as mission 1, or the main menu, or during multiplayer skirmish.

- Closed Date—note when the bug died.

- Verified By—the name of the tester who verified the bug fixed

- Notes—a free-form text area where the developers and QA folks may write short notes to each other in the pursuit of bug closure

- Bug Fixer—simply the person who corrected the bug

- Bug Change History—a little history noting the changes that a bug goes through in its lifetime

Defect Tracking Software

You will definitely want to track your bugs in a database of some kind. Many organizations build their own bug tracking databases using tools such as Microsoft Access, or you could use a professional quality tool like Merant's Tracker (http://www.merant.com/PVCS/products/tracker/index.html) or Mozilla's Bugzilla (http://bugzilla.mozilla.org).

Activision uses Tracker exclusively, and we have found it to be very productive with both a Windows client and a simple web browser client. The web browser client is relatively slow to use, but it does have the huge advantage of being able to check on the progress of SFC3 from my home or anywhere. Bugzilla also has a web interface.

The Testing Plan

The testing plan should detail what, how, who, and when the game will be tested. As for what to test, dust off the use case diagrams as they make an excellent checklist of the functionality the game is supposed to perform.

Additionally, set up lists to review each and every button for spelling and tool-tips, and check the alignment and positioning of all of your graphical assets. Check to be sure all of the assets are in the correct and final

‹ ‹

format. Be sure there are no extraneous files in the release build such as debug helper files and your lead artist's favorite MP3s!

The QA lead should build a large spreadsheet in Excel or some other handy application to track all the necessary tests that should be performed many times during the course of production.

Every button should be clicked, right-clicked, and double-clicked, the game should be run for days on end, the keyboard keys should all be mashed at once, and all of the controller buttons mashed. Now this sort of button smashing does not need to be tested often—at least one sweep after alpha or beta.

How Many Bugs Are Left to Find?

An extremely intriguing pair of ideas to estimate the number of bugs in your game can be found in Steve McConnell's *Software Project Survival Guide*. One is called defect pooling and the other is defect seeding; despite reading about these techniques in 1998, I have not yet been able to find a publisher's QA team willing to let me try them out on them! Read on to find out why.

Defect Pooling

The way defect pooling works is by taking your QA resources and dividing them into two separate pools—pool A and pool B. Pool A and pool B are then to go about their QA business as if the other team did not exist. All of the bugs pool A finds should be plugged into the bug database, and every bug pool B finds should be plugged into the database. Hopefully, *hopefully*, a great number of duplicate bug entries will show up in the bug database; and that

is a good thing? Yes. A simple pair of equations will illustrate how:

$$\text{Bugs}_{\text{Unique Identified Bugs}} = \text{Bugs}_{\text{Pool A}} + \text{Bugs}_{\text{Pool B}} - \text{Bugs}_{\text{Pool A \& B}}$$

$$\text{Bugs}_{\text{Total Unique Bugs That Exist}} = (\text{Bugs}_{\text{Pool A}} * \text{Bugs}_{\text{Pool B}}) / \text{Bugs}_{\text{Unique Identified Bugs}}$$

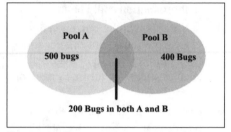

Using pools of bugs to estimate remaining bugs

To do this right the two QA pools must not become aware of the bugs already found by the other pool; otherwise you will not have an accurate count of the duplicate bug reports. It is common sense that this would work; imagine two end users who play your game for a year and they both find the same three bugs in the game. You would then be extremely confident that if you fix these three bugs, the game would be darn near bug-free. On the other hand, if these two players were finding about 50 new bugs a month in your game and there was absolutely zero overlap in their bug reports, then you should develop a deep and foreboding sense of apprehension as there appears to be no limit to the number of bugs in your game.

The reason why defect pooling has never worked for me is that no publisher was willing to double the size of the QA team for us. I am convinced this technique does not cost more; indeed I believe it would save the publishers a ton of money if they would test areas of

> >

the game until they met a certain over-lap requirement of, say, 75 percent bugs common to the two pools before shifting the attention of the QA team to another area of the game. To be handled efficiently, one would need to look into the feature set of the bug tracking software to set it up so that the testers in pool A would not be able to see the bugs in pool B, and some tool is needed to facilitate the marking of duplicate bugs between the pools (I am imagining some sort of neat 3D operating system where the QA lead could quickly draw spider-web-like connections between bugs).

Defect Seeding

Defect seeding is much easier to set up than defect pooling; in fact it does not require any work from the QA team to set up and monitor. Similar to defect pooling, the idea is to use a simple statistical modeling tool to estimate how many bugs could possibly be left to identify in the game.

To use defect seeding the development team must consciously *put bugs* into the game. All sorts of bugs: crash bugs, spelling errors, poor balance, etc. The more bugs placed throughout the game and at all levels of severity, the better the estimate it will produce.

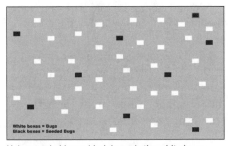

Using seeded bugs (dark boxes); the white boxes indicate normal bugs.

Now as QA discovers bugs in the game, the producer or lead programmer should track which of the seeded bugs have been identified by the QA team and which have yet to be identified. A simple equation shows how to use this information:

$$\text{Bugs}_{\text{Total Unique That Exist}} = (\text{Bugs}_{\text{Seeded Planted}} * \text{Bugs}_{\text{Seeded Found}}) * \text{Bugs}_{\text{All Reported So Far}}$$

A quick review of the seeded defects that have yet to be identified by the QA team will reveal a gap in their QA process, and the development team may then gently suggest focusing more time in the area of light coverage.

Notice that by carefully keeping track of the categorization of both the seeded and normal bugs you will be able to build estimates for the number of bugs total in portions of the game such as mission 1 vs. mission 10 or single-player versus multiplayer. This also is an excellent tool for guiding QA to areas that need more attention and for developing confidence that an area has received enough QA attention.

Political Resistance

Too many times on my game projects the QA team spends an inordinate amount of time testing the areas of the game *they want* to test and not enough time on this little corner here or over there. As I said earlier, I have yet to be able to get the QA teams I work with excited about either of these methods. It is just like trying to introduce UML or C++ to developers who do not use the tool currently; the resistance is caused by the perceived loss of time involved in learning the new method and some degree of fear that any formalized method of measuring the QA team's performance would reflect poorly on them. On the whole I find this ironic, as the QA team should be the most enthusiastic about identifying flaws in the process and wanting to improve them.

At Taldren we have occasionally placed a few seeded bugs, and we have informally tracked the overlap between our own QA folks and the publisher's folks and even compared that to the beta testers. Each of these casual efforts provided us with more information, and we felt that given time we should do this more rigorously. Of course it should be said that you must have a handy way of removing these seeded bugs from the game before release! This need to make the bugs easy to remove causes a slight distortion as regular bugs do not have this limitation, and thus the seeded bugs are not exactly statistically equivalent.

Automated Testing

Seeded defects are essentially tracking testing coverage. An efficient and reliable method of achieving testing coverage is to have a computer find the bugs automatically!

Various 3D first-person shooters have used this method by having the camera randomly teleport to a point in the level and pick a random direction to point at. This camera should just keep jumping around continuously looking for crash bugs.

There is also commercial testing software you can purchase that will do all of the random mouse clicking and button mashing you could hope for. To use automated testing well, you must challenge the creativity of your programmers to come up with scenarios that will tax your game's subsystems.

Beta Testing

You must have a plan for beta testing, not merely throw it out to whoever wants it, listen to the complaints, and fix the complaints until they stop. To use beta testers effectively you must be deliberate and spend a lot of time communicating with them.

Why are you using beta testers? Are you looking for free publicity for the game? Or are you looking for great compatibility testing? Or is your game a massively multiplayer game that simply must be beta tested by a great number of consumers? Are you looking for a second opinion on the interface or the game's balance? All of these are good reasons to use beta testers, and your plan for the beta testers must reflect the reason.

You should have at least one person who is given the responsibility of coordinating the activities with the beta testers and sorting through their complaints. (Note that this might be a second pool to use in a defect pooling system.) A web site should be set up with bug forms and other information such as a requested time to play the game online to get the player count on the servers up higher.

Essentially beta testers are untrained testers who want to be entertained and cannot be told to do anything specific as you are able to with a QA employee.

I may sound negative on beta testing but I am not! Taldren would not have enjoyed the success it has without the tremendous input from our beta testers at every step of the way.

When to Release the Game

The whole point of the QA plan is to develop an organized method for testing the game so that QA is able to give the thumbs-up to the rest of the team when the game is ready to be released, right? No. The QA plan and QA team exist only to identify flaws in the game and keep accurate records of the status of each bug. Too many games find themselves in an ugly period of war between the development team and the QA team. Sometimes games will sputter and stall while QA demands certain defects to be fixed and the development team practices some kind of passive-aggressive behavior and works on something else. The most critical element of the QA plan must be to articulate very clearly what objective, *measurable* quality goal the game must achieve before it is ready to be released.

For example, is the goal to ship the game with no known crash bugs, or no known crash bugs and no known text errors? Or perhaps ship with a mean gameplay time of six hours before a beta tester notices a bug? Or all high bugs fixed and 80 percent of the medium bugs fixed? All software and all games ship with bugs; knowing this, your QA plan cannot be to simply test and fix the game forever until someone feels enough pressure to ship the game (this is of course the normal method of determining when to ship a game). By making this an objective, measurable goal, the development and QA teams will be much more likely to work harmoniously together as they now have a common enemy: the release quality goal.

In the end do not let executive management shirk their duty. They are the ones who release software; development teams create software and QA teams test software. It is the executive management that is responsible for the business, and deciding when to release a game is as important a decision as they come.

> >

Chapter 19   > > > > > > > > > > > > > >

Time Estimates

The requirements analysis, game design, and technical design phases have us cover the most difficult part of project planning: identifying the tasks we must perform. Second to identifying the tasks is estimating how long it will take to complete them.

All great games are unique works of engineering and art carried out passionately by a team of game developers for an extended length of time. It is impossible at the start of the project to identify all the tasks that must be performed, and it is more than impossible to estimate exactly how long it will take to finish a creative effort that involves new bits of engineering and inspiration. Despite this challenge, if you walk into a publisher's office and announce at the end of your presentation that your project will take as long as it takes until the game is done, you will find yourself ushered out of the office after the publisher picks himself up off the ground. This calls for a story:

Recently Taldren required the services of an outside accounting firm; they quoted a price for their services that was a range, not a fixed bid. I dug a little deeper and it turned out they did not know if it was going to take them 20 or 40 hours to complete this accounting task for us. I gave it a moment's thought and realized that the accounting folks sure have their

business model more mature than the typical game developer. I am sure it is true that he does not know if it will take 20 hours, 40, or somewhere in between to perform this accounting work. However, I could not help being offended since the business model we game developers use is a fixed bid. I told the accountant that we must agree to a fixed price for projects between 30,000 and 60,000 man-hours! It should be common sense that it is far easier to estimate a task that a single person will be charged with and is expected to last less than a week compared to a project requiring two dozen developers for nearly two years. Yet if I used the same range as the accountant, I would quote our publisher's advances (fees) like this:

Publisher: "Congratulations, I believe in your game, and we will pick it up. But first, how long will it take to complete and how much in terms of advances will you require?"

Erik: "We have given it considerable thought and planning and have settled on a $2.6 million budget and ready in 18 months at the low end and $5.2 million and three years at the upper end; we will let you know as we progress."

And that is when the publisher falls off his chair laughing and I am ushered out of the building.

The funny thing is that in reality many, many game projects are actually run as in the scenario above. More often than not developers find out mid-project that they can no longer ignore the underbid, and the release date is looming near and the game is not ready. It is not uncommon for some games to receive multiple new infusions of time and cash. These failures to accurately bid a project force publishers to be even more defensive in their positions and demand even more profit from future game development deals.

I now realize why independent game companies are so much more efficient than the military and TV and movie industries—we have to be! That is something I am genuinely proud of—how much work we all get done with relatively modest resources. That being said we do need to do a better job of estimating our projects and slowly weaning our publishers off of time and money budgets that estimate the fewest dollars and have a non-zero probability of creating the game.

Now let us get on with the estimating.

Two Ways to Estimate a Task

I have a very simple view when estimating the time required for a task to be completed; it is always one of two answers: How much time will it take to complete the task *or* how long do we have to complete the task.

Time Boxing

I find that in practice it is a lot easier to deal with tasks that simply have to be executed by a certain time. I first heard the term "time boxing" from a technical director at Electronic Arts Sports when I asked him how he estimates how long it will take to do something that is technically very challenging when there is not a standard reference for how long it will take to complete. He replied that when you simply do not know how long a task will take, spend your estimating time figuring out how long you could *afford* to be working on the problem. That becomes your time estimate that you later plug into your Gantt chart. If you run out of time and the task is still not complete and you intend to honor

your time budget, you must abandon the task: Cut the feature, fall back to a less exciting version of the feature, or make some other cut to compensate for the loss. If you determine that you cannot perform a satisfactory cut and you are out of time, then you are stuck with going to your executive management team and advising them of your dilemma and requesting additional time and money, an activity you should avoid.

The elegant thing about time boxing is that you do not need to get bogged down in estimating something that is fundamentally unestimatable, and at the same time you have a powerful motivational tool for the developer(s) who must carry out the work. If someone knows that their work will simply be thrown away unless they complete it by a certain date, and that certain date is backed up by a rationally developed project plan, then they dig deep into themselves, concentrate, and usually find great satisfaction by pushing themselves to new levels of personal achievement to meet the deadline.

> **JARGON**: *Time boxing*—placing a rigid time constraint around a task that is based on the project not being able to afford more time on that particular task.

Task Estimating

The core of the chapter is estimating how long it will take to implement some software or create some artwork. The artwork side is considerably more reliable in predicting than the software side.

Art

Typically your game's art assets can be broken down into a certain number of models, textures, animations, rooms, levels, sprites, tiles, and so on. Estimating is then very straightforward; create one or two of these assets and assume that the rest will take as long or even a bit shorter as the team develops more experience with the tools and the desired artistic direction.

Have your artists keep careful records of how long it is actually taking to create the art assets. After about one month of production, stop and hold a meeting and review their data on how long it is taking them. Also follow up on anything that appears to be taking longer than expected and ask if there is anything that could be done to make them more productive. Usually at this point I find that the estimates are trending downward. It is vitally important to task the artists, like all developers, at less than 100 percent capacity to allow for the usual time loss of illness, vacation, system upgrades, and unusual family events. In the artists' case, however, there is also the inevitable need to

go back and iterate on specific areas of the game when an area is undergoing design drift or rapid technological development.

Design

My weakest area of task estimation is design. I have always led the design efforts at Taldren, and I am constantly undervaluing my time. As an entrepreneur I think it is perfectly normal to add another 10 hours of tasks to a 70-hour workweek. I say this glibly, without boasting, but it is the truth. This makes it difficult for the designers and producers below me, as I expect from them the same unflagging devotion to the company, and I feel I am not currently allocating enough time for design and production management. I recently returned from a visit to South Korea where I spent several days learning about how a game developer there, Makkoya, goes about its business of making games. One of the most striking impressions I had was that fully one-fourth of the company was devoted to game design! At Taldren, I am sure that one-fourth or more of the personnel enjoy significant responsibilities and authority in game design, but until this summer we never had a full-time employee exclusively devoted to game design. Game design is iterative and creative; this conspires to make it difficult to estimate how long it will take to *complete* a task. I generally allow approximately one man-day for the design of a screen or panel depending on its complexity. For larger systems such as how the combat system of an RPG system might work, a week might be appropriate to rough out the entire system and perhaps another two to three weeks to flesh out all of the details. In the end, you should have the designer responsible for the design task estimate how long it will take to complete the task. If game design is somewhat analogous to writing, then you should expect your designer to be able to generate three to ten pages of design a day. I feel uncomfortable attempting to distill the efforts of game design into too simplistic a metric. Please contact me if you have some better methods of estimating design tasks.

Programming

Programming tasks are notoriously difficult to estimate; in fact, it could be argued that the theme of this book revolves around the difficulty of planning software. There is no standardized method for predicting how long some programming task ought to take. There is no standard such as the number of lines of code per day per developer.

For example, if you create an incentive for programmers based on the number of lines of code, they will simply write more lines of code. This happened when Apple and IBM worked together on the Taligent operating system. The IBM engineers had labored under a number-of-lines-produced-per-day incentive program, while the Apple engineers were new to the system. The Apple engineers, being superb problem solvers and optimizers, realized they would be paid more money to write more lines of code, so they did—to the detriment to the project. Similar problems occur at the close of a project if management proposes bonuses based on the number of bugs closed per developer. Consciously or subconsciously, folks will realize that quality is not sought during development and

they might as well be sloppy and collect the bug fixing awards at the end of the month.

Hire the best folks you can and avoid using incentive programs that motivate your programmers to go into another direction besides making the best game possible, on time and on budget.

There are roughly four categories of programming tasks:

1. Difficult, due to the design being vague, a time risk
2. Tedious but not a time risk
3. Simple and not a time risk
4. Difficult and a time risk

Category number one: tasks are difficult and time-consuming because they are vague. In my opinion, this is the number one reason why schedules break in my firm opinion. Schedules do not break because the developer is pushing the envelope too hard or because the developer has explicitly agreed to too many features. Rather, the schedule breaks when the developer agrees to perform a task at a high level without digging deep enough to find all of the required subtasks.

This is also by far the most difficult process to consistently master: task identification. That is why so much of this book focuses on raising the formalism of the game development process by involving a separate requirements gathering phase and Unified Modeling Language for specifying software requirements—tasks.

So how do you know if a task has been broken down enough? My simple rule is to ask the programmer, "How are you going do X?"

The response "I don't know; when I get there I will figure it out," is an easy red flag to spot. This task requires immediate attention to break it down into smaller tasks.

Better is this response: "Um, I will start with looking at Y for inspiration and then I will plug away for a while until I am confident that this is the best method for performing X in a separate test-bed framework. Then I will integrate the new code." That response may well be detailed enough to feel comfortable depending on that task's unique circumstances. You will need to make the call if it requires deeper analysis.

Of course the reply "Oh that's easy. I wrote up my attack plan earlier in the day and sent it to you in an email; didn't you get it?" makes me feel all warm and fuzzy inside like a good beer.

Often the real difficulty is that the project is not far enough along to break down a task into finer resolution. To address this I demand much more resolution for the tasks upcoming in the next 60 days or so than I require of tasks much later in the schedule. I highly recommend meeting at the beginning of each milestone to assess the quality and depth of your game and technical design material for the upcoming milestone and quickly assign someone to drive to the required resolution in advance of the rest of the development team. In this manner your technical directors and art directors should act like scouts for an army scouring the future and reporting back and suggesting course changes.

Category two tasks are tedious and time consuming but low risk. These tasks are not especially difficult to estimate nor do they create much worry that something unexpected will occur to everyone's unpleasant surprise. The

danger that lies in these sorts of tasks is that due to their tedious, inglorious nature, the folks assigned to perform them will settle into a lower energy state, as their area is apparently not critical. This attitude could cause these tasks to go over budget, and again the resource assigned to the task may not understand the impact of running over schedule. There is not much trick in estimating these tasks; rather the challenge is maintaining a sense of importance and urgency in these tasks as the developer is working on them. You will need to show them what they will be working on next or how they could be helping out in other more exciting areas if they push through their slogful of tasks.

Category three tasks are simple and are not a time risk. Not much to be said here; these are straightforward. However, I do encourage you to load up your project with as many of these types of tasks as possible! As with long, tedious tasks, there is a minor danger of small, simple tasks seeming unimportant, and some time loss could occur here. However, I find this to be a relatively rare occurrence as most people derive pleasure from closing out their tasks, and the smaller tasks give them more apparent velocity on their task closure rate.

Category four tasks are the difficult, time-risk tasks that we touched on earlier with time boxing. These are the glory tasks usually assigned to your most senior programmers: create a new 3D engine, create a physics engine, reverse engineer something obscure, create a technique for doing anything no one has done before. The first thing to do with these types of tasks is be sure they are not masquerading as category one tasks, where the goals and design have been vaguely defined and that the current task appears difficult due to the breadth of the task. For example, "create a new 3D engine" is grossly vague as a task and could involve anywhere from the efforts of a few months to many man-years depending on the sophistication of the 3D engine requirements. This is clearly a candidate for breaking down into smaller steps. A better example of a category four task would be when John Carmack set out to put curved surfaces in Quake III. That would be an excellent task to wrap a time box around. (However, in John Carmack's case I would guess he just worked on it until he was satisfied with his efforts.)

At the end of the day you really want to eliminate as many of these types of tasks as possible from your game project. They act like festering boils on an otherwise healthy game project plan. Be sure each of these category four tasks that remain in your project are key features both in gameplay and in a marketing sense. If there is significant doubt that anyone will miss this particular feature, you should probably cut it and save yourself the schedule pressure.

Each Shall Estimate Thy Own Tasks

A key rule that I follow under all practical circumstances is to have my

programmers estimate their own tasks. This has several powerful benefits. The most powerful is that you have full buy-in from the developer that they have a reasonable schedule to follow. Another benefit is that you are growing your employee's strength in project planning and management by having them participate or, even better, shape the final game development schedule.

How will they derive their own time estimates? At the end it will come down to a very subjective calculation that distinguishes humans from computers. We are able to soak in data from a myriad of sources—past performance, expected performance, level of interest, motivation, and guesses—and in a relatively short period of time estimate how long it will take to perform a task.

Yep, that's it; at the end of the day it will come down to just a gut estimate. Of course the simpler the item is, such as implementing a dialog box, the more straightforward the estimating process is. However, I do not know of anyone who has a software-project-estimator-o-matic device for coming up with estimates.

Save Your Plans and Compare

To improve your developers' skill at estimating, take care not to throw away their original estimates, and take the time to compare them with the actual results achieved during production. This should always be educational no matter how senior the programmer.

Making the Plan

Now that we have identified all of our tasks and have generated time estimates for them, it is time to flip to the

next chapter and roll all of this data into a plan!

> >

Chapter 20 > > > > > > > > > > > > > > >

Putting It All Together into a Plan

A lot of game companies use Microsoft Project to plan their game project schedules. MS Project is decidedly stronger at planning schedules than maintaining schedules. There are many annoying difficulties getting a workable schedule out of MS Project, and it seems that maintaining the tasks is certainly the most time-consuming chore a producer will face.

There are a host of other project planning products that you may use, but from running my "Real Methods of Game Production" roundtables at the Game Developers Conference in 1999 and 2002, I have found there is no clearly superior tool to MS Project.

Project planning and task tracking are two separate activities in my mind, and all of the project planning software packages including MS Project purport to do both tasks well. The real truth is these software packages do a decent job at planning a project, but when it comes time to update the schedule by closing tasks and inserting new tasks, the process is slow and tedious. Many times I have simply started new schedules to plan out from that current point to the end of the project. Mind you, it is not impossible; it just takes a lot of time.

The larger game development teams schedule maintenance that is so time consuming they have a dedicated human on their team updating the schedule full time! Part of the problem is that game projects with 100 to 800 man-months lie somewhere between the two classes of project management software: the dozen or so man-months of effort for a marketing campaign (which MS Project is excellent for) and the hundreds of man-year efforts for major construction projects (for which you need very expensive software such as Primavera and a small group of dedicated project managers).

Okay, now on with the overview of MS Project.

The goal of a schedule is to organize all of the project's tasks, illustrate the dependencies between tasks, track progress, level tasks, and assist in scenario planning.

Dependencies need special care as you do not want some of your development team to stall for lack of art, for example, nor do you want a critical feature to fail to be completed on time for a given milestone because the key component of this critical feature must be completed by just one programmer who

< < < < < < < < < < < < < < < < < < < < < < < < < < < < <

is already tasked on *another* critical task.

Tracking progress is simply marking off tasks that have been completed.

Scenario planning is using the software to analyze different "what-if" scenarios such as "What if we cut the map editor altogether?"

Let's Create a Schedule for FishFood!

Go ahead and fire up your copy of MS Project. A wizard tool will pop up suggesting that you take up the wizard's offer; decline the offer, close, and close the window.

Create a New Project File

A blank project will be staring at you; dismiss this project and select File | New to create a new project file. A project information pop-up dialog will solicit either a start date or end date. Choose a start date to schedule from rather than an end date to schedule back from.

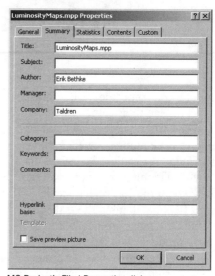

MS Project's File | Properties dialog

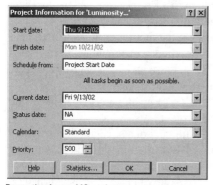

Properties for an MS project

Project, like all Office products, offers a properties dialog that you may fill out with a bunch of dull details such as author name, manager, company, etc. If you feel the need to decorate your files with such details, choose File | Properties.

What Is a PERT/Gantt Chart Anyway?

There are a myriad of diagrams, charts, and reports you are able to generate with Project. A good-sized project will be composed of thousands of bits of information from task names to assigned resources, start dates, priorities, and dependencies. The view you choose will reflect what you are trying to get a good look at. The two most common types of charts are Gantt and PERT. These were introduced in Chapter 10.

To review, the PERT chart is the visually simpler chart with boxes for tasks that are drawn left to right with

> >

dependency links between the boxes. The boxes may be detailed with duration and resource name.

The advantage of the PERT chart is that it displays the critical path of a project very well. It stands out like the trunk of a tree with non-critical path tasks stemming from the trunk as branches or sometimes as solitary boxes. PERT charts are fun to fill in as tasks are completed. The disadvantage to a PERT chart comes when you are charting more than just the high-level tasks, say fifty to a thousand tasks. When the number of tasks reaches that size, it takes a lot of paper to print out the chart, and the dependency lines may become too tangled to make much visual sense. Another minor disadvantage of the PERT chart is that since it is such a graphical layout, the project

manager might get distracted for an inordinate amount of time fiddling with the boxes and getting the layout of the boxes to look good. (This apparently remains a minor AI problem to solve someday: well-laid-out PERT charts.) Bottom line: PERT is good for overviews and easily constructed from the Gantt chart.

The Gantt chart consists of a spreadsheet of data on the left-hand side such as task ID, task name, start date, end date, duration, and resource name (who is going to do the job). On the right-hand side are the tasks graphically portrayed as bars of varying length proportional to their duration laid out left to right underneath the project calendar displayed at the top of the chart.

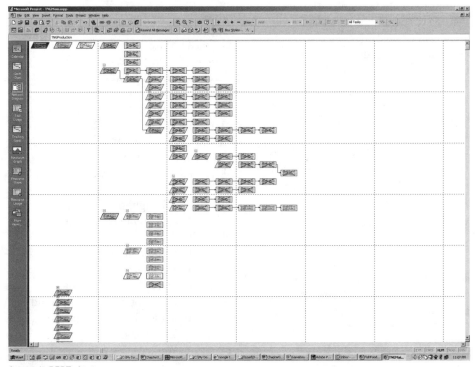

A sample PERT chart

< < < < < < < < < < < < < < < < < < < < < < < < < < < < < < < < <

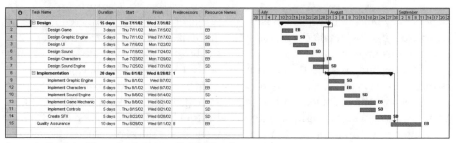

O	Task Name	Duration	Start	Finish	Predecessors	Resource Names
1	☐ Design	15 days	Thu 7/11/02	Wed 7/31/02		
2	Design Game	3 days	Thu 7/11/02	Mon 7/15/02		EB
4	Design Graphic Engine	5 days	Thu 7/11/02	Wed 7/17/02		SD
3	Design UI	5 days	Tue 7/16/02	Mon 7/22/02		EB
6	Design Sound	5 days	Thu 7/18/02	Wed 7/24/02		SD
5	Design Characters	5 days	Tue 7/23/02	Mon 7/29/02		EB
7	Design Sound Engine	5 days	Thu 7/25/02	Wed 7/31/02		SD
8	☐ Implementation	20 days	Thu 8/1/02	Wed 8/28/02	1	
9	Implement Graphic Engine	5 days	Thu 8/1/02	Wed 8/7/02		SD
12	Implement Characters	5 days	Thu 8/1/02	Wed 8/7/02		EB
10	Implement Sound Engine	5 days	Thu 8/8/02	Wed 8/14/02		SD
13	Implement Game Mechanic	10 days	Thu 8/8/02	Wed 8/21/02		EB
11	Implement Controls	5 days	Thu 8/15/02	Wed 8/21/02		SD
14	Create SFX	5 days	Thu 8/22/02	Wed 8/28/02		SD
15	Quality Assurance	10 days	Thu 8/29/02	Wed 9/11/02	8	EB

A sample Gantt chart for a simple game called FishFood!

The main advantage of the Gantt chart is that it is good for displaying up to several hundred tasks resulting in a finer granulation in your schedule. (The finer the granulation in your schedule, the more likely you are planning all of the required tasks, and thus the more likely you will be on time.)

Dependencies between tasks are drawn as simple arrows between the tasks. The Gantt chart is easy to read both from top to bottom, with the convention of the earlier tasks at the top, and from left to right as time passes.

The main disadvantage to the Gantt chart is, of course, the key strength of the PERT chart: that it is difficult to see at a glance the critical path of the project. Fortunately, with Project it is simple to enter your task information under the Gantt chart and later choose to view your scheduling information from any number of views such as the PERT chart.

Start Entering Tasks

Entering task information in Project really could not be easier. Pick a row and start by simply typing in the name of the task in the Task Name column, and enter the estimated time for duration. Bam, you have entered a basic task.

O	Task Name	Duration	Start	Finish	Predecessors	Resource Names
1	☐ Design	15 days	Thu 7/11/02	Wed 7/31/02		
2	Design Game	3 days	Thu 7/11/02	Mon 7/15/02		EB
4	Design Graphic Engine	5 days	Thu 7/11/02	Wed 7/17/02		SD
3	Design UI	5 days	Tue 7/16/02	Mon 7/22/02		EB
6	Design Sound	5 days	Thu 7/18/02	Wed 7/24/02		SD
5	Design Characters	5 days	Tue 7/23/02	Mon 7/29/02		EB
7	Design Sound Engine	5 days	Thu 7/25/02	Wed 7/31/02		SD
8	☐ Implementation	20 days	Thu 8/1/02	Wed 8/28/02	1	
9	Implement Graphic Engine	5 days	Thu 8/1/02	Wed 8/7/02		SD
12	Implement Characters	5 days	Thu 8/1/02	Wed 8/7/02		EB
10	Implement Sound Engine	5 days	Thu 8/8/02	Wed 8/14/02		SD
13	Implement Game Mechanic	10 days	Thu 8/8/02	Wed 8/21/02		EB
11	Implement Controls	5 days	Thu 8/15/02	Wed 8/21/02		SD
14	Create SFX	5 days	Thu 8/22/02	Wed 8/28/02		SD
15	Quality Assurance	10 days	Thu 8/29/02	Wed 9/11/02	8	EB

Focusing on a task name and duration

Now let's talk about task names. It is important to be sure the name of a task includes a strong verb like "purchase workstations" or "test logon protocol" or "implement save game" rather than the vague "workstations," "logon protocol," and "save game." The strong verb makes the difference between a task and a topic. I still make the mistake of using topic names rather than task names; this is usually a strong hint from my subconscious that this topic has not been thought out enough for me to feel comfortable articulating discrete tasks.

Another common mistake I see in game project schedules, including my own, is that the schedule is composed of only features to be implemented and assets to be created. You may be wondering what else there is to game production. Well, it does take actual time to test all of the deliverables in the milestone before you send it off to the publisher. It takes time to respond to the publisher's feedback, it takes time to go to E3, and it certainly takes loads of time creating the E3 build! It takes time to train developers on new tools such as when you switch from Character Studio to Maya. It takes time to create all of the documentation at the start of the project. It takes time to reconcile the schedule with reality. It takes time to submit a build to the license manager and get feedback. It takes time to plug in the sound effects and voice-overs. And it certainly takes time to balance and tweak your games.

Tasks Are Performed by Resources

The final key bit of information that you need to add to your task besides task name and duration is who will do the work—the resource. Enter the first name, last name, initials, job title, or alphanumeric string you want in the resource column.

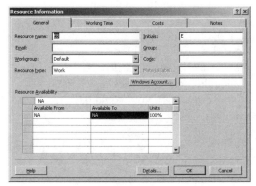

Adding a human resource to a project

If you do not know at this time who will be performing the task, as you want to see how things will stack up before deciding, guess, flip a coin, or choose somebody at this point. We will use Project's task leveling tool later to help us sort out who should be doing what for maximum productivity.

Where Does All of This Task Information Come From?

An excellent question to ask at this point is where these task names, time estimates, and durations are coming from.

Experienced game developers who have led large portions of games and who are tasked with creating a schedule for a type of game project they are familiar with will be able to sit down with Project and immediately dash off a few dozen tasks before pausing to think. However, at some point both the experienced project manager and the less experienced project manager will need to come up with tasks in a more formal manner. By far the best (and only) way to come up with the tasks is to get them from the people who will be carrying out the work, or at the very least the leads of each of the portions of the game project. For example, your lead animator should come up with estimates for all of your animation. I would advise against your lead programmer, who might specialize in graphics, coming up with the online multiplayer tasks; those should come from the multiplayer programmer herself.

You may choose to collect these tasks from a rather informal brainstorming session, or you might send an email out to everyone to review the design documents (game and technical) and come up with the tasks for their area of the project. The size and scope

< < < < < < < < < < < < < < < < < < < < < < < < < < < < < < <

of your project will determine what works best for your project. In general, if I am trying to execute a mini-project like getting a build ready for E3 or developing a demo for a brand-new game we will be pitching to publishers, the informal brainstorming approach works most efficiently for me. I reserve the more formal approach, where each resource is given perhaps a week to break down his area of the schedule into composite components, for the beginning of full production.

The reason it is so important to get the developers themselves to come up with the tasks is threefold: First, they are the experts in that field, and they will be better able to break the problem down into smaller pieces. Second, you want them to participate in the scheduling so that they understand better what they need to accomplish, why, and by when. Finally, by giving the developer the authority to set the time estimates you will achieve a far greater "buy-in" and sense of obligation to get the job done in a reasonable amount of time compared to when the schedule is passed down by a heavy (and often less knowledgeable) hand from above.

Organizing Tasks

I have to admit I like building MS Project Gantt charts (it is a good thing to like your job), and Project makes it easy to organize the tasks in your Gantt chart. There are nine levels of indentation to facilitate the logical grouping of tasks. As the tasks are coming in from your various team members, plug them into the chart, push them around, and indent them; have fun. Now is the time to make the schedule logical and clean. In fact, this aspect of project making is so easy I am able to do it in real time

for small projects with half a dozen of my guys riding shotgun over my shoulder, shouting out tasks and time estimates, and am able to keep up and cook a schedule together. Some people might shudder at the apparent lack of thought put into a schedule crafted in that manner; however, I have found that all schedules are merely estimates of what needs to happen. Also, most people's guesstimates of how long a task will take to complete will not be far off from a more carefully crafted estimate (both of which are bound to differ more relative to the actual time it took to complete the task compared to the difference between the two tasks).

Draw dependencies between tasks with reluctance; do not think that the more lines you draw on the Gantt chart the more accurate your schedule will become. Rather, group related tasks under super-tasks and draw dependencies between these chunkier bits.

Task Granularity

How fine in time resolution should your task estimations be—a day or a week or some other time? I have been back and forth across the issue and yes, the finer the resolution the more accurate and reliable the project is likely to be. If you could measure every task down to a quarter of a day, you would have tremendous resolution to work with, and you would have a Gantt chart that would impress the most jaded of executive management teams. The problem with schedules with ultra-fine task resolution is that they invariably become wrong quite quickly and require a tremendous amount of producer time to fix: Delete these 10 tasks, add these 20 tasks, modify the duration of these two dozen tasks, and so on.

> >

Thus, my new philosophy on task resolution for schedules is to cut the tasks into pieces as small as possible but no smaller than the producer has time to maintain. This is really just being honest with yourself and knowing what your time limitations are for maintaining the project plan. I would say that a schedule that has 15 developers working on a game for 15 months should have somewhere between 300 and 600 tasks in the project plan.

How to Account for Vacation and Sick Time

When creating your schedule you must account for vacation and sick time. I have to admit I was vexed for quite a while on how to best manage the planning for vacation and sick time. I mean, how would you know that your lead programmer would come down with bronchitis and lose seven days 13 months from now? If you try to stick tasks in the project plan called "vacation" or "sick days," you are creating a bunch of little falsehoods that will annoy you as you try to perform project leveling. Project will toss these tasks about all over the place, and you will start placing dependency lines or special instructions for the timing of each and every one of these tasks.

After thinking about the sick and vacation day problem for a long time, I have finally developed an elegant and easy solution: I modify the working calendar for all of the developers at Taldren and change Fridays to half-days. This effectively places two full days of fluff per month into the schedule, leaving 24 working days a year for sick and vacation time. Take whatever your company manual says about days off and adjust your Friday time off up

and down to suit your tastes (I recommend going a little bit conservative).

I like this method for handling unschedulable tasks so much I might start writing off part of Mondays for project maintenance, system upgrades, interviews, dog and pony shows, and other unplanned tasks that tend to affect everyone in the company at one time or another. By keeping these tasks separated on Mondays vs. Fridays, I will be able to adjust either one up or down as I develop more accurate historical data.

Remember Odd Tasks

Scour your collective brains to identify weird or odd tasks like trade shows, submission to hardware manufacturers, the installer, the auto-patcher, customer service, fan interaction, and so on. This is one area where experienced organizations have an edge on start-ups; the start-ups generally only plan for the absolute minimum of tasks yet still have to complete all the tasks that everyone else does as well.

Time Leveling in Project

The main advantage of a project tracking package such as MS Project over a task tracking database is the ability to analyze the loads between the various team members and perform task leveling.

There are two principal tools for performing task leveling in MS Project that complement each other in your quest for a clean, balanced schedule across your team: the automated leveling tool and the resource usage view.

After you plug in all of the tasks with the required bits of info of who and how long, click on Tools | Resource Leveling | Level Now….

‹ ‹

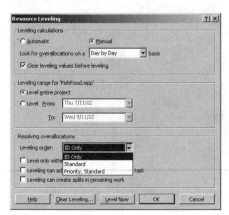

The Resource Leveling dialog in MS Project

cies between the tasks across all resources and lay them out in time in order to best accommodate a smooth path to completion. As you know, computers are not intelligent; as such, MS Project will make a finite number of dumb placements of tasks. Your job is to look over these errors and correct them through adding dependency lines, priority weightings, or time constraints such as "start no earlier than X date." After iterating for a while you will end up with a schedule that makes sense.

All done? No. If you click on the Resource Usage View button, you will discover that your task assignments have caused an uneven allocation of time across your team, as shown in the following figure.

Despite the intimidating number of choices on this dialog box, there are really only two meaningful options: to level by ID or to level by Priority, Stan-

	O	Resource Name	Work	Details	J	J	A	S	O	N	D	2003 J	F	M	A	M	J	J
		⊞ Unassigned	0 hrs	Work														
1		⊞ Alex	1,576 hrs	Work		132h	158h	152h	168h	148h	160h	164h	144h	152h	160h	40h		
2		⊞ Paul	1,504 hrs	Work		132h	158h	152h	168h	148h	160h	164h	144h	48h	160h	72h		
3		⊞ Scott	1,368 hrs	Work				144h	152h	168h	148h	160h	164h	144h	152h	136h		
4		⊞ Marc	1,384 hrs	Work				144h	152h	168h	148h	160h	164h	144h	152h	152h		
5		⊞ Joe	1,696 hrs	Work			144h	178h	168h	184h	168h	176h	184h	160h	168h	168h		
6		⊞ Ken	1,280 hrs	Work						60h	160h	164h	144h	152h	160h	156h	152h	132h
7		⊞ Zach	1,336 hrs	Work				152h	168h	148h	68h	64h	144h	152h	160h	156h	124h	
8		⊞ Sean	960 hrs	Work		108h	132h	126h	138h	126h	132h	138h	60h					
				Work														

The resource usage view before leveling

dard. For simple schedules with less than 300 tasks, I find that leveling by ID tends to work well as the Gantt chart will most likely be laid out with early tasks at the top of the chart and later tasks at the bottom of the chart. The Priority sort is useful when you have truly large project files and you have attached priority weighting to each of your tasks (if you do not weight individual tasks, then the leveling will behave as if you had chosen the ID sort).

What MS Project does during the leveling is look at all of the dependen-

You will see that some of your developers have large gaps of idle time in their schedule, and others are acting as the long pole and causing the game to sprawl out past the final delivery date. How do you fix this? You have to understand what MS Project is telling you. It is saying that the long pole folks have been assigned too many critical path tasks and the others with gaps in their schedules are twiddling their thumbs while waiting for the critical path folks to deliver the goods. The solution is to look for tasks belonging to the critical path folks that may be transferred to

> >

the people with gaps. This is very much an iterative process as you are looking for clever bits of reassignment that will neatly cover the gaps in some folks' schedules while eliminating the spikes in the critical path folks' schedules.

To solve the difference between developer A with a gap and developer B with a spike, you might have to rotate a subset of tasks through developer B and developer D to make it all work out. The goal is to massage your schedule until your resource usage view looks like a nice clean brick of time with all gaps filled and the whole team finishing up at the roughly the same time.

critical eye. Take the time to do this and you will make a schedule at least twice as strong as it was just a week previously. Novelists must do this with finished manuscripts; producers should also set aside their schedule for a time and revise.

How to Distribute the Schedule to the Team

A fine schedule that is locked up and kept in the oracle's tower is not very useful. A project plan must be a communication device used by the whole team. Every time I think of producers who keep the schedule information secret, I squint like Clint Eastwood and

0	Resource Name	Work	Details							2003					
				J	A	S	O	N	D	J	F	M	A	M	J
	⊞ Unassigned	0 hrs	Work												
1	⊞ Alex	1,576 hrs	Work	132h	156h	152h	168h	148h	160h	164h	144h	152h	160h	40h	
2	⊞ Paul	1,504 hrs	Work	132h	156h	152h	168h	148h	160h	164h	144h	48h	160h	72h	
3	⊞ Scott	1,368 hrs	Work		144h	152h	168h	148h	160h	164h	144h	152h	136h		
4	⊞ Marc	1,384 hrs	Work		144h	152h	168h	148h	160h	164h	144h	152h	152h		
5	⊞ Joe	1,696 hrs	Work	144h	176h	168h	184h	168h	176h	184h	160h	168h	168h		
6	⊞ Ken	1,280 hrs	Work		72h	152h	168h	88h	92h	164h	144h	152h	160h	88h	
7	⊞ Zach	1,336 hrs	Work			152h	168h	148h	160h	164h	144h	152h	160h	88h	
8	⊞ Sean	960 hrs	Work	108h	132h	126h	138h	126h	132h	138h	60h				

After leveling

Let it Jell

All freshly minted project plans are full of errors, inconsistencies, and omissions. All of my project plans needed several passes to get into shape, and the difference from the first draft to the first revision is always the most dramatic. You will not be able to fix these flaws the same day that you create the schedule. Instead you must let it jell for at least a week and then come back and read through the schedule carefully with the leads of your team with a

twitch my fingers looking for a gun. Managing a team is not a management vs. the developers contest! Take the schedule and paste it up on the wall! As the team members get tasks accomplished, have them go up and highlight completed tasks (more on measuring progress in the next chapter).

Take the time to create customized reports for each of your team members. MS Project boasts a number of reports including To Do Lists and a Who Does What list, as shown on the following page.

< < < < < < < < < < < < < < < < < < < < < < < < < <

To Do List as of Fri 9/13/02
FullSchedule-Joe

ID		Task Name	Duration	Start
Week of July 7				
6		Orientation with Unreal Tools (Joe)	7 days	Mon 7/8/02
Week of July 14				
6		Orientation with Unreal Tools (Joe)	7 days	Mon 7/8/02
11		PS2 Technical Design	10 days	Wed 7/17/02
Week of July 21				
11		PS2 Technical Design	10 days	Wed 7/17/02
Week of July 28				
11		PS2 Technical Design	10 days	Wed 7/17/02
97		Choose Game / Main Menu	3 days	Wed 7/31/02
Week of August 4				
98		Choose Character Archytpe	5 days	Mon 8/5/02
Week of August 11				
100		Improve attributes	2 days	Mon 8/12/02
101		Training intrinsic skills	3 days	Wed 8/14/02
Week of August 18				
102		Buying Gear, Weapons and Items	5 days	Mon 8/19/02
Week of August 25				
103		Information Terminals	3 days	Mon 8/26/02
104		Mission Briefing	4 days	Thu 8/29/02
Week of September 1				
104		Mission Briefing	4 days	Thu 8/29/02
105		Purchasing new (nanotech) skills	3 days	Wed 9/4/02
Week of September 8				
106		Illuminati Political Status	5 days	Mon 9/9/02
Week of September 15				
107		Selling Items	5 days	Mon 9/16/02
Week of September 22				
108		Load and Save Game	6 days	Mon 9/23/02
Week of September 29				
108		Load and Save Game	6 days	Mon 9/23/02
207		Test-Case Verification TestBot	8 days	Tue 10/1/02
Week of October 6				
207		Test-Case Verification TestBot	8 days	Tue 10/1/02
208		Automated engine stress case	7 days	Fri 10/11/02
Week of October 13				
208		Automated engine stress case	7 days	Fri 10/11/02
Week of October 20				
208		Automated engine stress case	7 days	Fri 10/11/02
Week of January 26				
277		Pickup Objects	7 days	Tue 1/28/03

Page 0

A sample To Do List report for the Black9 project

Also, you can sort the main Gantt chart by resource name and print out just that section of the schedule. Print out mini Gantt charts for each team member to stick up on their own walls— they'll love it!

> >

Chapter 21 > > > > > > > > > > > > > > >

Measuring Progress

On Leadership

There are many books you could buy on leadership, and I am sure many of them are worthwhile to read. In this section of the chapter I am putting down what I think leadership in game development is all about.

Know What Your Goal Is at All Times

As a leader your job is to be out in front and guide your troops to some goal. You will likely do a good job of leading towards the goal if you keep it in mind, and correspondingly you will do a crappy job if you cannot figure it out. This painfully straightforward fact is the number one responsibility of the leader.

Despite how obvious this rule is, it is all too easy to forget what the goal is. For the great majority of game projects it is to create a great game on time and on budget (three goals combined actually). I discussed in earlier chapters how to use your business parameters and how to shape these goals to reflect your specific goals. Here are a few examples of how the goal is sometimes forgotten:

As a leader you will sometimes come across employee behavior that is underwhelming. Specifically, you might have tasked an employee to perform a certain set of tasks only to learn later that he has not made good progress due to his claim of insufficient information to get the tasks completed. Your emotional reaction is to be defensive and point out all of the instruction you have already provided on the set of tasks and express your frustration that the employee is not telling the truth. Compounding this frustration, the conversation is taking place in front of other team members. You assert clearly that the employee is fibbing and is not recognizing the sufficient information you have provided to get the job done. Here you have blown it. The other employees are being presented with a choice of whom to believe—you or the employee in question. Is the employee lazy and not only shirking his work but lying and trying to shift blame to his supervisor? Or, are you being an arbitrary manager so insecure about yourself that you resort to being harsh on your employees in front of other team members? Either outcome is bad for the company; the employees lose a lot of respect for either you the manager or for their teammate. See? The leader in this case forgot the goal is to be sure the employee has all of the information and resources he needs to accomplish his task and was instead focused on defending himself at a considerable loss to the company.

What should the leader do? In most of the cases where employees are claiming that they are confused and do not have enough information to get the job done, the best policy is to provide them with more information until they understand what they need to do. If you are pressed for time and are unable to help them get this information, simply delegate the task directly to them! Ask them to figure out what the issues/goals/requirements for the task are and after they have figured out the task of what they are supposed to do, only then carry out the work. By far, most employees will respond well to this direction. If you have hired well (and I assume you have or you will have too many problems to be successful), then in the overwhelming majority of cases your employee is genuinely confused and it is indeed your fault that he does not know enough to make strong progress on the task.

In the game industry it is extremely common for most members of the development team to wear multiple hats and have quite a lot of responsibility. This is even truer of the managers on a game project. Most game industry managers must perform their management duties as well as a considerable amount of production work depending on the skill set of the manager and the needs of the project. I have seen several instances where the leader was overtasked and due to time pressure provided minimal guidance to his staff. In the end he got into a defensive argument with the staff over whether or not the employee had enough information to get the job done.

What do you do if the employee is truly lying and he *is* shirking his work and trying to blame it on you? This is a serious problem, and the best way to deal with this problem is to wait 24 hours to cool off and ask yourself again if his claim of not having enough information could be valid. If it still seems like an outright lie to you, then you must confront this employee and nip this bad behavior in the bud before it grows out of control. Specifically, do not dress him down in front of his teammates; instead, after the cooling-off period, take him into a private office and let him know that you are not losing your mind and that he is lying to you. Make this a verbal or written warning at your discretion and then be consistent. If he persists in this malevolent behavior, you will need to let him go before he corrupts the rest of your team.

There is a class of management problems similar to this I call *task rejection*. Naturally, you will want to minimize task rejection on your project, as it is extremely unproductive.

> **JARGON**: *Task rejection*—the author's term for the behavior of developers to sometimes carry out a task with some form of passive-aggressive behavior.

Employees practice task rejection due to a limited number of reasons:

1. They are simply employees with a poor work ethic.
2. They do not have enough information to carry out the task.
3. They feel that the goal as outlined to them is unattainable.
4. The employee is facing a problem in her personal life that is causing her a significant distraction.

I hesitated to list problem #4, because in my experience an otherwise competent employee even while faced with significant personal problems continues to perform her duties in good speed while under this distraction.

If you have an employee with a poor work ethic, I suggest you simply let him go. I find it impossible to instill a sense of work ethic in those who lack one. I believe that letting this type of worker go is honestly the best action you can take on behalf of the employee.

Problem #2 should be the easiest to solve and is by far the most common. I always find it amazing when I walk into an employee's office and ask what is going on with some task he is not getting done, and he pauses and thinks about the task, almost as if it was the first time he has given it deep thought. Then I discover that he does not have a key piece of information to get over some of hump. Your job is to simply supply the information or supply him with the path to the information and then he will be able to cheerfully carry on with the work.

The employee who feels he is facing an impossible task will usually feel defeat and will somewhat shut down. Some of your stronger employees will almost perversely focus in on a very narrow problem and solving that problem with superior quality. This is an issue you must resolve quickly. A key management task to keep your people happy and humming with bite-size achievable goals. It could be that the employee is correct and the goals you have outlined are too difficult to achieve, or it could be simply that he *perceives* that they are too much. In the case of the perception problem, it should be relatively straightforward to fix that impression. On the other hand, if the goal is truly unattainable, then you have a problem.

Why is the goal unattainable? Is it because you scheduled overaggressively in the desperate hope that your developers will chase your impossible deadline and will in turn be less late? Or is the goal simply unattainable? If you are between a rock and a hard place and you have no options, then I suggest you be open and honest and acknowledge to your employees that you know the goal is unattainable but you wish to press forward for some good reason. If you are a manager with a fake deadline approach, I implore you not to do this; it only burns out the development talent. Put more work into your scheduling and planning, and your projects should run smoother.

Set Goals, Not Hours

I got ahead of myself; why do I stress goals? Give your people specific targets such as "finish three character models by the end of the month" rather than set arbitrary hours. The reason is people pretty much finish what they are supposed to, whether that means finishing the character models or finishing their hours, and they optimize their work behavior to meet their goals. Which goal is more important to you: achieving some sort of milestone or being sure your team spends X number of hours working on your project?

Lately, I have been fond of setting achievable but difficult goals for my team such as "Clear 200 bugs from the database this week and you can all take Friday off." They enjoy the empowerment and dig in and focus.

Task Tracking

To measure project progress you must track the tasks that have been completed, the remaining tasks, and the newly identified tasks. Microsoft Project as a project management software solution, you would think, would be great for tracking what has been completed, what remains, and what is new. It turns out that it is fairly tedious to do all these activities. I swear I think Taldren could make a bunch of money by creating a truly easy-to-use and effective project tracking software package. In MS Project, tasks that are completed are difficult to move around; as soon as you mark them 100 percent complete, they are frozen in the schedule like boulders in the stream. If you are using the automated leveling tool (one of the main reasons to be using Project in the first place), these boulders act as annoying nuisances that must be manually moved about. If a task is marked completed but lies in the future, I think Project should shift it back in time behind "now," adjusting duration if need be; the task is done! So Project does not help much when it comes time to mark tasks complete. Entering new tasks is actually easier in my opinion than marking tasks complete. It still requires adjusting the dependencies between tasks and probably re-leveling work between resources. However, that work is appropriate and necessary as you want to understand the impact of the new tasks on the rest of the schedule.

What is the alternative to tracking a project in MS Project? From running my roundtable "Real Methods of Game Production" at the Game Developers Conference, I have found that most folks use MS Project to *plan* their game projects and use either Excel, a database application, or a bug tracking application to track their project tasks. All three of these treat a task as a record in a simple database, allowing the manager to quickly add records and modify existing records. It is easy to sort the records both in a spreadsheet and in a bug tracking system (note that database applications like FileMaker Pro and Access are used to create rough, internal bug/task tracking database applications).

The ease of use of these systems blows away MS Project in raw speed for the manager. The great negative of dispensing with MS Project is that you will not be able to identify critical paths, overloaded resources, or task dependencies. Those are powerful project management tools to set aside. In the real world it seems that all of the best-laid plans fall victim to the Pile-Of-Stuff-We-Must-Do-So-Why-Bother-With-Project philosophy. This is a heavy problem on my heart, and I have not yet figured out how to best solve this problem other than have better project management tools. Some teams literally have a full-time human devoted to updating MS Project files for large teams of 25+ developers; other smaller teams of 10 or fewer simply keep lists of things to do from high to low and work on the highs until they are all gone and then the mediums and then the lows. You need to measure the size of your team and figure out what level of methodology you require.

I do have a specific recommendation though: Use MS Project to create a skeleton of real, measurable tasks that

> >

are almost like a continuous string of micro-milestones each of your team members must achieve for the game to ship on time. Then use a spreadsheet or database application to track the thousands of minor bugs and tasks that come up during actual production of the game. This allows you to maintain an MS Project plan to do high-level project planning tasks like deciding you cannot afford to take the time to create the map editor so all of the tasks associated with the map editor should be pruned from the plan. Or you see that the animation work is falling behind and that you need to hire another animator.

As for specific bug tracking software to use, see the section on quality assurance in Chapter 18, "Technical Design."

Only Visible Tasks Are Completed

It might be a little extreme, but I feel it is a useful axiom of project management to assume that only visible tasks will be completed by the development team. I have a bagful of techniques that I use to make tasks visible.

The Daily Journal

Games are built a day at a time, and there are a surprising few number of days to complete a game. If you are slated to make a game in 18 months, then from a Wednesday to a Friday each of your developers must complete a full 1 percent of all they are going to put into the game. Each day counts. That is why I force my guys to figure out what they are going to get accomplished each day when they arrive in the morning and publish that information on our intranet application we call the Daily Journal. Below is a screen shot from one of my entries.

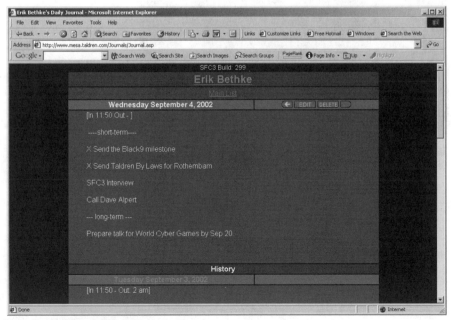

September 4, 2002, of my Daily Journal entry

< < < < < < < < < < < < < < < < < < < < < < < < < < < < < <

The Daily Journal is a simple application that stores your journal entries day by day. As you can see, it displays my name as a link so that anyone can click on it and go back and view the whole history of my daily entries as shown in the following screen shot:

Where the task visibility shows is in the view where each person's daily journal is automatically scanned for the first line and compiled into a what-everyone-is-doing-at-a-glance view, shown in the figure on the following page.

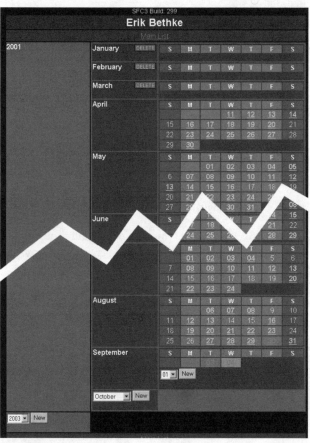

The Daily Journal provides a long history of activities.

> >

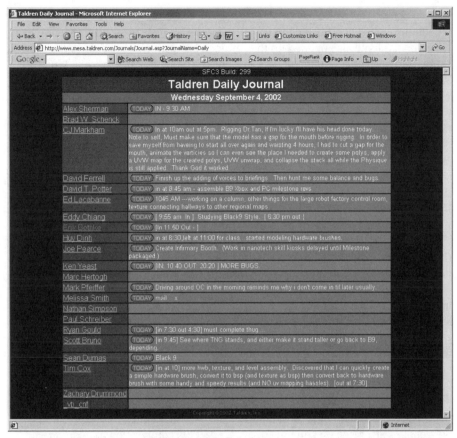

The what-everyone-is-doing-at-a-glance mode of the Daily Journal

You may notice that we are able to customize it at will and place such information as the SFC3 build number, which is automatically generated by our build machine. This assists people entering and reviewing bugs to be able to know the current build. Another custom we have is to note what time we came in that day and what time we left. We also use the notation of an X next to a task that has been completed and an O next to a task that is in progress (sometimes I only give myself the credit of a lowercase o if I do not feel that I have made significant progress on a task).

The whole team-at-a-glance mode has vastly increased the efficacy of my managers as well as myself for collecting the information about what everyone is working on that day. When I was working at the Dreamer's Guild they once tried a system where a producer with a clipboard would walk through, asking each person what he or she had accomplished that day or week. I remember how we resented that person and the clipboard as a waste of time and wondered why someone could not find a workstation for them and put them to work! Now with the Daily

Journal not only have we saved a tremendous amount of precious human time, but we have also opened up the Daily Journal to every single person in the company! You would be surprised what a morale booster it is for everyone to be able to check up on me or anyone else in the company and see what is going on. Some people are naturally positive and others are naturally suspicious. With full visibility up and down the chain, everyone is reassured what the rest are doing. Similarly, the Daily Journal acts as a polite forum for showing off what you have accomplished to the whole company without drawing undue attention to yourself.

Finally, the Daily Journal acts as a just-in-time troubleshooting device, as many times you will see someone working on task X that reminds you that you need task Y from him or her, or that, whoa, task X shouldn't start yet; work on task Z instead! I also encourage people to write in concerns that need airing team-wide to get multiple people's attention on solving difficult or vague problems.

In principle many of these functions could be accomplished by sending an email to the whole team; however, that would end up being more stuff in my email box for me to sort through compared to the elegant web display.

The Wall

The wall is in reference to a number of ways I plaster our walls with task lists. I discovered when I first started leading teams that people have a very flexible amount of energy and focus that they bring to their development day, and it is up to you as the project leader to harness the full value of their day.

I noticed that game developers love to *compete*. A healthy team loves to kick ass with the tasks and wants to clear them off and move on. Typically this exhibits itself with some members of the team checking off all their tasks and checking out early while other poor souls have their weekend doomed to finish up their tasks.

I started by extracting from MS Project or the bug list the tasks that had to be completed by the next milestone. I wrote them out on a whiteboard in my office with a column for each member of the team and asked my team members to come in and check off their tasks the moment they were completed—not in batches! The effect was to create a little game where people would come in and check off their tasks and simultaneously see how they stood compared to the others on the team. If they were "ahead" they would feel good, and if they were "behind" they would feel the pressure to focus and get stuff checked off.

This competition bit works really well. However, as every manager should admit, when the tasks were assigned they were only *estimated* to be leveled out between the developers; many surprises and details occur during development. I have always maintained that game development is a team effort, and I do not like people to gloat that they are way ahead of everyone else. Instead of allowing ugly disparities between team members, I continuously adjust task assignments to do real-time leveling. This relieves the pressure on the folks who were behind and were feeling that their load was unachievable, and it puts healthy pressure on the guys who were ahead to get back and put their shoulder into the problem.

> >

This is the key to the management style I have used throughout my career in leading games, and I feel it is the only fair way to manage the team. Of course this real-time task leveling requires a lot of judgment to be sure that all of the team members will not task reject and not take advantage of the "free leveling." This I have found not to be a real problem in practice, as we only hire excellent people.

I do not use whiteboards anymore as my handwriting is not very good and it is too slow to update. Instead, I use MS Excel to create lists in a spreadsheet to create punch lists of tasks that need rapid execution. See the following for a real example of a list of tasks on SFC3 during mid-production:

Status	Who	Art?	Priority	Est	Where	What
	MH		10	E	Skirmish	If I am the only human and I click start - auto ready all players and begin the game
	MH		10	E	Skirmish	All ships should default to higher officers
	MH		10	E	Skirmish	Need to supply the mission objectives for a skirmish game
	MH		6	E	Supply Ship	Do not display Trade-In or Cost of ship in a non-campaign game
	MH		7	M	Skirmish	Removing frustrating highlighting mechanic as per Scott's comment on the different player lines
	MH		7	M	Skirmish	Hang in skirmish setup when I was doing free-for-all between a Fed DN and a Kli DN and I clicked on all sub panels like Officers, Refit, Supply for both ships
	MH	Yes	3	M	Skirmish	Where do we put mission descriptions? Or just have longer more descriptive mission names
	MH	Yes	10	H	Skirmish	The clickable options need to be visibly clickable - suggest a shadow box or something????
	DF		10	E	Battlefest	Always default newly spawned ships in skirmish to Red Alert
	DF		10	E	Battlefest	Delay after the player dies before spawning new ship to savor the explosion
	DF		10	E	Battlefest	Battlefest ships should be created with good tractors, anti-cloak device, etc...
	DF		8	E	Tactical	Rear-firing torpedo arcs are too narrow
	Art	Yes	10	E	Everywhere	All weapon arc pie charts should have a bright color for the actual arc and darkness for out of arc.
	Art	Yes	10	E	Everywhere	Cloaking Devices need an icon
	Art	Yes	10	E	Tactical	Remove the target speed indicator hole in the bottom bar
	Art	Yes	10	E	Tactical	Weapon arc button needs to be reversed
	Art	Yes	10	E	Vessel Library / Refit	Weapon arc button needs to be reveresed
	Art	Yes	8	E	Everywhere	Warp system icon needs to be revisited
	Art	Yes	6	E	Tactical	Remove metal border around the tactical map
	Art	Yes	9	M	Vessel Library / Refit	Move the variant choose to just under the ship description at the top of the screen
	Art	Yes	8	M	Tactical	Open up the shield reinforcement click area
	Art	Yes	6	M	Tactical	Speed text at the bottom bar hole needs to stop jumping around
	SB		10	E	Reticule	Move all of the target related text under the tactical map
	SB		10	E	Reticule	Remove target name from the reticule
	SB		10	E	Reticule	Remove speed and range from the reticule

< < < < < < < < < < < < < < < < < < < < < < < < < < < <

Status	Who	Art?	Priority	Est	Where	What
	SB		10	E	Reticule	Change the reticule art to the art explored in Photoshop by Erik and Scott
	SB		10	E	Tactical	Firing probes will uncover cloaked ships within a radius of 5 around the probe
	SB		10	E	Weapon Text	Weapon text on the HUD screen should be separated for each weapon
	SB		10	E	Weapon Text	Weapon text shall be colored Green for Charged & in arc, Yellow for Charged and out of arc, and Red for uncharged, offline, or destroyed
	SB		10	E	Weapon Text	Weapon text status text should be "Ready", "No Arc", "No Charge", "Offline" and "Destroyed" with Offline, No Charge and Destroyed all sharing the red color state
	SB		9	E	Tactical	All ships' basic scanners should have a weak anti-cloak ability
	SB		9	E	Tactical	Verify that the battle report stats are accurate
	SB		9	E	Tactical	Remove player fleet loss stat from battle report
	SB		8	E	Tactical	Do not draw the multiple tube bar below weapon icons
	SB		8	E	Tactical	Have a greater penalty for losing cloak status if fly too close or too fast
	SB		8	E	Tactical	High forward speed and reverse need more penalties
	SB		8	E	Tactical	When tapping the Z key and you have no target or a friendly selected have an officer say "No enemy targeted, sir."
	SB		8	E	Tactical	Display the mission title
	SB		7	E	Tactical	Have an Officer warn the player that a ship has uncloaked nearby
	SB	Yes	7	E	Tactical	Add to the enemy schematic area the current subsystem target
	SB		7	E	Tactical	Torpedoes should explode on your hull
	SB		7	E	Tactical	Ship explosions should be less lethal, but do damage out to a farther range as per the effect
	SB	.	6	E	Debug	Add the ability to jump into an AI ship to see what is going on
	SB		5	E	Tactical	Remain targeted on the enemy while cloaked even if the player taps away on T and doesn't actually target anything else
	SB	Yes	4	E	Tactical	Chop up the bottom bar indicator lights into three states reflected no charge, charge, and finally when in arc, light the other two buttons
	SB		4	E	Tactical	Display the player's race logo when no target selected
	SB		10	M	Tactical	The weapon & systems icons shall go from Green to Yellow to Red and then to Black when destroyed
	SB		8	M	Multiplayer	Add a "shot-clock" to the game to prevent non-engaging idiots from delaying the game. After 10 turns of no activity a cloak appears and counts down 3 turns. If this timer passes without DAMAGE being scored the game is ruled a draw
	SB		8	M	Tactical	Everyone gets basic mines, use the mine layer device for big mines
	SB		8	M	Vessel Library / Refit	Reorganize the ship class as per Scott's recommendation
	SB		7	M	Tactical	Tone down the cloak effect for larger ships
	SB		7	M	Tactical	Tone down the warp effect for larger ships

A bit of this real-world spreadsheet

These spreadsheets I then post in a centralized hallway near my office and have the development team come by as tasks are completed and check them off. This creates the same visibility and competitiveness effect as with the whiteboard but with the added benefit that I am able to print out individual copies so the guys are able to have their own copy of what they are assigned at their desk.

On Starfleet Command 1 I took this to an extreme and prepared daily spreadsheets for each one of the team members and left their task lists on their keyboards like some sort of evil project tooth fairy. This worked out great for everyone and we had tremendous efficiency, but at a great cost of my time. Today I feel it is better to create lists once a week and update as required. The closer you are to final candidate, then of course you will need to update the lists more often.

Many of you might be surprised that we have this nifty web solution for our daily journal and at the same time use the relatively crude spreadsheet method of delivering tasks. Why do we not use a bug tracking application or some other web application? The answer is that we do use a bug tracking application, and it does that job very well. However, those bug tracking applications do not *focus* people on the tasks they must get accomplished and in what order.

To avoid the Sisyphus effect of constantly taking away people's accomplishments and replacing them with fresh new lists of stuff to finish, I simply leave on the spreadsheets a fair amount of what they have already accomplished. This looks great when visitors come by and look over these

heavily marked up lists of stuff, and the individual team members take pride in a pile of checked off tasks.

Team Meetings

Another necessary aspect of task visibility is to hold team meetings. I am on record for hating meetings. I hate seeing people stare at the ceiling and drool and the inevitable silly developer jokes that crop up in a meeting that is poorly focused and whose only purpose appears to be to steal everyone's life. I have been at my share of stupid meetings—Dilbert stuff. At Taldren we have no standing scheduled meetings; instead we have core hours, and other managers and I call meetings at will when required. Most of these meetings focus on a narrow problem that crosses the border between several team members. The type of meeting that is relevant for this discussion is the team meeting. Lately we have been calling meetings right after delivering a milestone for Black9 with the rough agenda of "What *exactly* are we going to accomplish for the upcoming milestone," followed a couple of weeks later with a meeting discussing "How are we going to finish up this milestone?" Despite the Daily Journal, email, the wall, and management by walking around, there seems to be some magical energy about the team meeting where people really do open up and share their problems and concerns and seek out help from the other team members.

I simply cannot count how many new tasks are discovered during a team meeting. I now have a ritual of asking each person to declare out loud how they interpret their milestone obligations and discuss in general terms how they are going to go about completing

‹ ‹

these obligations. This seems to have tremendous power in creating these verbal contracts between team members as I cannot ever recall hearing one of my guys express verbally what he will get accomplished and see him fail to finish it (maybe late, but always accomplished). It seems that folks in general are more worried about letting down their team members in a public forum than facing their manager in a private meeting in an office. I am sure some productivity consultant somewhere has a good explanation; please forward it to me if you come across one.

Of Leaves and Gutters

The final word I would like to say about measuring progress is that sometimes change for change's sake will increase your team's productivity. The way change can usefully be applied to task tracking is to sometimes change the focus of the team. Let me provide a healthy example:

I have noticed that game projects collect a great number of small and easy tasks that are clearly of less importance than the high-priority stuff the team has been grinding through. To harness the effect of change, every once in a while I will come in on a Monday morning and tell everyone, "Okay, this week I want every one of the text errors and stupid little bugs cleaned out of the bug database. Finish them and take Friday off!" The team loves the change of pace from working on tough bugs to tearing through a bunch of small stuff and seeing the overall bug count come down. As a manager you can feel good about this, for no matter how trivial a bug is, it takes time to fix. And you cannot allow the game to ship with easy-to-fix bugs, so you might as well clean them up. I would much rather fix 10 to 20 easy bugs than fix one medium bug that is obscure and difficult to fix. I call these bugs *leaves*, and I think of this switching of focus as clearing out the leaves from the *gutters*.

If you are having trouble with your publisher asking for an unending stream of new features and feature revisions, I feel it is entirely healthy for a project to stop and take measure of the true progress of the project by focusing the team on clearing the gutters of these leaves and seeing how much time is left for addressing new features and feature revisions.

> >

Chapter 22   > > > > > > > > > > > > > > >

Controlling Feature Creep

Making games well would be hard enough if we were challenged with just identifying the tasks and estimating them well at the outset of a project; however, it is made nearly impossible (and impossible for the cancelled projects) when someone goes about adding features during production of a game.

Now why would anyone do such an evil act?

The answer is they are not being evil, they are just trying to make the game better by adding something to the game. I will be the first to say that no game design ever laid to paper was ever complete before production began and that all games need to have their feature set tweaked, expanded, reduced, folded, and spindled during the course of production. That being said, this chapter focuses on how to best direct this creative energy to being more creative than destructive to your game project.

Great Games Satisfy Player Expectations

Careful analysis of all great games will show that they fully delivered on all expectations that the game developers planted in the minds of the players and then brought these expectations full circle with excellent implementation of these features. For example, Blizzard's Diablo is one of the more simple games ever created in the RPG genre, arguably only a slightly more sophisticated cousin of the arcade game Gauntlet, yet Diablo has enjoyed far more commercial success than the mega-RPGs that Bethesda has put out in the Elder Scrolls series. I have to admit, I love the Bethesda games and long to lose myself in game worlds that are larger than I am able to

explore. Yet the Bethesda games are distinctly weaker in execution than the Blizzard games. This weakness I feel is directly attributable to the sheer amount of expectations that the Bethesda games open up. For example, Bethesda games pride themselves on having huge worlds where you can step off the story path and explore anywhere you want. Well, I go exploring off the beaten path and quickly find the nonscripted fare to be pretty tame, canned, repetitive encounters that due to the complexity of the software are relatively buggy. Diablo, on the other hand, features one of the smallest game worlds in modern games that still somehow gets you from a quaint medieval village through 15 layers of underground dungeons complete with exploring hell itself!

id's games are the finest examples of small, tight feature sets that fully deliver. The reason feature creep happens is that while a game is in production it is often difficult to imagine how the final gameplay will feel, and out of anxiety or lack of confidence people start to suggest more and more stuff to throw into the pot. If you think about excellent cooking, it too tends to be simple in ingredients when the chef is confident about his craft, and tends to have the flavors and spices all run together in a muddy mess when the chef is lacking confidence.

My basic belief is that feature creep is bad and that every new feature proposed should have to claw its way through a gantlet of interrogation and examination before allowing the proposed feature to take its place upon the sacred schedule.

Feature Creep Occurs During Design

Feature creep actually starts during the earliest parts of the project: requirements gathering and game design. Here it is quite easy to lose track of the core game you are making (because it is still so fresh and new) and start sprawling a bit and tossing in ill-considered, distracting features. The solution to this problem is to let the game design document jell for a few days and then crack it back open and consciously mark each and every task as primary, secondary, or tertiary.

Primary, Secondary, and Tertiary

Right at the outset a lot of your features really are not as central and core to the game as other features. Aggressively push to move as many features into secondary and tertiary positions as you can, right up to the point where you feel you are compromising the game, and then push just a tad more. In Microsoft Project you will be able to make notes on the tasks and track the lower priority tasks by assigning them a low-priority weighting. For visual clarity consider using different colors for primary, secondary, and tertiary. Some managers feel this is the wrong framework for getting the most work out of their developers. They would instead rather consider every possible task a must-do task and reluctantly cut tasks when forced by reality at the end of the project. I have found through direct, hands-on management of my folks (of which there is a wide personality spectrum) that they relish checking off their primary task lists and love to then tear through their secondary and tertiary tasks rather than plug away at an impossibly long task list where the producer comes along every so often and cuts away tasks that are clearly low priority when there is no more overtime to give.

Feature Walking

Feature walking is where a single instance of feature creep sprawls into a whole new series of feature requests and bugs to be fixed. I find these situations to be the most frustrating. Here you are, successfully carving time out of the schedule to complete a feature request only to find out you are further behind than if you had never agreed to the feature in the first place. Be especially alert when you accept a new feature, and try as hard as possible to identify where this new feature may take you.

Publisher-Suggested Features

The most difficult features to cut are the features suggested by your publisher. These may come from their executive management, from their QA staff, or directly from your producer at the publisher. Most of these folks to some degree or another wish they were the designers on the game. This is actually a good thing; you want the folks working at the publisher's place to be passionate about the game and to have enough interest in games in general to execute their actual job descriptions. The side effect of this required skill set and passion is an ongoing list of feature suggestions and revisions from these publisher folks. Publishers hold the great majority of power in the game developer-game publisher relationship due to being the source of capital as well as access to market. This steady imbibing of subconscious power often makes it difficult for the publisher to constructively accept rejection of a feature suggestion they have made to the developer. As a publisher they feel it is morally within their right to request these changes.

My advice is to avoid outright rejection of these publisher feature requests. Instead, you should track them: Immediately tag a feature suggestion with a priority label of primary, secondary, or tertiary and also develop a time estimate for the suggestion if your resources have time to look into it

(the suggestion may be of such low priority it does not merit the distraction of your team members to estimate how long it will take to complete).

As these publisher suggestions begin to pile up, your publisher will likely begin to develop a sensitivity to the pile of work they have been suggesting and will likely become sympathetic and roll up their sleeves and participate with the feature cutting as well as the feature creeping.

No matter how the publisher tries to position their suggestions constructively, push back and do not allow them to develop the assertion that their suggestions (or QA's or the beta tester's) are somehow more objective than your own team's suggestions. In my opinion all of this game creation work is pretty messy gut-call decisions when you look closely.

In fact, the ugly truth of the matter is that many of these publisher (or QA or beta test) ideas are in fact simply bad ideas. This too will be politically difficult for the game developer to respond to. I do, however, have a technique I use that I feel works best for everyone and of course requires the most work. Instead of dismissing poor suggestions out of hand and getting into a shouting match with your publisher, stop and think to yourself *why* they made that particular suggestion. The *suggestion* itself may be crummy, but what you should be interested in discovering is why they made the suggestion in the first place. What was bothering them that they are trying to fix? Focus on that and develop a conversation with the publisher. This is good game design and excellent customer service. The publisher should respond to your genuine efforts to solve their identified problem and should be more than willing to drop their poor suggestion if you are able to mutually develop a truer solution to the problem they identified.

Push Independent Tasks to the End

No matter what the priority a given task may be assigned, strive to push newly suggested features as far back in the schedule as possible. Any new feature suggestion task that might be independently completed (and no other task would be dependent on that task being completed) should be pushed back. The reason for this is that so many suggested features tagged with a high priority under the relatively rosy-tinted glasses worn at the project's beginning phases will undergo rapid transformation into not-so-important tasks when it is closer to the end and time is running short. This critical hard tack must be held through development; otherwise the addition of these "high-priority" new features will cause the schedule to break and possibly jeopardize a planned, truly core feature later in the schedule. These dropped core features create the jarring lapses between creating player expectations and failing to fulfill these expectations. This is where great game ideas are turned into mediocre released games.

Regularly Practice Feature Cutting

I have talked a lot so far about how to manage the feature creeping phenomena, however I have not really provided any specific advice as to what to do with your secondary and tertiary features.

My rule of thumb: Be sure to implement fully all primary features, pretty much cut all tertiary features (unless they are trivial to execute), and use the secondary features as a source of morale and personal accomplishment for your developers to chew through as the schedule allows. In other words, as soon as you mark something as tertiary you are emotionally accepting it to be cancelled without further ado.

The producer should either call a meeting or just handle the feature cutting herself. I recommend at the beginning of the milestone phase that the producer review all of the outstanding secondary suggestions and determine if any of these need to become tertiary, and if the schedule is under pressure, determine which of the primary tasks must be converted to secondary for the project to remain on time. Remember, it is always far easier to resurrect a task if you find yourself running ahead again compared to saving the project after it has already run significantly over budget due to distractions of minor tasks.

If your tertiary task bucket is getting too full, I suggest the elegant solution of opening up a spreadsheet or database to track suggested features for version 2.0 of the game you have in production. This has the double effect of easing ugly pressure on the current game as well as creating the positive feeling of a sequel to the current work being planned. I call this activity flushing ideas to the dream pile.

How far should you cut back? If you are ahead of schedule, obviously the pressure to cut will not be that great. However, do not get too cocky as something down the road could always pop up and chew through your time surplus and more in short order. I recommend completing each milestone

> >

two to four weeks before it is due if at all possible.

If you are just on time, I would recommend being a bit more aggressive as your developers will actually work harder and with higher quality if you ease the schedule pressure on them and turn them into heroes.

Finally, if you are running late, you must act quickly and decisively to cut the feature suggestions down to a more reasonable size. Your developers are actually performing below their best, as they feel like losers for allowing the project to get behind schedule. You must remove this ugly feeling by pushing enough primary features to secondary to put you immediately back on schedule without any use of 80-hour workweeks.

> >

Chapter 23 > > > > > > > > > > > > > > >

Alpha, Beta, Go Final!

The Test of Well-Laid Plans

Requirements, planning, time estimates, Gantt charts, state diagrams, vectors, models, voice-over files, menus, meetings, staffing up, cutting features, adding features; all of these activities need to come together and produce a game starting with the alpha build.

Back up. There is a build before alpha called *first playable*, which is where the home stretch to making a game really kicks off. The game should at this time be essentially fun. It should be easy for any member of the team to play the latest build and immediately start rattling off features they would like to see in the game. The producer should be smiling at this point because the vast majority of these suggestions should be planned for content and features that are just around the corner before alpha is reached.

So your primary target during production should be to reach first playable as soon as possible but no sooner than it takes to create robust, healthy software along the way. Once you reach first playable, almost all "big scary risks" should be dealt with and you should be at mostly content creation and relatively well-contained programming tasks. I believe that first playable is the most important milestone in a

project. At first playable either you will see a fun game that simply needs more stuff or you will have engine technology bits that are poorly bolted together (and everyone is being polite and not discussing the obvious lack of a game).

The concept of first playable and alpha used to blend together; however, as the size of projects increases it is becoming clear that we need an earlier stage than feature complete to gauge the progress of a game project. Sure, there should be milestones all along the way that have specific deliverables, but there is a night and day difference between a milestone that has a laundry list of things that need to be accomplished versus being able to pick up a controller and *play a game*.

> **JARGON**: *First playable*—the first time all of the major gameplay elements are functional and playable.

Review your schedule and prune off all the "leaf tasks" that do not have any important dependencies and deprioritize them relative to any task that delivers core gameplay functionality. An easy example of this is to verify that your basic localization pathways are in place, but delay the actual localization of your game as long as possible.

< < < < < < < < < < < < < < < < < < < < < < < < < < < < < < < < < < <

On Alpha

Reaching alpha is the second most important milestone in my opinion (do you see a trend here?). The idea behind alpha is that your programmers should no longer be actively breaking the code base with new features but rather shifting their focus to cleaning up the code base.

To allow yourself to reach alpha you must have the courage to announce to the team and to executive management that you are feature complete. Announcing it really is not difficult; more difficult is resisting the urges from the team, beta testers, and executive management to add more features to the game. The only fair thing to do if a game reaches alpha and then new features are implemented is to drive the game back to alpha again before moving on and attempting to reach beta. That is, after adding a bunch of new features, you should ask out loud, "Are we good now? Feature lock?"

> **JARGON**: *Alpha*—the point at which a game is feature complete.

To determine whether or not you are at feature lock, you will need to do two tasks: Compare the alpha candidate build to the maintained design documents and determine if all of the planned features have been implemented. Next you need to play the game as a team and honestly determine if the game is fun or not. Feature-complete games will be fun with bugs and balance to address, and games that are not fun need something more or something less. Either way, you are not alpha on your way to beta, instead you are still in production.

If your budget allows, it is always good to perform some focus group ·

testing on your alpha build. Reportedly Microsoft is the king of focus groups with specialized focus group testing experts who use rooms with one-way mirrors and many other sophisticated techniques to ferret out the true opinions of the unbiased alpha testers.

Another group of alpha testers should be the marketing team. I know, I know, great salespeople are able to sell snow to Eskimos, but I always feel better when the marketing folks understand my games and really get behind them.

On to Beta

Between alpha and beta your team will focus on making the game stable, fixing crash bugs, cleaning out text bugs, and balancing the game. The classic high standard for beta is a feature-complete game with no known bugs (more commonly, no known show-stoppers or no known shippable bugs).

Different groups and different projects have their customized version of beta, and I suggest you use the strictest measure of beta your group will tolerate. Any relaxing of the standards at beta only invite more feature creep and feature revision as folks think, oh well, we will fix the bugs post-beta.

> **JARGON**: *Beta*—the point at which a game contains no known bugs (that are not shippable).

I highly suggest that folks treat all of the time after beta as being gone— unusable for tasking. With that attitude both the publisher and the developer will work together to keep the feature set tight and clean and avoid feature walking. With all your energy and focus, the beta candidate should be a shippable product.

> >

If you are working on a fixed time budget to release, you must carefully manage your time even more to focus on the bugs that have true high priority and not get distracted on the micro features or even bugs of low or medium importance. This might mean you will have to consciously start to close out trifling bugs that you know you can live with—not simple-to-fix bugs like spelling errors, but the little tiny suggestions that not many people would really notice.

If you want to save yourself a bunch of time, do not release your beta build to beta testers until you are beta! That might sound silly, but I disagree with Activision's policy of sending alpha builds to beta testers and responding to their bug reports until the game is of shippable quality. The reason I disagree is that your team and the publisher's QA department is more than qualified to find all the low-hanging fruit in the alpha build, and you should attack the alpha with zeal but still only release the beta with no known bugs to outside beta testers.

I advocate being even more conservative with your beta testing plan and release the beta in stages: Release a build to 25 testers for two weeks, fix bugs, then release to 100 testers for four weeks, fix bugs, and then open it all the way up to your final number amount of testers, perhaps 1,000 or so.

The beta testers are there to find bugs and flaws in balance that escaped the attention of the in-house QA teams. Outside of high-priority compatibility bugs, the beta testers should only be finding crash bugs by using the game in unexpected ways and finding other low-priority obscure bugs. You want to use the beta testing feedback to make

your game bulletproof. So if you release the beta build too early or to too many beta testers at the start, you will often be clobbered with reports on bugs your team already knows about and many duplicate reports.

You will also need at least one full-time person to handle the communication with the beta testers. It is far too easy to create the expectation with the beta testers that they are playing an important role in the development team and to dash that expectation with a demonstrated lack of coordination and communication.

The Finale

The road to the final gold master for all of my games is blurred with memories that I cannot recall with clarity. I remember making hot to-do lists two to three times a day and sleeping in the offices and wandering around Costa Mesa in the middle of the night, eating at the local International House of Pancakes or Denny's. Is there a method? Not really—it is just test, fix, test, fix, test, fix until you run out of time. Sure, the QA team will make a few regression tests to double-check that everything that was previously fixed stayed fixed (there are always surprises), and there may still be some feature revisions going on to accommodate beta tester feedback.

> **JARGON**: *Gold master*—the final candidate build that becomes the master used for production of the final game.

A big decision to make between beta and final is whether or not you are going to patch the game. It may sound unromantic, but I believe the majority of games that release patches knew before release that they would need to create a patch. So if you know you are going to create a patch, it is better to be honest with yourself and the team and be organized about the patch planning.

For example, on SFC1 we realized we were low on time about 60 days from release and decided to pull two of the six playable races from the single-player campaign; however, we left those two in for multiplayer missions. This allowed us to take those missions off the QA plan and the corresponding set of bugs to after release. This also allowed us to sweeten the eventual patch that had bug fixes with two new campaigns, making the game 50 percent larger from the single-player perspective.

If you are creating a console title that absolutely positively cannot have a patch, then your entire philosophy on how you will approach bugs will be different from a game with a patch. I recall having a phone conversation with a fairly highly placed Xbox executive, who was gushing with pride over the recent success of Morrowind for the Xbox. It was selling through like crazy despite being the buggiest game to date from the executive's own voluntary admission. He said the final eight weeks of testing was focused purely on identifying hang bugs and that the QA and development teams ruthlessly ignored all other bugs no matter how trivial to fix in the pursuit of shipping a crash-free Morrowind on the Xbox.

The real challenge in executing the final candidate well is to avoid creating new bugs while closing older bugs. Not only does this not help, but many times it may hurt as the new bugs could be of greater severity than the older bugs. One method to address this problem is to use what is called *pair programming*:

two programmers in front of one workstation. There is a philosophy of programming known as extreme programming that holds pair programming as one of its central techniques to creating reliable and robust code. I fully agree that pair programming produces reliable and robust code, but for the great majority of production time, this is a luxury that is really not required. However, during those final three weeks of code tweaking, it is of considerable comfort to have another person verify your changes. During production my teams tolerate pair programming only on very tough problems, but during the pursuit of the final candidate everyone welcomes the comfort of sharing the stress and responsibility of their bugs with another.

Even if you use pair programming, my final bit of advice on the pursuit of the final candidate is to not modify any code in the final ten days of production. Instead, document bugs and flaws and stick them in the readme. If you find trivial-to-fix bugs like errors in the text assets, fix them with caution. If you find serious bugs in the main game executable and you feel the game simply cannot ship with these bugs, perform the fix and then reset your clock for another ten days of testing before release. I thought I understood this well with SFC1, yet all of the major bugs the fans encountered with the final release were bugs introduced in the last ten days of the final candidate cycle. Even with pair programming errors sneaked through faster than the QA team could identify.

Obviously if you have no time limit on when you have to ship your game, then quality is the highest priority for your game. In that case, the pursuit of the final is much simpler, if not longer. You are free to iterate until all known bugs are fixed or the only ones remaining are below your quality threshold and the beta testers have stopped reporting new bugs.

Chapter 24

Point Releases vs. Patches

Patches—the bane of PC games. It seems it is impossible to buy a PC game without it requiring a patch shortly after release. Often a patch is available as soon as the game hits the store shelves; what gives? If the developers are able to have a patch ready by the time the boxes are on the shelves, why did they ship the game before it was finished?

Software Complexity and the Fragility of Computers

The basic problem is that software is far more complex than is apparent to both the consumer and the developers. Compounding this problem is that software is a digital system that usually works or does not work with nothing in between. Computers are very literal machines and have no ability to interpret what they should do when there are minor flaws in the software code or data. This is in contrast to things found in the real world. Most cars start off in great condition and then one day wind up at the junkyard, but along the way they malfunction and receive repairs. Along the way to malfunctioning, a car may develop a leak in a tire, be slow to start, make a strange noise at 4500 rpm, spill out too much smoke, drift to

the left, or just become dirty. None of these suboptimal behaviors will stop the car from performing its basic role in getting you to work. All of these bad behaviors are "bugs" that need to be fixed, but in stark contrast to software it is rare for a car to unexpectedly "crash"—except of course due to "user error" (or other "users"). Software often runs splendidly without the slightest hint of a problem and then crashes instantly with no possibility of recovery. This pathological behavior is the main culprit in our frustration with software.

Think of eating out at dinner; it doesn't always taste the same. The watermelon may be underripe at the salad bar, or the chicken may be a little too pink at the bone for comfort, or the baked potato was undercooked. None of these are issues that will prevent your meal from "functioning." In fact, most people will just deal with this without any thought and move on; others might send their chicken and potato back to the kitchen for more cooking. Either way the "user" of the dinner has a lot of flexibility and control in dealing with the "bugs" found in the dinner. None of these dinner "bugs" are tantamount to a crash. A crash would be more like

‹ ‹

going back for a second helping of egg salad at the company BBQ after it has been sitting in the sun for four hours; that will "crash" the user's "operating system." That bad egg salad will indeed irritate the average consumer, but for the most part, food products, while having many "bugs," cause very few "crashes" and result in very little "user" frustration.

Or take a used house that someone would be happy to buy. It will have hundreds of hairline cracks in the cement walkways, stains on the tile, rust in the gutters, squeaky floorboards, insects living inside, and so on, and all of this is normal. It is unreasonable to expect a house to be free from all errors and "bugs" of construction; even new homes will feature dozens of minor defects. The key again is that none of these minor problems will affect the value or function of the home in any material manner.

Back to software. Again our software is very fragile; feed it just a bit of unexpected data or wander off into user behavior not planned for and the software will usually fault in a way that is visible, material, and frustrating to the user. There are techniques for making software more robust such as exception handling, where the programmer purposely writes code for cases of use that are not supposed to ever occur (exceptions) that are handled by other blocks of code so the software is able to gracefully recover.

> **JARGON**: In C++ this is accomplished via a *try* block where the possibility of failure could occur, a *throw* statement when an exceptional case occurs, and a *catch* statement that provides the specific exception handling code.

The reason military, medical, and especially space mission software is so expensive to develop is the reliability and robustness requirements that software must fulfill. There have been many robotic spacecraft missions that were initially thought to be complete failures due to mechanical and/or software bugs that were overcome by solid software and/or updating the software on the spacecraft. The most positive example of this is perhaps the Galileo spacecraft with Jupiter as its target. After traveling through millions of miles of space, the high-gain transmitting antennae failed to deploy. This was a big tragedy; after spending nearly $2 billion and nearly two decades from conception to arrival at Jupiter, all was considered lost. All the rest of Galileo's instruments checked out, but what would it matter if Galileo were mute and could not send back the data and images of the truly awesome Jupiter and its own miniature solar system of satellites. The only way for Galileo to communicate was through its low-gain transmitter, which it used during the interplanetary journey. The problem with this antenna was that it was only capable of about 1/100th the bandwidth of the high-gain antennae. After much grief and anguish some rocket scientists and programmers got together and upgraded the compression algorithms that Galileo launched with, and in the end Galileo was able to transmit about one-tenth the data they had planned to send back. While still a disappointment, this simply required the various scientists to think more carefully about which images and data they truly wanted to download from the spacecraft. In the end, less science was

> >

performed, however, science *was* performed.

All game software that I know of has some bugs; even the simplest and most rigorously tested of console titles contain a few. I certainly agree and acknowledge that there are wide spans from the infamously failing Battlecruiser series to the near marvels of perfection that Nintendo released such as Mario64 and Zelda64. In the previous chapters we discussed how to best ship a game with the fewest flaws possible. This chapter discusses your options in dealing with patches, point releases, and fan-requested features after release.

The finest piece of modern PC game software from a high-quality ultra-low bug count point of view, in my opinion, is Counter-Strike. Counter-Strike enjoys an impeccable pedigree; the engine behind Counter-Strike is the Half-Life engine, which in turn is Valve's modification of id Software's Quake I engine. Both Quake and Half-Life were developed by the best developers in the world and received far more testing and revisions than the average PC game. On top of this marvelous technical foundation, Counter-Strike was in what seemed like interminable beta. I believe that is the truest reason why Counter-Strike runs so flawlessly: it was in open beta for over 18 months, and at a cost of $0 and loads of fun, it has become probably the single most tested game in the history of electronic gaming. Counter-Strike remains one of the world's most popular games despite its lack of any traditional marketing and distribution and after over three years of release!

It seems that to obtain truly bug-free, robust game code you must release the game to the public, respond to bug reports, and rerelease many times until the game is perfect or you run out of development resources or the public's interest. Again, the previous chapters dealt with how to make the highest quality software possible before release; at this point we are discussing post-release.

How About Those Console Games—They Don't Patch!?

It is horribly expensive to patch a console game. You must send a replacement CD/DVD/cartridge out to the consumer and pay for postage for both the returned and the new fixed media, as well as destroy the older media and build replacements. This has occurred a few rare times in console gaming history. The last time I was aware of this practice was with the first run of Gran Turismo 2 for the PlayStation 2. One critical bug that was found post-release erased the player's garage (save game). In general, it is true that consoles do not patch because it is financially impractical. Due to this, most developers and publishers spend relatively more money creating an arguably simpler game relative to their PC brethren. With the stakes so high, the publishers also staff up larger test teams and take more time. Finally, as discussed earlier, the hardware manufacturers add their own QA teams to verify that the game meets their standards.

Dark clouds of patches loom on the horizon of console games. First the Xbox started off with a hard drive to accommodate downloadable and incremental content, and now the PS2 also boasts an external hard drive. These hard drives were built for online content, but mark my words, these hard drives will hold patches in the near future. Of course, a console patch will never be called a patch; it will be called an update or an upgrade. Look under the hood and you will see that some flaws in the originally released game will be fixed in the update.

Online Games—the Perpetual Beta?

The other extreme from the console game is the online game in regard to the frequency of patches being released. It is not uncommon for massively multiplayer games to release a patch a week or even more often. Despite this frequency of patching, the better online games enjoy tremendous commercial success with gross margins in excess of 40 percent and a noticeable fraction of the GDP of South Korea. So if both console games and online games make a ton of money, what is the relevance of patches? At the end of the day you must do whatever it takes to make a consumer happy to buy something they do not have to buy—a luxury item. For the console game, that means making good on the expectation that the consumer will be able to pop the new game into the machine in the living room and be up and having fun in a matter of seconds. For the massively multiplayer online game, that means the developers will continuously improve the gameplay experience since the game is sold as a monthly service rather than a one-time product. This monthly service arrangement makes it not just okay to release patches but actually expected and demanded!

Point Release as a Sugarcoated Term for Patch

One day I realized that id Software used the term "point release" instead of patch, and while id Software deserves the reputation of making some of the world's finest games, I still felt the simple use of clean-sounding "point release" rather than the dull "patch" enhanced id's reputation in the public's eye. A point release sounds much more deliberate than a patch. After all, a patch is something you sew onto jeans or glue onto tires when you are too poor to buy new—definitely not glamorous. A point release indicates that you had this patch planned all along and it is the user's good fortune to get this update from the developer.

Now to be fair to id, the quality of their released games exceeds most any other developer's *after* being patched. id also deliberately adds more functionality to their point releases similar to how online games add features and improve functionality. Almost all users feel good about getting extra functionality after having paid for a game. The problem with patching games that are not massively multiplayer is that the user has to log onto the Internet, search for the patch, download the patch, and see if the patch addresses the particular bug that the user experienced that caused them to go out and look for the patch in the first place. Contrast this effort to playing an online game, where as part of the login process the game determines whether or not your version of the game is up to date, and if not your local copy of the game is auto-patched.

> >

Fan Requests

If you have made a good game and the word-of-mouth ball gets rolling, soon players will attempt to communicate to the developers what new features they would like to see in the game. I suggest you set up a message board such as Infopop's (http://www.infopop.com) Ultimate Bulletin Board software. Hosting a forum for players to discuss their experiences with your games is also a good idea and has been one of the best moves for Taldren (see our forums at www.taldren.com).

When dealing with fan requests you will receive a bunch of suggestions that might be roughly categorized into bad ideas, good ideas that are too big to bite off at this time, and good ideas that are just right in size. The best way to handle this is to address the bad ideas and say why you do not think they are good. Trust me, this builds respect and develops a better relationship with your fans as they will come to learn how your group approaches games and will likely learn something they did not know. Most obviously it will show that you are listening to their suggestions. For the good and ambitious ideas it is also best to acknowledge the idea and show that you support the idea on its merits, but at the same time shape their expectations that this feature is not likely to be added in the near future.

It is the good ideas that will not take much time to implement that are the real gems. At the risk of appearing crass, here is where the return on your time investment in the message boards will be returned in spades. The amount of gratitude you will receive from your fans for adding a few special requests (this stuff could literally take minutes if not hours—just bits of creative insight that the fans came up with) will demonstrate to them that you have a true dedication to their interests. This is the stuff that will produce a fan for as long as you are in the game business. This is also the "special sauce" that converts a mere "patch" into a "point release"!

The Publisher-Developer Post-Release Relationship

The business model of a game developer is under continuous challenge by the publisher. In short, the publisher distorts a business (the developer) into a business with a single customer, and the customer is the source of capital and the access to market. These three factors combine to make the publisher a dominant force of control for the developer. In regard to patches, almost all development contracts require the developer to warranty their work for some period of time after release. This is all reasonable, but if you look at the project's budget and milestone advances, you will never see an amount of money earmarked for post-release support. All publishers know that PC games require post-release support, and in fact they demand the developers provide this service. The leverage the publisher invariably leans on is "Hey, dontcha wanna earn royalties?" or "I don't want to work with someone who does shoddy work and is not willing to stand by it." Certainly publishers should not expose themselves to unnecessary work, and if they do their job by running their publishing company well and are careful in the selection of their developers and in their review of milestones, all should go well with the project. A publisher should advance the costs of post-release support as the developer is always the last one to receive royalty income to offset the costs of support.

I have tried (unsuccessfully) to use the online nature of a component SFC series to include a modest budget for post-release support. I recommend that others keep pushing for it. Any publisher in the world would bend over backwards to advance the funds necessary to create patches for Doom III or Warcraft III. It is smart money to support your games in post release. My point is all games require post-release support; even the most financially healthy and successful developers support their games after release. I would think lesser games deserve all the support they can get, no? At the bottom line, the publisher knows they are able to use the overtime efforts of a start-up developer trying to make their reputation to stand by their games. Developers should push back when they have times of leverage and also realize that it is their position to give and struggle while they are growing their businesses.

Tools for Creating Patches

So, okay you actually need to make a patch today. Listed below are two popular patching tools: the more established RT Patch by PocketSoft and the upstart Visual Patch by Indigo Rose. Both of these tools compare what you distributed to the users in the previous version to the binary bits of the new version and extract the differences. After extracting the differences it compresses it tightly and wraps it in a self-executing self-extracting patch-applying tool. Both of these tools allow you to wrap your own user interface to the process if you like, or you can use their standard user interface. I recommend that you download both and give them a try.

I also recommend that you provide a main menu level option in your game to get the latest patch. I like the auto-patcher in BioWare's Neverwinter Nights the best; it is verbose and visually pleasing to watch it go about its patching business.

Product name:	Visual Patch
Published by:	Indigo Rose, Inc.
URL:	http://www.indigorose.com/products/visual_patch1.php
Price:	$495

Product name:	RT Patch v. 6
Published by:	PocketSoft Inc.
URL:	http://www.pocketsoft.com/pr/rtpproc.html
Price:	$995

> >

User Extensibility—The Magical Patch

Another patching mechanism that we make use of at Taldren is to externalize as much of the game data as possible to facilitate user extensibility. Your fans will be able to generate far more ideas than you will be able to handle. It would be far better if you simply allow them to make their own changes to the game. I find it useful to think of it as their game. For example, in the SFC series all of the ship data has always been easily modifiable in the format of a simple spreadsheet readable by Excel.

There are many subtle benefits to user extensibility; one is that it gives your game legs without your continued effort. Half-Life and, by heritage, Quake are probably the most user-extended games in the history of games. Clearly an activity (providing for user extensibility in their games) that the highly successful Valve and id Software perform is an activity that any company should emulate. Too many companies think user extensibility robs sales from their own future sales. I am not going to proselytize further on this issue; for those of you who resist user extensibility, good, stay that way—more for Taldren!

> >

Chapter 25   > > > > > > > > > > > > > > >

Garage Development Spans the Internet

Mario64 enjoyed a reputed budget of $20M+, and Wing Commander IV, Return to Castle Wolfenstein, and Warcraft III all are rumored to have development budgets approaching $10M. Most modern AAA budgets are in the range of $2M to $5M. So what could a few inexperienced, passionate wannabe game developers accomplish when facing these seven- or eight-figure budgets expended on behalf of teams that have hundreds of years of collective game industry experience?

One company started out making electronic pinball games—Epic; another company cut up thick paper to make playing cards—Nintendo; another loaned an employee a computer over the weekends and he created a side-scroller featuring a kid wearing a football helmet—id Software.

Silver Creek Entertainment

In this chapter I profile Silver Creek Entertainment, as independent as you could imagine. They create, market, and distribute their own games and have never worked with another entity, let alone a publisher. This includes running their own online multiplayer service that they built and operate.

These guys started off by setting their sights on no less than Microsoft!

Profile of Jonas Stewart

hwsol@silvercrk.com
Jonas Stewart
Pixel Pusher and Game Design
Silver Creek Entertainment

Erik Bethke: How many developers are at Silver Creek Entertainment? How many programmers, artists, testers, and management?

Jonas Stewart: There are five folks and a boatload of gnomes in hamster wheels. This is broken down into three development staff members: two coders and an artist (that's me), one person who keeps the office in order and handles customer relations, and one person who deals with bipedal creatures outside our fortress who aren't customers.

We pretty much self-manage and don't have anyone but the marketplace to answer to. My idea of a true indie is a team that answers to no one but their own heart's desire and the customers they produce for.

What language is used for the development of SCE's games? C++? What tools do you use for creating the art of the SCE series of games?

Most everything is written in C++ with some Python scripting thrown in.

Almost all the art is done in Photoshop with a mouse (I know it sounds bad but you get the hang of it) and on occasion I've used trueSpace, Bryce, and Poser. But I find I can accomplish most of what I need now in Photoshop alone. Of course you don't exactly need Maya or Max to do card games yet.

Do you folks work on just one game at a time, or are you working on multiple games at a time?

We try to focus on one game, but we oftentimes float back to old projects to spruce them up a bit. We constantly try to improve our released games as we make new gizmos or see a way to improve something on our current project. Unless there is something making it incompatible with our current lineup, a lot of what we do can be applied to our older stuff with not too much pain. The players don't seem to mind getting a free new feature now and then either.

What is your general development process?

Our general development process... hmm. "Let's make a card game. Okay, and let's make it really cool with fairy dust and stuff." Months later a card game appears in all its glory. Of course there is the daily grind that does tend to wear down the team until it's done. It's really just a build and polish sort of thing. We do try to keep focused on what *add*s something to the game or at least the intended purpose of the games. So on our multiplayer games, we think in terms of helping players have fun together with Fooms (the fireballs and magic elements), whereas with Solitaire we try to keep in mind a state of solitude and enjoying just hanging out being yourself.

We do have a mental plan that encompasses what we want to do. But we are very flexible along the way to take in new ideas that lend to the cause.

Would you say your competitive advantage is the absolute total commitment of quality that you bring to your games?

Yes, that's probably true. We fill a niche for card games that are well crafted and steeped in a fantasy atmosphere. Not everyone cares, but for those who do, we have something to offer them. There are plenty of generic card games out there, but we try to take something that seems plain and see if we can breathe life into it. It's kinda like a No. 2 pencil—to one person it's just a stick with graphite that you can leave notes to get more milk, but in the hands of the right people that pencil is a gateway to wonderful worlds. They illustrate a place like the Shire or a post-apocalyptic LA. It's all perspective and the use of your craft; we are still working on it.

There is plenty of shovelware for the rest of the folks, but that's not what we want to make.

> >

If I may ask, what sort of sales figures for Hardwood Spades and/or other SCE games are you comfortable releasing?

We eat and aren't sleeping under the bridge so I can't complain. Our main mission is to make games all day and get paid to do it, although it would be nice to have a castle. I'll be saving my nickels for a while, though.

The way I see it, every day above ground is a GOOD day.

Have you considered retail distribution? What has been your experience with game publishers?

We may take a stab at retail when the time is right, but selling online has been a good and loyal friend. Retail is a fearsome beast that has chewed up and spat out more than its fair share of games. It's definitely not just about making the best game... there are a lot of other factors that can tank a project even after you release it. Online at least the power of success and failure is on our hands a tad more. Of course I read that "they" just found a 2km asteroid that may collide with the planet within the next 15 years...so maybe this is all a moot point.

What are your marketing budget and/or strategy for SCE games?

"If we build it, they will come." We just make stuff as good as we can and let folks know about it at download sites and in search engines. It's just Internet promotion 101.

Probably one of the best places to learn about online, direct to customer selling is the Association of Shareware Professionals. These folks are veteran indies.... they don't talk much about game development, but they know a lot about the business of selling online.

What is SCE's early story? How did you start the company?

Our early story, eh? Well after the fall of the dinosaurs and rodents ruled the earth...err wait, let's fast forward a tad. Basically Silver Creek started after two guys, Jonas Stewart (that's me) and Dan Edwards, decided that making games would be cool around '93-'94. So after we realized that some epic full person shooter Blade Runner game was a bit ambitious for two guys just learning this stuff, we tried a "weekend" project, which became the original Hardwood Solitaire.

Windows was still scoffed at as a medium for games at the time, but we were shooting for releasing on Win32 (95) since we were on the OS beta. Hardwood Solitaire turned into something far more complex than a weekend project as we tried to put together something that was truly different from the other dull implementations that were out there...the main culprit being the one that came with Windows or the other "application-like" card games. We wanted to bring our gamer attitude to a card game and try to make it LOOK like a game, not a spreadsheet or word processor app. Working during the summer and living at home eating lots of Top Ramen (chicken flavor is pretty tasty), we bought ourselves enough time to finish one of the first if not the first Windows Truecolor game released. Hardwood Solitaire evolved into HWS II: The Enchanted Decks, which was a much more refined product.

We also volunteered at the Game Developers Conference from '95-'99, which was pretty cool. That helped us keep exposed to aspects of the gaming industry, and it was pretty cool back then. Something any aspiring game developer should do at least once. After that we attended as Independent Game Developer finalists and even picked up an Indy award in 2001 for Hardwood Spades there.

After Solitaire we took the plunge into online games with Hearts, Spades, and Euchre. They are leaps and bounds more complex and trippy than Solitaire, but we grossly underestimated the effort that "tacking on" multiplayer meant. Needless to say, having a community of people is something that needs constant attention. Somewhat like being mayor of a small town and you soon realize that you don't ever want to be president of the U.S.

Anyhow...I guess that was the quickie version of "the beginning." I did leave out the absolutely massive amount of time playing Duke Nukem 3D and Doom and that we wore out quite a few joysticks playing Descent and flying guided missiles through the mines. But hey, we all did that back in the day, right?

What is the future for SCE? Do you feel the need to grow into more product lines?

For now we are sticking to card games. Trying to keep focused on what we seem to be pretty good at. Puzzle and card games are in nice small bite-sized chunks. We really don't want to become managers to a large team of people; we want to make games, and keeping project teams small allows us to do that.

Do you have any tips for aspiring indie developers?

An unfinished project is not a game. Try to finish everything you make unless it has a fatal error in concept or design.

If you are hooking up with buddies to make a game, make sure that it gets done. Most of the time it won't when you have to count on a bunch of free help; try to keep the team as small as you can. Ideally you can really only count on yourself, but working with a trusted friend as long as you both have passion will work. It might not be great, but you will learn plenty in the making.

Start small and finish it. Then make the next step; it's not realistic to think you will be making the next big thing on your first project.

Making games or any type of entertainment is really like a magic trick. There is a lot of preparation and sweat that goes into making folks who witness the magic believe in it. Make sure you enjoy knowing that magic won't be the same for you once you become the magician. You will know it's a trick but hopefully enjoy its construction. Err, I don't know if that made any sense, but basically there is a difference between enjoying the entertainment and creating it.

And above all else, have fun! If you don't have the burning desire to make games, and you don't spend nearly all of your waking hours at least thinking about games and game design, then find another thing to try that you are passionate about. We all will eventually cease to exist...enjoy the time you have; don't waste it on something you don't like.

Part IV >>>>>>>>>>>>>>>>>>>

Game Development Resource Guide

> >

Chapter 26 > > > > > > > > > > > > > > >

Getting a Job in the Game Industry

"You work in games, huh? That's cool; so, what
do you do, just play games all day, huh?"

—Most anyone outside the game industry

Who Is Trying to Get into Games?

As I write this chapter at Taldren we are conducting interviews for artists, from modelers and texture artists to riggers and animators. We are staffing up for our Black9 game that was announced in late 2002.

There are roughly three groups of people we are looking at: young people who have just finished school, people who have a lot of experience in a related industry, and people who have experience in the game industry. Naturally, the folks who have the experience in the game industry are generally more desirable to hire, as it will cost us less in training to get the maximum production out of the programmer, artist, or designer. The folks with experience in other industries such as stop-motion animation, 3D modeling for film, SQL business programming, or aerospace engineering generally all have a strong work ethic and an interesting background that might be of some value to your game shop. The younger people straight out of college, especially the newer game schools such as DigiPen and The Art Institute of California, are usually full of energy and raring to go as they have just finished paying tens of thousands of dollars to learn how to make games and are now eager to really make games.

Recently I had two folks come in from the animation/film industry. I asked them why they thought they would like to get into games. It was interesting that both of them said they were looking for a stable position. While game companies are not as solid as working for Sears or General Electric, apparently we are more stable than these film and animation houses that staff up for a project, put everyone on 1099s, rip through the work, and then lay them off.

So they want a nice, stable job? Hmm, I was hoping for something along the lines of having an everlasting burning passion for creating games and that they are pounding on my door to apply that passion to our games! We are not

< < < < < < < < < < < < < < < < < < < < < < < < < < < <

your local Department of Motor Vehicles where you can regain your confidence with a nice steady job and then wade back into film when you feel better. So first of all, express your passion for creating games.

You Want Me to Do What? Oh, I Would Rather Do This

The other sorts of misfits for the game industry are the folks who confuse working in the game industry with getting paid to play games. Twice I have employed guys who have reported to me that they are not "into" their current assignment, and that is their explanation for not getting their task completed. Sometimes I think all young people should join the military, work on a farm, or do asphalt roofing for a few years before entering the game industry. I have found over the years that the folks who have had crappy blue-collar jobs in the past truly appreciate sitting in air-conditioned offices being paid to be creative. The people without this background often confuse the word "hobby" with "work." While it is true you should enjoy your work, we all have jobs to get done, and there is quite likely at any given time something we would rather be doing!

Hours of the Game Industry

The truth behind the game industry is that most work is done at independent game development houses that are working against a milestone-advance payment schedule, and the work must simply be performed on time.

Anyone will tell you that employees who put in a solid 40 hours a week, with a full benefits program, who are well paid, and who spend their nonworking hours with friends, family, and other rewarding activities are most productive and happy. Working 120 hours a week is not very efficient and does not result in high-quality work. Most developers have hearts of gold with the best intentions, the author included, who start off each project with the simultaneous goals of making the best game possible while having sane and humane schedules for their staff. The game industry is a brutally competitive industry where folks all around the world love to make games and are willing and able to pour their souls into the games; we all are like this. It is like being a professional entertainer or athlete in that you must train hard for a long time, often poorly compensated, for the chance to become successful later in your career. Here at Taldren we are now three years old, and for each of our projects we have strived to improve our project estimation capabilities. However, we continue to find ourselves needing to work the occasional Saturday, and a few weekends a year we must work through the weekend at crunch time.

I have another axiom that covers this phenomenon: The younger the development house, the harder they must work to be competitive. The largest, highest profile projects are

> >

naturally going to be signed up with the more successful, well-established developers. These developers will have a lot more leverage and control over the relationship with their publisher and will most likely be able to achieve better advances, a longer schedule, and in general be able to develop with their more experienced team members at a more healthy pace than a start-up shop with their first contract. People looking into the game industry should understand this dynamic and find some other job if they are allergic to long hours and a load of work.

You Did Not Scare Me—I Love Games AND I Want In!

Okay, if the above comments did not dissuade you from wanting to enter the game industry, then come on in, the water's great!

So what do you know how to do and what would you like to do? Generally speaking there are six broad classes of skill sets in the industry:

1. Programming
2. Art
3. Testing
4. Producing
5. Audio
6. Design

I listed the skill sets in descending order of ease for breaking into the industry. Skilled programmers have the easiest time getting into games. However, Visual Basic programmers generally do not cut the mustard. Strong artists from other industries can often slide over without difficulty. The easiest way into games with the least skills is to become a tester at a publishing house; the only requirements seem to be a passion for games and some degree of written communication skills.

Producing jobs are both easy and difficult to get. Producers in the game industry often come from the testing or occasionally programming side of development; however, increasingly folks are being hired into producing slots at publishers who have some other management experience such as in the film or music industries.

Audio jobs are difficult to get in my opinion, due to the relatively low number of jobs industry-wide and the willingness of so many talented individuals to work for relatively low compensation.

Design is the single most difficult job to get in the industry and I am sure the hardest job to get as your break-in job. Some old-time paper RPG designers from TSR were able to transition into well-paying jobs at Interplay's Black Isle studio in the heyday of the Baldur's Gate series. The most common way for new people to get into design positions is in the 3D first-person genre where exceptionally talented and dedicated folks create compelling levels on their own that get picked up by fans and become popular. However, I argue these folks typically work for free on their own for a year or two before their work is noticed, so their first position is essentially as self-employed intern.

How to Get a Job as a Programmer

Program bunches. Learn C at a minimum—I highly recommend C++—and have a passing knowledge of assembly so that you are not ignorant of it. Pick a simple game such as Pac-Man, Frogger, Pitfall, or Sub-space and do your best to recreate the game on your PC with high frame rates and interesting improvements to the fundamental gameplay. Find an artist on the Internet to create some artwork for your game. Now you have your own game in your portfolio. Depending on your time and skill set this might take you one to six months to create. If your code is well written and your game plays well, you probably have enough demonstrable strength to get an entry-level job at a game company working with their internal scripting language to develop missions or scripts. This is your foot in the door, this is where the vast majority of programmers in the industry start: performing the coding work that is considered safe and tedious, allowing the more senior programmers to concentrate on the more challenging aspects of the project. As you demonstrate growth and ability, you will quickly be handed more and more challenging work—don't worry!

This has been my path into the game industry. I started as a scripter on I Have No Mouth And I Must Scream, developed by the Dreamer's Guild for Cyberdreams. When I was hired I came from space science work at JPL with a strong professional background in FORTRAN and a basic understanding of the syntax of the rest of the major languages including C and C++. For No Mouth, we used an internal scripting language called SAGA that worked

pretty much like an unreliable C without low-level abilities. I was steadily given more responsibility until two years later I led my own team on a gambling game project, Caesars Windows95. From that position I transitioned fully into management as a senior producer at Interplay on Starfleet Command I, and now I am fortunate to run my own development studio, Taldren.

Programming is a valuable skill set that is not about to go out of demand. As a game programmer you are also the ultimate arbitrator of how a feature will turn out, so to the closet game designers out there (that would probably be everyone), this is a great job to exercise your creativity.

When you go in for your interview, be prepared to answer programming questions in real time. The Internet is full of great sites with helpful hints on how to handle the programming test such as http://cplus.about.com/cs/careers/. Why am I pointing out a site to you that probably has spoilers for the questions I and other developers would have asked you? The reason is simply memorizing the solutions will not help you; you will be called upon to explain your code in front of the senior technical staff in the company, and if you are fudging they will notice. Go ahead and scour sites such as the one above, use it to prepare yourself, and become a stronger programmer.

Typical starting salary for an entry-level programmer is about $40,000. Various factors such as the relative wealth of the company and the cost of living in the area will cause this number to be higher or lower.

> >

Artists and Their Portfolios

Artists have it both easier and more difficult than programmers; on one hand, it is a lot easier for the interviewer to review a portfolio or a demo reel to see how strong the artist is, but on the other hand, it is all too easy to create an impression that may be incorrect if your portfolio and demo reel are not top quality.

Animators, modelers, texture guys, and riggers, the most convenient format for delivering your portfolio of work to a game company is in the form of a VHS tape. Take some time to plan out your demo reel; think about what impression you want to deliver. Will you take your existing work and arrange it, or will you create new work especially for the demo reel? Be careful not to show too much material from a single genre such as traditional fantasy, sci-fi, or comic book work unless that is all you are capable of performing. While showing your range of ability is important to be sure you are considered for every job you want, do not include weak material just for the sake of variety.

Trim your demo reel down until every bit of it is vital for demonstrating who you are and then cut just a little more. Having the eye to revise, edit, and trim your own work is the mark of a professional. One time I had to endure a demo reel that offered over 12 different walk animations for a cartoon dog. The only impression I developed was that the artist himself could not decide what his best take was, and he was shifting that burden to me!

Demo reels with a sound track to add an aural dimension almost always are received with much greater enthusiasm. A clever technique for animators is to use the voice track from a popular movie and animate a character to lip-synch a few lines from the movie. I recently saw the demo of an animator who did this to the famous righteousness of God speech Samuel L. Jackson delivered in *Pulp Fiction*. The character delivering the lines was a cross between a Chihuahua and a gremlin, with perfectly bugged-out eyes to pull off the anger in Samuel Jackson's line. This was brilliant for the production values of the line, the voice-over was AAA quality, and I was free to enjoy myself and appreciate the quality of the animation. In fact, I believe this was a strong demonstration of the guy's ability to animate to a given specification rather than a crutch or a cheat of any kind.

Bradley W. Schenck is Taldren's senior art director, and in his career he has seen about 5,000 resumes, has interviewed more than 500 people, and has directly hired about 50 people in positions of game artists. The key thing he looks for besides manifest skill and talent as shown in a reel or a portfolio is an emotional, bone-deep statement of why the artist loves the aspect of art he is pursuing. For animators, solemn statements about the weight of a body in motion make Brad crack a thin smile. He is looking for people who think about their art when they are driving, taking a shower—their quiet time.

Typical starting salaries for artists are about $35,000, with the usual factors at play.

How Do I Become a Tester?

Starting as a tester is a venerable tradition. All publishers have their own QA departments staffed with testers. While developers may or may not. Developer QA staffs, however, often double as a line producer/MIS guy or has some other double duty.

The easiest way to become a tester is to call up the publishers and simply ask if they have any openings. Most publishers will not hire testers who are not local, so if you are not local to the publisher you would like to work for, visit the city where the publisher is located and appear local.

I Have a Great Idea for a Game—I Want to Be a Designer!

If you have no experience in the game industry and you are not the creator of some intellectual property that is being adapted in the production of a game, then your only real avenue into straight game design is mod-making and level making. Find a game you love that facilitates user modification such as Neverwinter Nights, Dungeon Siege, Quake, or Unreal and think of something new and different you can create with these game engines and push

through and make a new game. The most famous example of this method is the mega-hit Counter-Strike, which is a mod of Half-Life; the Counter-Strike crew now have their choice of opportunities.

However, most game designers in the industry work their way through programming or art and have gradually assumed greater design responsibilities over the course of their projects.

So You Want to Be a Producer

The final job position I will discuss is the producer. The producer comes in many different flavors in the game industry such as coach, line producer, executive producer, associate producer, project leader, project planner, and project manager. Several of these titles are synonymous, and in general a producer is a person who gets everything else done that programmers, artists, designers, testers, and audio folks do not perform. Most producers start at the bottom as line producers and work their way up as they demonstrate that they can handle more responsibility. Another common method is for an art

director or a technical director to be promoted into a project leader role at a game development studio. However, at publishers it is increasingly common to hire senior producers from other industries where the individual held a management position.

Being a producer, I believe, is one of the most difficult jobs as you must relish pressure, have excellent communication skills, both written and oral, be able to resolve personality issues, be decisive, and thrive under constant task switching. It is true that the project leader usually has the most influence over the final shape of a game, but rather than a great prize, this is a heavy responsibility.

If you feel you were born to lead a team of creative folks, then start at the bottom and consistently demonstrate your willingness to work towards the best interest of your team and game, be proactive, and challenge yourself to solve new problems. If you do this, your leadership skills will be recognized rapidly, and no doubt you will be promoted to the role of a producer. The reason is that there is, at least in my opinion, a profound shortage of folks out there who truly have what it takes to inspire their teams to the greatest of efforts and make the best games.

Go to GDC—Free!

A great place to meet game developers is at the Game Developers Conference (http://www.gdconf.com/) held in the spring in San Jose. It is a little-known factoid that you can be a volunteer at the conference working several hours each day in exchange for a full pass to the event. This will save you about a thousand bucks!

At GDC there are two prime avenues for networking for a job in the industry; the most straightforward is of course the job fair. Here you will find dozens of companies looking for new people. Your resume will go into the pile, and if you wrote a good one, maybe you will get a call back. The problem with this approach is that your resume will go to the HR department and sit for a while, gathering dust.

The better way to network for a job is to actually go up and speak to developers. After attending one of the conference sessions go up to the speaker and ask a good question and then follow up with an introduction about yourself and state that you are looking to break in and would like some advice on where to start. If they know of a job opening, they will steer you there more quickly than your resume will in the HR department. The reason is simple: They will see you standing there and will be able to look you in the eye to gauge your determination and sincerity. Also, rank-and-file developers usually know of job openings well before HR does. The truth is that team members, recalling that a buddy of theirs over at this other game shop is wrapping up his project and is looking for a change, fill the vast majority of positions in the game industry. In other words, I believe 90+ percent of jobs in the industry are filled by word-of-mouth and shuffling about. The HR department only gets a job description if the company has been unable to fill a position through this word-of-mouth method. Also, it takes guts to walk right up to someone and ask for a job, and we developers like to find people with guts.

‹ ‹

What About Those Recruiters?

I will save you, the recruiters, and game companies a lot of time; if you are new to the industry, fresh out of school, just start knocking on doors yourself as you do not have enough material in your resume to sell yourself. If you have a lot of experience from another industry, you might benefit from the use of a recruiter, but knocking on doors may still be your best bet. Recruiters are somewhat difficult to digest for the smaller independent developers such as Taldren; recruiters not only charge 20 to 30 percent of the prospective employee's salary as a fee, but they also pump up that salary to the highest levels that wealthy and/or desperate publishers are paying for their internal teams. So when I see the resume of someone without experience in the industry come through a recruiter, I just toss it in the trash, as I do not want to pay such a premium for someone who still needs experience. The only resumes I want to see from a recruiter are from those with significant experience from another developer or publisher who is likely to make a significant contribution to Taldren; that is worth paying such a premium.

Resumes, Demo Reels, and the Interview

I am placing these logistical steps for how to get a job at the end of this chapter because I think they are the most mundane, overly discussed topics on the subject. I have already discussed how you will really find your path into the game industry. This section will just be a short section on how to present yourself.

Honesty vs. Modesty

No matter what, you must be honest when creating your resume or demo reel, or performing your interview. First of all, it is unlikely that you will be able to fool the people you are trying to get to hire you; second, even if you do manage to fool them, you are only setting yourself up for tragic disappointment all around when you do not live up to your own advertisement. Or perhaps worse, it is never discovered and you end up working for some marginal company who cannot properly evaluate your skills and talents for what they are.

Having said that, you are still responsible for selling yourself to the company. Focus on the skills, talents, energy, and interests you genuinely do have and display them in the most attractive light.

Make sure your resume's objective clearly focuses on the job position the company is offering. If there are multiple job openings you are interested in and they are not identical but you feel you would be strong at any one of them, then tailor your resume for each position. You should of course write a cover letter that positions you as perfectly suited for the job posting the employer has described.

A pet peeve of mine is programmer candidates who list six or more programming languages on their resume.

> >

The vast majority of programmers I know specialize in a language or possibly two, such as C and assembly, or C++ and assembly, or C++ and SQL. The game company wants to know what you are *excellent* at, not how many different programming language books you bought or whether or not you know FORTRAN77.

This goes beyond just programming languages and can be applied to the rest of the knowledge sets you might put down on your resume. I suggest you be sure your main skills and talents are highlighted on your resume, and the others you have had past exposure to, if you must list them, should include some qualification such as "familiarity with Unix scripting languages such as sed, awk, and Perl or "familiarity with the UI of LightWave."

Here is a listing of recruiting companies:

Interact
831 S. Douglas St. Suite 119
El Segundo, CA 90245
phone: (310) 643-4700
(800) 333-5751
fax: (310) 643-4750
Info@InteractJobs.com

Mary-Margaret.com Recruiting and Business Services
Specializing in Entertainment Software
toll-free voice: (877) 662-3777
toll-free fax: (877) 662-3888
robin@mary-margaret.com
www.mary-margaret.com

Prime Candidate, Inc.
Pat Bigley
phone: (818) 784-1976
fax: (818) 501-1853
paddi@ix.netcom.com
www.primecandidateinc.com

Instant Studio
Eric Wills
President
phone: (480) 358-1417
fax: (480) 358-1439
eric@instantstudio.net
www.instantstudio.net

> >

Chapter 27 > > > > > > > > > > > > > > >

Starting a Game Development Company

"You will always have a boss, Erik, no matter where you go."
—Trish Wright advising a pre-Taldren Erik Bethke

So you want to run your own game company, huh?

Why?

Why do you want to start a game company? Most likely you are bursting with creative energy; you have a game that is tearing itself out through your mind and is screaming to be shared with the world. Is that it?

Or maybe you have been working with some friends of yours for a while and have developed a deep sense of camaraderie and you are ready to put this team to the test as a game company.

Maybe you have been extremely hard working and have already developed a game in your spare time (or a good portion of the game) and are now looking for a way to capitalize on this effort.

Or, maybe one or two of you are a member of the idle rich and making

games sounds like a great way to pass the time.

While all of these are solid reasons to start a game company, none are *compelling* reasons to create a game company. For all of these reasons you would most likely be better off joining forces with an existing game company. Creating a game company and, more importantly, running a successful game company is *very hard*. The great majority of game development companies fail, even quite a few that have enjoyed great success.

Why does your game company need to exist? What unique niche or role will your company fulfill? Do you have a great idea, and you just need a publisher to hand you a pile of money so you can produce a great hit? If so, buddy, get in line—and boy is it a long line.

< < < < < < < < < < < < < <.< < < < < < < < < < < < < <

Find a Path

Why does the world need your game company?

If you are able to answer that question with strength you *should* create and run a game company.

Sure, point to any successful game development company and you will show me that all it took was a mega-hit: Warcraft, Doom, Final Fantasy. However, as I said earlier in the book, without diminishing the greatness of these games or the effort it took to execute them, I feel the truly interesting struggle was how Blizzard got to the point where they could create Warcraft. How did id get to Doom? Do you know why Square named the key franchise Final Fantasy?

Here are some specific examples. Epic and id started out creating small shareware titles that were addictive to play and always financed their early projects through sweat and shareware registrations. When they both became successful they started performing their own publishing functions and used their position of impeccable strength to have publishers bid for their games.

Treyarch Entertainment started off as a regular milestone developer for Interplay; however, Treyarch aggressively pursued console port projects from Electronic Arts. These port projects turned out to be fairly substantial and could be delivered with much stronger regularity compared to an original property such as their Die By The Sword. Just four years after implementing that strategy, Treyarch employs 130 developers and has been bought out by Activision.

You have two major transition points to manage: How will you launch your company, and after launching how will you transition your company into a sustainable, successful company?

Most game company developers would benefit from a few years' experience in the industry to formulate their plan; others are quite capable of just striking out on their own path on their first day. Think about your company; what are your key employees especially talented at? What are you especially passionate about? What opportunities are available from folks with whom you have established relationships?

I Have a Plan; Now How Do I Get Started?

Okay, I will assume for the rest of this chapter that you have at least a handful of developers who have banded together to create a game, modify a game, perform a port of a game, or have some other subcontract to sustain your team. (Again, if you have your own pile of money, much of the start-up phase loses its romantic challenge.)

Your first priority must be to execute your first project on time, on

budget, and with as much quality as you can muster. I list the priorities in roughly that order. As this is your first project, more than likely you have been commissioned to perform a relatively modest project on behalf of a publisher. This publisher is taking a chance on you, they believe in you, but it is more of a trust-but-verify type of trust. As your team is new and untried, it is doubtful the publisher is expecting you

> >

to light the world on fire with amazing new features not found anywhere else. What they *are* expecting is that you will conduct your company with professionalism, and deliver what you said you would deliver on time and on budget. That will be the truest strength of your team: how strong a game you are able to create while remaining true to your advance and time budgets.

The first step of delivering your contract on time and on budget is being sure you have the right developers to perform the work.

Um, Erik, what about forming a corporation and office space and my business cards; it seems like we need to cover this before I hire any employees. Yes, those *are* important; however, I like to be sure production is rolling before I attend to some of these niceties. When we started Taldren the existing Starfleet Command team first rolled straight into production on Starfleet Command II, while Zach, Sean, and I found office space, a payroll company, and tended to a hundred other details of setting up a company.

Rounding Out Your Development Team

So my philosophy is to get development rolling as quickly as possible and then follow up with the rest of your infrastructure. I am not suggesting you do anything illegal like not pay people or run without workman's compensation or liability insurance. Just move through these items as quickly as you can while keeping your mind focused on production.

Who are your key employees? Do you have everyone it will take to get the job done? Hopefully the truly key employees such as your lead programmer, lead artist, and lead designer are already filled and now you simply need more developers.

The best way to find new employees is through word of mouth. Perhaps you already know some developers or your employees do. As odd as it might sound at first, ask other game companies if they know of quality recruits they have passed on for some reason. This will generally provide you with excellent candidates as other developers would be loathe to recommend a

poor candidate for fear it would reflect badly on them.

After exhausting your personal contacts, the next place to look for people is on web sites that are community access points for different disciplines such as:

G.A.N.G.
Game Audio Network Guild
P.O. Box 1001
San Juan Capistrano, CA 92693
info@audiogang.org
www.audiogang.org

ProTools User Forum
Follow the links to the User Conference bulletin board at the Digidesign site:
http://www.digidesign.com/

The key benefit of using these sites is that they attract generally more proactive, more sincere candidates who are staying up to date with their skills by interacting with others in the industry.

< < < < < < < < < < < < < < < < < < < < < < < < < < < <

If you still have openings after that, then it is time to cast your net wider by perhaps using Gamasutra (www.gamasutra.com), a strong site dedicated to game development in general, which has robust resume and job posting facilities.

In general I would not use a site like Monster.com, but not because I feel it is not good; in fact I would consider using Monster.com for noncreative positions such as administration. However, I feel the above community sites that are dedicated to a creative discipline will find you much stronger recruits.

Another resource for finding new developers is straight out of one of the new game development schools such as DigiPen (www.digipen.edu) and The Art Institute of California (see Appendix B). At Taldren we have hired folks from both places and have been pleased with the energy these newly minted game developers bring to the company. Of course you should only hire these folks if you have entry-level art and programming positions. You will also sometimes have to put in extra work as their first professional employer to shape their work ethics and manage their expectations for the game industry. Most of the time these folks turn out to be good developers earning loyalty back and forth between the company and the employee.

The final suggestion on recruiting new developers is to use one of a number of professional recruiting firms such as Interact (www.interact.com). Recruiters are generally tapped into better information than you and act as a giant amplifier on your personal contacts network. In return for identifying and placing a candidate with your company, they will receive a commission of 20 percent of the candidate's salary within 60 or 90 days of placement. While this is expensive, nothing can beat filling a position in your company with the right person on time. Like most things in game development there exists a triangle between cost, timeliness, and quality. The recruiter will usually find you quality candidates quickly and therefore must charge a premium for this service. You may or may not need a recruiter. If you have a bunch of time to fill your position, you will probably be able to find your own quality candidates. However, if you are short on time, a recruiter can help you fill that critical hole before your project is endangered. Keep in mind that slipping just one month on a team project far outweighs the 20 percent recruiter fee, let alone the cost of not getting your game to market on time and tying up your team for another month.

Fill your positions!

Where to Locate Your Game Company

This is a question that does not apply to many of us when we are starting our company. More than likely the place where we start our company is where we are currently located. Usually the founding employees all know each other professionally and already live in the same city.

However, there are a few things to consider when deciding where to locate your company like local tax laws, availability of talent, and proximity to game publishers.

Optimizing for tax laws may be one of the more interesting ideas to think about. It is my understanding that Ireland has special promotions for film and game companies. According to my sources your company *and your employees* are currently not required to pay federal taxes in Ireland as an incentive to bring business to Ireland.

Similarly, there have been tax incentives from the Canadian government in the past. The South Korean government invests heavily in game companies, and I am sure there are a host of places you could locate your company to take advantage of the local tax laws. Westwood employees enjoy the no state income tax in Nevada. However, at the end of the day I do not believe that optimizing for tax purposes is a good reason to relocate your company to an offbeat locale. There is a basic reason why these tax breaks are offered; it is because that local economy is suffering from a lack of business in the hi-tech and entertainment fields.

It is most important to be near potential publishers, especially when you are starting your company. Publishers are risking real amounts of capital on young, creative people (the people it takes to make games), and more often than not they lose a bunch of money. For all publishers it is such a relief to be able to send their producer down to your shop for the afternoon on short notice that that alone could make or break your deal compared to if you set up shop in Montana. The West Coast is where it's at for major publishers: Seattle, the Bay Area of California, and Southern California. If you have space, employees, and some good

visual material, you should have no problem convincing several publishers to come out and visit you. However, if you are just a state away in Arizona, you might have to subsist on small contract work for quite a while before someone gets curious enough to want to come out and see your shop. Despite being located in Southern California, I think that this is an annoying attitude; a publisher should be willing to go to Shanghai, Moscow, or Santa Fe to find a developer, but the truth is Santa Monica is a car drive away from Activision, Sony, THQ, Infogrames, Interplay, Midway, Blizzard, Universal, Vivendi, TDK, Conspiracy, Crave, Encore, Sammy, and perhaps a couple more publishers that I could not recall off the top of my head. Do good work in one of the three main West Coast areas and you will continue to get good work.

The other aspect of locating your company is to find someplace where there is abundant talent for games. Conveniently enough, this happens to be the same place the game publishers are located. Plenty of strong universities and a deep, vibrant hi-tech industry base are the raw materials of the Southern California, Bay Area, and Seattle communities.

Of course, there are many examples of successful game companies that are not located in these areas. If you choose to live outside these areas, such as the game development scene in Texas, you and your employees should enjoy the lower costs of living and be able to have a greater command of the local development talent. Again, in the end you will likely start your company around the location of your founding opportunity.

Lawyer and Accountant

Game businesses are created to enter into business relationships with other entities and to make money while making games. Thus, you need a lawyer and an accountant.

Your lawyer is critical in helping negotiate your contracts. When you start out you will not have much leverage to bring to bear, but fundamentally if someone wants to fund you, you have *some* leverage. A competent lawyer with experience in the *game industry* will help you focus your negotiations on the parts of the contract that must be changed and let you know the parts you can likely let slide. At the end of the day however, your lawyer is a vendor providing you with a service, and you need to make your own decisions on how to best run your negotiations. The reason I stress the familiarity with games is that if you get just any old lawyer, or even a high-flying Hollywood lawyer, he will not be familiar with the current trends in game publisher-developer contracts, and you will end up paying him a lot of money to learn the ropes.

Your accountant will organize your books, help you structure your business accounting, and of course prepare your company's taxes. As your company grows you may need your accountant to assist in preparing financial statements for your capital raising instrument.

Your accountant should also be familiar with the game industry as she would be better able to advise you on how best to handle your tax obligations suited to the game development business model.

Below is a list of lawyers and accountants who are familiar with the game industry.

Accounting:

Khoo & Company, Inc.

Eng Kuan Khoo
2240 Union Street, Suite 101
San Francisco, CA 94123
Phone: (415) 776-7998
Fax: (415) 776-7610
mailto:eng@khoocpa.com
http://www.khoocpa.com

Legal:

Farella Braun + Martel, LLP

Bruce Maximov
Russ Building, 30th Floor
235 Montgomery Street
San Francisco, CA 94104
Phone: (415) 954-4400
Fax: (415) 954-4480
http://www.fbm.com

Fischbach, Perlstein & Lieberman, LLP

David Rosenbaum
1875 Century Park East, Suite 850
Los Angeles, CA 90067
Phone: (310) 556-1956
drosenbaum@fpllaw.com

> >

Stephen Rubin
15591 Second Street
Waterford, VA 20197
Phone: (540) 882-4911
Fax: (540) 882-4913
www.stephenrubin.com
rubinesq@aol.com

Russo & Hale, LLP
Tim Hale
401 Florence Street
Palo Alto, CA 94301
Voice: (650) 327-9800
Fax: (650) 327-3737
thale@computerlaw.com
http://www.computerlaw.com

Deciding on the Type of Company

An important step you must take when starting your game development company is to decide what type of organization it will be—sole proprietorship, partnership, or corporation.

First I should point out that I do not have a law degree; my only qualifications are that I have run a game development shop for a few years. Also, my comments pertain to U.S. legal structures; those of you in other countries will likely have similar structures available to choose from.

The questions that shape your organizational trust are: How do you want decisions to be made? How do you want to pay your taxes? What liability do you want? What other forms of flexibility do you require for your business plan?

Non-Corporation

The two basic structures are corporations and non-corporations. I will discuss the non-corporations first as they are the simplest. The first is sole proprietorship: You're the boss; hire employees or not. If you are the only owner, you are a sole proprietor. Very little legal paperwork needs to be set up. You will probably need a local business license; however, your own social security number will act as the Internal

Revenue Service's tracking number for your business's financials. You simply pay taxes as an individual on the profits and losses of your company.

The other non-corporation structure is the partnership. It is easy to form a partnership. If you work with anyone else and do not expressly document him or her as an independent contractor, employee, vendor, or client, then poof! Like magic, he becomes your partner. For example, a successful game developer could grow his business for five years up to the point that three publishers offer simultaneous projects. He now needs two more producers to run these projects and neglects for some reason to pay them an explicit salary and have them sign an employment contract. After just a year these two new producers decide they don't like the games industry and want out. Do they simply walk away? No, they talk to *their* lawyer and come to realize they are your partners and you now share the equity with them. How much equity you ask? Is it one-eighth each? (One part for each year of service from each of these individuals plus our founder.) No. They get one-third each! In fact, our hero now is a minority owner. These two turkeys decide they want cash and sell out their two-thirds of the company for $100 to their neighbor, and now our hero has lost control of his company for $100, and he did not even get the $100. Bad move. The moral of the story is *always, always* document the nature of the relationship between all people working at, working with, and working for your game company.

The other large problem with a non-corporation is that you are held personally liable for any and all debts and damages incurred on behalf of the company. This means you are personally exposed to any lawsuit or debt the company could incur. This is even worse with general partnerships, for in a general partnership each partner is held personally responsible for any and all debts and liabilities incurred on behalf of the company. For example, Mary and Bob form a game development company, and Bob secretly decides the company really needs custom-made desks for each employee. This turns out to be a $50,000 expense. When Mary finds out she blows her lid and declares that the company shall not make any such purchase of custom desks. No such luck; Mary is the proud owner of 20 custom-made desks whether she likes it or not. In fact, if the company does not have enough money to pay for the desks and Bob is flat broke, the woodworker has the legal right to come after Mary and liquidate her comic book collection to satisfy the debt.

A third drawback with a non-corporation is that it is difficult to sell equity in your company, which you might find desirable when raising capital or when structuring an employee compensation and golden handcuffs program. You can have some degree of investor liability protection with a limited partnership; however, if you are seeking capital, you will be much more successful as a corporation.

So why would anyone have a non-corporation? The main thing going for non-corporations is the simplicity of setting up shop; however, this is time well worth spending to be protected.

Corporation

Corporations come in three main flavors: standard subchapter C, subchapter S, and the relatively new LLC.

To understand what an LLC and a subchapter S is, we must first discuss what a vanilla subchapter C corporation is. The subchapter C corporation, like all corporations, is a separate legal entity distinct from any individuals and is responsible and liable for its own actions outright. Corporations incur debts and suffer liabilities all on their own without getting down into the pockets of the officers or shareholders of the corporation. This is a very positive quality in the eyes of officers and shareholders. (Just ask any executive of Worldcom, Enron, Rite-Aid, or any of the other 1,000 U.S. public corporations who have restated their income in the period of 1997 to mid-2002 whether or not they would enjoy losing the liability protection of the corporation!) This protection from the activities of the corporation makes it safe enough to encourage successful, wealthy, and/or energetic people to become committed to the organization and make an investment of money, time, or both.

> >

Taxes

A subchapter C corporation has the freedom to sell shares to anyone in the world and pays its own taxes. The employees of the corporation pay their own taxes on their salaries. That seems straightforward until you think about being a small business owner. How would you like to make a profit at your game company, pay your taxes, draw a salary, and then pay taxes *again* on that same money on your personal income taxes? That would usually suck. So President Eisenhower pushed the subchapter S entity through Congress in the 1950s to promote small business activity. The subchapter S is a corporation just the same as a subchapter C, but the corporation does not pay *any tax*! Wow! Neat. The profits the company makes is simply considered the personal income of the shareholders in proportion to their holdings in the company, thus you are only taxed once!

So why would anyone set up a subchapter C? Wouldn't Microsoft organize as a subchapter S in a heartbeat? Well, there are serious restrictions on being a subchapter S. First of all your company may only have 35 shareholders, effectively preventing you from raising capital through the public equity markets. Furthermore, a subchapter S may only have U.S. citizens and residents as shareholders. This might be a problem if a key founder of your company is foreign. Also, the shareholders of a subchapter S must be individuals and not other entities such as other corporations (with the exception of certain trusts). Finally, a subchapter S may not own any subsidiaries.

So with all of these restrictions, why would you form your company as a subchapter S? Eventually you may want to go public, or you might get a foreign founder, and so on… That is why the IRS makes forms; the subchapter S acts as an incubator as the best structure for the early years of your company, and later you simply fill out some paperwork and become a subchapter C.

So what is a limited liability company—the LLC? The LLC is really a refinement of the subchapter S entity without the subsidiary restriction and the restriction of U.S. residents and aliens. The catch with the LLC is that it involves just a tad bit more paperwork to set up.

Buy-Sell Agreements

Beyond your company's formal structure, you should also have your lawyer draft language that describes something called a buy-sell agreement between the major shareholders of the corporation. This is a critical agreement as I found out the hard way with my first subchapter S, which I co-founded before I entered the game industry. In a nutshell, the buy-sell agreement handles the procedures that will be taken when a major shareholder leaves the company through choice, termination, death, illness, or injury. It is critical to have this in place before the time comes to handle the individual's exit. At the time of exit it will be too late to handle the situation with grace, for the stakes are too high and the drama is happening in real time. Believe me; work this out when everybody is all full of good cheer at the start of the game company.

< < < < < < < < < < < < < < < < < < < < < < < < < < <

Insurance

Workman's Compensation

If you will have employees, you will need workman's compensation insurance. The good news for us is that our rates are very low as we employ people to just come in and sit down and enjoy themselves. No lifting or physical activity is required for a game developer! Your accountant will likely be able to get you in touch with a good insurance broker.

This insurance is absolutely required; if you are not prepared to pay for it, then you are not prepared to employ people.

Liability Insurance

Any good corporation should have a liability insurance policy to handle minor legal scrapes and other complaints against your company. Usually this is paired up with fire, theft, flood, and other disaster protection.

Liability insurance is not a strict legal requirement as in the case of workman's compensation insurance; however, this is the kind of insurance you want to buy!

Employee Compensation Programs

Employee compensation is the most pleasurable part of the legal/business side of running a game development company. I suppose selling your company for tens of millions of dollars would feel good too, but I genuinely enjoy trying to figure out how to best motivate and reward my people.

Like a lot of things, when designing your employee compensation plan, you must figure out what your true goals are before you make any decisions.

For example, getting strong employees at low salaries is great; your company will increase its profit margin. Maybe that is a goal for you—low salaries (low costs). Fair enough, no company would express as a goal to have high costs. However, the interesting question is how you will achieve your goal. For example, I once worked at a game development company that was very short on cash flow and was

heavily motivated to reduce costs through hiring young, inexperienced (cheap) developers. This is fine, it is a tried-and-true strategy; the problem was the company did not have a consistent pay scale. They would pay one person $12 an hour and another $8, where the $8 guy was performing at a level far above the $12 guy. And sometimes they paid $20 or even $25 an hour for other developers who were in turn less capable than some of their $10-an-hour guys. This creates a host of problems: People have a sense of fairness, and if they find out that Bob is earning more than they are and they *know* they are outperforming Bob, you have just created a disenfranchised employee, and it will be extremely difficult to regain that employee's confidence and productivity.

My solution to that problem is to establish an internal pay scale that fits

>>>>>>>>>>>>>>>>>>>>>>>>>>>>>>>

your finances and then stick to it. For instance, if I accidentally printed out the salaries of everyone at Taldren and it got posted over the water cooler, no one could be offended. (You will always have some people who have a difference of opinion with you, but as long as you are consistent in applying your pay scale it will be a defensible and comfortable payroll report. And at the end of the day, if someone is still bent out of shape and I honestly feel that they are being compensated fairly, I don't worry about it.)

The standard is of course to pay a salary. You could pay hourly, but I will be blunt and honest: To be competitive and successful in the game industry *especially* when you are starting up your game company, there will be a lot of overtime and it will be difficult to pay people for all those overtime hours.

The counterpoint to this suggestion is to have all independent contractors working for you on a 1099 basis. This is apparently how the overwhelming bulk of production work is done in Hollywood, where a production studio casts their net out wide pulling in independent contractors to perform the work when there is work and then lets them go again when there is no work. This cycles on forever. This also occurs in the art production houses in the game industry. I have also been advised to structure my business that way. I fundamentally disagree; I feel you should work hard to create a highly motivated well-oiled game production company. Games are different from film, and what works for film may not necessarily work for games. Games are so much more flexible than film in their

ability to absorb more and more tweaking and improvement. When can you really say a game could not stand another tweak, feature, asset, or improvement? A film, on the other hand, as a discrete piece of art that can be viewed and thought about, could be declared more comfortably finished than a game.

It takes a long time to master a craft, and in the case of games, every two years you must reinvent your technology, forcing you to always chase mastery. This alone dictates the model of making solid hires and retaining good people for as long as practical.

So how much should you pay your employees? The honest answer is that no one really knows; it is like the stock market. Certain positions like lead console programmers tend to make a bit more money than a texture artist, although I am sure there is more than one lead console programmer in the world earning less than some texture artists. You have your financing from somewhere, seed money or your first deal—that is your budget. Be honest and go out and find the strongest people you can within your budget. I am sure that if you have a solid management team and a good attitude, you will attract some good folks to work with you no matter what budget you have to work with at the beginning.

There are salary surveys that float around the industry, and I cringe somewhat when newcomers see the salary surveys and go, wow, I am a programmer; I will make $80,000+. Yes, it is true there are many game programmers who earn $80,000 a year and more; however, they all started at a much lower rate earlier in their career. The problem with these surveys is that they tend to be skewed towards the more established developers and internal publisher teams that answer these surveys.

At the risk of being crude, I will throw out some rough figures for a start-up game company. If you are a small start-up in Oregon and have a $300,000 annual budget and you need to perform two GBA titles, you are in a tight position, but you have to start somewhere (GBA title budgets are usually $200K in North America with only the most well-known GBA developers getting $500,000 for a single title; so on your first title you might be happy to get $150,000). If you turn around each project in six months, you will need at least two programmers, two artists, and a designer/producer. Assuming you have a very low overhead ratio, call it 20 percent, then you have a salary budget of $250,000 without considering bonuses. So your salary plan might look like this:

Lead programmer:	$55,000
Programmer:	$40,000
Lead artist:	$50,000
Artist:	$35,000
Designer/producer:	$45,000

This would leave $25,000 spare for end-of-the-year bonuses or slippage money. It is always a good idea to have spare money. These are actually reasonable salaries for people with relatively modest experience in the game industry.

Notice you have just a five-person team and only six months to execute your games; here again it is of the utmost importance to design your games to fit your business parameters.

Medical/Dental/Optical/IRA

After you have sorted out your salary levels, I suggest setting up your employees with health and dental benefits. This is pretty much normal at any development shop, although you might be thinking of cutting corners when you are starting up and feel this is a luxury you could provide later. I disagree; health care is expensive and only more so when the individual is forced to secure it on her own without the benefit of negotiating as part of a group plan. If at the end of your salary plan you do not have enough money to provide some level of medical and dental benefits, I strongly urge you to trim back your salaries enough to allow this coverage. Your employees will appreciate it and immediately feel a lot more comfortable with the professionalism you provide with a full medical benefits package. You may still choose what level of compensation you will pay towards the package, and there are other choices to make, as your insurance broker will be able to offer disability and other products.

> >

401K/IRA/Retirement Benefits

One benefit that I feel is a luxury is a 401K or SIMPLE-IRA plan; these are retirement plans where your company has the option to contribute some matching funds towards the employee's retirement account. We have a SIMPLE-IRA plan at Taldren. We started it up after one year in business, and there was a tangible increase in morale after the introduction of the program. Again, the folks here felt more comfortable and reassured that we are a professional organization.

Project Bonuses

A time-honored tradition in the game industry is to provide a completion bonus in the range of 5 to 20 percent of the employee's annual salary upon the final acceptance of the completed project. This is a good bonus program because it drives people towards completing the game. One problem I have with the completion bonus is that if the project slips beyond the employees' control they could become frustrated as they see the money running away from them. Furthermore, if they thought the project would last a year and then it lasts 16 months, their bonus has effectively been diluted. I do not disagree with the completion bonus, but I feel it should not be your only bonus program.

Milestone Bonuses

As a milestone developer you make money when you deliver milestones to the publisher and they are accepted and paid. I have to admit I am partial to extending that business model down to the employees in a minor way by attaching a bonus to the timely delivery of the milestones. The condition here is the timely delivery of the milestone; again, a single employee may do a great job and still be unable to collect the bonus because as a group we were late. The effect I hope to deliver to my team is that this is a group effort. The bonus should not be overly large, or you could potentially cause people to rush their work at the risk of quality.

Royalties

Older than project completion bonuses are sharing the project royalties among the employees. This worked much more often in the past when game budgets were in the $75,000 to $150,000 range. Now the costs of most games are so large that they do not recoup their advances, and all of the promised royalties do not happen. I am a great believer in delivering on the expectations you create, so my advice with project royalties is to not promise them until they actually happen. If there is no expectation, there can be no disappointment. This may be a problem for some start-up development companies as they do not have enough budget available to pay salaries so they turn instead to project royalties as a form of regular compensation. Nine cases out of ten you will only succeed in burning morale. Sure, if you make a breakaway hit and you are packing away the royalty checks, share the good fortune, but my advice is to not overhype the royalties until they happen.

Stock Options

Stock options, on the other hand, I do feel are an honorable compensation instrument even for small, privately held development studios. Stock options for a private company are not immediately liquid; however, if you do sell your company to a publisher some time in the future, it is a nice gesture to recognize the unique contributions of your employees with some equity.

Take the time to educate your employees on the mechanics of your stock option plan, as it will likely be their first experience with options and they might be too shy to admit they have questions about how they work.

Trademarks and URLs

You should of course trademark your company's name and logo as well as any significant chunks of intellectual property you own. Again, this is an area where your lawyer will make the process painless. I can offer this much advice: Try not to found your company with simple names like Studio One as no doubt the URL has been taken and the trademark office will already have a lot of similar sounding company names that could potentially confuse the consumer. Best to think of some word that is not an English word, yet people

would "get it" the first time they heard it.

Basically, if you have a mark or a brand you want to protect, wrap a ™ around it while you await the results of the trademark search. After a period of time you will be told whether or not you may go ahead with the ®. The © stands for copyright and you should attach that to any document you create unless you are in a work-for-hire arrangement. And even then it is common to own your code outright and provide the publisher with an unrestricted license.

War Chests

Finally, without ever losing the magic in your heart for the beauty of games, never forget that you are running a business. A business primarily exists to create money. It might make money unethically, ethically, in an environmentally friendly manner, or any other way, but at the end of each day your company has been created to make money.

That seems like an all-too-obvious statement; however, looking at the dot-com bust of the 1990s you will see that American business lost track of the bottom line and measured business

success in hype created and not wealth creation. For a short while you can spend hype, but it is not very liquid and it will disappear all too quickly.

You have to start somewhere, and for most game developers we have modest starting points. No matter how modest your early contracts must be to get started, structure your deals and company expenses to make money off each of your games. Your advances must be large enough to cover your costs as well as provide a small profit to add to your war chest.

Game development can sometimes be a grim game, where you and your guys work hard against milestones that pay 90 to 110 percent of your costs until the day you encounter a tough problem, such as no follow-up project, grave project slip, or a failed publisher.

You must work towards building a war chest. Your goal should be to first have one extra month of burn rate, then three months of burn rate, then six months, and finally a year of burn. I would imagine after you have piled up a year's worth of cash, you could entertain investing in other ventures rather than socking away more cash. War chests cannot be undervalued; the quality of your projects, contract language, and ultimately your profitability will be directly related to the amount of cash you have in your war chest. Without it, when you need the cash badly to pay the next payroll, you have no negotiating room.

Earning money is easy, just work; it is the saving of money that is truly difficult. There are always a bunch of compelling *things* that you must spend money on at any stage of your company; however, I sincerely advocate being as frugal as possible without impacting productivity, and build that war chest!

> >

Chapter 28   > > > > > > > > > > > > > > >

Outsourcing Music

"Audio is one-third the game!"

—Tommy Tallarico

Music for Games

As in the movie industry, music is a critical component of a successful game. It is the mood and tempo of the music that will add the elusive quality of emotion to your game. With all of the visual information a game pumps out to the player, the ear is a critical channel to reach deep into the player's soul to enthrall the player.

For me the eerie percussion instrumentals of MechWarrior 2 evoked the strongest response from me. I can recall only fragments of individual missions, but it is the haunting, militaristic beats of Mech II that I keep on my personal jukebox. And whenever I hear the beat I have a fierce feeling of belonging to a clan of warriors—a clan of mech warriors in the 31st century striving to become Khan. The music evokes images of life and death struggles on distant planets...ahem. Where was I? Oh yes, music in games. Strong, evocative music is as vital as strong gameplay to make a complete experience. Bad music, on the other hand, may be so detrimental to your game that the game experience suffers, or at best the player turns off your music and

pops in a CD of her own to listen while playing your game.

Presumably I do not need to spend too much time convincing you to put music in your game. I just wanted to be sure you know how important music is to your game. Any range of human emotion may be nurtured and reinforced through music: love, loss, hate, fear, and triumph, just to name a few. The music you commission for your game should have the whole range of game experience in mind. For every major event/situation/level/experience in your game, ideally, a musical piece should be there to flesh out the experience and make it complete.

When to Think About Music

Most games have many challenges: time pressures, budget constraints, fat technical risks, original game mechanics to tweak. Coming up with good original music is just not as challenging to the producer as the rest of the game project. Simply carve out what you can from the audio budget for music, find a competent composer, tell them the budget and deadline, and collect your tracks when they are done.

The issue I have with this approach to game music is that it is haphazard. As I pointed out at the beginning of this chapter, music is a critical aspect of the game to develop emotional bonding with the player, so why short-change the game with a rushed job?

There is a tendency for people to believe that early in the project there will not be enough visible or demonstrable to articulate well to the composer the game experience. Another reason I have heard is if you give someone too long to do the job, they will charge you more! (Only the reverse could possibly be true; give someone time to fit it into his downtime and perhaps you would be able to get a discount.)

In the budget planning stage you should involve your composer if at all practical. By starting this early, the composer may be able to point out to you options you did not know you had and thus be able to modify the budget when it is still in its malleable phase at the start of the project. Even without jumping into the work directly, the composer is respected as a project stakeholder and thus will naturally have greater buy-in and, more practically, will be able to munch on creative thoughts for your game in the background until it is time for music composition to formally begin. Perhaps the composer will keep his ears open for new sounds and equipment that will lend themselves well to your project. In short, talk to your composer and conduct your relationship with him as a two-way street, not just a request for bid from a collection of vendors who will do a quick job at the lowest price.

> **TOMMY TALLARICO SAYS**: For some reason audio doesn't seem to be taken as seriously or respected as other parts of a game. This is quickly changing now that we have live orchestras and 5.1 digital audio playing.
>
> Another interesting thing is that one of the reasons people dealt with audio last was because they have in their heads (from the movie and TV industries) that sound is POST-production. This just isn't the case at all with audio for games.

Music Formats

Switching gears from the philosophical to the practical, I should take a moment to outline the formats of music that are typically employed in games.

- **MIDI**—Musical Instrument Digital Interface is a format whose specification is published by the MIDI Manufacturer's Association (http://www.midi.org). MIDI is more than just a data format for music; it is actually three components to the MIDI specification, which are the communications protocol (language), the connector (hardware interface), and a distribution format called Standard MIDI Files. For your purposes as a producer of a game, you are really only interested in what the data format can do for you.

The MIDI format is a bit different from other methods of digitizing music. It does not attempt to digitize sound at all! Rather, MIDI digitizes, or encodes into a binary format, commands such as note on, note off, and note velocities that are comprehensible to a MIDI-capable device. What does this mean,

> >

and why should you care? MIDI files are very, very small. How small? A MIDI file I have close at hand happens to be 2 minutes and 24 seconds long and requires just 8 kilobytes to store. Compare this to an MP3 of "With a Little Help from My Friends" by the Beatles that requires 2.75 *mega*bytes of space for a 2 minute, 44 second song. Thus, a MIDI file is roughly 350 *times* smaller than an MP3 and roughly 3,500 times smaller than straight digital audio!

The catch with MIDI is of course quality. Anytime something is 300 to 3,000 times less expensive than something else in terms of space, money, or time, quality must be compromised to achieve that savings. The resulting quality of a MIDI file is determined more by the *sound samples* the playback device is employing to replicate the composer's musical instructions.

The days of MIDI music for mainstream games have passed within the last few years as the capabilities of the consoles and PC have soared and production values have increased dramatically. MIDI will remain a most compelling format on any platform where memory and storage are a premium such as mobile phones, PDAs, and handheld consoles.

What Is Better Than MIDI?

So if MIDI is limited in quality by being a mere set of instructions for instrument on and off, what would be a reasonable way to improve the quality?

The direction of improvement would have to lie along the road of incorporating actual sounds with the musical instructions. Four different formats have been developed to varying degrees of success by encoding

digitized sound snippets along with the musical score:

- **XMI**—a more powerful version of MIDI where the instrument samples are built into the music file. This results in a musical file that sounds the same on any compatible playback device.

- **SF2**—Sound Fonts, created by Creative Labs for use on their sound cards. Sound Fonts are sets of digitized instruments that are downloaded to the playback device. Thus, a musical file created for use with Sound Fonts will only sound the same on other devices that also have the same Sound Fonts installed.

- **SBK**—Sound Bank, a similar and competing standard to Creative Lab's Sound Fonts.

- **Tracker**—a set of related sound formats: MOD (Module), XM (Extended Module), IT (Impulse Tracker), STM/S3M (Scream Tracker). These originated on the Amiga and were popular in early DOS-based computer games. They contained built-in sound samples with the sequence information similar to the XMI format, but it was up to the computer CPU to mix the samples together to create the music. In the old days the better quality the tracker file was, the more taxing it was on the CPU. Lots of early Epic games used these, including Unreal and Unreal Tournament.

All of these formats sound better than MIDI but at a cost of either a significantly larger music file or the requirement to distribute and install a sound font library on the target machine. As

< < < < < < < < < < < < < < < < < < < < < < < < < <

memory and storage become less and less expensive, these costs dwindle away into little concerns on modern consoles and PCs.

Digitized Sound Formats

Sound effects like explosions tend to be noisier and more complicated than musical scores. This would explain why you cannot recall the last time you heard a MIDI explosion.

> **JARGON**: Compression techniques that throw away bits of information such as JPEG for images are termed *lossy*, as in to lose information. Conversely, compression techniques that never throw away information are termed non-lossy.

At first glance, why would anyone want a lossy format? What could possibly be good about throwing away information? The answer lies in the whole point of *compression:* to make something smaller. If we're trying to make a chunk of information smaller (images, music, sound effects, it does not matter), we might be clever and achieve some efficiencies, but to truly scrunch the information down we will have to toss out information.

Any form of lossy compression for sound effects will strip the richness and depth of the sound effect, creating a flat sound. That is why the sound effects side of game audio has enjoyed a larger budget of bytes over the years. Only in recent times have we moved to fully digitized sound formats for music. In fact, MIDI could be said to be aggressively lossy, as it throws away almost all bits of information of how the real instruments should actually *sound*.

- WAV—A very popular format for digitized sound and so widely employed for sound effects that

people often casually use the phrase "WAV file" to mean sound effects.

- **ADPCM**—Windows standard audio format, which is a compression algorithm on top of the WAV format.

- **VOC**—A predecessor to WAV for Sound Blaster cards. It was used in the early DOS days.

- **CD/Redbook Audio**—Redbook audio is the format used to record commercial music CDs that consumers purchase. Thus, Redbook audio enjoys the status of having the highest standard of quality accessible to consumers. As the CD format for games became widely accepted, there was plenty of storage on the media to hold the beefy Redbook audio files. However, now the production values of the rest of the game have grown a voracious appetite for more storage space. The heyday for Redbook audio on the game CD has for the most part passed on in favor of a much more popular format, a format that is *twelve times* smaller than Redbook audio with nearly identical quality: MP3.

- **MP3**—Otherwise known as Mpeg 3. By now everyone is familiar with MP3. The MP3 standard would seem like it is free and open, but the truth is that the MPEG development group manages the development of the MP3 standard. An interesting detail is that the Fraunhofer Institute is the principal source of engineering behind MP3 and, along with Thompson Multimedia, holds some 18 patents covering a wide spectrum of the MP3

> >

technology space. This means that most any commercial exploitation of the MP3 format appears to be liable for a royalty to Thompson Multimedia. Looking up the relevant information at http://www.mp3licensing.com/royalty/games.html, it appears that there is a $2,500 fee for games that distribute files in MP3 format. This fee is waived if you sell fewer than 5,000 copies or as an entity you gross less than $100,000 a year.

Full technical details on MP3 are found at the Fraunhofer Institute: http://www.iis.fhg.de/amm/techinf/layer3/index.html.

To address piracy, the Fraunhofer Institute has been working with others such as the Secure Digital Music Initiative (SDMI) to create the Audio Scrambler which selectively encodes bits of the music stream with annoying noise that will only be properly decoded with the right key. Check out http://www.iis.fhg.de/amm/techinf/ipmp/scrambling.html for more details on the Audio Scrambler.

The other technique is watermarking for digital rights management. This may be used to develop proof of ownership, access control, and tracing illegal copies. For more details, see http://www.iis.fhg.de/amm/techinf/ipmp/water.html.

- **WMA**—Windows Media Audio, Microsoft's answer to MP3, includes integrated support for digital rights management. Windows Media Audio is a portion of the codec that combined with Windows Media Video is called simply Windows Media. For a complete overview of the tools and technology behind the Windows Media site, visit http://www.microsoft.com/windows/windowsmedia/technologies.asp. Microsoft boasts that their compression is better than MP3 and RealAudio and offers a whole suite of tools for the creation, manipulation, playback, and distribution of media files.

- **RealAudio**—Another competing standard similar to MP3 and WMA from RealNetworks. I tried hard to find information on the RealNetworks site for some technical information about RealAudio; all I could find is commercial messages and information relevant to a user of their playback and recording software. However, RealNetworks also offers tools for both the creation and playback of rich media files.

> **TOMMY TALLARICO SAYS**: Don't forget Yellowbook or streaming audio. This is by far the most widely used way of doing music now and in the future. The newer platforms are also able to have multiple streams playing at once and mixable on the fly depending on the action.

How Do You Break Down the Music Bid?

Game music ranges quite a bit in cost, influenced by the composer's experience, the choice of performance (synthetic or live), and the total minutes of music purchased.

Most of the music work offered to composers is work for hire without any royalty arrangements. The more successful composers such as Tommy Tallarico have made strides in correcting that with bonuses when games reach different sales targets. Whether or not the composer has other distribution rights beyond the game is a matter of negotiation with the publisher of the game, the usual winner in that discussion.

Music created by a North American composer and delivered in high-quality synthesized MP3 or other digital formats runs between $600 and $1,500 per minute, with $1,000 being the industry norm. So what does $1,000 for a minute of music mean?

Most AAA games have the gameplay hours running at about 15 to 25 hours; we will call it 20 hours. (Usually you do not count multiplayer or user extensibility options such as map editors in gameplay hours. Only the single-player experience is used to calculate gameplay hours.) Does this mean you need to commission 20 hours of music, which would be 20 hours x 60 minutes x 1000 = $1.2M of music? Um, no. While there have certainly been game budgets large enough to accommodate that figure, that would be an outrageous amount of original music. I doubt that many composers have 1,200 minutes of great music on tap and ready to hand over to you. I would guess that many composers would be happy if they produced 20 hours of quality music in their professional careers!

Movies are scored throughout their 110 minutes of playtime with the usual action films using popular rock sans vocals and dramas using classical composers with long stretches of muted music. Movies are not rock videos and do not require music to be played throughout the experience.

Games are also not rock videos, and a constant stream of music is not only unwarranted, it is not desirable. Rather, the music must be placed to support the action, tension, and drama you are developing in the game.

Score Music for Triggered Events

Take Pac-Man, for example; for the most part there is a steady-state drumming of the wakka-wakka sound effect as Pac-Man eats the dots. When Pac-Man eats the power-up, a short, fast-paced aggressive musical tone reinforces the comical terror of the now-dark blue ghosts on the run from Pac-Man.

Another example is the simple act of Mario picking up a star in Mario64, triggering what is called a short *musical sting*. These are important aural reinforcements for a game action.

Exploration and Ambient Music

Ambient music is scored for the slow periods of gameplay that you need to have between the action sequences. This music should not be too driving or distracting; rather it should reinforce the aesthetic mood or setting in the game. For example, if you were making a game with intrigue between two rival warlords in feudal Japan where the character plays the role of an intrepid ninja assassin exploring the rival warlord's castle in the middle of the night, I think the haunting sounds of the Japanese shakuhachi would be the perfect instrument for the job. Liberally scattering doses of exploration music with dollops of silence mixed in between is great for the important quiet periods of the game.

> >

Chase/Battle/Hunting Music

This is the fast-paced hard-charging music that is reserved for the most exhilarating moments in a game. While this music is critical to nail, it is important not to overdo it and use it too liberally. If you do, you will totally spoil the impact when you really need to get the player's blood pumping.

Jump Lists

Each game handles its music differently. However at a high level, many AAA games employ some sort of context-sensitive music track switching. The specific technology employed determines its name; for Starfleet Command we used very small segments of just eight seconds each and jumped around dynamically in real time relative to the amount of combat action the player was facing in the game. So we called it jump lists.

You need to determine how you will transition between musical tracks and have that information handy at the start of your talks with the composer.

Menu Music

This upbeat but vague music is the equivalent of the credits music in a movie. This music needs to have enough aural impact to help overcome the relative lack of action as the player clicks through the menus.

TOMMY TALLARICO SAYS:
Cinematics are becoming a very important role in the storytelling aspect of a game. For FMV movies (mostly used in intros, between levels, and ending credits) the composer is able to completely score right to the picture.

How Many Minutes Do You Really Need?

Here is how we have broken down our musical minutes for our upcoming action/RPG Black9:

World Setting 1:
6 search and/or ambient songs @ 1:30 minutes = 9 minutes
4 chase and/or battle songs @ 1:30 = 6 minutes
5 musical stings @ 5 seconds = 25 seconds
3 cinematic songs @ 1 minute = 3 minutes

World Setting 2:
6 search and/or ambient songs @ 1:30 minutes = 9 minutes
4 chase and/or battle songs @ 1:30 = 6 minutes
5 musical stings @ 5 seconds = 25 seconds
3 cinematic songs @ 1 minute = 3 minutes

World Setting 3:
4 search and/or ambient songs @ 1:30 minutes = 6 minutes
4 chase and/or battle songs @ 1:30 = 6 minutes
4 musical stings @ 5 seconds = 20 seconds
2 cinematic songs @ 1 minute = 2 minutes

Menu Music
5 minutes of theme music = 5 minutes

This is a total of 53 minutes of music planned for a game with about 20 hours of gameplay. Taking the industry average of $1,000 a minute, we will expect to pay about $50,000 to $60,000 for the music in our game.

I think this is a good value when you consider that the music industry would typically advance a new, upcoming group $100,000 to $500,000 for their first record. You will get music composed by a professional, custom designed for your game, and you will have the distribution license for the material. A good deal I think.

Live Performance?

Ever wonder what all those folks who were studying violin and the tuba were going to end up doing after they graduated college? I wondered. Sure, if they turned out to be Yo-Yo Ma, life is good, but what about the rest of them? I don't know about you but I have only been to the Hollywood Bowl a handful of times, and I grew up within walking distance of the bowl. Well, it turns out the world has quite a bit of work for professional players of classical instruments. Movies, television, and games have all benefited from live performances, most often directed by the composer. How much does a live performance cost? For Starfleet Command I, Ron Jones, our composer, considered flying out to Prague to hire the world-famous but apparently inexpensive Prague Orchestra. In the end, Ron did fly, but a short

distance to the Salt Lake Orchestra. How much will it cost to have your music performed by a live orchestra? It varies by the venue and number of players of course, but a nice round number would be $25,000.

TOMMY TALLARICO SAYS: Another thing I think is important to say is that the nonunion buyout orchestras in Europe are the least expensive. The easy calculation is to add about $1,500 per minute of music to your budget. Depending on which orchestra you use that number can easily go up to $10,000 per minute.

You may also say that for one hour of an orchestra's time, the composer normally budgets for three minutes of finished music per hour of orchestra time.

When live orchestra is used it's not just the players/musicians that get hired. You need an arranger (arranges each part for every instrument), a copyist (writes out all of the music for every part of the orchestra to play), a conductor, an engineer, and a studio. You could have a great orchestra and a crappy room (studio) and it will still sound horrible. Rooms are VERY important when recording live orchestra.

With permission from Bill Brown, here is a survey on the use of live orchestras for games.

USING LIVE ORCHESTRA FOR GAMES
by Bill Brown

This article is a gathering of thoughts and news items from various sources regarding the use of live orchestral soundtracks and chorus in games with information for developers, publishers, and composers alike on the benefits of recording with live orchestras. Many of the games listed here have already seen very successful press and great creative results—with a tangible, positive impact on game and game soundtrack sales.

Emerging markets for soundtrack sales are currently being pioneered by G.A.N.G. in brand new territories and markets. G.A.N.G. has already convinced a major national retailer to create soundtrack displays in sections where games are sold, exponentially raising awareness of game soundtracks to potential buyers.

The intention of this presentation is to create an ongoing resource to educate and bring aware-ness about the benefits of using live orchestra for games. G.A.N.G. members are invited to submit orchestral game music news to Bill for future updates to this page.

Orchestral Soundtracks—Ancillary Market Opportunities:

When your soundtrack is recorded with a live orchestra, you automatically create media interest and word of mouth—people appreciate the immersive effect live orchestra brings to the experience. Filmmakers have known this for years—MIDI scores cannot compare to the magic that happens when an orchestra is hired to perform a soundtrack.

Standalone CD Soundtracks Soundtrack sales can quickly recoup session costs and can continue to bring in revenue for both the composer and publisher for years beyond the life of the game.

Marketing campaigns Movie trailers, TV, and Internet promotion creates community "buzz" and word of mouth via the Internet and between gamers—selling more games—exponentially. A big orchestral score is news, and news equals sales.

Bundling Opportunities Pre-Sales, Extra Features, Licensing Opportunities—Simultaneous release with game SKUs in new markets, or with simultaneous marketing campaigns (as in the case of the major motion picture *The Sum of All Fears* and the game of the same name, released in conjunction with the film).

NEWS FROM THE FRONT LINES:

Clive Barker's Undying: Bill Brown—Composer: (Excerpt from Gamasutra's Game Audio Gallery feature) "I was set to record a live chorus for a Game Boy commercial spot a couple years back and had just started talking with DreamWorks about Undying which later became Clive Barker's Undying. The day we were going to go record the chorus, I wrote a few ideas down that seemed to fit the mood of Undying, drawing from both Latin and Gaelic text that seemed to fit and brought them along just in case we had time to fit in a few lines. We recorded in a big church in the valley, which was noisy, but had a big sound to it. I just sang the

4-part harmony to the separate sections and then conducted them all wild to DAT (with no accompaniment). So I brought those tracks back to my studio and experimented with them. I arranged orchestra accompaniment around the vocal parts using my synths and samplers here. A year later, I was finally working on the project, and it all fell together in about three weeks of writing. This is a very good example of the wonderful results that can happen just by involving your composer as soon as your project gets the green light!"

Undying was nominated for the prestigious British Academy of Film and Television Arts (BAFTA) 2001 Interactive Entertainment Award in the Music category. "The music was very well-integrated into the game, successfully matching and enhancing the uncomfortable feel, helping to build the participant's tension at critical moments in the narrative. Intelligent sound woven into the fabric of a filmic genre."

Tommy Tallarico on Evil Dead; "My only fully live orchestra gig was Evil Dead (PS, Dreamcast, PC) for THQ. I used the National Hungarian Symphony Orchestra (64 pieces) and the Budapest Chamber Choir (30 people—15 male/15 female). I wrote the entire vocal score in Latin. I used Steve Salani's services at Forte Music. It was a VERY inexpensive alternative. Although the quality isn't as good as the stuff I've heard from Jack, Jeremy & Michael, it is definitely better than MIDI (in my opinion). The voices were really incredible!! I would highly recommend people use the choir!"

HEADHUNTER records in London

Abbey Road's famous Studio One has played host to innumerable big-budget orchestral recordings for film, but the final session before its refurbishment in 2001 saw it being used for a new purpose: to record the soundtrack for a video game.

The publishers of HEADHUNTER understood the business model for making money back by releasing the score soundtrack—which is still a huge seller in Japan. This commitment on the publisher's part opened a floodgate of creativity to flow into the scoring and implementation of music in the game. Our hats are off to composer Richard Jacques and the entire team!

> >

Orchestral Composers—GDC

Chance Thomas speaks out at the 2002 GDC orchestral seminar: The GDC program stated: "The live symphony orchestra is the palette of choice for many of today's top games. No amount of technology can match the magnificent power, range, skill, color, and sheer emotive strength of a live orchestra. With current game systems capable of delivering high-quality digital audio interactively, developers are increasingly turning to the orchestra to breathe life into their games. This GDC session offers education and informative discussion on just what it takes to produce a live orchestral game score." Couldn't have said it any better ourselves! Chance was joined on this panel by fellow composers Jeremy Soule and Jack Wall. Read Jack Wall's white paper "Using a Live Orchestra in Game Soundtracks" originally presented at the 2002 Game Developers Conference.

The panel exposed the benefits of releasing soundtracks independently from the game itself. Chance Thomas's soundtrack for Quest for Glory V is a great example of the potential benefits. The soundtrack was released before the game and included a playable demo of the project. **They sold 50,000 copies of the soundtrack** and made $500,000 from soundtrack sales. Chance said, "Music is the language of emotion. We draw people in." *Ironically the soundtrack outsold the game*. Quote from gamesdomain Quest for Glory V review: "The music was very well done, Sierra knows this is one of the highlights of the game, which is why they are selling the soundtrack."

More ideas from Jack Wall—Composer: Myst III Exile: (In regard to using live orchestra)... "The way I got Myst III Exile going was I talked up **ancillary markets** to the producer and to the marketing department. If you have great sounding music, you can sell this music as a **standalone CD**, you can use this music in your **marketing campaigns**, etc. They used the heck out of me for Myst III Exile. I basically crafted about 80% of their entire launch marketing campaign for them. It took a lot out of me, but obviously, it was worth it. They put the music on United Airlines flights. They used the Main Title in the **trailer that played nationwide in movie theaters**. But, more directly, I think it's how to educate publishers and developers that it will truly translate into sales—That's the bottom line!" Read Jack's Myst III: Exile article "The Evolution of a Videogame Soundtrack."

Medal of Honor Allied Assault and Medal of Honor Frontline Scores Recorded in Seattle

The next two scores for the DreamWorks Interactive Medal of Honor Series are complete. A 95-piece orchestra was used for the recording, which included a full choir. Michael Giacchino —Composer.

The Academy of Interactive Arts and Science Awards Medal of Honor Underground Best Original Score

At the 4th Annual Interactive Achievement Awards, Medal of Honor Underground won in both categories in which it was a finalist: "Outstanding Achievement in Original Musical Composition" and "Outstanding Achievement in Sound Design."

When you hear the phrase "video game score," what do you usually think of? MIDI? Eric Serra-style synth? Synthesized orchestras? Drum machines? How about "fully orchestral John Williams-style action scores?" Finally, the orchestral score has migrated to video and computer games, with the release of Medal of Honor. The game, based on the film *Saving Private Ryan*, was authorized by Steven Spielberg and turned out probably the best game music score ever heard up to this point. The music is in the percussive, swashbuckling vein of John Williams and it conjures up images of his *Indiana Jones* scores… Michael Giacchino—Composer.

Outcast Nominated for Aias Best Original Score 2001

The 60+ minute score recorded with a 105-piece Moscow Symphony Orchestra and Chorus was one of three finalists for the 2001 AIAS award for Best Original Score. Lennie Moore—Composer.

Infogrames subsequently released Outcast as a stand-alone soundtrack and marketed that soundtrack through their official web site. In 2001, in collaboration with **Vivendi/Universal** a re-mix CD was released which incorporated the soundtrack from Outcast into re-mixes done by European artists.

> >

2002 Aias Outstanding Achievement in Musical Composition Nominee—Myst III: Exile

AIAS nominates score for Myst III: Exile for 2002 "Outstanding Achievement in Musical Composition" award. The score for Myst III was recorded with the Northwest Symphony in Seattle. Jack Wall—Composer.

Myst III: Exile's score won the Game Industry News' Best Soundtrack award for 2002.

Game Soundtracks Using Live Orchestra and/or Live Chorus:

Sovereign (not yet released)	Jeremy Soule—Sony/Verant
Hitman 2 (not yet released)	Jesper Kyd—Eidos Microsoft
Medal of Honor: Frontline (5/2002)	Michael Giacchino—DreamWorks SKG
Headhunter (5/2002)	Richard Jacques—Sega
Medal of Honor: Allied Assault (1/2002)	Michael Giacchino—DreamWorks SKG
Myst III: Exile (5/2001)	Jack Wall—Mattel/Ubisoft
Azurik: Rise of Perathia (11/2001)	Jeremy Soule—Microsoft
Evil Dead (3/2001)	Tommy Tallarico—THQ
Clive Barker's Undying (2/2001)	Bill Brown—DreamWorks SKG
Mech Warrior 4 (11/2000)	Duane Decker—Microsoft
Medal of Honor: Underground (10/2000)	Michael Giacchino—DreamWorks SKG
Crimson Skies 1 & 2 (9/2000)	David Henry—Microsoft
Klingon Academy (06/2000)	Inon Zur—Interplay
Amen: The Awakening (4/2000)	Jeremy Soule—GT Interactive
Medal of Honor (11/1999)	Michael Giacchino—DreamWorks SKG
Outcast (8/1999)	Lennie Moore—Infogrames
Quest for Glory V: Dragon Fire (1999)	Chance Thomas—Sierra
Small Soldiers (1998)	Michael Giacchino—DreamWorks SKG
Heart of Darkness (1998)	Bruce Broughton—Infogrames
Total Annihilation (1997)	Jeremy Soule—Cave Dog
The Lost World (1997)	Michael Giacchino—DreamWorks SKG
StarFleet Academy (1997)	Ron Jones—Interplay

The above list is a work in progress, if you know of additions or corrections please email Bill.

Thanks go to http://www.music4games.net for some of the tidbits included here.

Chapter 29 > > > > > > > > > > > > > > >

Outsourcing Voice

> "Work com-plete."
>
> —Orc peon from the Warcraft series

When sitting down with Chris Borders to go over the budget for voice-over work for Starfleet Command, I was shocked to find out how reasonable it was to have celebrity actors such as George Takei (Mr. Sulu of course) perform lines that I wrote for my game!

Adding the human voice brings a special magic to your game. Think about the wonderful voices in the Warcraft series; how many of you reading this book can read these lines as they were delivered in the game?

> ORC PEON
>
> Work com-plete.
> I can do that.

The magic behind the voices is that we get the intelligence of a human driving the personality of these fantasy characters in our games! It really is the coolest thing. Also, voice work is ideally suited for outsourcing as it takes a highly specialized set of skills to cast the talent, direct the talent, record the voice, and post-process the voice. Only the larger publishers have enough work to employ their VO directors full-time. Alternatively, some game studios have a single amazingly talented audio guy who is able to handle all of the voice-over work for the games. This is a rare talent though; you would do better to outsource as you will not save any money having the VO director/producer on staff year round.

Voice is pretty much all positive. While there are still physical limits with the hardware we are using, the limits are very generous, so go out and get great voices for your games!

In the following interview Chris Borders tells us how it is all done.

Interview with Chris Borders

Erik Bethke: Would you provide a short background on yourself and what role you play in voice-over work in the game industry? Where did you learn to do voice-over work?

Chris Borders: I started working in video game voice-over (VO) back in 1995 as a VO editor for Interplay Productions. I edited VO recordings and attended many VO recording sessions for Interplay on such titles as Star Trek:

Judgment Rites, Stonekeep, and Descent.

Shortly thereafter I was quickly promoted to the title of VO supervisor simply because we were developing more and more titles and needed someone to handle all the VO work that was coming in. My job was to oversee all aspects of VO development for Interplay games including going over the script and characters, setting up auditions, hiring a VO casting director, studio director, and recording studio, scheduling VO talent, setting up union contracts (SAG/AFTRA), attending the sessions, and organizing the material for editing and implementation.

Being no one at the company had ever done this job before (and mostly relied on outside contractors), it was quite an undertaking. I literally had to almost start from scratch. First I started bare knuckles, making connections with the best possible people I could find in the VO industry. I spent many hours on the phone every day "schmoozing" with various Hollywood talent agents, VO directors, and recording studios.

After a year of doing this I realized I could do much of the talent casting and some of the lower budget titles' studio direction myself.

Eventually I took on the casting and studio directing for some major projects myself, and I only hired a contracted director when I couldn't take it on because of overlapping projects.

I now cast and direct the majority of all Interplay titles including the very successful Baldur's Gate series which has received many high-praised reviews for its high-quality voice-over acting.

What range of budgets are you seeing for voice-over work in today's games from low to high?

Most of the games I work on have good budgets that allow me to hire better than average VO talent and some celebrity film actors. However, I occasionally have to work with much smaller budgets that can sometimes affect the quality of the VO acting. On Baldur's Gate II I had to cast as many as 300 character roles with a budget that was better suited for 30 character roles. This became quite a challenge for me, being I wanted BG2 to have the best VO possible. I however managed to pull a few strings and pull it off.

Typically I see most game VO budgets ranging from $20,000 to $100,000 depending on how many characters are in the game, how much dialogue there is, and if the producer calls for celebrity actors.

What in your opinion was a good value? What was simply overspending?

In the past before I became a director, I noticed that when poor quality actors were hired to save money it always ended up costing more in the long run. Thus, budgets had to be raised to accommodate better actors to make the part work. This is, in my opinion, a huge waste, being the work had to be done twice thus costing more, when just hiring a professional actor in the first place and recording it once would have saved studio cost, director cost, editor cost, not to mention having to still pay the poor quality actors (that will never be used in the final production) their session fee.

However, just hiring a bunch of famous celebrity actors so you can have

> >

big names on your title is not always a good idea either. Most great games (unlike motion pictures and TV) don't rely on famous box office actors to make them sell. I will hire a celebrity actor mostly because I know it will make the character part really shine due to that actor's abilities. And if the game player recognizes that actor's voice while playing the game, then all the better.

On the other hand, if you are making a game based on a famous motion picture or TV show, etc., then it might be in your best interest to hire the same actors (if obtainable) that originally acted in the film, TV show, etc. This will make the gaming experience similar to the original product. But again, one must use discretion when doing this, especially if the original actor will cost you your entire game budget.

All in all, I try to hire experienced professional VO actors that fit the parts well. There is a huge amount of talented VO actors out there. They may not have recognizable names that the general public will know, but they will do the job well and will not cost you your entire budget.

What preparation should the developer and producer have on hand before they approach you for voice work?

The most important thing to start with is a good script with well-defined characters. This is half the battle. One thing I have seen over and over through the years is a great game with a poorly written script. I heard this great quote by rock singer Iggy Pop that I always use when asked about why some scripts should be rewritten: "A stale

waffle with a bunch of syrup on it will still taste like a stale waffle." In other words, if the script does not read well, no actor on earth will make it better. Of course, many game developers don't always have a prolific scriptwriter on staff. For this reason I suggest contracting a professional "script doctor." A script doctor will take your script and make it better for an actor to read so it sounds more natural or funnier (depending on what type of game script it is) and will not change the main idea that the original writer was trying to achieve.

Also, have a budget in mind. If you don't know how much it will cost to record the VO, your designers may create a monster. In other words, designers will add voice-over parts as much as can fit into the games' system limits. If you don't have enough money to fulfill this much VO, things may have to be greatly refigured, taking up valuable development time.

If you already have a rough idea of how much money it will cost to accomplish what your designers are designing, you will be better prepared in keeping on track and on budget.

What preparation do you do? How do you plan the voice-over work? How do you do the casting for the different roles?

I first start by meeting with the development team to discuss the title and to give them an idea of what kind of budget they will be looking at based on what they are trying to achieve. Once I have character descriptions I can start the process of casting actors. I do this two different ways depending on the title and how much time I have to complete the VO work. If I know exactly what the designers are looking for and have little time, I can just cast actors that I know will work well for the various characters. On the other hand, if the designers have very intricate character descriptions or don't exactly know what they are looking for, I will set up voice auditions so they can listen to many different actors voicing sample lines for each character. This will take slightly more time, though the end result usually is dead-on to what the character designer was thinking originally.

Once I have a final script in hand and actors have been cast in the various roles, I then proceed to schedule the various actors for work. This is very involved, being I have to schedule the proper amount of time with each actor to complete the part, negotiate the actor's session fee (within budget), and schedule studio time.

Then from there we start recording the parts. This can take anywhere from a couple of hours to a month depending on how many characters there are and how much dialogue needs to be recorded.

Once all the scripted dialogue (VO) is recorded, picks are made and the VO files are edited and implemented into the game for testing.

You use SAG actors, right? How does that work?

The term SAG stands for Screen Actors Guild. SAG is an actors union that the majority of professional screen actors in America belong to. So in order for a game company to hire a union actor, someone must be affiliated as a SAG union payroll service or signatory. Many game companies do this themselves, which is very simple to set up with SAG.

However, it is not impossible to do it sideways using a SAG payroll signatory service. This service will create all the contracts based on the deals that have been made with each actor's manager or agent.

There are, however, extra fees involved with hiring a union actor.

12.65 percent on top of the actor's fee is for the actor's pension and health benefits (this fee goes directly to SAG). Many agents charge a 10 percent fee on top of the actor fee, being they are the ones who are representing the actor. And of course if you use a union signatory, they will also charge a small fee for their services.

AFTRA (American Federation of Television and Radio Artists) is also an actors union that can be used to hire union talent (many actors belong to both SAG and AFTRA). All the rates and fees are the same as SAG.

> **TOMMY TALLARICO SAYS:** A lot of games record with non-SAG actors as well; it's just a lot harder to find talented non-SAG people to act. Although it may seem cheaper to go non-SAG in the beginning, it could end up costing you a lot more because of the amount of time and takes.
>
> For a smaller project (couple of hundred lines), you're safe going the non-SAG route. If you have 500 lines or more you definitely want to consider doing it union. In the long run you'll be a lot happier.

> >

What happens at a voice recording session? What facilities does the studio have to make it a voice-recording studio? How do you evaluate a studio?

When looking for a recording studio to record voice-over, quality should be your first objective.

The studio should have a professional staff, state-of-the-art digital recording equipment, and a very quiet and dead sound booth. Things like a nice lounge, good food, and a sexy receptionist are not important unless entertaining your expensive talent is more important to you than the recordings you will get from them. Most of today's professional voice-over recording studios should have the ability to record voice-over digitally to hard disk or digital tape (DAT), and a sound booth that is designed for VO.

Most music recording studios have ambient rooms so musical intruments like drums and guitars sound better. This is not what you want to record VO for CD-ROM games. If you are supposed to be listening to your VO character in an outdoor setting, recording them in an ambient VO booth will not sound like it was recorded outside, but in an ambient room. And there are no special studio tricks that can remove this "room ambiance" well. However, if you start with a dead room with no ambience, it is simple to later add a room ambience or a stadium ambience using a digital reverb.

The recording process is fairly simple. The actor or actors sit in the VO booth, and the director and recording engineer sit in the control room, usually with a thick piece of glass between them so they can see each other. The actor will talk directly into a high-quality condenser microphone and listen to him or herself back with headphones (this is optional as some actors prefer not to hear themselves through the mixer). In the control room, the director has a small microphone that can be turned on or off from a button near the director seat that patches into the mixer so he or she can talk back to the actor to give direction. The recording engineer makes sure all the recording levels are correct by monitoring the session and also watches the tape counter and sometimes takes notes as to how many takes were done per line and what time each take was recorded, so later the editor can reference these recording notes. A good studio will also record the director's voice as well; this way the editor has a second reference as to what take is what and what is going on in the session.

How actors are recorded is slightly different depending on the script and how the game's characters interact with each other and the player.

In many games, VO characters interact with each other throughout the script. It is sometimes best to record many actors together at the same time. This is known as an ensemble session. Each actor is set up in the booth with his or her own mic and patched into the mixer on a separate recording track. This way the scripted character interaction sounds more natural, yet there is still enough separation to allow the editor to edit the various characters' takes, so different reads can be implemented.

The other type is just recording one actor at a time. This is the most common style of recording for CD-ROM games, as you are in a one-on-one situation and can pay close attention to just one character at a time. This is also a much more cost-effective way to record, being that it is far easier to schedule an actor for four hours (or less) to complete the part versus having to block out a full eight-hour day using multiple actors only reading their occasional parts over that long time span.

How many takes does it require for the talent to get their lines? How much voice work can an actor do in a session?

Generally a standard VO session is four hours as per most actor union rules and regulations. After four hours the talent can charge more for an additional four hours (or less) and is required to have a one-hour lunch break. After eight hours, again more fees will apply and a one-hour dinner break.

Most actors will require as little as two takes and as many as ten takes to read the part to the satisfaction of the director. Some actors take longer just because, and some can hit it "right on the head" after the first take. If the casting director and the recording director do their work correctly, there is no reason it should have to go beyond ten completely read takes. After that you might have a very frustrated actor on your hands. Many seasoned VO actors will ask you if they are really the right person for the job if you just can't get what you are trying to get. And rightfully so, being that actor may have other VO jobs that same day, and it is very hard on their voice to keep repeating the line over and over

when they may not be the right performer in the first place.

> **TOMMY TALLARICO SAYS**: Remember, a SAG actor can only do three different characters within those four hours. You have to pay extra if you want them to do other characters, even if it's only a few lines.
>
> The other thing you may want to mention is that you can't mix SAG and non-SAG actors on a project. If you go SAG, *everyone* has to be SAG.

What is the most unusual thing about your job that not many other people in the industry have much awareness about?

Well in general, the entertainment industry is a far cry from your average desk job. However, there are many similarities as well. On one side I get to work with some of the most talented actors on earth, and I get to hear some really great stories firsthand (sorry, *National Enquirer*, my lips are sealed). On the other, I have very detailed schedules I have to maintain; I must keep up a professional outlook, and not every actor is a pleasure to work with (however, this is not the norm). So, when people say to me, "Gee it must be cool doing what you do for a living," I am quick to remind them that it's not all what it sounds like, and even I have frustrating days like anyone.

Here is a funny story I like to tell about how strange my job can be. I was working on the Interplay game title Star Trek: Starfleet Academy, and we were shooting full motion video on a green screen at a well-known Hollywood set just across the street from Paramount Studios. I had to be up by 4:00 A.M. and on the set by 6:00 A.M.,

> >

and I was leaving the set by as late as 10:00 at night. So needless to say I was very tired. We were in the middle of a break and I was looking over some of the dailies, and up walks actor William Shatner from his private trailer/dressing room. Being we were filming Mr. Shatner for this production, this was fairly normal; however, I was in one of those strange (too much caffeine, not enough sleep) trances, and Mr. Shatner (in full Starfleet dress uniform, I might add) starts asking me about the technology we are using to make this game, and at that moment I freaked in my mind and thought to myself, "Crap! Captain Kirk is standing here asking me about technology, what a strange life!"

What trends are you seeing in voice-over work in games?

With the sound quality in games getting better and better every year, gamers are noticing game sound more than ever before. Just five years ago when I started in this business, not one game reviewer ever mentioned the sound in a game, much less gave it a review. Now in 2001 it is fairly normal to read many game reviews on voice-over, music, and sound design. So it is more important than ever for a game to have high-quality VO done by professional actors, rather than just grabbing the 2D artist down the hall and having him record his best impersonation to the portable DAT recorder.

My goal is to try to achieve a similar quality that a great motion picture has when it comes to voice-over acting in the games I work on. Though our game budgets are far less than a multi-million-dollar film, it can still be done

within reason. I keep reading reviews on what the gamer did not like about the VO, and I try to improve it within the boundaries that I am stuck with.

What are some mistakes you or projects you have worked on made in regards to voice; can you avoid them now?

The biggest pitfall I have to deal with is the VO programming in a game. On some titles the character keeps repeating the same line over and over every time the player clicks on the character. I can't tell you how often I read a review where the reviewer says, "I got so sick of hearing that character say the same thing over and over, I just turned down the volume to zero so I could finish the game." I am trying my best to combat these types of problems beforehand with the designers and programmers so this does not happen on future titles. VO programming is getting better, however it is still not perfect.

How do you control the creeping nature of many game projects from affecting your budgets, specifically in requesting retakes or rescheduling of talent time?

It is always tough when you propose a VO budget early for a game and it turns out that you needed more money to complete the VO once it is near completion. I always try to pad my VO budgets best as I can so there is no "we can't afford any more" from the producer if it looks like a part has to be redone or some of the actors ended up costing more than I anticipated. It doesn't always work in every case; however, most of the times I have to ask for more budget monies it was because the designers decided to add ten more characters at the last minute.

What was your most challenging game project? Which game were you most proud of?

I am always proud of everything I work on, however a couple projects I am especially proud of are: Baldur's Gate II: Shadows of Amn, Baldur's Gate II: Throne of Bhaal, Baldur's Gate: Dark Alliance, Star Trek: Klingon Academy, Star Trek: Starfleet Command, and Fallout: Tactics.

My most challenging project was by far Star Trek: Klingon Academy. It was a huge undertaking finding as many as thirty actors that could sound like a true Star Trek Klingon. Auditions went on for weeks before I found the right actors. The studio sessions were even tougher… "No, no, more Huuq in that line, and more anger!" I even had to fly all the way to Toronto, Canada, to

record extra VO and ADR (Automated Dialogue Replacement) with famed actor Christopher Plummer, who voiced and acted the part of General Chang. Christopher Plummer is a very talented actor! This game took almost a year to complete just my work.

> **TOMMY TALLARICO SAYS:** I think one very important element that is not addressed here is the actual script writing itself!! You can have the best actors in the world, but if the script is terrible it doesn't matter how many Academy Awards they've won. A lot of times the designer is put in charge of writing a script. Unless the designer is very talented, this really shouldn't be done!
>
> The designer could certainly provide a treatment or first draft for a script, but I would highly recommend hiring a proper scriptwriter to at least check over the work. Scriptwriting is a lot harder and more important than most people think!

Voice-Over Script for the Orc Peon from Warcraft III

As Chris Borders discussed in his interview, one of the most common mistakes is to record only one line for an action that will occur repeatedly in a game. This is doubly painful since it is relatively inexpensive to record multiple lines, and some basic scripting provides the logic for choosing which line to say. For example, Blizzard has always placed cute one-liners that are triggered each time the player clicks on one of their units in the Warcraft series of real-time strategy games. The game chooses the lines randomly from a set of common phrases and notices when the player clicks on a single unit too

much and triggers a different set of lines. In the tradition of the reverse design document, here is the script for the orc peon in Warcraft III:

ORC PEON: A character that sounds like a good-natured, but slow younger brother of Yoda.

ORC PEON

In response to the player's clicking to select.

Yes?
What you want?
Humm?
Hrmp?

> >

ORC PEON

In response to the player's harassment through clicking.

What!?
Me busy. Leave me alone!
No time for play!
Me not that kind of Orc!

ORC PEON

In response to the player's direction to carry out a task:

Work. Work.
I can do that.
Okey dokey.
Be happy to.

ORC PEON

Announcing that he has finished constructing a building.

Work com-plete.

And finally, I leave you with the immortal words of the orc grunt:

ORC GRUNT

Zug. Zug.

> >

Chapter 30 > > > > > > > > > > > > > >

Outsourcing Sound Effects

"Gulp, uhh, huh-huh, gulp! Bleh ---"
—Trent Reznor of Nine-Inch Nails—absolutely nailing
the sound of a drowning man for id Software's Quake

Sound effects are tremendously important for games as they are in cartoons and even more so in movies. As Tommy Tallarico is apt to wax on about, games are one-third audio (for the accountants among us, the gameplay and the graphics would be the other two). So much attention with game making is placed on making the graphics scream through your eyes and grab hold of the back of your skull and glue you to the screen that sound effects are never properly appreciated for the indispensable impact they deliver in a game.

It seems appropriate to me then, that id Software with technical genius John Carmack at the helm would be a pioneer with audio and join up with Trent Reznor of Nine-Inch Nails to produce all of the sound effects for Quake. I must have played hundreds of hours of deathmatch Quake with Sean and Zach, and I will never be able to forget just how incredibly clean Trent Reznor produced the sound of a nail gun's nails ricocheting off the stonework in the halls of Quake. Or the painfully real sound of a man who has stayed underwater for too long gulping down precious air. (My understanding is that Trent did some method acting for this one!)

So, let's dig into sound effects!

Interview with Adam Levenson

Erik Bethke: Would you provide a short background on yourself and what role you play in audio work in the game industry?

Adam Levenson: I started playing music at about six years old. Yes, I was a drummer. I was also fascinated by cassette machines and liked to create collage style recordings of just about anything I could find. Many years later, after surviving adolescence, I completed my bachelor's degree in orchestral music at Boston University. While studying at BU, I worked as a freelance orchestral percussionist in Boston area orchestras and toured internationally playing avant-garde contemporary music. After graduating, I rebelled against the staid classical world, moved to New York, and played in a rock 'n roll band. Eventually, the East Coast weather and the groveling existence of a drummer in a rock band got the best of me, and I decided I needed a more satisfying creative life. I moved out to LA to study in a cutting-edge masters degree program in world music at CalArts. During my time at CalArts, I commuted up to San Rafael, California, to study North Indian classical drumming on the tabla. After CalArts, I thoroughly immersed myself in the study of Indian and Middle Eastern music for about five years. I worked as a dance accompanist, playing live for ballet and modern dance classes in San Francisco and Berkeley. Accompanying eventually led to composing for dance companies. One of the choreographers I was working with had a husband who was leading up development on an edutainment title for Broderbund (now I'm dating myself). He heard my music and decided to offer me a gig to produce sound and music for his game. I had never even seen an Apple computer. Soon I was freelancing for several game companies and finally landed a full-time gig at Trilobyte in Oregon in 1996. Since joining the Interplay audio team about four and a half years ago as a sound designer, I am now audio director at the company. Continuing my pursuit of educational masochism, I recently finished a certificate degree in C++ programming.

My role in game audio production is directorial while remaining very much hands-on with respect to technical design, music supervision, sound design, and post production.

What range of budgets are you seeing for audio in general and sound effects specifically in today's games from low to high?

The sound effects portion of game audio production is enjoying a higher profile on next generation platforms, and budgets are increasing to meet the demand. Consumers expect to be entertained by today's game sounds; it no longer serves a solely utilitarian role. Smart developers are careful to customize each project's sound effect budget to meet the needs of the game, so budgets vary widely depending on the demand for sounds.

Average budgets for sound effects production, not including game audio mixing and implementation, range from $20K to $60K. Some AAA titles come in with much larger sound effects budgets at over $100K, and there are a few publishers and developers with far more limited resources coming in at lower than $20K.

What preparation should the developer and producer have on hand before they approach you for sound work?

Creating an entertaining sound effects experience for the end user means creating mood, stirring emotion, and delivering believability. All of this relies on getting as much detail as possible from the developer regarding each element of the game you'll be dealing with. For example, your next fabulous RPG game has a gigantic white dragon in it. The thing is so huge that the game practically crawls to a complete stop whenever it appears. Sure, anyone can go in, get some dragon sounds pulled from various libraries, and slap them into the game engine. You've got sound now, but who cares; it has nothing specific to do with the character design. The trick is to ask the designer questions about the creature. Is it a good dragon, is it a bad dragon, is it a very, very bad dragon? What is its motivation? Seriously. If you know something about who this dragon is, then you can make sound design decisions that will build character into the voice and create something that when matched up with picture, raises the little hairs on your forearm.

Producers and designers should be ready to answer your detailed questions about areas, creatures, weapons, vehicles, about every aspect of the game. Their answers will help you create a more immersive sound experience and may even help them to sharpen their vision of the game.

What preparation do you do?

Preparation for sound effects production is the most important stage in the sound development process. Without two or three weeks dedicated to preparation, you are usually flying by the seat of your pants and coming in for a crash landing. As I said in the previous question, you need to take the time to ask a lot of detailed questions, seek out what's between the lines, and start formulating an aesthetic and technical approach to your sound design.

As you learn more about the design and contents of your game project, you'll have to make suggestions regarding sound effect interactivity and playback. This is the sound designer's job, not really a programmer's job. You know how things will need to work to sound great, so come up with a vision, and use your technical creativity to discover a way to make it happen. Taking

the time to learn as much about your project as possible will only make you a better salesperson when it comes to presenting your ideas.

How do you plan the audio work?

Planning? This is the video game industry, not auto manufacturing, right? Not really. Sound effect production is just one part of a much larger audio development process involving dialog, music, ambient sound, and more. You not only need to coordinate your delivery and payment schedules with the developer and other audio creators, but you need to coordinate how your sounds are going to aesthetically fit into the overall game mix. It's a production line just like an auto factory. People working on putting cars together don't just randomly pump rivets into metal, well, at least we hope not. Everything they do is based on a predetermined plan. We can be more flexible than that since this is a creative process, but be careful; lack of planning is going to keep you at the office into the wee hours pulling your hair out, and there's a limited supply of hair for many people.

Where did you learn to do audio work?

From early tinkering with cassette machines, to layers and layers of lossy four-track bouncing, to the first version of Protools, most of my audio education has been hands on. Put aside my master's degree in music and a summer of audio engineering classes in Sonoma, California, and really it comes down to getting hands on and getting humble. Humility will allow you to learn from the talented people you meet. Audio production is creative work; there are no rules with the exception of some basic technical requirements, and you can learn from almost anybody. I've been extremely lucky to have worked with some of the most talented people in the industry, so I've absorbed the most from them.

How do you evaluate a studio?

We're talking specifically about sound editing and design here so studio is only an issue in that you want to see a rig that is compatible with standard formats, can produce a high-quality sound, and provides sufficient tools to work with sounds. Yes, I going to say it: Protools. Digidesign has spent years working on this juggernaut of sound design. It provides multiplatform compatibility, is an extremely portable and widely used format, and doesn't necessarily burn a hole in your wallet. Well, not such a big hole anymore.

What is the most unusual thing about your job that not many other people in the industry have much awareness about?

There is a stunning lack of awareness in the video game industry when it comes to sound. Most producers have no idea how complex, work intensive, and intriguing audio work can be. Post-production is like black magic to most industry people where strange terms like foley and headroom are thrown together with acronyms like PL2, AES/EBU, and SD2. Then there's 3D audio, but don't get me started. Audio production combines programming, audio engineering, music composition, post-production, acting, directing, and the kitchen sink. Sound designers, of course, have it the hardest, since most people can relate

somewhat to music. They're familiar with music studios, sort of. But they're probably not familiar with recording the family dog, grunging it up in your favorite DAW, harmonizing, adding a layer of your own recorded voice perversions, and matching the whole mess to picture. No.

What trends are you seeing in sound effects work in games?

Yes, I'm biased, but this is exciting. Sound effects playback in games is changing, and the changes are revolutionary. The age of games with all prerendered sounds is ending, and real-time mixing is taking over. This will bring more interactivity, more believability, and since sounds are being mixed for specific conditions, more emotional impact for the player. Everything we talked about at the beginning of the interview.

The other trend for SFX is higher production values in game movies. Users want cinematic experiences when they've got their Xbox hooked up to their Sony Dream home theater system. They just watched *Saving Private Ryan*, and their popcorn butter-stained fingers are reaching for your latest game project—don't disappoint!

What are some mistakes you or projects you have worked on made in regards to sound; can you avoid them now?

Tons of mistakes. It's a cliché, but that's how you learn, and I don't think mistakes are ever really avoidable in such a large and complex undertaking as game SFX. You just learn how to deal with the problems better.

> >

How do you control the creeping nature of many game projects from affecting your budgets, specifically in requesting retakes or rescheduling of talent time?

Real estate people talk about location, location, location, right? You need to talk planning, planning, planning. Like we talked about before, preparation is the key to success. Now, there will always be unexpected things like dialog pick-ups and changes to game design that make you hit your head against the wall repeatedly, but first make sure you record the sound of your head smashing into the wall. Take the time to carefully document during the preparation phase, not just a sound effects doc but also an audio programming doc. Everyone needs to be on the same page going into a project; it's your responsibility to make sure everyone understands what sounds need to be done, and to try to cover contingencies.

Below is a list of amazingly talented folks. All of them come highly recommended and will make your game a better game through sound.

Tommy Tallarico Studios, Inc.
Tommy Tallarico
President
President/Founder, G.A.N.G. (Game Audio Network Guild)
[www.audiogang.org]
Host, writer, co-producer, "The Electric Playground" and "Judgment Day" television shows
tallarico@aol.com

Immersive
Adam Levenson
Audio Director
6 Vista Cielo
Rancho Santa Margarita, CA 92688
Phone: (949) 433-9079
adam@immersive-sound.com

TikiMan Casting
Chris Borders
Dialogue Director
Phone: (949) 363-9548

Huge Sound
Chance Thomas
Phone: (559) 658-9266
Fax: (559) 658-9267
Cell: (559) 283-HUGE
www.HUGEsound.com

Jesper Kyd Productions
New York City
Game clients: Activision, EA, Eidos, Microsoft, BioWare, Shiny, IO Interactive.
Latest game scores: Brute Force, Hitman 1 and 2, Minority Report, Freedom, MDK2, Messiah
Studio: 212-987-9441
www.jesperkyd.com
Representation:
kirsten@jesperkyd.com

Owner/Composer: kyd@jesperkyd.com

Chapter 31 > > > > > > > > > > > > > > >

Outsourcing Writing

"It's a good day to die."

—The 113th Klingon lacking an original line in a Star Trek story

I am taking a step off the stage, and I am grateful to hand this chapter's baton over to Scott Bennie, the designer, writer, and producer for *Star Trek*: 25th Anniversary and Judgment Rites, as well as a frequent writer for the Starfleet Command series.

Computer Game Writing

By Scott Bennie

A book could probably be written on writing for computer games, but a few paragraphs are going to have to suffice. So here's some advice for prospective writers in the electronic game industry. These laws are absolute, unfailing, applicable in all circumstances, and if you fail to pay heed to every single word, you will not only suck as a game writer, you'll fail at life in general.

In other words, use your discretion when applying these rules.

Know Your Game; Know Your Business

This should go without saying, but it's best to start with the basics. If you're an outside contractor, it's quite possible that you may not understand the game you are writing. This is a problem. Fix it.

A writer who's uninvolved in the game industry may find the process of making games intimidating. Relax. You don't need to understand the code or the AI. What you do need to understand is every feature of gameplay and how they interrelate. You need to understand what the player will likely be seeing and experiencing when your dialogue plays.

Play games similar to the ones you are writing. Talk to fans of the genre and determine what they like. Grab as much of the developer's time as you can get and discuss what they're expecting to see. Understand that bad things happen in the development cycle. Computer games are complicated by the fact that nothing's written in stone until the game ships. So even if you know the product that you're designing for, some kid down in Q&A may walk up to the producer and tell him, "this game sucks!" and the whole game could change overnight. Or some guy in a business suit who's never played a game in his life because it might have distracted him from his shark-like quest to achieve his MBA may call a meeting and announce: "Your game Xanadu is just like Nimrod. We just saw Nimrod's sales figures, and it tanked. But Hamsterquest is a huge seller. Make Xanadu like Hamsterquest."

The really sad thing is that this can (and often does) happen multiple times on a project. Don't get too attached to your work.

Brevity is Bliss

The biggest problem people encounter when writing for games is that they WRITE TOO DAMN MUCH! They write truckloads of unbroken exposition. They write characters who don't know how to shut the hell up and take a breath. I know they do this because I've done it too.

Okay, so now that I've confessed my shameful secret, let me tell you how to break the habit.

First, be ruthless with your prose. Get together with other authors, read it out loud, and accept their recommendations on what to cut. In everything you write, there's going to be "cool bits," lines of which you are particularly proud. Do not exempt them. If you can, distill the cool bits into smaller but equally cool bits.

Second, study screenplays, especially action film screenplays or animation storyboards. They're the closest popular medium to games when it comes to storytelling; both are primarily visual experiences, and in both mediums excess dialogue kills the pace.

With rare exceptions, condense each speaking part to three or four lines of dialogue. *Thirty words at a time,*

maximum. If you need to exceed that in order to deliver exposition, try to break it up between multiple characters.

Remember the *seven-second rule.* Studies have shown that in any visual medium, you can only hold the audience's attention for an average of seven seconds before their minds begin to wander, so you need to cut to a new visual or event to keep their attention. No matter how good your dialogue is, if you dedicate 20 seconds to a long speech, it will die. So treat wordiness like a disease.

Speak the Speech I Pray You

(Okay, I had to get a Shakespeare reference in here somewhere.) When you write dialogue, speak it out loud. Act it out, over and over again. Perform it loudly, convincingly, as an actor would do it in a studio. Nurse your inner William Shatner. Then, after your throat's gone hoarse, take everything that was hard to pronounce, everything that ran together without a breath, everything that sounded awkward and hokey, highlight it on your word processor, and hit the Delete key and don't look back. Confine those words to the graveyard of things that didn't deserve to be released into the world.

Then do it again until you've got it right.

Develop an ear for interesting, natural dialogue. Record a call-in radio show, then transcribe it. It's amazing how different people sound in real life as opposed to a story. You probably don't want to fully adopt the cadences of the real world in your dialogue (fiction is after all, *not* real life but the condensation of interesting bits), but it doesn't hurt to infuse your dialogue with more natural patterns.

> >

Sometimes your genre (say, a medieval fantasy game) will require you to write period or anachronistic dialogue to evoke the proper mood. You should try to capture it. However, if you're required to make a choice between beautifully written evocative period dialogue and clearly explaining a game concept or giving direction to the player, *choose the clear explanation*. Keep things close enough to a modern tenor that you will be understood. The needs of the game outweigh the needs of setting a pretty mood.

On Dialogue Trees

Some games, such as computer RPGs, have dialogue trees where the player has to choose between a number of dialogue selections. Too often the dialogue's scripted with one obviously correct answer (almost always "the nice approach" or "the smartass approach," etc.) Unfortunately this can make a game too predictable. The answer should not always be the obvious one. You need to mix attitudes; make it so Character A responds best to threats, Character B will always try to stall for time, Character C values politeness and respect, and Character D respects people who get into insult duels with him. Character E likes a chance to talk tough, but he'll settle down if you acknowledge him once he's had a chance to display his manhood. Character F will be panicked, but if you carefully calm him down, you can then have a reasonable conversation, etc.

Once you've got your character matched to the personality that's needed to "win" the dialogue tree, you need to leave hints about the character's personality in the environment. Players can hear stories about people

from other people, find legends in ancient tomes, spot the graves of the people who were killed by Character D because he thought he was being patronized, etc.

In teaching, a multiple-choice test is defined as "a test where the correct answer is obvious to an *informed* student." Dialogue trees are multiple-choice tests. There needs to be a way for the player to learn what's the best approach to a problem aside from trial and error, because trial and error *sucks*.

Use Story as a Reward

Reduced to a behavior, games are all about the cycle of challenge and reward. If that makes a game designer sound like B.F. Skinner or Pavlov, if the shoe fits, wear it. In a game, a designer sets a goal, which the player is encouraged to meet. When they meet that goal, they receive a reward.

Treat the story as one of the most important rewards. Take your story and break it down into segments. Make sure they are regularly fed new revelations and more significant plot points as one of the rewards of the story. Whenever you can, cultivate mystery and use foreshadowing to build the player's expectation that something big is going to happen, then make sure the payoff is big enough to meet the player's expectations.

When you can, make the story (and the game) tied to the character's actions. Don't just reference future events, reference past events, player accomplishments, and failures.

The 80 Percent Stereotype Rule

If you're working in an established genre, you need to fulfill the gamer's expectations, and like it or not, the player expects archetypal (meaning cliché) characters to act in expected ways. On the other hand, the overuse of stereotypes is not only offensive from an artistic standpoint, their overuse can destroy the drama. In *Star Trek*, the first time a Klingon ever said, "It's a good day to die" it was good drama; but by the thirtieth time it had become bad comedy.

Whenever you can, take the cliché and twist it a little: "I don't care if it's a good day to die or not, today one of us is NOT walking away!" references the cliché and thus gives the player a sense of familiarity but is better at maintaining the drama.

I'd like to suggest the 80 percent stereotype rule. If you can make a stereotypical situation or character play out differently than expected 20 percent of the time, you preserve the comfortable feeling of the expected while still providing the player with surprises. However, when you set up an expectation and break it, the player eventually needs to understand why.

Hint, Hint, and Hint

And that leads us to the second really big mistake writers make: A computer game lives or dies depending on how well it provides the player with clear direction. Nothing frustrates a player more than not knowing where to go and what to do. It's okay to hurt them, to surprise them, to annoy them, but never *ever* confuse them. Players do like to explore, but they also want a safety net, so make sure there's always a clear task available for them to perform when they get bored with exploring the world.

If your game is mission based, all major mission objectives need to be codified and available to the player at all times through the scenario. Mission objectives need to be crystal clear. If you can, get hold of some blind testers while you're writing the scenario, read the scenario objectives to them, and ask them for feedback on what they think the scenario wants them to do. You should know within five minutes if your directions are clear enough.

A mission success should never depend on fulfilling a hidden objective. On paper, finding the hidden objective to solve the scenario sounds great; the reality is that it's a recipe for frustration. (A better way to achieve this desired effect is to tell the player, "We want you to explore the area; if you find something interesting, we'll get back to you with further instructions.")

Time related hints to help players who haven't solved a puzzle (or items in the environment such as hint books) are usually good things. The designers may not want to use this approach, but it's better to cover too many bases than too few.

Expect Schizophrenia

The most frustrating thing for writers coming into the industry to understand is that you're not writing a linear story. You are not writing a screenplay; you are writing sequences of possible events that will not become a story until the player puts them together.

You can (and probably should) limit the number of possible outcomes, but (except for linear action games) you're not likely to have control over the exact sequence of events. You (or the designer) can set up special events triggered by other events so you know that some events will follow others, but you need to know that sometimes the

> >

player will go to Location A first and then Location B, and sometimes it'll be the other way. You need to adjust the attitudes of game characters to reflect the fact.

If You Have Time in a Bottle, Don't Uncork It

Computer games sometimes break basic rules of storytelling, and that's okay. Yes, it makes no sense that Villain X would not advance his evil plan while Our Hero spends two years in the wilderness looking for gold pieces under mulberry bushes, so you'd normally expect some pretty serious consequences for that time wastage. However, players *hate* to be pushed. Great story ideas don't always translate into great game ideas, so it's better to give them what they want than to do the game your way and have them take it back to the store because they hate it.

It's okay to do an occasional "countdown to escape" or a "you have a short amount of time to defeat this particular foe" sequence to add dramatic tension, but otherwise, a writer should accept that "we will not use time limits as a way to increase the tension" and learn to live with the smaller palette.

Scott Bennie
33509 Mayfair Ave.
Abbotsford BC Canada
V2S 1P6
(604) 870-1113

(Contact the author at erik@taldren.com for more information about freelance writers.)

> >

Chapter 32   > > > > > > > > > > > > > > >

Outsourcing Cinematics and Models

"They want Star Wars for a nickel."

—Anonymous art house producer

Game development houses are defined as a collection of programmers and artists who get together to make a game. So why would it be a good idea to outsource art from your studio and lose out on developing the experience with your own employees?

The basic answer is that you do not have the artists on staff who have the expertise or you simply have too much work to carry out with the artists you do have. Either way, you would go out of house only when you do not have the talent in-house. The classic case is of cinematics, which require the skill sets of creating high-res models, texturing them, animating them, creating high-res backdrops, and creating the cinematic sequence. Finally, the cinematic crew will go back and add special effects like explosions or laser blasts and then hand off the finished cinematic to the audio team. This is a considerably different skill set than creating low-res 3D models for your game. Even houses such as Blizzard and Square, who are world renowned for their cinematics, effectively outsource their movies, as these cinematic teams are nearly separate entities from the game teams.

The following interview with Mark Gambiano covers all aspects of working with an art house from his experience at Mondo Media. In the interest of full disclosure, Mark was the art director for our in-game low-poly ships on Starfleet Command I, when my art team was under three artists.

< < < < < < < < < < < < < < < < < < < < < < < < < < < <

Interview with Mark Gambiano

Erik Bethke: Would you provide a short background on yourself and what role you play in art production in the game industry?

Mark Gambiano: Growing up, my interests were divided between art and electronics, which was a pretty odd combination back in the '60s and '70s. I couldn't seem to settle on either one as a career and majored in both in college. Video gaming had just hit the scene, and I spent a lot of time in video arcades. I had also bought a Mattel Intellivision console about that time and was learning my first painful lesson about game addiction and repetitive stress injuries. Later, when personal computers started to become more affordable in the mid-'80s, I bought an Atari 800, and computer graphics looked to me to be a great way to combine both of my long-time interests. I messed around with 2D paint programs and even some very crude 3D packages. Moving up to an Atari 512ST and later a Mac IIcx, I continued to teach myself more about 2D and 3D computer graphics and began to create some portfolio work.

When I decided to get into computer graphics as a profession back in 1990, one of my early clients was Mondo Media, a company in San Francisco that was doing 2D point-of-sale retail demos and speaker support presentation work at the time. I came in as one of their first 3D artists, although much of the work at that time was 2D NAPLPS vector artwork for the original Prodigy online service. After a couple years freelancing, I went to work for them full time, and we stepped into the field of game production with a full

motion video title called Critical Path. That was followed by another full motion video title The Daedalus Encounter (featuring Tia Carrere of *Wayne's World* fame). Although it wasn't my call to do the games with video, I was creative director on both projects and pushed hard to make the 3D as high quality and cutting edge as possible. FMV games never really caught on, but the company used the 3D skills developed on our game projects to solicit contract work from other developers, either creating game assets or doing high-res 3D intro cinematics. Some of the projects I was involved with as a 3D artist included Zork: Nemesis, Blade Runner, Civilization: Evolution, and Hot Shots Golf. In addition, I directed or art directed game assets for Star Fleet Command I and II, and high-res cinematics for MechWarrior 3, Alpha Centauri: Alien Crossfire, and a Japanese Dreamcast game called Under Cover.

Could you break down what sort of outsourcing you see going to an art house? Models, movies, and?

It runs the gamut. Most of the time, we would get high-res cinematic work from developers that either didn't have the time or resources to do them in-house or felt that we could do a superior job. The work usually consisted of designing or redesigning opening, interstitial, and ending cinematics. Sometimes the client wanted us to use rezzed-up game assets, as with Aliens vs. Predator, but most of the time it was like MechWarrior 3 and Under Cover, where we built high-res models and environments from scratch. On other games like

> >

Zork: Nemesis and Blade Runner, we produced high-res 3D environments for use as stills or Quicktime VR-style panaramas. On Hot Shots Golf, Starfleet Command, Nerf Arena Blast, and others, we created low-poly in-game assets. On a couple of the low-poly jobs, we also did animation, either key-framed or motion-captured.

What range of budgets are you seeing for art production in today's games from low to high?

Mondo Media moved away from doing that kind of contract a couple of years ago in order to pursue doing original content for the web, so my figures are a few years old. Budgets ran from about $10K to as much as $450K. Most seemed to be in the $25 to $75K range, though.

What in your opinion was a good value? What was simply overspending?

I think nearly all of our clients got more than they paid for, so for them it was a good value. There were very few jobs that came in where we felt the budget was even adequate, let alone "fat." As to whether their budgets for this work were excessive in relation to the game development costs overall, I can't say, since we were never privy to that kind of information.

What preparation should the developer and producer have on hand before they approach you for art production?

It depends on whether the job is for in-game assets or for cinematics. With cinematics, we usually get the job towards the end of the production cycle, so the look and feel has been

well defined. The problem here was usually that the client has come up with a *Titanic*-level script but has only a *Blair Witch* budget. We nearly always have to adjust their expectations and come up with timesaving alternatives to get the work done on budget. In these cases, it would be better for the clients to present a general idea of what they want and let us come up with a script and approach that provides the most bang for the buck.

On real-time 3D jobs where we're doing game assets, the client really needs to have their art specs down *solid* before handing them off to an art house. On nearly every project we were involved in that used custom 3D engines, many aspects of the model and mapping specs were either unknowns or still in flux at the time the client wanted us to get started. In the worst cases, they changed well into the art production cycle and required substantial revisions to the work that everyone thought was completed. This usually resulted in delays and additional charges back to the client for the revisions.

What preparation do you do? How do you plan the motion capture work? Where did you learn to do art production?

The director or art director usually does general research on the project and puts together a file of reference materials. If the project involves real-time assets, we assign a technical director to keep an eye on those aspects. The TD pours over the specs with a fine-tooth comb, making sure that every aspect of what we have to deliver has been defined. We create spreadsheets that list all of the assets and use them to keep track of progress. Often we end up doing some design work as well, developing visual concepts for the assets and running them by the client for revisions and approvals. When it gets close to production time, we select the best artists for the type of work and schedule their time.

For mo-cap, we subcontract to a firm that specializes in that kind of work. We come up with a complete shot list and discuss the technical challenges of pulling off the capture session. We work with them to select the performers and then attend the session to direct the action. The toughest one we had to do was for a hockey game—setting up on a frozen ice rink in the wee hours of the morning for several days in a row. Ice is reflective and the shavings tend to obscure the markers, so it was a real challenge. Plus, all the moves had to begin and end in a default position and take place within a relatively small perimeter.

Much of our art production skills came from on-the-job training and plain old painful experience. Every job was an "opportunity" to learn—the specs or process or client expectations were always a bit different on every job. It was up to the directors to make sure they had a solid grasp of every aspect of a project, or had specialists in place to handle those things they could not.

What is the most unusual thing about your job that not many other people in the industry have much awareness about?

Probably the misconception that we are just some kind of "art factory," and the client just puts the script they want in one end and the animation they envisioned comes out the other side. We

much prefer to be thought of as a partner in a client's project, and after years of experience doing very similar things for a lot of different clients, we've come up with a lot of ways to save them money and get maximum impact out of the shots that we produce. What we need in return is for them to have an open mind and not expect, as one producer aptly put it, "*Star Wars* for a nickel." Most of the time, the clients do understand this, and ultimately, the level of quality of the finished product pleasantly surprises nearly all.

What trends are you seeing in art production in games?

First, there's been a huge consolidation in the game industry—publishers being acquired by large corporations and ultimately doing fewer titles. Also, the huge shift in titles towards real-time 3D and away from 2D and prerendered 3D has meant a big drop-off in the number of clients looking for high-res prerendered intros for their titles. Many are trying to use their 3D engines and game assets to do the cinematics, which is both a blessing and a curse. They can do more of the work in-house, but it usually doesn't look as good. Still, with the new GPU-based 3D cards like the NVIDIA GeForce and ATi Radeon getting so powerful, it's only a matter of time before real-time 3D really does look like prerendered work, and at that point we'll have the best of both worlds.

What are some mistakes you or projects you have worked on made in regards to art production; can you avoid them now?

For real-time 3D, the worst one was doing artwork for clients whose

> >

programming teams didn't have their act together and either delayed art production or caused unnecessary extra work by changing specs after models had been built and mapped. I found the best way to avoid getting caught in this trap was to produce a small representative sample of the models requested and not proceed with production on the rest until the client had signed off on them (and agreed that any further changes could be back-charged). That way, if the specs changed, we only had to fix one set of models instead of dozens, and the specter of additional charges helped motivate them to make sure their engine was going to be happy with the models presented.

On high-res work, the biggest trap was trying to do *too much*—either in quantity of shots, quality of shots, or both—given the budget. Sadly, too often the budgets were very tight to begin with. Sometimes management would have to trim them after the design was done to close the deal, yet the expectations had not changed in the least. Also, it seemed like the budgets were always a "best case" scenario; there was little wiggle room in them for unforeseen problems, and problems almost always showed up.

One of the worst dangers was with client-provided models. The client would tell us they had this or that model available, so we would cut that out of the budget. On one project we really got stung because the models had been converted from Alias for use in 3D Studio Max, and they were a *mess*—all kinds of extra faces and junk clogging up the works. Ultimately we had to rebuild them from scratch, because it was actually faster than trying to fix them. The project was a fixed

bid, so we got screwed. After that, whenever a client said they had a model we could use, we insisted on approving the model before we would discount the bid.

How do you control the creeping nature of many game projects from affecting your budgets, specifically in requesting retakes or rescheduling of talent time?

With cinematic projects, it was rarely an issue. Usually most of the assets were available, or we used stand-ins and waited for the models before doing the final renders. If the wait got excessive, we were often able to get the client to turn production of that asset over to us for an additional charge. They were usually in crunch mode at the time and it was one less thing for them to deal with.

Retakes could be a problem with some clients. We usually did one or two retakes per shot as a matter of course, but every once in a while we got a client who was a real pain to please. Usually this was because they were one of the "I don't know what I want, but I'll know it when I see it" variety. As artists, we did the best we could to make them happy. If it really started to get excessive, we let the producer or management work out some kind of agreement. Thankfully, that rarely happened; the vast majority of our clients were very pleased with our work and would come back to us for their next project.

What was your most challenging game project? Which game were you most proud of?

The most challenging one was probably Critical Path, although The Daedalus Encounter and MechWarrior 3 are close runners-up. It was the first time we had done a game and also the first time we had tried to combine actors shot on bluescreen with high-res, animated environments. We had a motley collection of 486 PCs, and renders took forever. To cap it off, we had to design and produce the game (which was really only supposed to be a demo) in only four and a half months. We worked outrageous hours (my personal best was 36 hours straight during a 119-hour week) and were there nearly every weekend.

I think the work I'm most proud of from a visual standpoint were the five-and-a-quarter minutes of high-res cinematics we did for Under Cover. I was given a lot of control over the project, and as a big *anime* fan, I was able to fulfill a dream by traveling to Japan to meet with the clients and do some sightseeing and shopping. The work was challenging since it contained a lot of human character work, but I think we produced some really beautiful shots. I was also really pleased with the MechWarrior 3 work. It was great going to E3 that year and seeing our stuff blown up to wall-size proportions and slathered all over the convention hall.

Following are some art houses:

Mondo Media
135 Mississippi
San Francisco, CA 94107
Phone: (415) 865-2700
Fax: (415) 865-2645

Dragonlight Productions, Inc.
19100 Ventura Blvd., Suite 10
Tarzana, CA 91356
Phone: (818) 343-1701
bizdev@dragonlight.com
krissie@dragonlight.com
http://www.dragonlight.com

> >

Chapter 33 > > > > > > > > > > > > > > > >

Outsourcing Motion Capture and Animation

"Can you motion capture a snake or water falling?"

—The author when on tour of the House of Moves facility

Animation in Games

The overwhelming majority of games have characters that need to be animated. The exceptions to this would be games such as racing and flight simulations, or even the author's own Starfleet Command series, which use 3D vehicle models that do not require any animation work.

So if you have kids with football helmets, monkeys inside of glass balls, space marines on a ringworld, or undead zombies, then you need animation. Animation work is as well suited to outsourcing as any other art task. In other words, it is better to have the talent in house; however, if you have too much work or just do not have the talent, then by all means look outside to solve your animation needs.

The first question you must determine is whether or not you will employ artists to key-frame the animation or retain a motion capture studio and use motion actors to perform moves and capture them digitally.

The answer to this question is really easy if you are animating spiders, six-legged robots, sharks, snakes, and blobs; all of these make excellent candidates for key-framing due to the difficulty of training spiders and blobs to be motion capture performers. When I was given a tour of the House of Moves facility, I asked Jarod Phillips all sorts of annoying questions like, "Have you motion captured a snake or a waterfall?" His answer was that they tried motion capturing a dog at the insistence of a client, but it did not work out well and a skilled key-framer would have performed a far superior job and faster.

Key Framing

Outsourcing your animation work is actually straightforward. Take the finished model and textured model and hand it over to the animation house. In addition to the model and texture, you will need to supply your technical requirements such as number of bones and in what data format you want to receive your animation. You must also supply a move list that describes in as much detail as possible the moves that you want the character to perform.

Typically a key-framer should be able to perform at a rate of between one to two moves a day, varying considerably upon the complexity of the moves. Be sure to indicate in your move list what moves are intended to be looping and which are not to loop.

Animation work is priced on the per-move basis with rates ranging from $25 to $150 a move or more.

Motion Capture

Motion capture is the digital science and art of recording the movement of humans with multiple cameras and using it to drive animated 3D models. In principle, one would be able to quickly obtain perfectly natural and fluid animation and drop it right on top of your model.

In practice, motion capture rivals the cost in both time and money of key framing and may cost even more. In addition, it has been common in the past for the motion-captured results to be very poor and require man-months of cleanup before being usable by the 3D model and game engine.

How Does Motion Capture Work?

The basic idea is to suit up a motion actor who has some expertise in the motions to be recorded. For example, for a SWAT game you choose to motion capture a police SWAT officer or for a basketball game you may record how an NBA star dribbles. The suit is of some

black, stretchy fabric. A couple dozen little balls are glued to the suit. These balls are covered with tons of tiny reflective glass beads, the same sort of stuff you see on reflective sporting equipment such as bags for the rack on the back of a bicycle. These glass balls are designed to be efficient in reflecting light of a certain color.

Next in the setup are a bunch of cameras. The number of cameras varies depending on the facility, with a typical number being 18. These cameras do not record the movement of the actor; they record the movement of those reflective white balls.

The motion is captured in what is called the *volume*, the 3D box of space that the cameras are set up to view. Outside of the capture volume, the cameras are blind. To record moves such as an athlete performing a pole vault you would probably need to spend a lot of money setting up the motion capture cameras in a big open building such as a large hangar, which would also involve the costs for transporting and tuning the system. This is a good example of when you should probably break out a key-framer for the job.

Typical volumes are 16 feet by 20 feet—large enough for complete walk and run cycles. Too small a volume and useful captures cannot be performed. Quite a few companies set up their own facilities and end up creating a space that is too small and have to go out of house for some of their moves!

Motion capture has come a long way in quality from the early years with most advances in the proprietary software that runs the cameras in real time as the data is being collected as well as software that is run in post-production to "clean up" the motion captured data.

> >

Cleaning up the Motion Data

After spending tens of thousands of dollars for your motion capture sessions, it would be nice if the data were to just drop in and work. The truth is the data is full of noise and errors that must be cleaned up. Each of the motion capture systems has automated tools that smooth out some of the noise in the motion and perhaps do some boundary checks. A common error is when a character makes contact with the ground, as in a tumble, and the cameras lose track of a few balls. When this happens the system will often make a poor guess as to what the motion really ought to be. This is fixed by a human in the post-processing phase where they are looking at the skeleton of a character and watching it move through its range of motions.

A large proportion of the outsourced motion capture work is performed by House of Moves using the standard Vicon cameras and its Deva system for post-processing. However, many publishers and some of the largest independent developers have their own systems.

One of the more interesting motion capture studios is Giant. Giant uses a fundamentally different motion capture system. Instead of using the expensive proprietary Vicon cameras, Giant employs 18 or so regular black-and-white security-type video cameras. These cameras then feed the real-time data into Giant's processing software called Motion Reality. One of the appeals of Giant's system is that *before* you capture any motion data, you provide your character's model, textures, and skeletal structure to Giant for *pre*processing. This preprocessing involves using some neat-o biometrically correct algorithms that learn the parameters of motion for your specific character. This provides two distinct advantages: first, when taking the actual motion capture shoot, instead of the director looking at a constellation of balls on the playback monitor, he is able to see the motion as *applied* to the actual character while in the motion capture studio, without waiting days for the data to be cleaned up and applied to the character. Second, because the biometrically correct algorithms are applied to the motion capture data in real time, you save yourself a lot of cleanup processing that occurs when balls go out of the camera's view, due to the algorithm's ability to extrapolate and interpolate where those missing balls *ought* to be.

So Giant's system sounds like the best one to use, right? I honestly cannot give you a final answer. We have used both data from Giant, sourced from a motion capture session just for us, as well as some library footage from House of Moves. To our surprise, while Giant's post-processing software was relatively easy to use, there was more cleanup involved than I expected for the advanced system. As for the House of Moves data, it was data that was about two or three years old by the time we were able to play with it, and it showed its age. The data was noisy and not all that cool feeling when applied to our models.

I would have to say that both of these motion capture studios deserve consideration for your next project.

Planning Your Motion Capture Shoot

To be successful with motion capture I suggest you seek out your eventual motion capture vendor early in production to establish budget. Shop around, as one facility may be booked and another might be happy to sell time at a minimal margin. The motion capture studios tend to build their bid by counting the total number of moves and actors you are requiring. Next they classify your moves into several categories of difficulty from routine to very difficult. For example, routine moves would be running, shooting a weapon, and sneaking about. Moderately complex moves would involve light stunt work such as falling to a mat. From there, the shots can get pretty expensive, especially if you are hiring a stunt coordinator and stunt men to perform wire work.

You should prepare a list of all of the moves you need your characters to perform. Then meet with one or more of the motion capture studios and ask them how would they approach the project. Do they see room for collapsing some of the requested moves? Do they suggest some killer moves that you overlooked? Who do they suggest you hire as the motion actor?

One of the first things a motion capture studio will tell you if you are listening is that celebrities often make poor motion capture actors. For example, the going rate for a motion capture actor with modest stunt abilities is around $1,000 for the day. Some projects have spent $500,000 capturing the motion of star athletes only to throw the data away because the motion was poor relative to what a motion actor is able to perform.

After you have your budget and animation plan, it is best to go back and work on your characters for a while and be sure you have worked out all of your technical requirements and that your game design is final (e.g., you know if you need climbing or swimming motions). Only then come back to the motion capture studio to perform the data collection.

You will need to allocate at least three months in your schedule to allow the motion capture studio to perform a first-pass cleanup to the data and then turn over the data to your team for further refinement.

Best Use of Motion Capture

In my opinion, motion capture really shines in recording the subtle movements a human makes that are difficult to notice and thus difficult to get into your key-framing. Fortunately, to me, this means that aggressively acrobatic work for which Hollywood might use human performers and wires should instead be done by key-frames. I love to see motion capture used for the idle animations of the character. We have amazing motion of the female protagonist for the upcoming Black9 stretching and limbering up for battle—wow! And on the sublime side of the spectrum, it should be trivial to key-frame simple walks and run cycles.

In the future I expect the software side of motion capture to make large strides; soon I believe the data will just drop in, and in the end motion capture will provide us with amazingly quick and amazingly good motion for our characters.

> >

Here is a list of motion capture studios:

House of Moves
Jarrod Phillips
Vice-President, Sales and Marketing
5318 McConnell Ave.
Los Angeles, CA 90066
Phone: (310) 306-6131
Fax: (310) 306-1351
jarrodp@moves.com
http://www.moves.com

Giant Studios West
Chip Mosher
West Coast Sales Manager
Giant Studios West
3100 Donald Douglas Loop North,
Hangar 7
Santa Monica, CA 90405
Phone: (310) 392-7001

> >

Chapter 34   > > > > > > > > > > > > > > >

Fan-Generated Material

"I Have No Debugger and I Must Script."
—The author, circa 1995

Game Development with Your Fans

Outsourcing game development to fans—an interesting idea, huh? Taldren has experimented with outsourcing parts of our game development to fans; while we are not currently engaging any fans, we would consider it in the future.

> **WARNING**: Remember to always secure all of the intellectual property rights when working with external contractors, most especially when working with fans. Any hole, ambiguity, or looseness in your agreement with the fan contractor will generally be ruled in favor of the fan in any courtroom dispute. This is discussed in more detail at the end of this chapter.

Design Critique

So what sort of work is useful to have fans look at? The most straightforward and common is design critique. This happens during the closed or open betas at the end of a project where the fans will tell you whether or not you have made the game fun to play. Fans will of course do this work for free, not really for access to a free game, but rather for the novelty of influencing a game they care about in progress.

Money is an interesting thing; we use it as the medium of exchange for the bulk of human industry in the modern world. I have to admit I find it very refreshing to interact directly with our fans and customize our games to their liking. Of course it is far more challenging to adjust a game to fit some sort of balance between the wave functions of all these people's opinions. It is much simpler to design, implement, and test without having to verify if it truly entertains your customers. Beta testing solves that problem, but at the cost of quite a bit of communication and iteration.

At Taldren we also experimented with a more intimate form of fan design critique by way of a private forum we called The Inner Circle. For Starfleet Command II we actually sent these folks candidate design documents early in development where it would be a lot easier for us to respond to their comments before actually implementing parts of the game. I think this technique should be reserved for careful use. It worked well for SFC2, as it was an established game with fairly narrow interpretation of the licensed material to maneuver the game design through. The licensed material from the *Star Trek* shows and the Star Fleet Battles board game provided both ourselves and the fans a lot of structure to draw from when defining the game mechanics and the subsequent balancing. I would imagine this technique might be useful when creating other high-fidelity simulations such as a tank warfare sim. This is certainly not a useful technique when exploring gameplay of a totally new creation that would provide poor guidance for outsiders to base their input on. Finally, no matter what anyone else says, at the end of the day someone on your team (most likely the lead designer or project leader) must make the final call.

Levels and Missions

There are many examples of fans creating content for their favorite games back to the very innovation of electronic games. Indeed, the bulk of the early development of games was the result of mainframe programs taking over from each other and incrementally improving on the earlier games. However, it would have to be the advent of id Software's Doom that inaugurated the modern era of fan extensibility and content creation for commercial games.

id Software constructed Doom to be extremely easy for players to create new levels (called WADs) to further extend the deliciously 3D carnage of Doom into a never-ending nightmare. The quality of these levels ranged from mind numbingly underwhelming to levels that met or even exceeded the original shipping levels for Doom. In fact, a mini cottage industry sprang up around Doom with unlicensed collections of levels for sale on cheaply produced CDs in jewel cases and a game programming book dedicated to Doom with a level editor for Doom. Soon, better level editors were made for Doom than the level editors that shipped with Doom.

Games such as Counter-Strike and Day of Defeat are the most visible and successful of these fan mods, as they are called. There are at any given time hundreds of fan groups working together across the Internet to develop new games based on the engines and tools of their favorite games.

All of this technical ability and energy are a potential resource for your game. The first step in considering this path is to develop a strong tool for implementing new missions or levels for your game. Strong, reliable tools that end users are able to use with efficiency and confidence requiring little or no technical support is what you need to create. With a poor tool your technical support burden from your tools programmer will quickly outstrip the cost savings of having your own designer implement a few more levels. Of course, a strong, reliable tool is just what you *should* build for your own internal team. Thus, I argue the cost of making a strong reliable tool for end users is free.

For the Starfleet Command series we experimented with hiring fan programmers to write a few mission scripts. We ended up hiring three or four programmers, and we paid them as independent contractors. Programming missions for Starfleet Command required a passing knowledge of C++ as each mission was built as a dynamic linked library (DLL). We chose to program our missions in C++, largely due to my earlier experience as script programmer on I Have No Mouth And I Must Scream. At that time we used a C-like proprietary programming language named SAGA. As a scripter working with SAGA, I was continuously frustrated with some features promised in the language that didn't quite work. The goal of SAGA was to create a C-like language that was very safe with built-in memory and bounds checking, array types—the sort of features you would find in Visual Basic or Java. As I ran into problems with SAGA, the tools programmer(s) would stop and take the time to fix the bug. It struck me that the rest of the team and I were working very hard to implement a new programming language that was missing all the common tools of a standard programming language like a debugger! From that experience I developed the opinion that you must have a *really* good reason why you need to create a new programming language to script your missions.

As I said, we simply used C++ as the language for Starfleet Command; we wrote a mission scripting API that developed support for creating ship entities, a set of engine callbacks, and a host of other goodies that were required to make fun missions. This system worked out much better for our internal mission programmers as C++ has a plethora of handy tools already developed. It allowed for rapid tweaking of the scripting API, required less maintenance by more senior

programmers to support the scripting API, and our internal programmers were able to continue progressing in their C++ skills rather than work with a proprietary language with little future reuse.

This C++ scripting API worked out less well for our external fan scripters. This is due less to the language being C++ and more to our constant, dribbling changes to the API. We never noticed the cost of making changes to the API with our internal team as it was nearly effortless to communicate the required changes in the calling parameters or other change details, and we promptly had newly rebuilt scripts. For the external scripters working across a hemisphere, all communication occurred by way of email. In principle, we could write up our changes in the scripting API and distribute them in email to the external scripters; however, that would only work out *if we wrote down* the changes we made to the API. With internal folks it is so much easier and faster to communicate late-breaking changes by holding an impromptu water-cooler meeting or popping into another employee's office. After all, rapid, liquid communication is the main benefit for working in an office in the first place! In the end the missions we received from the external scripters required significant maintenance on our part and overall was probably not a net benefit. The remedy of course would have been to reserve working with the external scripters until after the scripting API settled down into its final form. We have always released this scripting API to the consumers who buy our Starfleet Command games, and waiting until the

API settled into its final form and only then releasing it to external fan scripters would have been an improvement.

3D Models

Outsourcing 3D character models to fans is an order of magnitude more straightforward than outsourcing mission programming. Fans have an innate attraction to making models, whether they are starships and airplanes that do not require animation or human and non-human animated characters. Your first job is to screen the fan for the requisite talent and skill required to create a 3D model of the same high quality that your internal team is producing. I advise you to review their skills as you would with a potential artist you might hire. The general procedure is to provide the fan modeler with a sketch or even better a color comp of the model to be created and provide them with all of the technical details such as polygon budget, whether or not all of the polygons must be triangles, the limits on the size of the texture map, and perhaps details on other possible texture maps such as the bump, luminosity, or damage textures. It would be unreasonable to hold the fan to the same sort of rigors as your employees, although it is completely appropriate to have a deadline. You may still have an issue with quality, and it may not be immediately apparent that there are technical problems with the model until you drop the model into your game engine and try it out. It is important to drop the model into the engine and perform your other quality check procedures as soon as possible when working with fan modelers. It will be much more effective to provide the fans with rapid feedback while the work is still fresh in their mind and while they have the energy to work on your project. You must remember that even if you do pay these fans a decent rate for this outsourced work, they know that they do not work for you and are not motivated in the same way as employees.

Other Potential Activities to Outsource

3D models, missions, and levels are just a few of the assets or activities that you could outsource to fans. To identify these opportunities, be open minded when fans contact you and offer help, and think about the possible holes you might have in production. For example, David Perry has a volunteer staff that works on his dperry.com web site. Perhaps you have a musically talented fan who is happy to flesh out your musical scores—maybe sound effects. Or perhaps running the news update for your web site. If you end up with a relationship with a fan, I think in the end it strengthens your organization; you will be provided with a new ally, a strong source of information, and who knows what other potential opportunities!

Legal Matters When Working with Fans

Important disclaimer: Again I remind you that I am not a lawyer, and I am not qualified to provide legal advice. The simple rule of thumb is to not treat fans any less formally than you would treat other independent contractors. That means you should agree to a fee for their services. I strongly suggest a fixed fee payable upon satisfactory completion of the work. Second, you really

> >

must develop the agreement that the work they perform is a work for hire and that the fan contractor relinquishes any claim to the work. This waiver of rights is obviously important to avoid surprising and ugly claims causing costly litigation to resolve. Acquiring this agreement becomes even more important in the likely event that you are developing this work as a work for hire for a publisher and *you* are promising to hand over all rights to the publisher.

Talk to your lawyer and ask her to draw up a boilerplate independent contractor agreement for you. You will end up using this agreement many times—well worth the investment.

> >

Epilogue

I recently heard a talk by Mark Terrano of Microsoft in Daejon, South Korea. His talk was titled "What is Life?" It was simply the most information-dense, most wonderful talk I have ever heard given about the games business. Mark opened and closed his talk by referring to himself both as teacher and as student. Mark is an accomplished developer with a good number of great games.

Honestly, I feel more on the student side than the teacher side, myself.

A year and a half and over 200,000 words went into this book. This was my first attempt to write a book, and I apologize to you, dear readers, for having to endure my clumsy efforts. While writing this book our company has grown from 15 employees to 25, and we have started and shipped SFC3. We are now working on our first console title, a multiplatform sci-fi action/RPG called Black9. And I became a father.

After eight years of game development, personally leading the shipping of five games, I feel like I am just beginning to understand what I need to focus on to become a stronger game producer.

The tools are getting better, the machines are faster, the games are much bigger, and this will only accelerate. The future of games is amazingly bright, and I just cannot wait to play your games!

Please consider this book as just my humble efforts to begin a conversation with all of you on how to make games better.

Please send all your thoughts, information, and criticisms to me at erik@taldren.com so I may learn from you.

> >

Appendix A > > > > > > > > > > > > > > >

Suggested Reading

I am addicted to books; book buying is easily my largest discretionary form of spending. My personal library is quite extensive on the topics of software development, the game industry, chess, science, science fiction, role-playing games, world affairs, and the Chinese and Japanese languages. May you benefit from my reading (and spending) and choose the best titles for you. Of course this book list makes no recommendations for chess or Asian languages—email me if you are interested in those topics!

Project Management

Jacobson, Ivar et al., *The Unified Software Development Process*, Addison Wesley, ISBN 0201571692, 1998

Here is the software development methodology that is espoused by the three amigos: Jacobson, Booch, and Rumbaugh. This book goes beyond software modeling and discusses how best to customize a methodology for your project.

McConnell, Steve C., *Rapid Development: Taming Wild Software Schedules,* Microsoft Press, ISBN 1556159005, 1996

Rapid Development is the larger work that Steve McConnell drew upon to create his *Software Project Survival Guide*. If you have already digested the *Survival Guide* and are hungering for more, read this large work at 647 pages! At the same time I can no longer recommend reading McConnell's older work, *Code Complete*. While it is somewhat different than *Rapid Development*, there is not much material that is unique between the two works and what is unique in *Code Complete* is somewhat dated—its focus on the C programming language may be of interest to some of your technical teammates.

McConnell, Steve C., *Software Project Survival Guide,* Microsoft Press, ISBN 1572316217, 1997

A most excellent distillation of Steve McConnell's work in improving the software development process, every manager and developer of a game project should be required to read this short book—just 250 pages!

< < < < < < < < < < < < < < < < < < < < < < < < < < < < < < <

Game Industry

Abrash, Michael, *Michael Abrash's Graphics Programming Black Book,* Coriolis Group Books, ISBN 1576101746, 1997

> Previously published as: *Zen of Graphics Programming: The Ultimate Guide to Writing Fast PC Graphics,* Coriolis Group Books, ISBN 188357708X, 1994.

Abrash, Michael, *Zen of Code Optimization: The Ultimate Guide to Writing Software That Pushes PCs to the Limit,* Coriolis Group Books, ISBN 1883577039, 1994

> Michael Abrash is one of my all-time favorite authors. The text of his Zen of Graphics series of books is material from magazine articles he has written for years. Michael Abrash remains the only author whose books I have reread just for the sheer pleasure of his writing—the material itself was bonus material. The Zen books I feel are must-reads for all of your programmers. Even though the bulk of his material is outdated due to advances in technology, the clarity of logic that he brings to bear on an algorithmic problem deserves to be studied.

Deloura, Mark, *Game Programming Gems volume 1*, Charles River Media, ISBN 1584500492, 2000

Deloura, Mark, *Game Programming Gems volume 2*, Charles River Media, ISBN 1584500549, 2001

Deloura, Mark, *Game Programming Gems volume 3*, Charles River Media, ISBN 1584502339, 2002

> Mark Deloura is the director of developer relations at Sony PlayStation and was previously editor-in-chief of *Game Developer* magazine. Deloura's *Game Programming Gems* have been edited with excellence, making each article of each volume in the series a must-read for the programmers on your team.

Hallford, Neal, and Jana Hallford, *Swords & Circuitry: A Designer's Guide to Computer Role-Playing Games,* Prima Tech, ISBN 0761532994, 2001

> This 524-page book is nicely focused on one genre—computer RPGs. The highlights of the Hallfords' book include interviews with Trent Oster, the lead designer (among many hats) of Neverwinter Nights representing BioWare Corp.; Chris Taylor, the lead designer of Dungeon Siege and CEO of Gas Powered Games; as well as four other interviews of lead designers of hit RPGs. The Hallfords also do a nice job of trying to analyze game design issues that are specific to the computer RPG. I would like to see a series of books myself that focus on different genres such as sports, extreme sports, platform, first-person shooter, etc. There is not very much specific that you will be able to make immediate use of; however, it is a pleasure to read.

> >

Olson, Jennifer (Editor-in-chief) et al., *Game Developer* magazine, CMP Media LLC

This magazine is the only and best print magazine for game development. Postmortems of games are key regular features such as "Black & White" by Peter Molyneux and "Deus Ex" by Warren Spector. Visit their web site at http://www.gdmag.com/ to subscribe to the magazine. It is also free to qualified professional game developers.

Rollings, Andrew, and Dave Morris, *Game Architecture and Design,* Coriolis Group Books, ISBN 1576104257, 2000

While I do believe this book is fundamentally worth reading, I could not escape the feeling that neither of the two authors have personally led a major game project. The positives of the book include some specific thoughts on how you might want to organize your team and some game design templates.

Sawyer, Ben et. al., *Game Developer's Marketplace,* Coriolis Group Books, ISBN 1576101770, 1998

This 728-page tome covers a wide selection of game development topics from the history of game development and the business of game development to design and audio. A lot of the specific tools mentioned in the book are now outdated; however, it is easy reading and the careful producer will gain some knowledge from the book.

Sawyer, Ben, *Game Developer's Source Book,* Coriolis Group Books, ISBN 1883577594, 1996

This is Ben Sawyer's 824-page predecessor to *Game Developer's Marketplace.* Several chapters were reproduced in the *Marketplace* title. If you own *Marketplace* there should be no driving reason to purchase *Source Book.*

Yu, Alan (Director of Conferences and Events) et al., *Game Developers Conference Proceedings*, CMP Media LLC

These proceedings are the collected papers on a wide variety of topics from programming and art to design and legal that are presented each year at the Game Developers Conference in March in the United States. Selected topics from 2000-2002 are available for free at http://www.gdconf.com/archives/. The full proceedings are available for purchase at the GamaSutra Store at https://www.gamasutra.com/php-bin/store.php (also a CMP Media LLC holding).

‹ ‹

Software Development

Booch, Grady et. al., *The Unified Modeling Language User Guide,* Addison Wesley, ISBN 020165783X, 1999

This is the definitive overview of the Unified Modeling Language. Each of the three amigos was lead author on a UML book: Booch wrote the *User Guide*, Jacobson, *Development Process*, and Rumbaugh, the *Reference Manual*. The *Reference Manual* and *User Guide* really should be purchased as a set after you have digested *UML Distilled*. I highly encourage reading *Development Process* before digging into the *User Guide* and *Reference Manual*.

Cline, Marshall et. al., *C++ FAQs 2nd Ed.*, Addison Wesley, ISBN 0201309831, 1998

The moderators of the online C++ FAQ at comp.lang.c++ collect and answer the questions most often asked by professional programmers on USENET. Every advanced C++ programmer I know has learned something from the book, an excellent read for your junior and intermediate developers with bite-sized chunks of information.

Fowler, Martin, with Kendall Scott, *UML Distilled 2nd Ed., A Brief Guide to the Standard Object Modeling Language*, Addison Wesley, ISBN 020165783X, 2000

Unlike most technical books, *UML Distilled* manages to cover something important in less than 200 pages. I consider this book a must-read for all of my developers, producers, and designers.

Lakos, John, *Large-Scale C++ Software Design,* Addison Wesley, ISBN 0201633620, 1997

This is a very important book; every programmer on your game development team should be exposed to this unique book. Game projects are now quite large pieces of software and the majority of game developers are self-taught or academically taught with no formal background in software engineering in a practical sense from working on large teams. This book discusses how to *physically* design your software, a topic that I believe is not covered anywhere else.

Maguire, Steve, *Writing Solid Code: Microsoft's Techniques for Developing Bug-Free C Programs,* Microsoft Press, ISBN 1556155514, 1993

The other Steve writing for Microsoft Press on good software development. Maguire presents many practical tips on writing solid code. This book contains especially lucid writing on debugging and how to integrate code

> >

team-wide. All junior and most intermediate programmers will benefit greatly from this book, and advanced programmers might be reminded of a safety technique that they have allowed to fall into disrepair.

Meyers, Scott, *Effective C++ CD: 85 Specific Ways to Improve Your Programs and Designs,* Addison Wesley, ISBN 0201310155, 1999

Meyers, Scott, *Effective STL: 50 Specific Ways to Improve Your Use of the Standard Template Library,* Addison Wesley, ISBN 0201749629, 2001

Meyers, Scott, *Effective C++: 50 Specific Ways to Improve Your Programs and Design 2nd Ed.,* Addison Wesley, ISBN 0201924889, 1997

Meyers, Scott, *More Effective C++: 35 New Ways to Improve Your Programs and Designs,* Addison Wesley, ISBN 020163371X, 1995

Scott Meyers is a very lucid author and perhaps the most popular C++ author. The Effective C++ series is most thoughtfully written, and Meyers shows an uncommon sensitivity of what the beginning to intermediate programmer would need to understand about C++. All of Meyers' books can be recommended without hesitation; however, the CD version of the two Effective C++ books and the STL book seem like the best buys. To get an idea how popular the Effective C++ books have been, notice the other C++ books at your local bookstore that attempt to capitalize on the title such as Essential C++, Efficient C++, and Exceptional C++.

Musser, David R., *STL Tutorial and Reference Guide: C++ Programming with the Standard Template Library (2nd Ed.),* Addison Wesley, ISBN 0201379236, 2001

The original edition of this book stood out to me as the only book able to explain to me how to use STL! For some reason, at the time that I was learning STL, either I was dense, or the other texts were poor, or an unfortunate synergy of the two conspired to make this a slower process than it needs to be. Your C++ programmers must have an introduction to the Standard Template Library that is part of C++. Lists, vectors, sets, and more complex data structures and algorithms have already been developed to a rigorously high quality. Your developers should not be reinventing their wheels when good ones are available for free!

Rumbaugh, James et. al., *The Unified Modeling Language Reference Guide,* Addison Wesley, ISBN 020130998X, 1999

This is the definitive reference for the Unified Modeling Language.

> >

Appendix B > > > > > > > > > > > > > > > >

The Art Institute of California—Orange County

Ai The Art Institute of California℠-Orange County

Thanks to The Art Institute of California—Orange County for providing the following information about the school.

Background

Opened in July 2000, The Art Institute of California—Orange County is an applied arts institute providing Bachelor's and Associate's degrees in Graphic Design, Media Arts & Animation, Game Art & Design, Multimedia & Web Design, Interior Design, and Culinary Arts. Located in the heart of Orange County's South Coast Metro region, The Art Institute is ideally situated in close proximity to Orange County's thriving business community, cultural attractions, shopping, entertainment and its famous beaches, not to mention the Los Angeles metropolitan area. The school is one of The Art Institutes, www.artinstitutes.edu, a system of 24 education institutions located nationwide, providing an important source of design, media arts, fashion, and culinary professionals. The Art

Institutes have provided career-oriented education programs for over 35 years, with more than 125,000 graduates.

Each program is offered on a year-round basis, allowing students to continue to work uninterrupted toward their degrees. Academic programs are carefully defined with the support and contributions of members of the professional community through Program Advisory Committees. Curricula are further reviewed periodically to ensure they meet the needs of a changing marketplace to qualify graduates for entry-level positions in their chosen fields.

The Art Institute is comprised of more than 50 faculty members who are working professionals in their respective fields. By tapping industry professionals, The Art Institute is able to bring a real-world perspective work setting and industry standards into the classroom preparing students for entry-level positions upon graduation.

The Art Institute of California—Orange County is accredited as a branch of The Art Institute of Colorado (Denver) by the Accrediting Council for Independent Colleges and Schools to award the Bachelor of Science and Associate of Science degrees. ACICS is listed as a nationally recognized accrediting agency by the U.S. Department of Education. Its accreditation of degree-granting institutions is recognized by the Council for Higher Education Accreditation. The Art Institute of California—Orange County is granted approval by the Bureau of Private Postsecondary and Vocational Education as a California private postsecondary degree-granting institution.

Game Art & Design Bachelor of Science Program

The Art Institute of California—Orange County (along with its sister schools in San Francisco and Los Angeles) offers a unique new Bachelor's degree program in Game Art & Design to bring a new generation of talent to the computer game industry.

The Game Art & Design Bachelor of Science degree program is designed for students who want to prepare for entry-level art positions in the game development field. Geared toward 3D animation and game level design, the program's students will learn character animation techniques, complex modeling, computer mapping, game level design, and how to script within the game. Through traditional art and design courses like life drawing, color theory, illustration, and sculpture, students also will create interactive game levels and learn to make computer game animation come alive with movement, color, and action characters.

Students will apply knowledge of video and animation to produce game products using 2D software to create backgrounds, 3D modeling and animation software to create game art, and 3D software to apply textures. The students also will receive a broad-based education that will include classes in art history and the humanities. By exposing students to classic art forms, they are able to incorporate more variety into their writing styles and animation sequences.

The curriculum will prepare future game developers to produce story lines and animations filled with creativity and inventive cleverness. The action and suspense that challenge people as they play video games can be accomplished through intelligent story writing. The curriculum also includes general education courses in areas such as mathematics and the social sciences.

The growing field of companies producing computer games is actively seeking artists trained in the art of computer animation and experienced with computer technologies—in Orange County alone there are game entertainment companies like Interplay Entertainment, Blizzard Entertainment, Taldren, Shiny Entertainment, and GameSpy Industries. Computer and video game sales could approach

> >

$17 billion in 2003, with another $1.1 billion in online gaming revenues, according to IDC. The game industry includes video games played on console game systems, personal computers, and handhelds. According to Forrester Research, nearly 49 million American homes today have at least one video game system. Nearly 75 million homes are projected to have systems by 2005, achieving a 70 percent penetration level.

The Art Institutes' Game Art & Design program was designed by a faculty curriculum committee and professional advisory boards of industry experts, including specialists with work experience at Sega of America, Macromedia, Konami, Pixar, LucasArts, Sonique, Terra Lycos, PDI/Dream-Works, and Apple. The program gives students a curriculum that responds to the ongoing changes in the game development and multimedia industries, ensuring that students graduate with the skills and knowledge that employers need. Furthermore, students learn about the changing demands in the business world through a regular series of guest speakers.

Potential students interested in the Game Art & Design, Media Arts & Animation, or another program offered by The Art Institute of California—Orange County are invited to call (888) 549-3055 or (714) 830-0200 or visit www.aicaoc.aii.edu for curriculum and admissions information.

For more information on The Art Institute of California—Orange County, please contact Anne Mack at (714) 830-0254 or macka@aii.edu.

Index

> >

> >

Check out Wordware's market-leading Game Developer's Library featuring the following new releases.

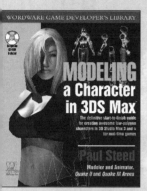

Modeling a Character in 3DS Max

1-55622-815-5
$44.95
7½ x 9¼   544 pp.

Direct3D ShaderX Vertex and Pixel Shader Tips and Tricks

1-55622-041-3
$59.95
7½ x 9¼   520 pp.

Vector Game Math Processors

1-55622-921-6
$59.95
6 x 9   528 pp.

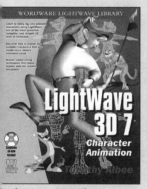

LightWave 3D 7 Character Animation

1-55622-901-1
$49.95
7½ x 9¼   360 pp.

Advanced 3-D Game Programming Using DirectX 8.0

1-55622-513-X
$59.95
7½ x 9¼   592 pp.

3D Math Primer for Graphics and Game Development

1-55622-911-9
$49.95
7½ x 9¼   448 pp.

Visit us online at **www.wordware.com** for more information.

Use the following coupon code for online specials: **gamedev9518**

www.GameInstitute.com

A Superior Way to Learn Computer Game Development

The Game Institute provides a convenient, high-quality game development curriculum at a very affordable tuition. Our expert faculty has developed a series of courses designed to teach you fundamental and advanced game programming techniques so that you can design and develop your own computer games. Best of all, in our unique virtual classrooms you can interact with instructors and fellow students in ways that will ensure you get a firm grasp of the material. Whether you are a beginner or a game development professional, the Game Institute is the superior choice for your game development education.

Quality Courses at a Great Price

◇ **Weekly Online Voice Lectures** delivered by your instructor with accompanying slides and other visuals.

◇ **Downloadable Electronic Textbook** provides in-depth coverage of the entire curriculum with additional voice-overs from instructors.

◇ **Student-Teacher Interaction** both live in weekly chat sessions and via message boards where you can post your questions and solutions to exercises.

◇ **Downloadable Certificates** suitable for printing and framing indicate successful completion of your coursework.

◇ **Source Code** and sample applications for study and integration into your own gaming projects.

"The leap in required knowledge from competent general-purpose coder to games coder has grown significantly. The Game Institute provides an enormous advantage with a focused curriculum and attention to detail."

—Tom Forsyth
Lead Developer
Muckyfoot Productions, Ltd.

3D Graphics Programming With Direct3D

Examines the premier 3D graphics programming API on the Microsoft Windows platform. Create a complete 3D game engine with animated characters, light maps, special effects, and more.

3D Graphics Programming With OpenGL

An excellent course for newcomers to 3D graphics programming. Also includes advanced topics like shadows, curved surfaces, environment mapping, particle systems, and more.

Advanced BSP/PVS/CSG Techniques

A strong understanding of spatial partitioning algorithms is important for 3D graphics programmers. Learn how to leverage the BSP tree data structure for fast visibility processing and collision detection as well as powerful CSG algorithms.

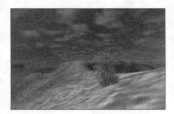

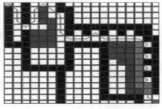

Real-Time 3D Terrain Rendering

Take your 3D engine into the great outdoors. This course takes a serious look at popular terrain generation and rendering algorithms including ROAM, Rottger, and Lindstrom.

Path Finding Algorithms

Study the fundamental art of maneuver in 2D and 3D environments. Course covers the most popular academic algorithms in use today. Also includes an in-depth look at the venerable A*.

Network Game Programming With DirectPlay

Microsoft DirectPlay takes your games online quickly. Course includes coverage of basic networking, lobbies, matchmaking and session management.

MORE COURSES AVAILABLE AT

www.GameInstitute.com

Windows, DirectPlay, Direct3D are registered trademarks of Microsoft Corp. OpenGL is a registered trademark of Silicon Graphics Inc.

Gamedev.net

The most comprehensive game development resource

- ◌ The latest news in game development
- ◌ The most active forums and chatrooms anywhere, with insights and tips from experienced game developers
- ◌ Links to thousands of additional game development resources
- ◌ Thorough book and product reviews
- ◌ Over 1000 game development articles!
  Game design
  Graphics
  DirectX
  OpenGL
  AI
  Art
  Music
  Physics
  Source Code
  Sound
  Assembly
  And More!

 **Gamedev.net**

OpenGL is a registered trademark of Silicon Graphics, Inc.
Microsoft, DirectX are registered trademarks of Microsoft Corp. in the United States and/or other countries.

About the CD

The contents of the companion CD are not the usual bits of programming code one would expect in a traditional computer programming book. Instead, you will find three tools that are very useful in the production and development of your games.

The following folders are on the CD:

- Perforce—Perforce is a very powerful asset and source code control system. Asset management and version control are critical bits of day-to-day housekeeping in the development of a game. Most folks start out with Microsoft's very modestly priced Visual Source Safe. After your team grows you will begin to feel the limits of VSS, and Perforce is an excellent solution. Perforce is somewhat expensive; however, the version included on the CD is a free two-client and server license to use as long as you like.

- Perforce has also graciously supplied a Best Practices White Paper on version control.

- Daily Journal—The Daily Journal is a tool we developed and use internally at Taldren to track and publish the company's activities on a daily basis. As you will see, it is a very thin web applet with no additional bells or whistles. Feel free to modify the Daily Journal to your needs.

- Describe—Describe is by far the easiest to use of the forward and backward code generation UML tools that I have used. A full-featured demo of Describe is included on the CD.

CAUTION: By opening the CD package, you accept the terms and conditions of the CD/Source Code Usage License Agreement.

Additionally, opening the CD package makes this book nonreturnable.

VERMONT STATE COLLEGES

0 0003 0748367 7

CD/Source Code Usage License Agreement

Please read the following CD/Source Code usage license agreement before opening the CD and using the contents therein:

1. By opening the accompanying software package, you are indicating that you have read and agree to be bound by all terms and conditions of this CD/Source Code usage license agreement.

2. The compilation of code and utilities contained on the CD and in the book are copyrighted and protected by both U.S. copyright law and international copyright treaties, and is owned by Wordware Publishing, Inc. Individual source code, example programs, help files, freeware, shareware, utilities, and evaluation packages, including their copyrights, are owned by the respective authors.

3. No part of the enclosed CD or this book, including all source code, help files, shareware, freeware, utilities, example programs, or evaluation programs, may be made available on a public forum (such as a World Wide Web page, FTP site, bulletin board, or Internet news group) without the express written permission of Wordware Publishing, Inc. or the author of the respective source code, help files, shareware, freeware, utilities, example programs, or evaluation programs.

4. You may not decompile, reverse engineer, disassemble, create a derivative work, or otherwise use the enclosed programs, help files, freeware, shareware, utilities, or evaluation programs except as stated in this agreement.

5. The software, contained on the CD and/or as source code in this book, is sold without warranty of any kind. Wordware Publishing, Inc. and the authors specifically disclaim all other warranties, express or implied, including but not limited to implied warranties of merchantability and fitness for a particular purpose with respect to defects in the disk, the program, source code, sample files, help files, freeware, shareware, utilities, and evaluation programs contained therein, and/or the techniques described in the book and implemented in the example programs. In no event shall Wordware Publishing, Inc., its dealers, its distributors, or the authors be liable or held responsible for any loss of profit or any other alleged or actual private or commercial damage, including but not limited to special, incidental, consequential, or other damages.

6. One (1) copy of the CD or any source code therein may be created for backup purposes. The CD and all accompanying source code, sample files, help files, freeware, shareware, utilities, and evaluation programs may be copied to your hard drive. With the exception of freeware and shareware programs, at no time can any part of the contents of this CD reside on more than one computer at one time. The contents of the CD can be copied to another computer, as long as the contents of the CD contained on the original computer are deleted.

7. You may not include any part of the CD contents, including all source code, example programs, shareware, freeware, help files, utilities, or evaluation programs in any compilation of source code, utilities, help files, example programs, freeware, shareware, or evaluation programs on any media, including but not limited to CD, disk, or Internet distribution, without the express written permission of Wordware Publishing, Inc. or the owner of the individual source code, utilities, help files, example programs, freeware, shareware, or evaluation programs.

8. You may use the source code, techniques, and example programs in your own commercial or private applications unless otherwise noted by additional usage agreements as found on the CD.

CAUTION: By opening the CD package, you accept the terms and conditions of the CD/Source Code Usage License Agreement.

Additionally, opening the CD package makes this book nonreturnable.

DISCARD